THOMISM AND TRADITION

From Rivulets to the Fountain's Source

THE AMERICAN MARITAIN ASSOCIATION
BOOK SERIES VOLUME 32

I0892980

AMERICAN MARITAIN ASSOCIATION BOOK SERIES

GENERAL EDITOR

Giuseppe Butera

Since 1988, when the American Maritain Association Book Series was founded by Anthony O. Simon, the American Maritain Association has annually published a collection of essays based largely (although not exclusively) on papers presented at its international meetings. The many volumes of the series range over the entire span of themes and problems found not only in Maritain's writings but also in those of St. Thomas Aquinas, and are intended for specialists and non-specialists, alike. In Maritain we find a Thomist who is fully engaged with his times and an encouragement to do the same with our own. So encouraged, these volumes are offered in the same spirit of friendship for which Jacques and his wife, Raïssa, had so notable a genius.

THOMISM AND TRADITION

FROM RIVULETS TO THE FOUNTAIN'S SOURCE

EDITED BY HEATHER M. ERB

AMERICAN MARITAIN ASSOCIATION

Distributed by

THE CATHOLIC UNIVERSITY OF AMERICA PRESS

Washington, D.C.

Copyright © 2025 American Maritain Association
All rights reserved
Manufactured in the United States of America

Distributed by the Catholic University of America Press
620 Michigan Avenue, N.E., 240 Leahy Hall
Washington, D.C. 20064

Cataloguing-in-Publication Data available
from the Library of Congress
ISBN 978-0-9972205-6-8

For Frederick

The future is bright!

The American Maritain Association gratefully acknowledges the generous financial support of the following contributors in support of the publication of this book series.

Anonymous Sponsor
Anonymous Sponsor
John Cahalan
Marie George
Herbert Hartmann
James Jacobs
Walter Raubicheck
Denis Scrandis
Michael Torre
John Trapani
J. Raymond Zimmer

Contents

Acknowledgements

My special thanks to those who provided invaluable insights, reviews, corrections and suggestions which have ultimately culminated in this book. In particular, I owe a debt of gratitude to Giuseppe Butera, who finishes his task as the series editor with this volume. In addition, I am grateful to James Hanink, who promoted the conference theme which bases the book's contents, and who has provided a leadership that combines the search for meaning with the grace of mystery, joining, as did Maritain, the pursuit of truth and human fellowship under the guidance of love.

HEATHER M. ERB

Introduction

Fidelity to Truth and Intellectual Fellowship

SEVERAL MODERN THOMISTS have written on the nature of tradition, aware, as G. B. Phelan describes it, that the history of philosophy is its life in human minds. Unlike thinkers such as Nietzsche, who cultivated an inhumane "forgetfulness" and considered tradition as a type of slavery opposed to the autonomy of the sovereign individual, Aquinas's thought moves freely among traditions, drawing on and extending them in an act of receptive contemplation that echoes Greek meditations on the nature of wisdom.

Whether one defines tradition in the merely secular sense of actions and practices that are received and given, or in the stricter sense understood by Plato and expanded on by Josef Pieper, as having a divine origin and meaning, tradition in the philosophical sense involves memory (Augustinian *anamnesis*), a dialectic of doctrinal fidelity to a school of thought, and a receptivity to new interpretations and adumbrations. A zeal for truth that welcomes intellectual fellowship characterizes Maritain's ideal of the catholicity of reason and love. Philosophers calling themselves Thomists differ widely on the irreducible set of principles defining their tradition. For both Maritain and Gilson, it is the mystery of existence itself which is the heart of Thomist philosophy and tradition. It is the act of being's abundance and generosity that establishes the dignity of the person and his capacity for fraternal dialogue. For many, it is a realist, communal, theologically directed metaphysics shorn of any remnant of Cartesian idealism and individualism which generates the Thomist tradition.

Aquinas developed his thought within the framework of a variety of intersecting and often opposing intellectual traditions. Although he views philosophical progress as possible only through reckoning with those traditions, which supplement the frailty of our intellects, he uses his own criteria to reach the truth concerning rival traditions, such as the consistency and explanatory power of the accounts.

Complementing his debt to the ancients is the integral unity of his heart and mind, protecting his work from the errors of the uncritical use of traditions, on the one hand, and the illusory presumption of independence from authorities, on the other. The philosophical discourses he draws on are common opinions subjected to dialectical analysis, yet his intellectual edifice does not suffer from the dry abstractionism so often attributed to him. Gilson reminds us that a philosophy is not defined principally by the elements it borrows but from the spirit that quickens it. The Christian spirit permeates both the rhythm of Aquinas's prayer and the structure of his thought, even though the authority of revelation is conclusive, while that of philosophical traditions is only pedagogical.

For Aquinas, intellectual traditions serve as authorities and starting points for his own creative syntheses and interpretations of philosophical and scriptural topics. Some of the more notable traditions spurred his investigation of the discipline of *sacra doctrina* which opens his *Summa Theologiae*. Whether that theology is a science in the Aristotelian sense, and how it transcends traditional science, displays his application of Augustinian wisdom to a philosophical tradition, and his synthesizing of traditions of science, wisdom, and even wisdom literature. He also uses the tradition of using philosophy in theology ("changing water into wine"), and that of the threefold nature of wisdom (viz., the acquired natural wisdom of metaphysics, the revealed wisdom of theology, and the infused wisdom from the Spirit), as well as the fourfold mode of Biblical interpretation. His reviews of the history of philosophy reveal both his respect for, and deft handling of, traditions as redirected by the purposes of his own metaphysics and epistemology. In contrast to simplistic explanations of knowledge as either material or accessed through separate substances in the tradition of some *antiqui* and Avicenna, he shows how our knowing involves forms originating in sense and coming to be in us immaterially. Moreover, the Dionysian tradition of the emanation and return (*exitus/reditus*) structure of reality forms the architectonic of his *Summa*, a sapiential ordering complemented by various narratives of causality, exemplars, and types of grace, offering occasions for his evaluation of rival traditions.

If Aquinas sees himself as an interpreter who extends, reconciles, and corrects various intellectual traditions, there is also the question of mapping out the traditions of Thomism, and discerning the ways in which St. Thomas himself conveys a tradition of thought—a task involving more than the unknowing, comfortable familiarity of the craftsman with his tools; it is the knowledge of an artist who knows the causes and is ready to give an account through universal principles. The philosophical art is a search for principles by the raising of topics and difficulties. In reflecting on the intellectual unity of topics presented here, Aquinas's image of living water, taken from his *Commentary on the Gospel of John*, comes to mind. "Living water," he states, is "connected with its source and flows from it," while "non-living water" is disconnected from the source from which it stands, and collects in ponds and cisterns (*In 4 Joann.*, lect. 2, no. 577). It's my hope that the traditions of Thomism, far from being a series of deaf mens' quarrels, may bear some remote and analogical similarity to the Creator Himself, the "living fountain that is not diminished in spite of its continuous flow outwards" (*In 1 Joann.*, lect. 1, no. 3).

Part I of the book, "Living Water: The Integrative Framework," provides an integrative framework of ideas that recur in many discussions of the nature of Thomism, namely, the concept of Christian philosophy and the relationship between philosophy and theology. In the first chapter, "An Exercise in Christian Philosophy: W. Norris Clarke on Receptivity as a Positive Perfection of Being," Hannah Woldum Ragusa extends the question of Christian philosophy in her discussion of W. Norris Clarke's "creative retrieval" of Aquinas's metaphysics, and in particular, to ways in which both theological data and philosophical method inform Clarke's personalist interpretation of Aquinas. Against the background of Jacques Maritain's and John Wippel's discussions of Christian philosophy, Clarke's fidelity to Thomas's theologically inspired metaphysics is outlined. Along with a meditation on the deliverances of the metaphysical judgment of separation, she ably argues for Clarke's defense of receptivity as a positive perfection of being as an application of contemporary Christian philosophy developed within a relational metaphysics of being and person.

The integrative framework of Thomism is also girded by the topic of the relation of philosophy and theology. Four chapters are devoted to this topic. In his chapter "Catechetical Thomism: Metaphysics and Sacraments," John Conley rhapsodically presents the case for the return to the Thomistic metaphysical scaffolding in catechesis, citing its boon to the "philosophical texture" of Catholic culture and to the practice of catechetics. He walks us through the Roman Catechism's (1566, often called the Catechism of the Council of Trent) deployment of the categories of matter and form as they can be applied with varying degrees of precision to the seven sacraments. Balancing a metaphysical examination of sign and signified with his discussion of spiritual transformation through revealed sources, he astutely retains an emphasis on mystery that characterizes all good catechesis, not just in those associated with the post-conciliar period. In his chapter "The Ontology of the Divine Indwelling: A Hard-Headed Thomist Meets with Palamas," Matthew Minerd defends a Byzantine version of Thomism which joins a philosophical examination of divine immensity and ontological presence to a theological analysis of the relation between persons on the level of grace. For Minerd, a Thomist adopts Aquinas as the occasion for, and as the animating spirit of, their philosophical and theological inquiry. Taking the fourteenth-century debate of the hesychasts on our divinization and the essence of God as his point of departure, Minerd begins by exposing the philosophical dangers in interpretations of Palamas. He then argues for a resemblance between Eastern (Palamas) and Western (Ambrose Gardiel) versions of the divine indwelling of the Holy Trinity, using both philosophical and theological evidence, appealing to Aquinas's theory of the divine missions, and appealing to a wide swath of interpreters, from Vasquez, Suarez, and John of St. Thomas to Maritain, Nicolas, and Journet.

In his chapter "St. Thomas Aquinas on the Individuation of the Intellectual Soul," Marco Stango offers an interpretation of Aquinas in which bodily and intellectual habits play distinct but equally essential roles. A fascinating set of implications for the status of the separated soul are drawn in terms of how a disembodied soul can be said to maintain its personal identity, a problem Stango investigates against the backdrop of Aquinas's insistence, in *De Ente* 5, that the soul remains individual after death, and in contrast to the Gilsonian view concerning the role of *esse* in individuation. A final topic on the boundary of philosophical and theological reasoning is found in Dumsday's "Alexander of Hales on the Irremediable Demons." In this formidable textual treatment of the twelfth-century Franciscan theologian's work on soteriology found in his *Summa Theologica*, Dumsday pits

Hales against modern universalists who claim that all souls will most likely be saved from eternal damnation. Since the metaphysical principles of human and angelic souls are related to each other, Dumsday launches the test case of the question of the irremediable demons, both in the case of Lucifer and in that of the lesser demons. His discussion illumines Alexander's deft use of philosophical and theological reasoning in a sweeping analysis that includes meditations on free will in spiritual creatures, the nature of sin, and the reconciliation of divine justice and mercy.

Part II, "From a Table of Solid Rock: Moral, Social and Political Theory," engages a key debate in social and political theory, namely, the relation of the person and the common good, and the twin dangers of totalitarianism and individualism. In "Personalism and the Common Good: Evaluating the Maritain-De Koninck Controversy," Francis Feingold identifies the points of agreement and disagreement between the two Thomists and offers a resolution of the tension between the dangers of individualism and totalitarianism through Aquinas's emphasis on friendship-love as the motivation for our desire-love of the common good. Individualism is avoided through love of God and city above self in the realization of our radical dependence on them in various ways; totalitarian tendencies are averted in that the primary sense of "good" involves the person and his degree of perfection. In "The Right Rights: Whose Aquinas? Which Natural Law?", Christopher Ragusa turns to the issue of the ground and scope of human rights, navigating between the views of Finnis, who grants us rights but *no* sphere of autonomy, Tierney and Villey, who deny Aquinas has a concept of either individual rights *or* a sphere of autonomy, and Porter, who ascribes *both* to human persons. Emphasizing Aquinas's participatory understanding of natural law avoids the modern competition between freedom and rights, on the one hand, and the common good and justice, on the other, and Ragusa defends a view of rights as relational in justice, and not as independent of concerns for the common good. In this, he identifies MacIntyre's invective against modern rights talk as stemming from the myth of the radical and autonomous individual.

The Thomist teaching regarding the dignity and end of the human person is often associated with Yves Simon, who carried the contribution of Pope Leo XIII to the Church's social teaching into his analysis of modern democracies and capitalism. In "Yves R. Simon, MacIntyre, and Distributism: Justice in Exchange in the Contemporary Market Economy",

Thomas Rourke contrasts three critiques of modern industrial capitalism. The first critique focuses narrowly on the economic problems (Marxism). The second critiques the profit motive from the incompatibility of thinkers such as David Hume and Adam Smith with the distinction between reason and desire in classical and medieval thought (MacIntyre). The third critique is staged from the viewpoint of a robust Thomistic concept of the common good, offering the solution of distributism as a corrective to the problems of exploitation and to unbridled capitalism's perversions of desire and the good life (Simon).

Part III, "The Sound of Mighty Waters: MacIntyre on Desire for the Good," includes two accounts of the views of the twentieth-century Thomist Alisdair MacIntyre. Characterizing all rational enquiry as tradition-dependent accounts and philosophical theories as constructed histories of the struggles and successes of those accounts, is a hallmark of the work of Alisdair MacIntyre. In "God and the Good: MacIntyre, Ur-Platonism, and the Retrospective Rational Vindication of Trinitarian Theism," Mark Moes applies MacIntyre's insight to the Greek tradition of philosophical theism, defending the view that Plato, Aristotle, and the NeoPlatonists Plotinus and Proclus form an unbroken transmission of various positions. Moes bases his argument on these thinkers' views on the immateriality of the soul, on a causal interpretation of goodness and the human good, and on his observation that Trinitarian theology introduced metaphysical solutions that extended and transformed the Greek tradition of philosophical theism. In "MacIntyre and Meno: *After Virtue* vs. a Socratic Objection," Kelsey Tuning continues the account of MacIntyre on tradition, applying it to the Socratic question in Plato's *Meno* of whether the good life can be sought both justly and unjustly. Tuning then develops MacIntyre's notion of virtue as a quality that allows man to obtain goods internal to a practice, directing his concept of the good life. While Meno's focus was on external goods, MacIntyre's depiction of the communal search for happiness involves practices that relate primarily to internal goods. Because these cannot be sought unjustly on pain of disappearing entirely, Tuning argues that MacIntyre's view of tradition and virtue as necessarily stemming from goods internal to these practices, makes Socrates' objection that we must add the consideration of justice to the pursuit of the good life, redundant.

The fourth part of the book, "The Cascade's Rhyme: Twentieth-Century Thomism," introduces the topic of contemporary accounts of Aquinas's thought as it engages with various movements in recent philosophy. Twentieth-century Thomism includes a wide variety of approaches, its divisions being a topic of sharp debate among Thomists. A select number of topics are broached without the aim of exhausting the varieties that could be listed. Christopher Lutz tackles the modern notions of law, obligation, and obedience that can generate a "moral alienation" if ungrounded in Aquinas's account of teleology as applied to human acts and flourishing. His "Thomistic Aristotelianism vs. Moral Alienation: A Response to Bernard Williams" offers a MacIntyrean Thomist response, based on the rationality of traditions, to the complaint that moderns such as Kant muddle moral philosophy by divorcing it from inclinations.

There has been much debate on the status of "analytic" Thomism, with various scholars giving degrees of breadth to the concept in terms of method and content. In "Anscombe, Causality, and the Play of Creation," James Hanink displays the scope of Elizabeth Anscombe's analytic approach in his lucid discussion of her "causal provocation" with respect to necessity and chance. Distinguishing between levels and types of causality, he introduces the notion of "range causality" to steer us out of the false dichotomy of strict causal necessity and pure contingency and chance. Appealing to the personalist account of John Henry Newman, and to the notion of creation as "play", he points us towards an arena where the essential nature of the Logos reflects a freedom associated with human flourishing.

In "Truth and Contexts of Intelligibility in Maritain's Early Work," Alice M. Ramos considers the importance of contexts in relation to the concepts of intelligibility and traditions in the thought of Alasdair MacIntyre. For MacIntyre, a failure to reference and evaluate contexts of various types results in what we witness today, namely, moral discourse that has become an indefensible and unintelligible set of dead-end debates, in a "graveyard for fragments of culturally large-scale philosophical systems." Ramos tracks the progress of the secularization of Christian ethics, including an analysis of its Protestant and Jansenist catalysts which rupture the harmony of faith and reason. The radical repercussions of Descartes' revolt against tradition in the thought of Hume and Kant are contrasted with a MacIntyrean view of the role of contexts and traditions in the common search for the good life. James Capehart gives a broad yet penetrating outline of the evolution of a central Thomistic theme in his chapter, "The Christian Philosophy of Gilson, Maritain, and St. John Paul II as Principle of Unity for a

Twenty-First Century Thomism". He presents us with the richly cultivated fields of Christian philosophy from its earliest notion in Saints Justin Martyr and Augustine as the love of true wisdom itself, and its development by Étienne Gilson and Jacques Maritain, who articulate the formal, objective, as well as subjective influences of Christian revelation on the life of reason. He leads us through the rationalist and on occasion, Thomist objections to the concept of Christian philosophy, and to the defense of its identity as both *ancilla* and *amicus theologiae,* warning us with Maritain against creating an "ideological monster" of an abstract Christian philosophy shorn of any existential moorings or influences. In "Integrating Neo-Thomism and Ressourcement Against Modernism: Garrigou-Lagrange's *Christ the Savior* as a Test-Case," Matthew Levering discerns a broad family resemblance between two streams of twentieth-century Thomist theology. Connecting diverse theologies under the broad banner of Thomism, Levering makes the argument that Garrigou-Lagrange (sometimes called a Thomist "of the strict observance"), who develops his view from within the Thomistic-Scotistic debate regarding the relation between the Incarnation and the Cross, is in this respect parallel to Ratzinger's similar project undertaken in dialogue with biblical scholars. Christology and soteriology are intertwined in the Thomist tradition, even as this union is developed within widely varying contexts.

The fifth and final part of this volume, "As If God Poured Thee: Is there a 'True' Thomism?", takes up the challenging question of the criteria for the designation of "Thomism", whether in its philosophical or theological guises. The topic of Maritain's interpretation of Aquinas's metaphysics is treated in Denis Scrandis' trenchant defense of Maritain's "intuition of being" as faithful to Aquinas's texts, in his "Is Maritain's Metaphysics Authentically Thomistic?" Scrandis tracks the evolution of Maritain's metaphysics, in its inception, inspired by Bergson's anti-mechanistic philosophy, but flourishing by aid of the "luminous flood" of Aquinas's *Summa.* Scrandis reviews Aquinas's divisions of the speculative sciences, illumines the points of contact between Aquinas and the commentatorial tradition on the degrees of abstraction, and interprets Aquinas's subject of metaphysics (*ens inquantum ens*) in light of Maritain's intuition of being and its "infinity of analogates." Taking aim at John Wippel's theory of the subject of metaphysics as the fruit of the negative judgment of *separatio,* Scrandis defends his conviction that Maritain's intuition of being is an authentic instance of Thomistic realism, undergirded by a non-subjectivist epistemology.

Given the variety of approaches labeled "Thomistic", ranging from Laval Thomism, existentialist Thomism, River Forest Thomism, transcendental Thomism, analytical Thomism, and palaeo-Thomism, to name just a few, some scholars, such as Ralph McInerny, object to limiting the tradition by means of a strict list of criteria. Some view list-making as an extension of the anti-modernist tactics favored by Pope Pius IX (*Syllabus of Errors* [1864]), Pope Pius X (the "24 *Theses*" [1914]) and their followers. This objection is discussed and put to the test by Sr. Anne Frances Ai Le's contribution, "A Thomist is a Thomist: A Must? A Must!: A Quest for 'Mere Thomism.'" Contrasting McInerny's broad understanding of the tradition with Romanus Cessario's stricter and more purist criteria, she finds they both discern a unity among Thomists based on their acts of philosophizing embodying a conception of philosophical and theological enquiry, and raises the question of the legitimacy of a plurality of Thomisms, given their realist focus.

The defining documents of Pope John Paul the Great's pontificate recommend Aquinas as a guide in philosophy, making Thomism, as Michael Torre shows, in his "Modest Reflections on Being a Thomist Today," the "focal center" of a broader philosophical conversation with many traditions. The "joyously difficult project" of Thomism today, Torre argues, is one involving the seminal insights of the Aristotelian-Neoplatonic tradition and penetrated by a spirit of dialectical engagement and historical awareness, in a communal struggle across place and time towards the truth of things.

The theme of "Thomism and tradition," while ambitious and far-reaching, has been visited before by Thomists such as Sr. Helen James John, Jean-Pierre Torrell, Romanus Cessario, and Cajetan Cuddy, and even by non-Thomist scholars of religion, such as Bernard McGinn, to name just a few. Aquinas's theological and philosophical "heritage of truth," to use a phrase of Pieper, both drew from the well of prior intellectual traditions and gave birth to a commentatorial tradition and a school of thought rich in complexity and innumerable in its refined and detailed reflections. While continually drawn back towards the unity of their source, Thomists resemble the cascading beauty of a living fountain undiminished by its continuous flow outwards.

I

LIVING WATER

The Integrative Framework

HANNAH WOLDUM RAGUSA

An Exercise in Christian Philosophy

W. Norris Clarke on Receptivity as a Positive Perfection of Being

I. Introduction

IN *AN ESSAY ON CHRISTIAN PHILOSOPHY*, Jacques Maritain weighs in on one of the key debates of the twentieth century, namely, the debate about the possibility of Christian philosophy. Maritain takes Thomas Aquinas to be a model of a Christian philosopher whose Christian faith illuminates the philosophical quest in multiple positive ways without compromising the fundamental nature or method of philosophy.[1] Maritain's understanding of Christian philosophy implicitly suggests that Thomas Aquinas's approach is still open to the philosophers of today. Christian faith and life can and should continue to illuminate the philosophical quest, leading to new philosophical insights that can eventually be defended from a purely philosophical standpoint, but which would be unlikely to be discovered without the aid of Christian revelation.

I would like to examine the twentieth-century, Thomistically inspired philosopher W. Norris Clarke as an example of a contemporary philosopher who has consciously engaged in this very project of Christian phi-

1. See Jacques Maritain, *An Essay on Christian Philosophy* (New York: Philosophical Library, 1955), 30. "Christian philosophy is not a determinate body of truths, although, in my opinion, the doctrine of St. Thomas exemplifies its amplest and purest form. Christian philosophy is philosophy itself in so far as it is situated in those utterly distinctive conditions of existence and exercise into which Christianity has ushered the thinking subject, and as a result of which philosophy perceives certain objects and validly demonstrates certain propositions, which in any other circumstances would to a greater or lesser extent elude it."

losophy.[2] Clarke developed his own unique Thomistically inspired metaphysics while also drawing on phenomenology and identifying himself with the late-twentieth-century movement of "Personalist Thomism," of which Karol Wojtyla (Pope Saint John Paul II) is the best representative.[3] In my view, Clarke resembles Thomas Aquinas as a philosopher in two ways: First, he wants to remain open to the genuine insights of pagan and contemporary philosophy, synthesizing the best of it into his overall project, insofar as it sheds light on the truth. Second, he brings to the surface certain philosophical insights from Christian revelation which would have been very difficult to discover on their own through reason alone, although in the end they can be supported by purely philosophical arguments.

It is Clarke's work in this second arena that will be my focus here. In other words, I want to examine Clarke's work as an example of Christian philosophy in our own era. I will do this precisely by focusing on one particular philosophical insight that Clarke made central to his own thought from about 1993 until his death in 2008 (although you can see intimations of it much earlier), namely his trademark position that receptivity is a positive perfection of being.

Clarke argues that receptivity at its highest level does not involve any limitation or passive potency but is rather a positive perfection of being. He defends this unusual metaphysical position as "an exercise in 'Christian philosophy'" that is intended to be a "creative retrieval and completion" of St. Thomas's own thought.[4] Although he ultimately defends his position with philosophical arguments, he admits that this insight first occurred to him through his experience with contemporary theologians.[5]

2. See, for instance, W. Norris Clarke, SJ, "The Future of Thomism," in *New Themes in Christian Philosophy*, edited by Ralph McInerny (Notre Dame, Indiana: University of Notre Dame Press, 1968), 189, and "Introduction" in *Explorations in Metaphysics* (Notre Dame, Indiana: University of Notre Dame Press, 1994), ix. In the latter work, Clarke describes his own project as a two-fold one that includes both a "creative retrieval" of the philosophy of St. Thomas, conducted "under the stimulus of ... the authentic contributions of later, especially twentieth-century, philosophy" and a "creative completion" of those lines of thought present in the works of St. Thomas, but never fully articulated by him (x).

3. See Clarke, "The Future of Thomism," 204–205; "Introduction," in *Explorations in Metaphysics*, ix–xv; "The Integration of Personalism and Thomistic Metaphysics in Twenty-First-Century Thomism," in *The Creative Retrieval of Saint Thomas Aquinas: Essays in Thomistic Philosophy, New and Old* (New York: Fordham University Press, 2009), 226–27.

4. Clarke, "Person, Being, and St. Thomas," *Communio* 19 (Winter 1992): 613; Clarke, "Reply to Stephen Long," *The Thomist* 61, no. 4 (October 1997): 624.

5. See Clarke, "Person, Being, and St. Thomas," in *Explorations in Metaphysics*, 220. He cites

Clarke's position, first developed in a 1992 *Communio* article and in his 1993 Aquinas Lecture *Person and Being,* was clarified in numerous articles throughout the 1990s and maintained until his death. And although his views met with criticism from several fellow Thomists, Clarke continued to defend his position as a real exercise in Christian philosophy in the tradition of Aquinas. He also argued that this understanding of receptivity as a positive perfection was implicit in Aquinas's thought and just waiting to be illumined. By analyzing his two primary arguments in defense of his position, I will show how Clarke is indeed a model of Thomistic Christian philosophy in our own day.

II. On Christian Philosophy

Before analyzing Clarke's account of receptivity as a positive perfection, I must briefly explain the notion of Christian philosophy. Some of Clarke's critics, including Steven Long and George Blair, have—in my view—failed in their critiques because they leave the notion of legitimate Christian philosophy vague. They have not sufficiently examined the relationship between divine revelation and philosophy, and they end up accusing Clarke of making philosophical mistakes that he does not in fact make, misunderstanding the way in which Clarke uses theological discoveries in his philosophical endeavors, or even stumbling into unorthodox statements that Clarke himself is careful to avoid.[6] It is therefore important to preface my examination of Clarke's philosophy with a brief account of Christian philosophy. Both Maritain and Wippel identify two possible meanings of "Christian philosophy," only one of which they see as viable. Despite a difference

Joseph Ratzinger, Hans Urs von Balthasar, and John Cobb as theological inspirations (212; 220). It should be noted that this chapter in his 1994 book *Explorations in Metaphysics* is a slight reworking of the article by the same title that Clarke first published in 1992 in *Communio*. Hereafter, the two versions of the same article will be referred to as "Person, Being, and St. Thomas" (1992) and "Person, Being, and St. Thomas" (1994).

6. See Steven A. Long, "Divine and Creaturely 'Receptivity': The Search for a Middle Term," *Communio* 21 (Spring 1994): 151–61; Long, "Personal Receptivity and Act: A Thomistic Critique," *The Thomist* 61 (1997): 1–31; George A. Blair, "On Esse and Relation," *Communio* 21 (Spring 1994): 162–64. Blair implies that Clarke uses the revealed mystery of the Trinity as a premise in an argument intended to derive conclusions about being, although Clarke does not in fact do this. In rejecting the notion that *any* perfection can ever be received fully, Long inadvertently arrives at an unorthodox Christian theological position because his view implies that the Son does not perfectly receive from the Father all that the Father gives. Clarke explicitly points out this theologically pertinent error. Both Long's critique of Clarke, as well as Clarke's response to Long's critique, will be further examined later in this paper.

in terminology, their views are complimentary and together they offer a helpful lens through which to understand Clarke's project.[7]

In *An Essay on Christian Philosophy,* Maritain distinguishes between a philosophy that is Christian in the "order of specification" and one that is Christian in the "order of exercise."[8] A philosophy cannot be Christian in its order of specification (i.e., in its nature), since its object is the truth attainable through the natural power of reason. In other words, to remain genuine philosophy, Christian philosophy must rely upon a strictly philosophical method, using arguments based on reason alone.[9] However, philosophy *can* be Christian in its "order of exercise," in terms of the *state in which* human beings philosophize.[10] Because the whole human being is the one who philosophizes, his Christian faith will influence his exercise of philosophy by offering to him both objective and subjective aids.

By "subjective aids" Maritain is referring to grace and the infused virtues, which illumine and strengthen an intellect darkened by original sin. Grace also fortifies conclusions reached through natural reason.[11] For instance, Maritain brings up the way in which the theological virtue of faith nourishes and supports the philosophical knowledge of God: "Now the higher virtues succor the lowlier in the proper sphere of the latter. The virtue of faith, for example, enables the philosopher, who knows of the existence of God by purely natural means, to adhere rationally to this truth with a sturdier grasp."[12] Christian revelation is also able to provide "objective aids" to philosophy in three ways, as the history of philosophy amply demonstrates. First, Christian revelation is able to reveal some things that, although by nature belonging to the field of philosophy, might not be recognized as such. This was certainly the case prior to the Christian era, one example being the doctrine of creation. As soon as philosophy learns of these new elements, "it scrutinize[s] them according to its own order, which *ascends* from experience toward things divine (whereas revelation *descends* from God)."[13] Secondly, Christian revelation can serve to corroborate some things that

7. See Wippel, "The Possibility of a Christian Philosophy," *Faith and Philosophy* 1, no. 3 (July 1984): 289–90n28. Wippel acknowledges that his own understanding of Christian philosophy is basically in line with that of Maritain.

8. See Maritain, *An Essay on Christian Philosophy*, 11.

9. See Ibid., 14–15.

10. See Ibid., 17.

11. See Ibid., 26–28.

12. Ibid., 26.

13. Ibid., 19–20.

philosophers can discover on their own but which they might approach only with the greatest caution. In this category Maritain includes the validity of reason and the reasonableness of faith.[14] Third and last, Christian revelation is able to expand philosophy's field of inquiry since theology utilizes reason as an instrument to examine genuinely supernatural mysteries like the Trinity and the Incarnation. In this process, philosophy can come to realize certain truths even while being "led along paths which are not its own." Without philosophical reflection of this sort into the Christian mysteries, Maritain thinks it would have been "exceedingly unlikely that the philosophers would have come to an awareness of the metaphysical problem of the person."[15] It is worth emphasizing that each of these three kinds of objective aids still pertains to what Maritain calls the "state" or "order of exercise" of philosophy, and not to the "order of specification." In other words, a Christian philosophy that makes use of such aids truly remains a *philosophy*.[16]

Wippel's understanding of Christian philosophy is similar to and compatible with Maritain's. He distinguishes between the influence of Christian faith on philosophy in the "moment of discovery" and the "moment of proof."[17] Wippel accepts Gilson's point that medieval Christian thinkers, including Thomas Aquinas, first accepted certain beliefs on faith that they later investigated philosophically.[18] This influence of one's Christian faith in the moment of the *discovery* of truth can rightly be called Christian philosophy. What is not possible, however, is a "philosophy" that relies upon divine revelation in the *moment of proof*:

14. See Ibid., 21–22. "We come across another class of objective data which philosophy knew well but which it approached with much hesitancy, and which, though not a part of revelation, was corroborated by revelation. In the noetic order, for instance, the Christian sees the validity of reason divinely confirmed—recall St. Augustine's controversies with the Academicians—by the fact that the act of faith, notwithstanding its supra-rational character, is eminently reasonable. In this confirmation of the validity of reason he sees by implication the validity of many certitudes of the rational sphere which relate to discerning the motives of credibility."

15. Maritain, *An Essay on Christian Philosophy*, 23. It is interesting to note that Maritain refers to the possibility of the philosophers grasping the metaphysical notion of the person apart from Christian revelation as "exceedingly unlikely" but not impossible.

16. As a side note, Pope John Paul II lists Maritain by name as a recent thinker who has properly understood the relationship between faith and reason. The pope's explanation of the relationship between philosophy and theology owes much to Maritain's approach. See John Paul II, *Fides et Ratio* (1998): no. 74.

17. See John F. Wippel, *Metaphysical Themes in Thomas Aquinas* (Washington, D.C.: The Catholic University of America Press, 1984), 23–24, and Wippel, "The Possibility of a Christian Philosophy," 280–81.

18. See Ibid., 280.

> [A] medieval thinker could never, of course, admit a revealed premise into his attempted philosophical demonstration of a given conclusion without thereby passing from philosophy to theology. The proper name for any such procedure would no longer be Christian philosophy but Christian theology.[19]

Yet a Christian who reached a philosophical conclusion by way of his experience of faith, could then submit it to philosophical proof. If the thinker succeeds in finding rational evidence, "to that extent his procedure will be strictly philosophical in the moment of proof."[20]

Wippel and Maritain agree that Christian philosophy must rely upon philosophical arguments (Wippel's "moment of proof)"[21] and abjure the use of revealed doctrines as premises in a strictly philosophical argument. Even if a particular truth first comes to be known through divine revelation, if it is to become a part of philosophy, it must be defended philosophically. Thus, the only kind of Christian philosophy that is actually possible is a philosophy that is Christian in the "order of exercise" (to use Maritain's terminology) and in the "moment of discovery" (to use Wippel's phrase).

III. Receptivity as a Positive Perfection

The traditional view of receptivity is that it corresponds with poverty, potentiality, and change.[22] If an entity receives something, it is because that entity is lacking in some way and has the potential to become something that it was not previously. On this view, only imperfect, finite, limited creatures could be "receptive"; God as "pure act" could not.

Against this view, Clarke argues that "receptivity" ultimately designates a positive perfection of being, rather than a deficiency. He first articulated this position in *Person and Being* (1993) and in an article called "Person, Being, and St. Thomas" (first published in 1992 and revised in 1994), thereby

19. Wippel, *Metaphysical Themes*, 24.

20. Wippel, "The Possibility of a Christian Philosophy," 280.

21. See Wippel, *Metaphysical Themes*, 32; Maritain, *An Essay on Christian Philosophy*, 19–20.

22. See Clarke, *Person and Being*, 83. Clarke himself admits that metaphysicians, following Aristotle's lead, "have identified receptivity with the deficiency side of being, i.e., with poverty, potentiality, a prior lack that is later filled up." He does not cite any passages from Aristotle, but Aristotle's discussion of sense perception and thinking in the *De Anima* is relevant to his point. See *De Anima* 2.12, 424a16–20 and 3.4, 429a10–18, where Aristotle compares sensing and thinking in that both involve "receiving" the (sensible or intelligible) form of an object. In both instances, the sensing animal or thinking human is in potency to the object sensed or thought. Receptivity is thus associated with a prior potentiality that is actualized by some object.

beginning a debate that unfolded sporadically in the journals *Communio* and *The Thomist* from 1992 to 1997.[23] The interlocutors included the theologians David Schindler and Steven Long, as well as several others. After receiving both supportive and critical feedback from various thinkers, most of whom were theologians, Clarke tweaked and clarified his original position as well as his arguments in several direct follow-up essays. At its heart, the debate was about more than the notion of receptivity; it was a debate about the possibility of Christian philosophy and about the methodology and sources that a Christian philosopher—especially a Thomist philosopher—can and should use.

I will analyze Clarke's reasons for his position by distinguishing two basic arguments, one of which is a generally philosophical argument that he verifies with Christian revelation (the "theologically inspired" argument), and the other of which is a strictly metaphysical argument using the negative judgment of "separation." It is notable that Clarke's method for defending receptivity as a positive perfection is the same as the method that he recognizes in St. Thomas's own thought.

In discussing Aquinas's defense of free creation against a Neoplatonic emanationist doctrine in *De potentia,* q. 3, a. 15, Clarke notes that Aquinas not only makes a reasonable argument that draws upon divine revelation, but also provides another strictly philosophical argument.[24] In an explicit appeal to revelation, Aquinas states that the Trinity's self-communicating love is already complete in itself; God does not need to create a world in order to be complete. Clarke describes this first theologically-inspired argument thus: "This is a perfect example, to me, of what it means to have a properly Christian philosophy, where one can draw when necessary on a higher revealed source of truth to illumine and help to solve a problem incapable of adequate solution on the level of a metaphysics of purely natural reason."[25] Yet St. Thomas also offers another strictly philosophical argument for the same position, showing that no particular finite effect (viz., the universe) could be logically deduced from an infinite cause. From an

23. This particular debate was first brought to my attention by the chapter on Clarke's Christian philosophy of the person in John Winkowitsch, "W. Norris Clarke's Relational Metaphysics: Being and Person," (ProQuest Dissertations Publishing, The Catholic University of America, Washington, D.C., 2016), 257–71.

24. See Clarke, "Person, Being and St. Thomas" (1994), 223–24. Clarke references the *De potentia,* q. 3, a. 15 although he does not engage directly with the text.

25. Clarke, "Person, Being and St. Thomas" (1994), 223.

infinite cause, an infinite number of effects is always possible. Clarke summarizes the conclusion of this second argument: "thus whatever finite created order exists must be the result of a free choice on God's part."[26] Here Clarke shows that St. Thomas was a thinker who was inspired philosophically by divine revelation, but who supplemented revelation with rigorous, strictly philosophical arguments. This is exactly the method that Clarke uses in his writings on the topic of receptivity. He first acknowledges his theologically-inspired discovery that receptivity is a positive perfection of being and crafts a corresponding theologically-inspired argument, and then he offers a philosophical argument for the same position.

Clarke's first argument—the one that I am calling his "theologically-inspired" argument—begins with St. Thomas's understanding of being as dynamic act. Then, through a series of inferences, Clarke draws forth additional conclusions that he believes are latent (but not explicit) in Thomas's metaphysics. Clarke shows that St. Thomas understands that real being, as possessing an act of existence (*esse*), is intrinsically active and self-communicating.[27] He cites *De potentia*, q. 2, a. 1 to illustrate St. Thomas's view that action and self-communication follow upon being:

> I answer that it is in the nature of every act to communicate itself as far as possible. Wherefore every agent acts forasmuch as it is in act: while to act is nothing else than to communicate as far as possible that whereby the agent is in act.[28]

Clarke thus views the active and self-communicative nature of being to be a position held explicitly by St. Thomas.[29]

Next, Clarke argues that the intrinsic *relationality* of being is directly implied by the active and self-communicative nature of being, even though this implication is not explicitly recognized by Aquinas: "if a being naturally

26. Ibid., 224.

27. See Clarke, *Person and Being*, 6–7.

28. Thomas Aquinas, *Quaestiones disputatae de potentia Dei*, q. 2, a. 1, translated by the English Dominican Fathers (Westminster, Maryland: The Newman Press, 1952). See also *Summa contra gentiles* III, chap. 69, no. 15, translated by Vernon J. Bourke (New York: Hanover House, 1955–57): "Furthermore, the perfection of the effect demonstrates the perfection of the cause, for a greater power brings about a more perfect effect. But God is the most perfect agent. Therefore, things created by Him obtain perfection from Him. So, to detract from the perfection of creatures is to detract from the perfection of divine power. But, if no creature has any active role in the production of any effect, much is detracted from the perfection of the creature. Indeed, it is part of the fullness of perfection to be able to communicate to another being the perfection which one possesses."

29. See Clarke, *Person and Being*, 13.

flows over into self-communicating action toward others, and also receives from them, then it cannot help but generate a network of relations with all its recipients."[30] In other words, the relational dimension of being follows from the fact that self-communication is action toward others. Consequently, Clarke describes being as having a "dyadic" structure in that it involves both an "in-itself" dimension (as substance) and a "towards-others" dimension (as relational through its action).[31]

Clarke's final move is to argue that *receptivity* is the corollary of the self-communication and relationality of being: "Without receptivity no communication can become actual and complete itself."[32] Receptivity is "in itself a positive aspect or *perfection* of being," for even though it is intermingled with poverty and potentiality in lower levels of being, in higher levels of being (such as persons), receptivity does not necessarily involve any change or temporal succession, and in fact is associated with the mutuality of love among persons.[33] He explicitly appeals to the "intra-Trinitarian life of God" and especially to the Second Person of the Trinity (as fully divine, consubstantial with the Father, and eternally begotten by the Father) as proof that "this welcoming, active receptivity is a mode of actuality and perfection, not of potentiality and imperfection."[34] Stripped of every notion of change and imperfection, receptivity at its height refers to the perfect and actively receptive love that is the counterpart of self-communicative giving. Clarke thus takes receptivity to belong to both God and creatures analogously. It is found in its highest and most perfect form in the intra-Trinitarian life of God, but "analogously and proportionately, with increasing imperfection, down through creation."[35] It is also worth remembering that although Clarke describes this understanding of receptivity as latent in Aquinas's

30. Ibid., 14. Clarke is also careful to note that although not all relations are generated by actions, it is nonetheless true that all actions and passions generate relations.

31. See Clarke, *Person and Being*, 15–16; "Person, Being, and St. Thomas" (1994), 216; italics in original. See also David L. Schindler, "Norris Clarke on Person, Being, and St Thomas," *Communio* 20 (Fall 1993): 586, and Clarke, "Response to David Schindler's Comments," *Communio* 20 (1993): 593, 596. Schindler is concerned that Clarke has located relationality and receptivity in the second act of a being (operation), rather than in a being's first act (*esse*). Clarke clarifies his own position as follows: "I hold that the relationality dimension of any real being, its dynamic tendency toward self-communicative action, is rooted in the very substantial act of *esse* itself."

32. Clarke, *Person and Being*, 20.

33. Clarke, *Person and Being*, 20–21; See also Clarke, "Person, Being, and St. Thomas" (1994), 218.

34. Clarke, "Person, Being, and St. Thomas" (1994), 221.

35. Ibid., 221.

own metaphysics, he also admits its heritage in contemporary Catholic theologians Joseph Ratzinger, Hans Urs von Balthasar, and process theologians such as Charles Hartshorne and John Cobb.[36]

Inspecting this first argument, we can see that it is a philosophical argument that involves drawing corollaries from propositions that have already been proven and relies on revelation to corroborate its final move. To confirm his conclusion that receptivity is a positive perfection of being, Clarke appeals directly to the intra-Trinitarian life, to the divine person of the Son—a clear appeal to divine revelation. Furthermore, Clarke believes that the divine revelation of God as a Trinity of Persons should illuminate our understanding of the way in which all created and finite beings participate in and image God's perfections, including receptivity. Here, Clarke follows the theological order by proceeding from what we know about God (as Trinity) to our understanding of God's creatures,[37] thus relying on revelation in the order of proof, as opposed to the order of discovery. Even when criticized, he repeats this reliance.[38] So, to characterize the first argument as a strictly "philosophical" one does not accurately capture its motivating force.

However, Clarke's second argument is a metaphysical one that uses Aquinas's negative judgment of "separation,"[39] a negative judgment by

36. See Clarke, "Person, Being, and St. Thomas" (1994), 212; 220–21; *Person and Being*, 2, 22.

37. See Aquinas, SCG II, chap. 4, no. 5. Thomas distinguishes the philosophical order from the theological order thus: "For in the teaching of philosophy, which considers creatures in themselves and leads us from them to the knowledge of God, the first consideration is about creatures; the last, of God. But in the teaching of faith, which considers creatures only in their relation to God, the consideration of God comes first, that of creatures afterwards." Thomas states that he has been following the theological order in the SCG, beginning with a discussion of God in Book I and proceeding to the treatment of creatures after that. However, in Book I, chap. 9, nos. 2–3, St. Thomas explains that he will not rely solely upon the authority of Scripture, but will in fact offer demonstrative arguments to convince his audience of the truths about God that can be known through reason, even though these truths have also been revealed by God. Thus the *Summa contra gentiles* provides an example of St. Thomas following the theological order, although he relies on philosophical arguments when possible. I think Clarke's first argument follows a similar methodology: he understands receptivity as a positive perfection first of all from a theological perspective, taking into account what we know about God as a Trinity of Persons through divine revelation, but in order to explain receptivity in its connection to the self-communication and relationality of being, he offers philosophical arguments. The difference between St. Thomas's approach in the SCG and Clarke's approach here, however, is that St. Thomas is not intending the SCG to be a work of philosophy, whereas Clarke is intending to do metaphysics.

38. See Clarke, "Reply to Stephen Long," 622.

39. See Thomas Aquinas, *Commentary on the De Trinitate of Boethius* q. 5, a. 3, in *The Division and Methods of the Sciences*, translated by Armand Mauer (Toronto: Pontifical Institute of Mediaeval Studies, 1986). "Separation" belongs to the second operation of the intellect (judgment),

which we explicitly free *being* (the subject of metaphysics) from any necessary connection with matter and motion.[40] Being need not be material, or changing, or living, etc. Hence it is through "separation" that we can come to an understanding of being *qua* being, the subject of metaphysics.[41] Other things of this type—things that can exist without matter and motion, although they are sometimes found with matter and motion—include substance, potency, and act.[42]

Clarke makes this argument explicit in *Person and Being* and restates it with even greater clarity in responses to his critics.[43] He does not overtly describe the method he employs as "separation," although he does call it "metaphysical analysis"[44] and characterizes it as a process of taking steps "to detach [a] concept from identification with the imperfections of its lower modes."[45] He uses this metaphysical analysis[46] to detach the concept of receptivity first from temporal change and then from limitation.

Ordinarily, the receptivity of a perfection is understood to involve temporal change in that the subject goes from a prior non-possession of the perfection (such as love) to a posterior possession of it.[47] However, Clarke

---

whereas "abstraction" in the narrow sense refers to the first operation of the intellect and pertains to mathematics and the natural sciences rather than to metaphysics.

40. For a further explanation of separation, see Wippel, *Metaphysical Themes*, 30–31.

41. See John F. Wippel, *The Metaphysical Thought of Thomas Aquinas: from Finite Being to Uncreated Being* (Washington, D.C.: The Catholic University of America Press, 2000), 48–49.

42. See Aquinas, *De Trinitate*, q. 5, a. 4; See also Wippel, *The Metaphysical Thought of Thomas Aquinas*, 7–8.

43. See Clarke, *Person and Being*, 84–85. For a criticism of Clarke's argument, see George A. Blair, "On Esse and Relation," *Communio* 21 (Spring 1994): 164. Blair critiques Clarke for arguing from revealed Christian mysteries to the conclusion that receptivity is a positive perfection. For Clarke's response to this critique and a reiteration of his reliance on "metaphysical analysis" (the judgment of separation), see his "Response to Blair's Comments," *Communio* 21 (Spring 1994): 170–71. He denies that Blair has accurately characterized his method. He agrees with Blair that "deducing from the revealed doctrine of the Trinity the general metaphysical truth that all being in act is by nature self-communicative and relational" is "invalid philosophically, even for a Christian philosopher" (170). He adds that his own position "is put forward as a strictly metaphysical truth of universal validity arrived at by a strictly philosophical analysis open to any metaphysician, whether he accepts the Trinity or not" (170).

44. Clarke, "Response to Blair's Comments," 170.

45. Clarke, "Response to Long's Comments," *Communio* 21 (Spring 1994): 166.

46. See Long, "Divine and Creaturely 'Receptivity'," 157–58; "Personal Receptivity and Act," 27–28. Long explicitly characterizes Clarke's method as a "judgment of separation" and agrees that this methodology is the correct one for a metaphysician to use. However, he disagrees with Clarke's affirmation that a negative judgment of separation can *actually yield* a concept of receptivity that is stripped of all potentiality and limitation.

47. See Clarke, *Person and Being*, 84.

shows that it is possible to conceptually detach the aspects of motion and temporal change from the notion of receptivity: "Thus if person A timelessly gives perfection X to person B, then B does not first lack perfection and then later receive it, but *always* possesses it in *act*."[48] Usually a temporal passage from potentiality to act does accompany receptivity, but there is nothing about the concept of receptivity in itself that requires temporal change; receptivity is intelligible apart from a temporal before and after. Next, Clarke shows that receptivity can also be understood apart from limitation: "to *receive* a perfection does not assert that the perfection is *not received fully*, but only that it is received *from another*; whether fully or partially is not specified by the concept itself."[49] The fact that a perfection is received from another does not thereby indicate only a limited reception of or partial sharing in that perfection. Clarke's point is that nothing about the notion of receptivity itself involves limitation. According to Aquinas, "act is not limited except by reception in a distinct potency."[50] In other words, an act that is communicated to another is limited only by the potency of the other. This principle in its most generic expression simply states that "whatever is received in something is received in accord with the mode of that which receives it."[51] Whether an act is received fully or only in a limited and partial way is dependent upon the nature of the recipient. Having thus removed both the notion of temporal change and the notion of limitation from receptivity, Clarke concludes: "receptivity can be seen as an analogous concept transcending all its various possible modes."[52] In other words, receptivity has been shown to be the sort of thing that does not need to be tied to matter and motion, even if we have not yet proven its existence in some actually existing immaterial being.

To this last point one could perhaps raise the following objection: Although the negative judgment of "separation" allows us to see that receptivity *could* exist apart from all temporal change and limitation, we have not

48. Ibid., 85; italics in original.

49. Clarke, "Response to Long's Comments," 166; italics in original. See also Clarke, *Person and Being*, 85.

50. Clarke, "The Limitation of Act by Potency: Aristotelianism or Neoplatonism," *The New Scholasticism* 26, no. 2 (1952): 190. Instances where this principle appears in the works of Aquinas include SCG I, chap. 43, no. 5, and *Compendium theologiae*,18. In both of these passages St. Thomas uses this principle to argue that God is infinite.

51. John F. Wippel, *Metaphysical Themes in Thomas Aquinas II* (Washington, D.C.: The Catholic University of America Press, 2007), 113.

52. Clarke, "Response to Long's Comments," 166–67.

yet discovered that it *does* in fact exist in such a mode, and unless we know that it does exist in such a mode, Clarke's argument is problematic. Such an objection is similar to one that Wippel acknowledges has been raised against St. Thomas's own use of "separation" to grasp being, since some interpreters do not think it is justified to use "separation" unless it has already been demonstrated that being *does* exist apart from matter and motion in at least one instance. In other words, these objectors think that the actual existence of an immaterial being must be proven first before we can judge that being as such need not be material.[53] Wippel, however, does not think that St. Thomas believes that one must have prior knowledge that a positively immaterial being *actually exists* in order to use the judgment of separation to grasp being *qua* being. Pointing to the *De Trinitate*, q. 5, a. 4, Wippel argues that the metaphysician must first use separation to discover the subject of his science (being *qua* being) and only then "will be in position to inquire about the principles of that subject, that is, about divine things or the positively immaterial."[54] I think that this response is also applicable to the potential objection raised against Clarke's use of separation. Clarke does not need to prove that receptivity *actually exists* in a mode apart from temporal change and limitation; all he must do (and this he has done) is to show that receptivity *qua* receptivity does not involve any temporal change or limitation, since it *could* exist apart from these things.

To summarize this second philosophical argument, Clarke uses the method that St. Thomas himself associates with metaphysical analysis—a negative judgment of separation—to detach the aspects of temporal change and limitation from the notion of receptivity. Clarke also believes that this argument is valid independently of any reference to Christian revelation.[55]

Is Norris Clarke's proposal that receptivity is a positive perfection of being a genuine exercise in Christian philosophy? We are now in a place to say that it is. Clarke's approach is best characterized as one in which Christian revelation is involved in what Wippel calls the "moment of discovery." As previously noted, Clarke himself admits that he first arrived at the notion of receptivity as a positive perfection through the insights of contemporary theologians.[56] Clarke is also forthcoming about his belief that Christian rev-

53. See Wippel, *The Metaphysical Thought of Thomas Aquinas*, 51–53.

54. Ibid., 53.

55. See Clarke, "Response to Blair's Comments," 170.

56. See Clarke, "Person, Being, and St. Thomas," 612; *Person and Being*, 86.

elation can illumine our understanding of being, person, receptivity, and other metaphysical concepts.

Furthermore, Clarke's use of divine revelation seems to correspond most closely to the third kind of "objective aid" that Maritain believes Christianity can offer to philosophy. Using reason to investigate the revealed mystery of the Trinity, Clarke has discovered that receptivity is a positive perfection, and it is unlikely that philosophers would ever have reached this conclusion without divine revelation, just as Maritain notes that the discovery of the person would have been likewise unlikely apart from Christian revelation.

It is thus evident that Clarke's project has involved the use of Christian revelation in the "moment of discovery." What about his usage of revealed truths in the "moment of proof"? Although even Clarke's first argument uses philosophical reasoning, ultimately it rests on a consideration of the intra-Trinitarian life of God (specifically the Son's perfect receptivity of the divine nature from the Father) as the greatest evidence in defense of receptivity as a positive perfection. Hence Clarke's first argument is probably best characterized as a theological one that makes use of philosophical reasoning. However, his second argument relies upon a strictly metaphysical analysis in the "moment of proof." An insight first provided by Christian revelation has now been worked out in a strictly philosophical way.

One last aspect of Clarke's defense of receptivity as a positive perfection remains to be considered. In addition to these two arguments in support of his position, Clarke appeals to the idea that Christian revelation must function as a "negative norm," preventing Christian philosophers from drawing conclusions that appear to contradict the Christian faith.[57] Consequently, at the very least, no philosopher who is a Christian can argue that the converse of Clarke's position is true—that receptivity *always* involves temporal change, potentiality, and limitation. Clarke explicitly makes this point after a somewhat heated exchange with the theologian Steven A. Long.

Long, who accepts that a negative judgment of separation is a valid method for the metaphysician, nevertheless disagrees with Clarke that a judgment of separation *actually* yields a concept of receptivity that is stripped of all potentiality and limitation. Contra Clarke, Long concludes the following:

57. See Clarke, "Reply to Stephen Long," 623. ". . . theology is always taken as a negative norm, in the sense that no statement in philosophy will be allowed that contradicts or renders unintelligible a statement from theology, at least in its formally defined parts."

If the receiving subject does not originate the perfection, it would seem that even on the hypothesis of a 'complete reception' of a perfection the subject would stand in an atemporal relation of potency vis-à-vis the originating principle of the perfection: 'atemporal' because not every receiving is temporal, and here we are concerned with the pure definition of 'receiving'; 'potency' because in some respect—that of the perfection received—the subject is actualized by another (whether temporally or nontemporally) and hence is not simply self-actualizing. From this very datum it becomes manifest that a received pure perfection *cannot be received in its totality*.[58]

In other words, although Long agrees with Clarke that the notion of receptivity can be detached from temporal change, he does not agree with Clarke that the notion of receptivity can be detached from limitation and potency. Rather, he argues that potency belongs to the very definition of receptivity.[59] It is simply not possible in Long's view to "receive" a perfection fully, because reception always involves limitation and potency.[60] He does acknowledge that Catholic thinkers sometimes speak of the "receptivity" of the Son, who receives the divine nature from the Father in virtue of being the eternally generated Son of the Father.[61] But Long argues that such an understanding of receptivity is "complete equivocation." [62] The same term might be used to describe the receptivity of creatures and the Son's receptivity to the Father, but the meaning of the term in each case is completely unrelated. He thinks that "receptivity" in its ordinary sense implies ontological imperfection and pertains to creatures composed of essence and existence, which receive their perfections from another and are not self-actualized.

Clarke, however, argues that receptivity is to be understood analogously, not equivocally, as it pertains to creatures and to the divine person of the Son.[63] In the most perfect of beings (persons), receptivity indicates "one whole side of the richness of being-together, as intrinsically ordered toward

58. Long, "Personal Receptivity and Act," 27–28; italics in original. See also Long, "Divine and Creaturely 'Receptivity'," 157.

59. See Long, "Divine and Creaturely 'Receptivity'," 157.

60. Although neither Long nor Clarke brings up the Thomistic distinction between univocal, equivocal, and analogical efficient causes, I think it would be helpful to do so. See Aquinas, ST I, q. 4, a. 2; q. 6, a. 2. Univocal causes are efficient causes whose effects are of the same species as themselves. In other words, the same perfection is found according to the same formality in both the cause and the effect, and the effect is equal to the power of the cause. Surely univocal causality provides a clear philosophical example of the idea that receptivity does not always involve limitation on the side of the recipient.

61. See Long, "Divine and Creaturely 'Receptivity'," 155–56, 158.

62. See Ibid., 158.

63. See Clarke, "Response to Long's Comments," 165; 168; "Reply to Stephen Long," 619.

communion—an aspect of being which the Second Person of the Trinity is the supreme and totally positive example."[64] The example that Clarke returns to again and again is the "active receptivity" involved in a communion of love between persons.[65] This is found perfectly in the Trinity, but analogously in human relationships. Clarke therefore takes issue with Long's conclusion about the nature of receptivity not only for philosophical reasons, but ultimately because Long's conclusion conflicts with the Christian revelation of the divine person of the Son. Clarke explains:

> But it is not obvious—nor does [Long] attempt to prove it—that all receiving of perfection by one subject from another implies potency, nor that 'a received perfection cannot be received in its totality.' For the latter is precisely what happens in the Trinity, in the communication of the divine nature from the Father to the Son.... Long does not draw these essential distinctions, but makes an unqualified general statement that is clearly false when applied to the Trinity.[66]

Clarke critiques Long's position because it implies that theology and revelation are irrelevant for philosophy. Divine revelation shows that receptivity belongs to God insofar as it belongs to the divine person of the Son, and in the Son there is no limitation or imperfection. The Son receives the divine nature from the Father *eternally, fully, and perfectly*. In short, to insist that all receptivity involves imperfection and potency is to insist on something that flies in the face of Christian revelation.[67] Clarke ends his final contribution to the five-year debate on this note: "It may seem that I have been somewhat harsh in my reply to my critic. I am not accustomed to writing in this way. I did so only because I consider it so important today to make it clear how incomplete, even misleading, it can be when a Christian philosopher tries to ignore, or take no account of, the distinctively new and powerful light that Christian revelation, in particular that of the Trinity, sheds on what it means both to be and to be a person."[68]

64. Clarke, "Response to Long's Comments," 166.

65. Ibid., 168; See also "Reply to Stephen Long," 618.

66. Clarke, "Reply to Stephen Long," 622.

67. In defense of Clarke's position that receptivity is to be understood analogously as it pertains to the Son and to creatures, and that the Son's perfect and eternal receptivity of the fullness of the divine nature from the Father—without any implication of potentiality or limitation on the part of the Son—is a genuine part of the Christian revelation, I point to the words of Aquinas, who speaks of the Son's perfect "receptivity" of the divine nature in many places, e.g. *De potentia*, q. 3, a. 15, ad 17; q. 10, a. 2. Cf. ST I, q. 33, a. 3, ad 2, where he describes "receptivity"—the ability to receive (*accipere*)—as an analogous term that applies both to the Son and to creatures.

68. Clarke, "Reply to Stephen Long," 624.

IV. Conclusion

If we take a step back and view Clarke's understanding of receptivity from a distance, we see that it is one of his lasting contributions to Thomistic philosophy. In one of the last articles that he wrote in his lifetime, entitled "The Integration of Personalism and Thomistic Metaphysics in Twenty-First Century Thomism" (2009), Clarke characterizes his theory of receptivity as a contribution that has helped to complete the project of Thomistic personalism, a project that began especially with Karol Wojtyla (Pope John Paul II) and the Lublin School.[69] As Clarke understands it, Thomistic personalism brings together the interpersonal phenomenology of twentieth-century Christian personalism (e.g., Mounier, Marcel, Scheler, and Buber) with the traditional existential metaphysics of the Thomistic tradition. Clarke insists that a personalist dimension is already latent within Thomistic metaphysics and has only to be brought into the light. Clarke's insight that receptivity is a positive ontological perfection helps to make possible the "*personalization of being itself* from within Thomistic metaphysics" in that it helps us to see that the fullness of being is "persons-in-communion."[70] In this same article, Clarke reiterates his conviction that his project has been an exercise in Christian philosophy.[71]

If we return to where we began, we can now understand the way in which Clarke's philosophical project concerning receptivity and metaphysics serves as a contemporary model of Christian philosophy. Clarke, like St. Thomas Aquinas and others before him, believes that the Christian revelation can illuminate our philosophical inquiry by bringing to light certain insights that we would not necessarily have arrived at through unaided reason. Would St. Thomas himself have come to his elegant and highly-developed understanding of the essence/existence distinction and to his understanding of God as "*Ipsum Esse*" without prior exposure to Exodus 3:14 and to God's self-revelation there as the "I AM"? Would early medieval philosophers ever have come to a notion of the "person" without

69. See Clarke, "The Integration of Personalism and Thomistic Metaphysics," 226.

70. Ibid., 230; italics in original.

71. See Ibid., 231: "This self-revelation on God's own part confirms from above that our philosophical personalization of metaphysics is precisely on the right track. This is the very nature of Being itself at its highest level, to be Persons-in-communion, although philosophy cannot take us all the way to this secure affirmation on its own. The mystery unveiled by revelation makes the last step for our limited rational resources."

the ecumenical councils of the early Church and their Trinitarian formulations? Would anyone have realized that receptivity is a positive perfection of being without reflecting on the mystery of the intra-Trinitarian life? The answer to all of these questions is likely in the negative. Yet, despite theological influence, these insights also contribute to the great philosophical tradition as insights into the nature of being. There is need in our own era for Christian philosophers who will ponder in "alert receptivity"[72] the rich Christian theological tradition, ready to receive insights that can bear fruit in the philosophical realm.

72. See Jacques Maritain, *Creative Intuition in Art and Poetry* (Cleveland, Ohio: The World Publishing Company, 1953), 103.

JOHN J. CONLEY, SJ

Catechetical Thomism

Metaphysics and Sacraments

One of the parlor games of Catholic intellectuals involves classifying the various types of Thomism. Common candidates are paleo-Thomism (the Dominicans of the Angelicum), existential Thomism (Maritain and Gilson), transcendental Thomism (Jesuits Maréchal and Lonergan), neo-Aristotelian Thomism (De Koninck and the Laval school), and analytical Thomism (Brian Davies). Two of my personal homegrown American favorites are Shake-and-Bake Thomism ("Mix Thomistic metaphysics with the Southern military academy and stir") and Rage Thomism ("Bring back the 1950s, especially the parochial-school 1950s, as a Thomistic revival.") Both of the latter exhibit a suspicious nostalgia for the old Confederacy. Discretion indicates that I should not name names associated with the two latter categories.

Often forgotten, however, is the pastoral rather than scholarly circuit by which Thomism has shaped the rhetoric, the beliefs, and the practices of millions of modern Catholics. This is the catechetical circuit. It is through the catechetical text, rather than through the *Summa Theologica* or a commentary thereof, that we learned to perceive reality in terms of form and matter, substance and accident, the cardinal virtues, and cosmological arguments for God's existence. I will focus in particular on the Roman Catechism of 1566 (often called the Catechism of the Council of Trent and the Catechism of Pius V),[1] since it served as the text of reference and template

1. See *The Catechism of the Council of Trent or The Catechism for Parish Priests*, translated by John A. McHugh and Charles J. Callan (New York: Joseph F. Wagner, 1923), cited hereafter as

for thousands of diocesan and scholastic catechisms composed well into the twentieth century, including the various editions of the Baltimore Catechism.[2] I will study in particular the presence of Thomistic metaphysics in the catechetical presentation of the Catholic doctrine of the sacraments.

I. Sacraments in a Metaphysical Framework: Baptism

Modern catechetical texts commonly used the Aristotelian-Thomistic metaphysical categories of form and matter to explain the Catholic doctrine of the sacraments. Each of the seven sacraments is ascribed a precise type of form and matter. Not only is this form and matter central in explaining the nature of sacrament to neophytes; it is crucial in determining the validity and the liceity of a real or attempted sacramental action. The Roman Catechism's treatment of baptism and the Holy Eucharist illustrates this metaphysical procedure.

The matter of the sacrament of baptism is water. "The matter, then, or element of this Sacrament, is any sort of natural water, which is simply and without qualification called water, be it sea water, river water, water from a pond, well or fountain." (*CCT*, 119) Although water baptism was instituted by Christ to effect—and not only to symbolize—redemption from sin, the choice of water is not arbitrary. In the discussion of signs which constitutes the preamble to the analysis of the seven sacraments, the Catechism differentiates among three types of signs: those which bear a natural resemblance to the spiritual truth signified, those which bear a conventional (or social or human-made) resemblance to the spiritual quality signified, and those signs explicitly created by God to signify some spiritual reality.[3] The difference of the sacrament in this forest of symbols, of course, is that the sacrament brings about, and not only points to, the spiritual reality it signifies.

The Catechism specifies how the baptismal water is fitting or appro-

---

CCT. Promulgated by Pope St. Pius V in 1566, the Catechism was composed by a committee under the direction of St. Charles Borromeo and followed a mandate for its composition issued by the Council of Trent. This English translation is based on the fourth Roman edition of the Latin text, issued in 1907.

2. First published in 1885, *A Catechism of Christian Doctrine*, popularly known as the Baltimore Catechism, was based on Robert Bellarmine's *Small Catechism*, a condensation of the Roman Catechism.

3. The Catechism's discussion of three types of signs (*CCT*, 108) acknowledges its explicit debt to Saint Augustine, presumably his *De Doctrina Christiana*.

priate matter for this sacrament due to its natural qualities and due to its repeated use by God in the history of salvation. "In the first place, water, which is always at hand and within the reach of all, was the fittest matter of a Sacrament which is necessary to all for salvation. In the next place water is best adapted to signify the effect of Baptism. It washes away uncleanness, and is, therefore, strikingly illustrative of the virtue and efficacy of Baptism, which washes away the stains of sin. We may also add that, like water which cools the body, Baptism in great measure extinguishes the fires of concupiscence." (*CCT*, 119) Due to its natural purifying and cooling quality and due to its ubiquity on earth, water is uniquely disposed to signify and to effect the spiritual ablution from sin destined for all humanity.

It is not only its natural qualities that dispose water to serve as the matter for a sacrament of spiritual cleansing and purification. It is its repeated use by God in salvation history to signify repentance, healing, and liberation that makes water the apt matter for baptism. The Great Flood of Genesis is illustrative of moral cleansing. "The deluge which cleansed the world because the wickedness of men was great on the earth, and all the thought of their heart was bent upon evil, was a figure and image of this water." (*CCT*, 119) The water-connected healings in the New Testament testify to the use of water in divine healing. "The cleansing of Naaman the Syrian, and the admirable virtue of the pool of Bethsaida, and many similar types, are manifestly symbolic of this mystery." (*CCT*, 119) The waters of Exodus point to liberation from oppression. "The passage through the Red Sea was typical of this same water." (*CCT*, 119) All the biblical incidents cited by the Catechism involve the use of water by God in a supernatural manner to bring about a spiritual repentance, healing, and liberation which water in its undisturbed natural state could not effect. The matter used in baptism is more than matter, since God has repeatedly used the matter of water to bring about spiritual goods which go beyond the reach of material nature although they fall short of the redemption from sin which is the telos of sacramental baptism. Even more than the order of nature, the order and economy of salvation, where water has been repeatedly used by God to effect supernatural changes, indicates the appropriateness of water as the matter for sacramental baptism.

The form of the sacrament of baptism consists of a verbal formula: "I baptize thee in the name of the Father, and of the Son, and of the Holy Ghost." (*CCT*, 120) The water is to be poured on the forehead of the candidate for baptism as the minister pronounces the trinitarian formula. The Catechism is indifferent as to the mode of this ablution – immersion, infusion, or aspersion is acceptable.

The trinitarian formula is based on the authority of Christ. "It was so delivered by Our Lord and Savior when, as we read in St. Matthew, He gave to His Apostles the command: Go and teach ye all nations, baptizing them in the name of the Father, and of the Son, and of the Holy Ghost." (*CCT*, 121) But the trinitarian formula is not based on authority alone. The formula points to the baptism of Christ by John the Baptist, the seminal moment in the institution of the sacrament. The presence of the Trinity at the baptism of Christ is echoed in every new baptism of a Christian. "A very strong argument to prove that Baptism was then instituted by our Lord might be afforded by the fact that the most holy Trinity, in whose name Baptism is conferred, manifested its divine essence on that occasion. The voice of the Father was heard, the Person of the Son was present, the Holy Ghost descended in the form of a dove; and the heavens, into which we are enabled to enter by Baptism, were thrown open." (*CCT*, 122) The verbal form of the sacrament manifests the interior identity of Christ as the Son in the concert of three divine persons.

Annexed to the question of matter and form in the sacrament of baptism is the question of the appropriate minister. Following longstanding tradition, the Catechism provides an expansive answer. The ordinary minister is the bishop and priest. A deacon may also baptize. But in cases of necessity, virtually anyone with the right intention may perform a baptism. "Those who administer Baptism in cases of necessity … includes all, even the laity, men and women, to whatever sect they may belong. This office extends, in cases of necessity, even to Jews, infidels and heretics, provided, however, they intend to do what the Catholic Church does in that act of ministry." (*CCT*, 124) The Catechism defends the practice of baptism by midwives and exhorts priests to deliver detailed sermons on baptism since this is the one sacrament where laity, especially women, can function as ministers.

II. Holy Eucharist

The Roman Catechism's treatment of the sacrament of the Holy Eucharist follows a similar structure of argumentation. The sacrament is explained through the metaphysical principles of form and matter, but the explanation receives a metaphysical expansion through the introduction of the principles of substance and accident.

The matter of the Eucharist are bread and wine. The bread and wine are used by authority of the command of Christ to his apostles at the Last Supper. But again, this command is not arbitrary. These elements have a natural aptitude to signify and actually become the Body and Blood of Christ. "Observing as we do, that the bread and wine are every day changed by the power of nature into human flesh and blood, we are led the more easily by this analogy to believe that the substance of the bread and wine is changed, by the heavenly benediction, into the real flesh and blood of Christ." (*CCT*, 136) The daily experience of how bread and wine, common food staples, are changed into the flesh and blood of the human body makes them apt for use as elements transformed into Christ's Body and Blood. Biological transformation is linked to spiritual transformation.

This natural resemblance is enhanced by specifically theological resemblances. In the New Testament, Christ explicitly refers to himself as our food and drink. Physical food and drink are apt to represent this spiritual reality. "Our Lord Himself says: My flesh is food indeed and my blood is drink indeed. As, then, the body of Christ the Lord turns nourishment unto eternal life to those who receive this sacrament with purity and holiness, rightly is the matter composed chiefly of those elements by which our present life is sustained." (*CCT*, 136) The eucharistic matter is linked to Christological titles.

There are also ecclesiological reasons for the appropriateness of bread and wine as the matter for the sacrament. "The body of the Church, which is one, consists of many members, and of this union nothing is more strikingly illustrative than the elements of bread and wine; for bread is made through many grains and wine is pressed from many clusters of grapes. Thus, they signify that we, though many, are closely bound together by the bond of this divine mystery and, made as it were, one body." (*CCT*, 137) The bread and wine transformed into the Body and Blood of Christ also serve to transform isolated believers into one spiritual body, the Church. The composite nature of bread and wine, both of which are created by the patient molding together of disparate ingredients into a new single substance, renders them appropriate to signify the ecclesial union wrought by the Eucharist.

The form of the sacrament resides in the words of consecration of the bread and wine, based on the words of institution at the Lord's Supper found in the synoptic gospels. "The form consists of these words: This is my body, for it is written: Whilst they were at supper, Jesus took bread, and blessed it, and brake it and gave it to his disciples, and said: Take and eat. This is my body" (*CCT*, 137). Based on Saint Luke and Saint Paul, the words of consecration for the wine are "This is the chalice of my blood, of the new and eternal testament, the mystery of faith, which shall be shed for you and for many, to the remission of sins" (*CCT*, 138).

The form of the eucharistic prayer is not based on the authority of Christ and the Scriptures alone. The Catechism examines in detail the theological truths veiled beneath the exact words. The chalice indicates that Christ's blood has become the drink of the faithful. The reference to the New Testament indicates that this testament is sealed in blood; it is not just a figure of sacrifice. The reference to eternity indicates the eternal inheritance which is the destiny of the faithful. Interestingly, in light of our current controversy over the translation of *pro multis*, the Catechism argues that "if we look to its value, we must confess that the Redeemer shed his blood for the salvation of all; but if we look to the fruit which mankind have received from it, we shall easily find that it pertains not unto all, but to many of the human race" (*CCT*, 139). The verbal form of the sacrament carries its own theological weight and inevitability.

In one fundamental respect, the sacrament of the Eucharist operates differently from the other sacraments. It not only effects a spiritual change in the soul of the recipient; it actually changes the bread and wine into the body and blood of Christ. To explain this transformation, the Catechism resorts to another Aristotelian-Thomistic metaphysical principle: substance and accident.

The Catechism describes the eucharistic change as one where the substance of bread and wine is changed into the substance of the body and blood of Christ. The substance changes but the accidents of bread and wine remain. "The whole substance of the bread is changed by the power of God into the whole substance of the body of Christ, and the whole substance of the wine into the whole substance of His blood, and this without any change in our Lord himself. He is neither begotten, nor changed, nor increased, but remains entire in his substance" (*CCT*, 146.) This change operated during the Eucharist differs from a generic transformation in an object. Only the term *transubstantiation* captures what makes this particular change different—and miraculous. "Since natural changes are rightly called transformations, because they involve a change of form; so likewise our predecessors in the faith wisely and appropriately introduced the term transubstantiation, in order to signify that in the Sacrament of the Eucharist the whole substance of one thing passes into the whole substance of another" (*CCT*, 146).

The Catechism refutes other explanations of how the body and blood of Christ can be present under the appearances of bread and wine. This change cannot represent a change of place, as if the glorified body of Christ in heaven suddenly moved to the altar or tabernacle. The idea that the body of Christ is created anew during each consecration is absurd. Only the doctrine of transubstantiation can explain how the bread and wine actually became the body and blood of Christ. "In order that the body of our Lord be present in the Sacrament, it remains, therefore, that it be rendered present by the change of the bread into it. Wherefore it is necessary that none of the substance of bread remain" (*CCT*, 145).

The Catechism admits that the doctrine of transubstantiation leads to metaphysical anomalies. It explicitly refers to "the mystery of accidents without a subject" (*CCT*, 147). What could it mean to claim that the accidents of bread and wine remain when there is no bread and wine? To bolster this obscure dogma, it resorts to arguments from ecclesial authority. It cites the famous anathema of the Council of Trent: "If anyone shall say in this most Holy Sacrament of the Eucharist the substance of bread and wine remains, together with the body and blood of our Lord Jesus Christ, let him be anathema" (*CCT*, 145). It cites passages from Scripture and the church fathers which, while not using explicitly the term transubstantiation, indicate that transubstantiation has occurred in the Eucharist and that this transubstantiation permits no co-existence between the substance of bread and wine and the substance of the body and blood of Christ.

An exhortation to pastors, a central public of the Roman Catechism, underscores the opacity of the dogma of transubstantiation the Catechism has taken pains to prove. "The faithful are to be admonished against curious searching into the manner in which this change is effected. It defies the powers of conception; nor can we find any example of it in natural transmutations, or even in the very work of creation. That such a change takes place must be recognized by faith; how it takes place we must not curiously inquire" (*CCT*, 147). The philosophical and theological demonstration of the truth of the dogma of transubstantiation is covered by a cloud of piety.

Using the metaphysical principles of substance and accident, the Church leads the believer to an obscure affirmation rooted in faith alone. The eucharistic hymns of Aquinas elaborate on the role of faith alone in discerning the presence of the body and blood of Christ in the eucharistic species: "Lo, the Sacred host we hail. / Lo, o'er ancient forms departing / Newer rites of grace prevail, / Faith for all defects supplying / When the feeble senses fail" (*Pange lingua*). "We do not believe because of what we see or taste or touch. / We believe only because of what God the Son has said. / That Word of truth will last forever" (*Adoro te devote*).

III. Confirmation, Extreme Unction, Penance

The Catechism analyzes the other five sacraments through the metaphysical grid of form and matter. This Aristotelian-Thomistic analytic approach, however, does not operate with equal effectiveness over all the sacraments. If certain sacraments can be easily studied in this framework, others prove resistant to this binary analysis.

Confirmation clearly indicates its composition of form and matter. The form lies in the words used by the consecrating bishop: "I sign thee with the sign of the cross, and I confirm thee with the chrism of salvation, in the name of the Father and of the Son and of the Holy Ghost" (*CCT*, 144). This verbal formula indicates three powers communicated to the confirmed through the sacrament: the divine power of transformation; the new strength of mind and soul oriented toward salvation; the new commitment to spiritual combat as a soldier of Christ.

The matter is dual: the chrism and balsam used in the anointing. As elsewhere, the Catechism underscores the natural and scriptural appropriateness of the matter for a gesture that infuses the three preceding gifts into the soul of the confirmand. "Oil, by its nature rich, unctuous and fluid expresses the fulness of grace, which, through the Holy Spirit, overflows and is poured into others from Christ the head, like the ointment that ran down upon the beard of Aaron, to the skirt of his garment." (*CCT*, 143). Similarly, the fragrant balsam appropriately points out to the moral effects of confirmation: the growth in virtue and the protection from sin during spiritual combat. "Balsam, the odor of which is most fragrant, can signify naught save that the faithful, when made perfect by the grace of Confirmation, diffuse around them such a sweet odor of all virtues, that they may say with the Apostle:

We are unto God the good odor of Christ. Balsam also has the power of preserving from corruption whatever it is used to anoint" (*CCT*, 143).

Similarly, the sacrament of Extreme Unction can be analyzed through the form/matter prism. The matter of the sacrament is olive oil blessed by the bishop. This oil is naturally appropriate for this sacrament, since it has natural properties of healing and comforting those who are ill or injured. "Oil is very efficacious in soothing bodily pain, and the power of this Sacrament lessens the pain and anguish of the soul. Oil also restores health, brings joy, feeds light, and is very efficacious in refreshing bodily fatigue. All these effects signify what the divine power accomplishes in the sick man through the administration of this sacrament" (*CCT*, 206). The natural healing properties of oil appropriately symbolize the supernatural healing and pardon effected by God in the sacrament.

The form of the sacrament resides in the words used by the anointing priest: "By this Holy Unction may God pardon thee whatever sins thou hast committed by the evil use of sight, smell, or touch" (*CCT*, 206). The warrant for this formula is the exhortation in the epistle of Saint James that priests (presbyters) should anoint the sick in the church and pray over them. "That this is the true form of this Sacrament we learn from these words of St. James. Let them pray over him ... and the prayer of faith shall save the sick man" (*CCT*, 206). Although it is church tradition that establishes the particular prayers to be uttered, these formulae were created in response to a divinely inspired command.

The sacrament of Penance is less susceptible to form/matter analysis. If the form of the sacrament is evident, its matter proves elusive.

The form of Penance is the formula of absolution used by the priest in absolving the penitent from sin. "The form is: 'I absolve thee,' as may be inferred not only from the words, 'Whatsoever you shall bind on earth shall be bound also in heaven,' but also from the teaching of Christ Our Lord, handed down to us from the Apostles" (*CCT*, 181). The power of the priest to absolve sins is rooted in the divine commission of Christ to his disciples to do so on the evening of the Resurrection (John 20: 22–23).

The Catechism's elaboration of the form of Penance reflects an anti-Protestant polemic. Whereas many Protestant churches had argued that the ordained minister had the power and the office to declare that God had forgiven our sins, the Catechism insists that the priest-confessor actually has the actual power to absolve sins when he pronounces the words of absolution on a properly disposed penitent. "Since the Sacraments signify what they effect, the words, I absolve thee, signify that the remission of sin is effected by the administration of this Sacrament" (*CCT*, 181). The Catechism reinforces this view of the efficacy of sacramental absolution by distinguishing the power of the Catholic priest from the power of the priesthood of the Old Covenant. "How thankful, then, should not sinners be to God for having bestowed such power on the priests of His Church! Unlike the priests of the Old Law, who merely declared the leper cleansed from his leprosy, the power now given to the priest of the new law is not limited to declaring the sinner absolved from his sins, but, as a minister of God, he truly absolves from sin" (*CCT*, 181). The absolution from sin is effected, and not only symbolized or affirmed or recalled, by the priest's verbal act in the administration of the sacrament. The Catechism compares this to the lifting of the chains of sin which had bound the captive soul.

The matter of the sacrament of Penance is less clear because unlike the other sacraments, there is no material object required for the administration of this sacrament. Neither bread nor wine nor water nor chrism nor oil are used. The Catechism argues that the matter for this sacrament is of a spiritual, psychological nature within the soul of the penitent. "Penance differs from the other sacraments in this: that the matter of the other Sacraments is some thing, whether natural or artificial, the matter, as it were, of the Sacrament of Penance is the acts of the penitent, namely, contrition, confession, and satisfaction" (*CCT*, 181). Clearly, the Catechism can offer no commentary on the natural or supernatural appropriateness of this matter, since there is nothing tangible or visible to it. It functions very differently from the material substances used in the other sacraments.

Just as the Catechism's presentation of transubstantiation in the Holy Eucharist strains against the form/matter grid, the presentation on Penance also indicates the limits of this binary metaphysical approach. The concept of immaterial matter can appear as opaque as the concept of accidents that exist without inhering in any substance.

IV. Holy Orders and Matrimony

The Catechism's treatment of Holy Orders and Matrimony further illustrates the ease and the difficulty with which particular sacraments can be analyzed through the metaphysical lens of form and matter.

The analysis of Holy Orders (*CCT*, 207) is straightforward. The matter of the sacrament involves a physical substance and a physical gesture: the oil of chrism and the bishop's laying on of hands. The form is the long consecratory prayer uttered by the bishop, which delineates the nature and mission of the priesthood to which the Church is ordaining the candidate.

The metaphysical analysis of Matrimony (*CCT*, 209) is more elusive. The matter is an interior disposition rather than a physical substance. The matter is the mutual consent of the couple to live together as husband and wife in a lifelong, exclusive union of love. The form is the verbal promise made by the couple during the course of the ceremony: "I, N., take you, N., as my lawful husband/wife until death do us part." An unusual feature of this sacrament concerns the minister of the sacrament. It is the bride and groom themselves—and not the presiding priest, who acts only as a witness—who act as the minister of the sacrament.

V. Conclusion

The centrality of Thomistic metaphysics in presenting the sacraments in the Roman Catechism and its offspring indicates the reach of Thomistic philosophy far beyond the bounds of philosophy departments and academic publications. The time for studying the sociology of Thomism may have arrived. Notre Dame's Philip Gleason has recounted how Thomistic philosophy, and not theology, gave coherence and integrating structure to Catholic higher education until the 1960s.[4] Joseph McShane has documented the role of Thomism in the rise of the Catholic labor schools during the Depression.[5] Several political scientists have examined the role of Thomistic philosophy in the rise of Christian Democratic parties in Europe and Latin America.[6] Catechesis is only one area where modern Catholics outside of academic philosophy spoke Thomism as their default language.

The Roman Catechism also indicates how Thomism co-exists with other philosophical traditions within the Church. If the Thomistic metaphysical categories of matter/form and substance/accident are central to the

4. See Philip Gleason, *Catholic Higher Education in the Twentieth Century* (New York: Oxford University Press, 1995.)

5. See Joseph M. McShane, "A Survey of Jesuit Labor Schools in New York," *Records of the American Catholic Historical Society of Philadelphia*, 102, no. 4 (1991): 37–64.

6. See Steven Van Hecke and Emmanuel Gerard, *Christian Democracy: Principles and Policy-Making* (Berlin: Konrad-Adenauer Stiflung, 2011).

analysis of the sacraments, they co-exist with concepts drawn from other philosophical sources. The prelude to the treatise on the sacraments in the catechism is a study in semiotics, with an explicit debt to Augustine. The tripartite analysis of signs as natural, social-conventional, and theological is taken directly from the works of Augustine. Indeed, Augustine is cited far more frequently in the catechetical text than is Aquinas. The elaborate and occasionally fanciful discussions of how the matter and form of a particular sacrament is fitting or appropriate owes far more to patristic exegetical sources, abundantly cited in the text, than to Aquinas or to his modern commentators.

Finally, the study of the presence of Thomism in Catholic catechesis involves a painful nostalgia. Several years ago, a colleague at the American Philosophical Association asked me what the title of my memoirs would be if I lived long enough to write them. My spontaneous reply was *I Was a Teenage Thomist*. This is not because I ever read the *Summa* or a commentary on it as an adolescent. I did not even read Chesterton's life of Aquinas until I had entered the Jesuits. It is because I am old enough to have been prepared for first communion and confirmation with a religious education with a heavy Thomistic, metaphysical scaffolding. So thick was the Thomistic universe of my parochial school that I won a spelling bee by correctly spelling transubstantiation.

That world obviously has disappeared. During my high school years (1965–69) a new, more historicist approach to catechesis had replaced the earlier, metaphysical approach. This "history of salvation" approach presented basic Christian doctrine in terms of evolutionary development. We moved from the Old Testament (freshman year) to the New Testament (sophomore year), to the Church (junior year), to contemporary moral teaching (senior year). In freshman year, each student received a brightly colored, fold-out "salvation history" timeline that showed the progressive revelation of religious truth from creation until the Parousia. This approach was perfectly attuned to Vatican II's affirmation of "the development of doctrine" in *Dignitatis Humanae*, the conciliar decree on religious liberty. It provided solid historical information on the sources of basic Catholic doctrine and practice. But without a metaphysical structure, it served little apologetic purpose. It could only describe, and not persuade.

During my pastoral year as a newly ordained priest, I worked in a large parish with a grade school. One of my pastoral duties was preparing second graders for first confession and Holy Communion. Although I was not responsible for their religious instruction, I received a copy of the text used for their catechesis. As I recall, the section on Holy Communion focused on Beth, a young girl celebrating her birthday. Beth wanted to include everyone and reach out to onery Uncle Harry, alienated from the family. The text then linked this charitable meal to the sacred meal at Mass, where Jesus lovingly invited us to his dinner party. This inductive approach was easy to follow and rightly emphasized the role of charity in the eucharistic banquet. But more than metaphysics had disappeared. The sacrifice of the cross had faded into the background. The infinite distance between Beth's birthday party and the Holy Sacrifice of the Mass had receded.

The eclipse of a neo-scholastic metaphysical approach to catechesis has not only weakened religious instruction; it has weakened the philosophical texture of Catholic culture in general. The avenue by which every Catholic was once introduced to arguments for God's existence, broad moral principles, and metaphysical categories has vanished. The collapse of core curricula at Catholic colleges, in which philosophy once enjoyed pride of place, has further deepened this philosophical recession in Catholic culture. So far, the successor to catechetical Thomism is amorphous.

MATTHEW MINERD

The Ontology of the Divine Indwelling

A Hard-Headed Thomist Meets with Palamas

I. Introduction

THERE ARE MANY KINDS OF THOMISM. What about "Byzantine Thomism?" The expression, no doubt, will strike some as odd. Once upon a time, it was a title readily given to—arguably foisted upon—the Patriarch of Constantinople, Gennadios Scholarios (1400–1473): a Byzantine Thomist.[1] In the hopes of finding a point of dialogue with the Western Church, this defender of Eastern prerogatives and of certain aspects of Palamite theology was presented (by some, at least) as being a ready dialogue partner with the Thomists of the Latin world. Nonetheless, we know today[2] that for all the true and positive affection he

1. With various shades of nuance, see John Demetracopoulos, "George Scholarios (Gennadios II)," in *Encyclopedia of Medieval Philosophy*, edited by H. Lagerlund (Dordrecht: Springer, 2011); Hugh Christopher Barbour, *The Byzantine Thomism of Gennadios Scholarios: And His Translation of the Commentary of Armandus de Bellovisu on the "De Ente et Essentia" of Thomas Aquinas* (Vatican: Pontificia Accademia di S. Tommaso e di religione cattolica, 1993); A. N. Williams, *Ground of Union: Deification in Aquinas and Palamas* (Oxford: Oxford University Press, 1999), 11; Matthew C. Briel, *A Greek Thomist: Providence in Gennadios Scholarios* (Notre Dame, Indiana: University of Notre Dame Press, 2020); ———, "A Palamite Thomist? Gennadios Scholarios and the Reception of Thomas Aquinas in Byzantium," *St. Vladimir's Theological Quarterly* 62, no. 3 (2018): 267–85; Marcus Plested, *Orthodox Readings of Aquinas* (Oxford: Oxford University Press, 2012), 127–34.

2. See Christiaan Kappes, "The Latin Sources of the Palamite Theology of George-Gennadios Scholarios," *Nicolaus* 40 (2013): 71–114. Though, it is important to recall that Martin Jugie, in his well-known (and, arguably *infamous*, given its polemical tone) article acknowledges the Scotist resonances in Scholarios's thought. See Jugie, Martin, "Palamite (controverse), les antipalamites," in *Dictionnaire de Théologie Catholique*, vol. 11, pt. 2 (Paris: Letouzey et Ané, 1932), cols. 1777–1818 (esp. cols. 1800–1801).

had for Aquinas's thought, Scholarios was not hesitant to draw on many of the non-Thomist sources that he encountered during his travels in the West during the time surrounding the Council of Florence. Merely to cite one example, in the vexed question concerning the distinction between the divine names (as well as between the divine essence and the divine activities or "operations") Scholarios readily drew on Scotistic influences, some of which were hidden away in the thought of the Dominican Hervaeus Natalis, whose work he encountered while abroad in the West.[3] To my eyes, such Scotism causes grave problems for the use of the adjective "Thomist," given the many topics connected with the divine simplicity: creation, the granting of grace to spiritual creatures, the divine freedom, the divine missions, and so forth.[4]

We need only flip through the texts by Gerald McCool to remind ourselves that the meaning of "being a Thomist" was quite elusive in the twentieth century,[5] let alone in the earlier history of the Dominican order.[6] We need titles for general trends of thought, and I remain convinced that all those who view Thomas a true point of departure[7] and animating

3. See "The Latin Sources of the Palamite Theology of George-Gennadios Scholarios" cited above; also, "The Theology of the Divine Essence and Energies in George-Gennadios Scholarios" (Ph.D. diss., Aristotle University of Thessaloniki, Greece, 2018).

4. For a good summary of the Thomist position, viewed from the perspective of the problem of the "divine names", see Reginald Garrigou-Lagrange, "On the Eminence of the Deity: In What Sense the Divine Perfections are 'Formally and Eminently' in God," in *Philosophizing in Faith*, translated by Matthew K. Minerd (Providence, Rhode Island: Cluny Press, 2019), 341–60. For a consideration of a number of the other themes, see Peter Totleben, "The Palamite Controversy: A Thomistic Analysis" (S.T.L. thesis, Dominican House of Studies, Washington, D.C., 2015). For counter-indications, viewed from his own synthesis of Palamite, Thomist, and Personalist metaphysics on these points, see Mark K. Spencer, "The Flexibility of Divine Simplicity: Aquinas, Scotus, and Palamas," *International Philosophical Quarterly* 57, no. 2 (2017): 123–39. I see no way to make this rapprochement.

5. See Gerald McCool, *From Unity to Pluralism: The Internal Evolution of Thomism* (New York: Fordham University Press, 1991); *The Neo-Thomists* (Milwaukee, Wisconsin: Marquette University Press, 1993). McCool arguably simplifies this history a bit; however, the general point remains: merely within the neo-scholastic period, the term "Thomism" has been used to cover a whole host of speculative and exegetical bents.

6. See Frederick J. Roensch, *The Early Thomistic School* (Dubuque, Iowa: The Prior Press, 1964); Romanus Cessario, *A Short History of Thomism* (Washington, D.C.: The Catholic University of America Press, 2005); Romanus Cessario and Cajetan Cuddy, *Thomas and the Thomists: The Achievement of Thomas Aquinas and His Interpreters* (Minneapolis, Minnesota: Fortress Press, 2017); *The Oxford Handbook of the Reception of Aquinas*, edited by Matthew Levering and Marcus Plested (Oxford: Oxford University Press, 2021). To my eyes, the work of McCool needs to be balanced by the basic insights of works like these volumes.

7. In the sense expressed in John Deely, "Quid sit postmodernismus?," in *Postmodernism and*

spirit[8] for philosophical and theological inquiry merit some form of the name "Thomist."

But, is being a "Byzantine Thomist" possible? Rightly many Eastern Catholics strive to respond to the Second Vatican Council's call to fully embrace their particular traditions. Yet, as someone who personally has changed my ascriptions from the Roman Catholic Church to the Ruthenian Catholic Church, I must admit that I cannot quickly turn my back on the intellectual formation that I received in former days. While I am not sure if there is a ready answer to the question, "What is a Byzantine Thomist?," or even "A Ruthenian Byzantine Thomist," I would like here to make a try at the latter by doing a bit of philosophizing and theologizing on the "borders" of Thomism and Palamism. It is like proving the possibility of movement by walking.

I will perform this task by meditating on the nature of the divine indwelling, doing so in light of the Thomist teaching on these matters, reflected in particular in the line descending from Ambroise Gardeil and Reginald Garrigou-Lagrange.[9] My style will be personal—the meeting of my particular "tribe" of Thomists with Palamas's thought concerning the divine indwelling—though not engaging in a kind of point-by-point textual analysis. Rather, my sole desire is to show how it is that a Byzantine Thomist—a term that is at least "sociologically" applicable to myself—has been edified by his contact with Palamas.

II. An Overview Concerning the "Palamas Affair"

First, I will outline the famed controversy surrounding St. Gregory Palamas, in his immediate historical context, and thematically in relation to cer-

Christian Philosophy, edited by Roman T. Ciapalo (Washington, D.C.: The Catholic University of America Press, 1997), 68–96; also, briefly but well put, see Raymond Léopold Bruckberger's introduction to the collected volume *Dialogue théologique: Pièces du débat entre "La Revue Thomiste" d'une part et les R.R. P.P. de Lubac, Daniélou, Bouillard, Fessard, von Balthasar, S.J., d'autre part* (Saint-Maximin : Les Arcades, 1947), 9–18.

8. The second point is of importance too, for one may well argue that Aquinas is a kind of point of departure for Francisco Suarez, though to much different ends—to the point of ultimately causing a new division of *scholae* in the Roman Catholic world.

9. The reader will also detect, in the footnotes, my dependence on Fr. Jean-Hervé Nicolas, who on this point stands in line with his Thomist predecessors. For an excellent study of Thomas himself on the divine missions (a key element in the background of the problems discussed in this essay), see Gilles Emery, *The Trinitarian Theology of St. Thomas Aquinas*, translated by Francesca Aran Murphy (Oxford: Oxford University Press, 2007), 360–419.

tain Thomist concerns regarding his articulated theological positions, hoping to set them aside (without dismissing them, however). I merely wish to give you some bearings in a controversy that is not well known by all in the Catholic West, namely that concerning St. Gregory Palamas and the distinction, *intra divinis*, of God's unknowable essence and His "energies" (or "activities"). As we will see, this particular issue of "natural theology" is connected to St. Gregory's concerns regarding the uncreated character of grace. For those interested in more details than what I can provide here, I recommend the recent, excellent monographs by Norman Russell[10] and Marcus Plested,[11] as well as the somewhat dated, though informative study by Meyendorff, *A Study of Gregory Palamas*.[12] Despite its polemical tone, Martin Jugie's infamous article remains very readable,[13] and a quite excellent state of the literature can be found in Fr. Peter Totleben's as-now-unpublished S.T.L. thesis.[14]

To pick up *in medias res*, c. 1340, we find the Byzantine monk, Gregory Palamas, faced with an Orthodox adversary coming from the West, Barlaam of Calabria (c. 1290–1348). Many titles have been thrown at Barlaam: he is a Latinizer, a Thomist, a rationalist, a nominalist, a humanist, etc. None of these titles provide fair characterizations. What is certain, however, is that the prayer practices of certain hesychasts in the proximity of Mount Athos seemed quite odd to him, as well as their assertion that they were able to experience God in a kind of sensual way, in kinds of lights experienced at the terminus of their exercises of prayer.[15] To Barlaam's eyes, this all seemed

10. See Norman Russell, *Gregory Palamas and the Making of Palamism in the Modern Age* (Oxford: Oxford University Press, 2019).

11. See Marcus Plested, *Orthodox Readings of Aquinas* (Oxford: Oxford University Press, 2012).

12. See John Meyendorff, *A Study of Gregory Palamas*, translated by George Lawrence (Crestwood, New York: St. Vladimir's Seminary Press, 1998); also see the review of this text by Charles Journet, who on occasion there tries to save Palamas from Meyendorff's polemical presentation: "Palamisme et Thomisme, À propos d'un livre récent," *Revue Thomiste* 60 (1960): 429–52.

13. See n. 2 above.

14. See Totleben, "The Palamite Controversy: A Thomistic Analysis," 5–48.

15. Such perplexity at the language of the hesychasts is reflected, as well, in texts attesting to the relations between the Churches during the Council of Florence, in an amusing anecdote recounted in Russell, *Gregory Palamas and the Making of Palamism in the Modern Age*, 25: "But the Greeks, [Cesarini goes on to say] were holding that they do not see God himself, but certain lights, and in this there was great difficulty, indeed, such as nearly upset the whole business. At length, they yielded to argument and recognized that the souls of the blessed will see God, Three and One, as he is, but they wanted to have put into the *cedula* that some would see less and others more, and it was thought good that this should be included, since "in our Father's house, there are many mansions."

to be a form of Messalianism—an ancient error in matters moral or spiritual, having affinities (and, in some cases, historical ties) with Manichaeism, Catharism / Albigensianism, and the Slavic form that may have been of influence in Palamas's own circles of contact, Bogomilism.[16]

Moreover, Barlaam was scandalized at the claims made by St. Gregory Palamas regarding the way that God is present through grace. The hesychastic theologian asserted quite strongly the supernatural character of grace, even though it is received by a finite subject.[17] To restate this in somewhat Thomist terms, he would seem to be denying what would be called "created grace" as the *means by which* our divinization takes place.[18] (It does seem that Palamas did make room for a sense of created grace, as the *effect* of our divinization.[19]) However, his great concern was to emphasize the uncreated character of the new life communicated to us through grace. For his own part, Barlaam here saw something like a danger of pantheism, placing the divine transcendence in danger (and, by consequence, the finitude of the creature).

Now, Palamas had at hand another device which would cause even more woe for him, something that also remains, truth be told, problematic for Thomists as well,[20] namely the so-called distinction between God's

16. Given the limitations of space imposed upon us here, the reader can consult the following texts for more details concerning Messalianism and its various forms: Bradley Nassif, "Concerning Those Who Imagine that They are Justified by Works: The Gospel according to St. Mark—the Monk," in *The Philokalia: A Classic Text of Orthodox Spirituality*, edited by Brock Bingaman and Bradley Nassif (Oxford: Oxford University Press, 2012), 87–101 (esp. 90–92); Russell, *Gregory Palamas and the Making of Palamism in the Modern Age*, 101–107; Antonio Rigo, *Monaci esicasti e monaci bogomili* (Florence: Leo S. Olschki, 1989)

17. Citations on this point would be legion, throughout the *Triads, The Hundred and Fifty Chapters*, and *The Dialogue between and Orthodox and a Barlaamite*.

18. To the degree that it is possible, however, we could take Palamas as representing the apotheosis of a theological trend directly (and sanely, we Thomists would say) opposed to the profoundly problematic trend in certain theologians, holding (even after Trent's decree on justification and, in some cases, the decrees in *Dei filius* at Vatican I!) that there is no distinction of formal objects between natural and supernatural acts. One can at least understand Scotus holding this at his time before this matter became further reflected on by the Church, but it is striking to see even Billot holding this opinion after Vatican I! Concerning this particular line of thought, see the following remarks cited from a letter by the Jesuit Master General, Wlodimir Ledochowski, SJ (1866–1942) in Reginald Garrigou-Lagrange, *The Order of Things: The Realism of the Principle of Finality*, translated by Matthew K. Minerd (Steubenville, Ohio: Emmaus Academic Press, 2020), 294n10.

19. This claim is made on a number of occasions (with textual basis, especially in the correspondence between Gregory Akindynos and Palamas) by Russell in *Gregory Palamas and the Making of Palamism in the Modern Age*.

20. In the most learned form recently, see Fr. Totleben's study cited above.

unknowable essence and His energies. Developing certain themes in the Cappadocian Fathers raised against the "rationalism" of the Eunomians (or, Anomoeans)[21]—arguably, pushing Basil and Gregory of Nyssa to their most apophatic limits[22]—along with similar texts in Pseudo-Dionysius and Maximus the Confessor, Palamas would come to hold that a distinction must be made between, on the one hand, God's transcendent essence and, on the other hand, the "energies" by which He manifests Himself, both in the order of nature and that of grace, on the other.[23] Palamas held, no doubt on grounds similar to those of Pseudo-Dionysius,[24] that this ineffable distinction—which arguably cannot be reduced to the distinctions deployed in later Latin scholasticism[25]—ultimately resolved into the eminent unity of the Godhead, thereby not putting at risk the unity of the Godhead. Nonetheless, the hesychastic theologian expresses little doubt that this distinction alone preserves the transcendence of God beyond all creaturely participation, while also preserving the truly divine character of those participations.

Through His "energies," God is present to creation and to those whom He graces. In this way, they are akin to what one would think of in Latin terms as "divine operations or activities." Beyond this, there are other texts (indeed of Patristic provenance) asserting that even the "Divine Names" are

21. For a clear summary of this, see Vladimir Lossky, *The Vision of God*, translated by Asheleigh Moorhouse (Crestwood, New York: St. Vladimir's Seminary Press, 1963), 73–89; also, see J. -H. Nicolas, *Synthèse dogmatique* (Fribourg: Éditions Universitaires, 1985), §175.

22. See Andrew Radde-Gallwitz, *Basil of Caesarea, Gregory of Nyssa, and the Transformation of Divine Simplicity* (Oxford: Oxford University Press, 2009); for a different read of the relationship between Palamas and the Cappadocians (more in line with strands of neo-Palamism), see Torstein Theodor Tollefsen, *Activity and Participation in Late Antique and Early Christian Thought* (Oxford: Oxford University Press, 2012).

23. Interestingly, Palamas *does* seem to make firmer-than-expected distinctions between these two orders. For example, see Palamas, *Triads*, edited by John Meyendorff, translated by Nicholas Gendle (Mahwah, New Jersey: Paulist Press, 1983), 2.3.15–16. Also, if one consults the Athonite statement on behalf of Palamas (and also signed by him), it is clear that the controversy deeply engages questions concerning the distinction between nature and grace, with the Palamites drawing clear lines between the two orders. See "The Declaration of the Holy Mountain in Defense of those who Devoutly Practice a Life of Stillness," *The Philokolia*, compiled by Nikodimos of the Holy Mountain and Makarios of Corinth, ed. and trans. G. E. H. Palmer, Philip Sherrard, and Kallistos Ware (London: Faber and Faber, 1995), 418–25.

24. See Pseudo-Dionysius, *On the Divine Names*, in *Pseudo-Dionysius: The Complete Works*, translated by Paul Rorem (Mahwah, New Jersey: Paulist Press, 1987), chaps. 1–2. For a brief critique of this reading, see Nicolas, *Synthèse dogmatique*, §175.

25. See Basil Krivoshein, "The Ascetic and Theological Teaching of Gregory Palamas: II. Substance and Energy," *The Eastern Churches Quarterly* 3 (1938): 151–52.

energies in this way as well.[26] Reading with Western-informed lenses this supposed distinction among the various divine "operations" and names, certain Byzantine theologians, such as Gennadios Scholarios (Patriarch of Constantinople on-and-off during 1450s and 1460s), there saw something akin to the Scotist formal distinction,[27] and others held that it was less than a real distinction, even to the point of holding that it is akin to a conceptual distinction *cum fundamento in re*.[28] Though this is not the forum for adjudicating this matter, it seems, in the end, that a number of Palamas's texts lean in the direction of a real but "ineffable" distinction.[29]

Thus, maintaining the distinction between God's ineffable self-presence in His divine nature and His manifestation to creatures, it would seem—in a lamentable expression used by Palamas in a private letter and, seemingly, maintained in the course of later polemics—that God-present-in-grace is a kind of "lower divinity"[30] in comparison with the ineffable God who remains unknown in His essence, even in the vision of God in the hereafter.[31]

26. For the purposes of this essay, see the sources gathered in Radde-Gallewitz above.

27. This was, in part at least, mediated through his knowledge of the Dominican Hervaeus Natalis, whose thought contained certain Scotist resonances. See the texts by Kappes, cited in n. 1 above, as well as Jugie's own recognition of Scotist similarities, cited in n. 2. Interestingly, this emerges in an unexpected aside in Austin Woodbury, *Ostensive Metaphysics: Natural Theology* (The John N. Deely and Anthony F. Russell Collection, Latimer Family Library, St. Vincent College Library, Latrobe, Pennsylvania), no. 1685 (Distinction of the Divine Attributes, Scotist Formalism): "For this reason, the Scotist theory is logically reduced to the assertion—made by the Palamite sect among the Greeks in the fourteenth century—of a real distinction between the divine attributes, something that contradicts the divine simplicity" (lightly edited).

28. See John Demetracopoulos, "Palamas Transformed. Palamite Interpretations of the Distinction Between God's 'Essence' and 'Energies' in Late Byzantium," in *Greeks, Latins, and Intellectual History 1204–1500*, edited by M. Hinterberger and C. Schabel (Leuven: Peeters, 2011), 263–372. For a summary of this dense essay, see Russell, *Gregory Palamas and the Making of Palamism in the Modern Age*, 118–19.

29. See Krivoshein, "The Ascetic and Theological Teaching of Gregory Palamas: II. Substance and Energy," 138-56. Along these lines, perhaps with some over-emphasis, though, see John Romanides, "Notes on the Palamite Controversy and Related Topics," *Greek Orthodox Theological Review* 6 (1960-1961): 186-205; 9 (1963-1964): 225-27; Meyendorff, *A Study of Gregory Palamas*, 225.

30. See Russell, *Gregory Palamas and the Making of Palamism in the Modern Age*, 177–83.

31. Some, such as Vladimir Lossky, would have this be a central element to all Eastern Mystical theology. See Vladimir Lossky, "The Divine Darkness," in *The Mystical Theology of the Eastern Church*, translated by Members of St. Alban and St. Sergius (Crestwood, New York: St. Vladimir's Seminary Press, 1997), 23–43. The closest point of reference is the Thomist position concerning the non-comprehensive nature of the beatific vision in the blessed (see ST I, q. 12, a. 7). However, significant differences likely remain between the two positions. It would be of use to consider the relationship (and differences) between the two outlooks in light of Karl Rahner, "The Concept of Mystery in Catholic Theology," in *More Recent Writings*, vol. 4 of *Theological Investigations*, translated by Kevin Smyth (Crossroad: New York, 1982), 36–73.

This was the source of a number of additional arguments, not only with Barlaam of Calabria but also with Palamas's former-defender, Gregoras Akyndinos.[32] At best, the divine simplicity was at risk, and at worst it seemed that Palamas's thought implied a kind of polytheism.

Ultimately, however, Palamas's position won out in the Orthodox world through a series of councils held in Constantinople, culminating in his 1351 vindication, then, ultimately followed by the definitive defeat of the anti-Palamites in the Orthodox world when he was canonized in 1368. Anathemas against Barlaam and Akyndinos were included liturgically in the texts proclaimed on the first Sunday of Lent in some Orthodox Churches (and, from what I understand, in an altered, union-friendly form by certain Melkite Catholic parishes as well).

Looking on this as a Thomist, it seems, in the end, that we find ourselves faced here with two different theological vocabularies that never can be wholly squared with each other. They are, indeed, languages based upon two different metaphysical bents. Even though they deceptively share a great deal, in particular through their mutual "friend," Pseudo-Dionysius—cited with well-known frequency by Aquinas,[33] and described by Palamas as being second only to the apostles[34]—they are not compatible precisely as theological explanations concerning the various matters tied up in this debate.[35] St. Gregory Palamas leans Pseudo-Dionyisus in his native Proclean direction, whereas St. Thomas tilts him toward the Aristotelian doctrine of analogy.[36] However, insofar as we read their properly theological arguments

32. For an accounting of this, see Russell, *Gregory Palamas and the Making of Palamism in the Modern Age*, 231–37; Totleben, "The Palamite Controversy: A Thomistic Analysis," 35–44. For a recent attempt to defend Akyndinos against Palamas, see the texts and commentary in Juan Nadal Cañellas, *La Résistance d'Akindynos à Grégoire Palamas: enquête historique, avec traduction et commentaire de quatre traités édités récemment*, vol. 2. (*Commentaire historique*) (Leuven: Peeters, 2006).

33. See Fran O'Rourke, *Pseudo-Dionysius and the Metaphysics of Aquinas* (Notre Dame, Indiana: University of Notre Dame Press, 2005).

34. See, for example Gregory Palamas, *The One Hundred and Fifty Chapters*, edited and translated by Robert E. Sinkewicz (Toronto: Pontifical Institute of Mediaeval Studies, 1988), no. 85: "Dionysius the Areopagite, the most prominent of theologians next to the divine apostles ..."

35. Here, I share in the judgment rendered in Jean-Hervé Nicolas, *Synthèse dogmatique*, §173–75.

36. And yet, there are these striking texts in Palamas which I believe show that there is conceptual overlap even on questions of analogy, such as are found in *Triads* 2.3.16: "Therefore, not every man who possesses the knowledge of created things, or who sees through the mediation of such knowledge has God dwelling in him; but he merely possesses knowledge of creatures and from this, by means of analogy he infers the existence of God. As to him who mysteriously possesses and sees this light, he knows and possesses God in himself, no longer by analogy, but by a true contemplation, transcendent to all creatures, for he is never separated from the eternal glory."

as being marshaled in defense of the supernatural and intimate character of grace alongside God's incomprehensibility, we can say that followers of Palamas and of Aquinas agree on the level of faith. The difference exists on the level of virtual, not formal, revelation.[37]

The problems involved with divine unity are too great to be overcome, at least in my opinion, and I take consolation in the erudition on this point in Fr. Peter Totleben's thesis on this topic.[38] But there is much room for agreement on the fundamental concern regarding the life of grace, for here, the inspiration for Palamas's insistence upon the *true and real,* divinizing character of grace, is close to the very realistic theology of grace which represents one of the glories of Thomistic theology. I propose, therefore, without getting too caught up on the question of the language of created or uncreated grace,[39] to shift our focus away from the problem concerning divine unity and to be concerned with the "thickness" of the divine indwelling according to the Thomist position. This rapprochement provides an extrinsic theological justification[40] for a position I had originally drawn from

37. For an explanation of this distinction, see Reginald Garrigou-Lagrange, "Remarks Concerning the Metaphysical Character of St. Thomas's Moral Theology, in Particular as It Is Related to Prudence and Conscience," translated by Matthew K. Minerd, *Nova et Vetera* 17, no. 1 (2019): 261–66 ("Translator's Appendix 1: Concerning the Formal Object of Acquired Theology"). However, see the important additional remarks in Matthew K. Minerd, "Wisdom be Attentive: The Noetic Structure of Sapiential Knowledge," *Nova et Vetera* 18, no. 4 (Fall 2020): 1103–146.

38. Thus, on this point, I disagree with the hopeful (and insightful) attempts marshalled, for example, by Mark Spencer in the text cited in n. 4 above. See n. 4 above for Totleben's thesis.

39. Though, allow a comment here regarding the path forward here as well. For the Thomist, we could call the Hypostatic Union the uncreated gracing of the human nature of Christ, a gracing in which the whole uncreated reality of the second person is *subjectively* given to this nature. See ST III, q. 2, a. 10; Reginald Garrigou-Lagrange, 139–40. Also, grace, considered actively (on God's side), could also be considered uncreated (see ibid., 3, 113, 114). Parallels could be drawn here to the notions of "active creation" and "passive creation" (noting, however, here that unlike creation, the giving of grace presupposes something, namely the nature that is graced). Subjectively, our grace is created (just as is also the case for the grace in Christ's human nature, even though it derives from the grace of union), though objectively it opens out through knowledge and love on to the uncreated divine life indwelling within us. Cf. H.-D. Gardeil and Ambroise Gardeil, *La vraie vie chrétienne* (Paris: Desclée de Brouwer, 1935), 19–20. And this Thomist position may seem unacceptable to the followers of Palamas, but here, they should bear in mind the discussion reported above in footnote 18. Many, following the way of Scotus to various degrees, held a position that *infinitely* separates them from the Palamites, for on this Scotist path, it would seem that grace must ultimately lose its *objective* supernaturality, no matter what its defenders may say. On this, see also, Reginald Garrigou-Lagrange, *The Sense of Mystery*, translated by Matthew K. Minerd (Steubenville, Ohio: Emmaus Academic, 2017), 217–47; *The Order of Things: The Realism of the Principle of Finality*, translated by Matthew K. Minerd (Steubenville, Ohio: Emmaus Academic, 2020), 293–97.

40. That is, by way of authority derived from a theologian of weight.

the line of Fr. Ambroise Gardeil. And I will argue that this dialogue will be beneficial to the Palamite position as well.

III. One Meeting Ground for the Thomist and the Palamite: The Indwelling of the Trinity

John Meyendorff proposes an opposition in an article in the *Dictionnaire de spiritualité ascétique et mystique, histoire et doctrine*:

> Is this participation [in the divine life] only *analogical* and *intentional*, as the Latin scholastics would have it, in conformity with their philosophy of the created *habitus* and the divine simplicity? Or is it an *entitative* and immediate communion with the divine life itself?[41]

We here have an opposition: analogical-intentional (or "operative") vs. entitative-immediate. Is this all that fair? Is God's presence in grace merely entitative (and, ultimately, something like a "supernaturally upgraded" version of His creative presence of immensity to all things)? Or is it something else, akin to that of a friend present to the soul? Are these distinct modes of presence? How should we understand them? In Palamas's words, himself citing Gregory of Nazianzus:

> This is why the Divine One purifies the man who desires Him: by this purification, He creates men of divine character, conversing as with friends with those who have attained this state. And (to use a daring expression) uniting Himself as God with gods, and making Himself known to them perhaps to the same extent that He knows those who are known to Him.[42]

There is a presence here that is "more" than ontological. It is inter-personal, like that had through friendship and love. Palamas's position is both ontological and interpersonal, and in this, he is quite close to Gardeil. We find both of these aspects in a text which can be taken as bearing witness to these two aspects. On the "merely ontological" register—to anticipate a name to be discussed soon, we might say, "in the Vasquezian register"—we have Palamas stating: "[The purified and illuminated mind] does not simply contemplate some other object or simply its own image but, rath-

41. John Meyendorff, "Palamas (Grégoire)," *Dictionnaire de spiritualité ascétique et mystique, histoire et doctrine* 12 (1984), 105.

42. Palamas, *Triads*, 3.3.12.

er, the glory impressed on its own image by the grace of God." And yet, in his continued remarks, we can find Palamas tilting in the direction of operative-intentional union: "This radiance reinforces the mind's power to transcend itself, and accomplish that union with those better things which is beyond understanding. By this union, the mind sees God in the Spirit in a manner transcending human powers."[43]

To show that this is not an idle question, allow me to summarize a great theological question, one that led to the production of hosts of theological texts in the late-nineteenth and early-twentieth century:[44] in what manner does God come to dwell in righteous souls through grace? In Francis Cunningham's direct study of Aquinas, it is impossible not to sense that the debates noted at length in his own footnotes are, in fact, driving his narrative, which purports only to be a historical study of the problem up to Aquinas's own time, providing a historical study of the Angelic Doctor's own textual evidence. Without some awareness of the great inter- (and intra-) *scholae* divisions at play in this swirling theological debate, it is like stumbling into the middle of a conversation.

La structure de l' âme et l'experience mystique, by Fr. Ambroise Gardeil[45]—lays out the basic stakes of the matter. His position is substantially that of Garrigou-Lagrange,[46] Maritain,[47] Jean-Hervé Nicolas,[48] and Charles Journet,[49] and it is very close to that of Cunningham, whose study, cited above, remains the most learned Thomistic text concerning this topic (and its surrounding debates) published in English.[50] However, let's step back so

43. Ibid., 2.3.11.

44. See Karl Rahner, "Some Implications of the Scholastic Concept of Uncreated Grace," in *Christ, God, Mary and Grace*, vol. 1 of *Theological Investigations*, translated by Cornelius Ernst (New York: Seabury Press, 1974), 319–46; Francis Cunningham, *The Indwelling of the Trinity: A Historico-Doctrinal Study of the Theory of St. Thomas Aquinas* (Dubuque, Iowa: The Prior Press, 1955).

45. "The Great Gardeil," as Yves Simon once referred to him. See Jacques Maritain and Yves Simon, *Correspondance*, vol. 1 (*Les années françaises*, 1927–1940), edited by Florian Michel (Paris: CLD, 2008), 56.

46. For example, see Reginald Garrigou-Lagrange, *Love of God and the Cross of Jesus*, translated by Jeanne Marie, vol. 1 (St. Louis, Missouri: B. Herder, 1948), 136–173.

47. Jacques Maritain, *The Degrees of Knowledge*, translated by Gerald Phelan et al. (Notre Dame, Indiana: University of Notre Dame Press, 2002), 273–75.

48. Nicolas, *Synthèse Dogmatique*, §217ff; *Les Profondeurs de la Grace* (Paris: Beauchesne, 1969), 126–141.

49. See Charles Journet, *L'église du verbe incarné*, vol. 2 (Fribourg, Switzerland: Éditions Saint-Augustin, 1999), chap. 4 (p. 760–927). An English translation of this text is expected in 2025 by Emmaus Academic.

50. A small difference separates Cunningham from Gardeil, however. For details, see Cunningham, *The Indwelling of the Trinity*, 207 and 228n29.

that I might I lay out all of these matters, which likely are very cryptic at this moment.

A classic scholastic divide on this question lays between Gabriel Vasquez and Francisco Suarez. However, in order to help in understanding their difference on the question of the divine indwelling, I should explain a point of terminology.[51] What are the modes of divine presence? Here, I think we can benefit by charitably drawing on a comment by Vladimir Lossky regarding Palamas' use of the distinction between God's essence and His energies:

> Essence and energies are not, for Palamas, two parts of God, as some modern critics still imagine, but two different modes of the existence of God, within His nature and outside His nature; the same God remains totally inaccessible in His essence—and communicates himself totally by grace.[52]

Thus, first and foremost, there is the divine self-presence: "God in His nature," to use Lossky's expression. Here, we have the uncreated being of God, self-present in the Triune, eternal refulgence of actuality that is the Godhead as such—not as manifesting Himself, but rather, Triunely Self-Present *in Himself*. In Palamas' terminology, we here have the transcendent Divine Essence, unknowable by humans (according to Palamas). According to Thomist parlance, this is God's *comprehensive* self-presence, alone His, a knowledge (and love) infinitely exceeding even the beatific knowledge and love had by the blessed who are subjectively "capacitated" by the light of glory.[53] It is the entire, interrelational life of the Trinity of persons *ad intra*, each personally outpouring and perichoretically within each other.[54]

There is also "God turned outward," or again using Lossky's terminology: "God outside of His nature", or *God's presence ad extra*.[55] Here, according-

51. Here, I am slightly developing St. Thomas, though I lay in line with the presentation of these matters by thinkers like Gardeil and others in his line. See Aquinas, *In I Sent.*, d. 14, q. 2, a. 1, sol. 1, ad 1; ST I, q. 43, a. 3; Ambroise Gardeil, *La Structure de l'âme et l'expérience mystique*, 3rd ed., vol. 2 (Paris: Gabalda, 1927), 7–12.

52. Lossky, *Vision of God*, 157.

53. ST, I, q. 12, aa. 2, 6, and 7; Nicolas, *Synthèse dogmatique*, §174. Also see the amusing anecdote from the time of Florence cited above in n. 15.

54. On the notion of perichoresis (and its Christological origins, in a domain akin to what is now referred to as the "communication of idioms"), see Nicolas, *Synthèse dogmatique*, §§157–58.

55. I have chosen the word "presence" quite carefully, for rigorously in accord with the adage, *omnia opera Trinitatis ad extra sunt indivisa*, the acts of the Godhead *ad extra* must involve all three persons. And yet, this does not rule all of our knowledge of (and relation to) the divine Persons, for through the presence of God in grace, we can relate to each person distinctly as a *terminus* of mystical knowledge and love (cf. Nicolas, *Synthèse*, §§214–16). Moreover, as *terminus* (in contrast

ing to Thomist terminology, there are three modes of presence to be distinguished: God's presence through "immensity" (or, His efficient-causal presence), His interpersonal presence through grace, and His "personalizing" presence through the Hypostatic Union. Through the new relation to God[56] established by each of these gifts—(1) as unified efficient-causal principle (the presence of "immensity" in both the orders of nature and of grace[57]), (2) as terminus[58] of knowledge and love ("operative" presence rendered possible through grace), and (3) as terminus of the hypostatic union ("personalizing" presence through hypostatic unity)—God is present in a different way to His creatures. God "goes forth"—or, better, *He draws to Himself*—in three different ways: as causing nature and grace, as being known and loved (in each Person, uniquely) through grace, and as drawing Christ's human nature to the Second Person. In ascending degrees, we have unions of increasing profundity, culminating in the greatest of all unions, presupposing no mediating principle between nature and person: the Hypostatic Union.[59]

When it comes to the divine indwelling in the souls of *wayfarers* in the

---

with causal principle) of the Hypostatic Union, Christ's human nature is present to the *hypostasis* of the Second Person.

56. And this point is of great importance, as remarked upon by Gardeil, concerning St. Thomas, *In I Sent.*, d. 14, q. 2, a. 1, sol. 1, ad 1; cf. John of St. Thomas, *Cursus theologicus, In ST* I, q. 43, d. 17, a. 3, no. 7. See Gardeil, *La Structure*, vol. 2, 8–9: "Therefore, according to St. Thomas, the various forms of God's presence in the creature involve only diversity in *the creature's relation to God*, coming from the diversity of the gifts which are given to it. In order to rule out all ambiguity regarding the true cause of various modes of presence, St. Thomas takes care to insist and to note immediately that a new presence is not produced by *the diversity of gifts precisely as gifts* but, rather, by the new relation to God Himself which emerges from certain gifts. Indeed, if we confined ourselves to the gifts *inasmuch as they are effects of God*, they would be, in their diversity, *multiple participations* in the various divine perfections, the likeness of which is found in every created effect, although the relation of the creature to God Himself would not change.... In other words, God is newly present to the soul only when, through certain effects of His, a new and original relation to Him emerges, one that is distinct from the relation of effect to cause, something that is a property of every one of His effects, including grace. A new and special presence is begotten not by *the production of a new effect* but, rather, by *the new relation to God that follows upon the specific nature of this new effect*" (italics in original).

57. Because of Aquinas's own wording, some seem to hold that the presence of immensity is only natural. However, see Cunningham, *The Indwelling of the Trinity*, 191–95. Also, Gardeil, *La Structure*, vol. 2, 58–60.

58. The language of *principle* and *terminus* used here is being deployed very knowingly, drawing on a text from Jean-Baptiste Terrien (himself a follower of Vasquez), who in one explanation sets forth something almost the same as Gardeil's own position, though ultimately abandoning it for a purely Vasquezian postion. See J.-B. Terrien, *La grâce et gloire*, vol. 1, bk. 4, ch. 4 (Paris: Lethielleux, 1901; cited in Gardeil, *La structure*, vol. 2, 18).

59. See ST III, q. 2, aa. 6–10.

state of grace, the first two modes are necessary (ontological presence of immensity and intentional-interpersonal presence through grace). The whole difficulty is involved in how one integrates these two elements without explaining either of them away. Exegetically,[60] Thomas's own texts present some problem here, for early in his career, he seems to lean in the direction of explaining the presence of grace in terms ultimately drawn from the presence of immensity,[61] whereas in the *Summa Theologiae*, in his treatment of the divine missions in ST I, q. 43 (a. 3), he is clear that what is unique about the indwelling of God in souls in a state of grace is His presence as known in knower and beloved in lover.[62]

It is tempting to lean in one direction or the other, and this division (presence of immensity vs. union through knowledge and love) orients us in the same way as does that proposed by Meyendorff (entitative vs. intentional). Now, it seems that in the course of their mutual teaching and disputation,[63] the two Jesuits Gabriel Vasquez and Francisco Suaréz made such a choice to "lean" toward one of these two manners of explaining the divine indwelling. Understandably, Vasquez wished to maintain the realism of grace—a matter of no small importance, following upon the decrees of Trent concerning how grace is the formal cause of justification, something more than a merely moral attribution like what was held by Luther (and certain prior nominalists).[64] For this reason, he ultimately came to assimilate God's interpersonal presence through grace to the presence through immensity:

> (Thus, in order to account for the real presence of grace, we must say ...) With God already existing in us, He moreover deigns *to appear* in us through a new effect, namely, grace. And given that this gift is *appropriated* to the Holy Spirit, *we say* that He Himself is given and sent to us and that the entire Trinity comes with Him.[65]

60. On this problem, see Cunningham, *The Indwelling of the Trinity*, 230–90.

61. See Aquinas, *In I Sent*, d. 15 and 16.

62. Here, however, I suspect, that there is room for *some* meeting between myself (and a strict Thomism) and the positions held by someone like Mark Spencer in the text cited in n. 4 above.

63. On the historical relationships, see Gardeil, *La structure*, vol. 2, 15n2.

64. Trent, *Decree on Justification*, ch. 7 (Denzinger, no. 1529). Also see the 42nd condemned proposition in Pius V, *Ex omnibus afflictionibus*: "The justice by which the sinner is justified through faith consists formally in the observance of the commandments; it is the justice of works. It does not consist in any sort of grace in the soul by which man ... is internally renewed and is made a sharer in the divine nature." Denzinger, no. 1942.

65. Gabriel Vasquez, *Commentariorum ac Disp. In I Part. D. Thomae*, q. 8, disp. 30, ch. 3 (Ingolstadt: 1[6]09), vol. 1, 175–76 (cited in Gardeil, *La structure*, 13–14).

Here, we have an ontological presence, God's causal presence as the cause of grace in the soul—present *in this new effect*. And here, too, the human person's relations with the Trinity can be nothing more than appropriated, for as the old adage runs: *omnia opera Trinitatis ad extra sunt indivisa*. Perhaps one could trod down a Vasquezian path in the hopes of meeting Palamas there.[66] However, that would be like reading only half of the text from Palamas cited above, "He creates men of divine character," without fully appreciating the meaning of the second half: "... conversing as with friends with those who have attained this state."

Now, does this mean that we must lean in the other direction, saying that the interpersonal presence of grace is *only* intentional, that it would be possible, even if (*per impossibile*) God were not present through His immensity? It sounds strange, but this was the path taken by Suarez, no doubt thinking that this honored the insight expressed in ST I, q. 43, a. 3.[67]

Suarez develops what could be called a *merely intentional* presence. It is the presence of friends in the love of charity which would of itself call for fulfillment. Now, it is indeed true that love stretches out toward the beloved, who through the act of love is rendered intentionally present as the principle of love within the lover. When possession occurs, desire-love turns to joy, but joy is not possession. It is profound rest-in-possession. Possession comes from elsewhere, it comes from the beloved's gift of self.[68]

And here we come to Gardeil's profound point.[69] To understand God's indwelling in the souls of the just, we must see that it includes the presence of immensity as a necessarily presupposed part, though it formally is the

66. However, it is also possible that one would liken the Palamite position to that of Fr. Paul Galtier, whose use of a kind of intermediary between efficient causality and extrinsic formal (exemplar) causality. See Paul Galtier, *L'habitation en nous de trois Personnes* (Roma: Pontificia Universita Gregoriana, 1950), 217–19. This connection to Palamas is explicitly noted in Nicolas, *Synthèse*, §210.

67. Suarez, *De trinitate*, bk. 12, ch. 5, no. 12 (cited in Gardeil, *La structure*, 32–33). This position seems so strange a thought experiment that I am following Gardeil's interpretation of it. Even if it is ultimately not fair to Suarez, it provides us a kind of liminal possibility: intentional presence without causal presence.

68. See Nicolas, *Synthèse dogmatique*, §75: "In fact, love is a tendency and a union—a tendential union. This union, which is affective, must be carefully distinguished from the effective grasp. The former can exist without the latter (i.e. in the case wherein the beloved being is beyond the reach of the lover). However, even when they are realized together, they remain different from each other. It is not by love that the lover grasps one's beloved. It is by one's gaze. It is by a gesture of one's hands. It is by (experiential) knowledge."

69. A point which sets him openly at odds with eminent Thomists like the *Salmanticenses* and Fr. Barthélemy Froget's *De I'inhabitation du S. Esprit dans les âmes justes, d'apres la Doctrine de S. Thomas d Aquin*, 4th ed. (Paris: 1900).

personal, "dynamic assimilation"[70] of the Divine Persons through knowledge and love—a presence of persons to and in each other.[71] Here, in this kind of presence, we have the dwelling of persons in each other, while retaining their alterity: "God is love, and he who abides in love abides in God, and God abides in him" (1 Jn. 4:16, RSV). In the words of Journet: "Now, if every being that is the object of love dwells within him who loves him, in virtue of the Holy Spirit's indwelling, not only does God dwell within us, but we ourselves also dwell in God, thus plunged down into Him."[72] Or, as Palamas says, interpreting a text from St. Gregory of Nazianzus:

> Gregory is saying that they know God as well as God knows them. How? Not by the feeble efforts of reason, of which Barlaam was speaking at the start of this chapter, but *by virtue of the fact that they know God in God, that they are united to Him and so have already acquired the form of God.*[73]

However, let us take care to be clear, for even here below, this indwelling is not merely the moral indwelling of persons in each other, like lovers separated at a distance. Rather, it is a presence through knowledge and love rendered *existentially* present, like a lover truly present as a person here and now, for the very means by which we know of God's personal presence are the gifts of grace (bestowed through God's causal activity and, hence, present through "immensity").[74] We can refer to two supportive views at this point. First, that of Maritain:

> This is not just any knowledge and love. No! Rather, it is a fruitful, experiential knowledge and love, putting us in possession of God and uniting us to Him, not at a distance, but instead, really. For if the Divine Persons give themselves to us, they do so in order that we may possess them, that they may be *ours*. The gift of God is such that, according to St. Thomas's expression, it enables us to freely enjoy the Divine Persons. Would that be possible if they were not really and ontologically present there, offering themselves to us in our very depths?[75]

70. See Nicolas, *Synthèse*, §213.

71. See ST I-II, q. 28, aa. 1–3.

72. Charles Journet, *Entretiens sur la charité* (Paris: Parole et Silence, 1999), 111.

73. Palamas, *Triads*, 3.3.12; italics added.

74. This is why the chosen model used by John of St. Thomas for this knowledge is the self-knowledge we have of our own souls, existentially present as the source of our activities. There is one important difference, however, namely that God, present in grace, is personally present in alterity as the vital source of our divine life. See Gardeil, *La structure*, vol. 2, 82–84. Also, see Reginald Garrigou-Lagrange, "Whether the Mind knows Itself Through its Essence or Through Some *Species*" in *Philosophizing in Faith*, 79–80.

75. Maritain, *The Degrees of Knowledge*, 274–75 (translation slightly modified for clarity).

Then Jean-Hervé Nicolas, OP:

> In this way, we find knotted together, on the one hand, ontological there-being [i.e., through immensity] (without which one person is not really present to another) and on the other, interpersonal relations (without which this "there-being" is not a true form of presence). It is a fully supernatural knowledge, a kind of experience of the Divine Persons already present at the source of being, at the very source of the believer's knowledge and love, and this explains how grace makes the Three Persons really and personally present to the created person.[76]

Thus, while it is understandable why someone like Congar (and, in a way, Meyendorff in the text cited above) would contrast the *ontological* to the *operative* when considering matters East and West respectively,[77] must we not say, instead, that God's ontological gift of grace (as an ontological principle, present causally through immensity) is given so that we might, as persons, engage in the fully spiritual, free joy of being present to God by means of the very power of God? Or, in a powerful expression from Journet: "He comes in order to give Himself to me in His love, thus becoming my own, and if I possess Him, He is at my disposal, enabling me to return Him to God: to give God to God."[78] That is, through grace (and most especially charity), we are given the "operative" ability to return all things to God precisely by making the divine love of charity radiate in each and all of our acts. Again, as Journet summarizes so well:

> If one seeks out the supreme reason for this intercommunication of charity, we believe that one must ultimately return to the mystery that, in charity, God is the one who lends His indivisible and omnipresent Love to each person, so that in this Love each can embrace the whole Church and the whole universe. We must be identified with God in a certain way, that is, through the immaterial super-existence of love, so that we might be able to grasp all things from God, even those that belong most closely to Him, even His Christ, even His own deity, in order to offer them to Him as a gift, for He loves us in such an incredible way that He desires to receive them all, even His Christ, and even His deity, from our own hands.[79]

For the Thomist, the "presence" given through grace is at once entitative (as a radiation of the divine light causing created grace in the soul) and

76. Nicolas, *Synthèse*, §217.

77. See Yves Congar, "Deification in the Spiritual Tradition of the East," in *Dialogue Between Christians: Catholic Contributions to Ecumenism*, edited by Yves Congar, translated by Philip Loretz (London: Chapman, 1966) 217–31.

78. Charles Journet, *Entretiens sur la charité*, 29

79. Journet, *Église*, vol. 2, 921–922.

intentional-operative (as enabling us to be the vital source of divinized acts, above all those of the theological virtues). And in making this summary observation, I feel quite close to those words from Palamas cited at the beginning of this section:

> This is why the Divine One purifies the man who desires Him: by this purification, He creates men of divine character, conversing as with friends with those who have attained this state. And (to use a daring expression) uniting Himself as God with gods, and making Himself known to them perhaps to the same extent that He knows those who are known to Him.[80]

And just before this in the *Triads*:

> (Language akin to that of "presence of immensity":) [The purified and illuminated mind] does not simply contemplate some other object or simply its own image but, rather, the glory impressed on its own image by the grace of God. . . .
>
> (Language akin to personal-intentional presence:) This radiance reinforces the mind's power to transcend itself and accomplish that union with those better things which is beyond understanding. By this union, the mind sees God in the Spirit in a manner transcending human powers.

IV. Conclusion

Have I succeeded in showing the mutual concerns of Thomism and Palamas concerning the divine indwelling? At most, I've tried to place the two alongside each other without striving to show that they are making the same argument. My goal has been to present, in brief form, the reflections of a Thomist who retains the thought of the Thomist school while, nonetheless, seeing its kindred spirit in the great Byzantine Saint, Gregory Palamas. As a Thomist, I remain convinced that the line coming from Gardeil, holding that we must here deploy both God's presence of immensity and His intentional-personal presence, is utterly essential if we are to account for both the entitative and the personal-intentional-operative nature of the divine indwelling. However, to the degree that I have read my Thomist masters with an ear that is aware of Palamas's concerns (though not aiming to provide an explicitly "Palamite" solution based on his own texts in detail), my interpretation opens new pathways and points of discussion for Palamites as well.

80. Palamas, *Triads*, 3.3.12.

Some may dispute whether or not this is Byzantine, let alone the thought of a "Byzantine Thomist." Eastern Catholic Churches are a strange breed, perhaps, difficult to peg. But, for my part, I can say that I have at least honestly borne witness here to my recent reflections as a Thomist who spiritually lives in Catholic Byzantium.

MARCO STANGO

St. Thomas Aquinas on the Individuation of the Intellectual Soul

I. Introduction

ANTHONY KENNY COMPLAINS THAT St. Thomas Aquinas's metaphysics does not have the resources to support the belief that the intellectual soul maintains its individuation after the corruption of the body. In fact, he reasons, if for St. Thomas the body causes the individuation of the soul, then the soul loses its individuation once a human being dies a biological death. It is no surprise that for him the Thomistic idea of "disembodied individuation" is a hotbed of difficulties and contradictions.[1] On the opposite extreme, Montague Brown intends to solve the problem by saying that for St. Thomas the human soul is originally individuated in itself apart from the body at the moment of creation and then destined to a corresponding particular body. Since each soul is simply "commensurated" or "proportioned" to a particular body but not individuated by it, the body is not the "prior cause" of individuation and the separation of the soul from the body does not jeopardize its individuation.[2]

However, Kenny's perplexity and Brown's alleged solution are the result of a problematic reading of St. Thomas, due I believe to what Étienne Gilson has denounced as a "natural desire for an oversimplified Thomism—one

1. Anthony Kenny, *Aquinas on Mind* (New York: Routledge, 1993), 153.

2. Montague Brown, "Aquinas and the Individuation of Human Persons Revisited," *International Philosophical Quarterly* 2 (2003): 170–71; see also his "St. Thomas Aquinas and the Individuation of Persons," *American Catholic Philosophical Quarterly* 1 (1991): 29–44.

thing for each concept, one concept for each thing."[3] I have chosen Kenny and Brown out of convenience, simply because they represent nicely two opposed interpretations. While considerable work has been done on this much troubled aspect of St. Thomas's philosophy, the debate is still mired in the opposition between versions of the two views presented by Kenny[4] and Brown.[5]

The aim of the present essay is to advance a different interpretation of St. Thomas's doctrine of the individuation of the intellectual soul, helping to move this quandary forward. My interpretation can be roughly put as follows: while for St. Thomas at the beginning of life the individuation of the soul is caused by the idiosyncratic dispositions of one's body, the following stages of its individuation are determined *also* in other ways – and "in a more special and perfect way"[6] by intellectual habits. In other words, idiosyncratic or individual-specific dispositions, both bodily and intellectual, are the cause of the individuation of the soul and therefore of the human substance as a whole. Richard L. Purtill has developed independently a similar account of the individuation of a disembodied soul: "It might be argued that a disembodied spirit could be identified as the soul of a dead man, either because each person has a unique 'personality pattern' which persists after death, or because a disembodied spirit retains a capacity for animating a certain body even after the death of that body."[7] In the following pages I try to show that this is also St. Thomas's view.

3. Étienne Gilson, *Thomism: The Philosophy of Saint Thomas* (Toronto: Pontifical Institute of Mediaeval Studies, 2002), 229.

4. See especially, among many interpreters, John F. Wippel, *Metaphysical Themes in Aquinas II* (Washington, D.C.: The Catholic University of America Press, 2007), 126; Christopher Hughes, "Matter and Individuation," *History of Philosophy Quarterly* 1 (1996): 1–16; Joseph Bobik, "La doctrine de saint Thomas sur l'individuation des substances corporelles," *Revue Philosophique de Louvain* 29 (1953): 5–41; Anton Pegis, *St. Thomas and the Problem of the Soul in the Thirteenth Century* (Toronto: Pontifical Institute of Mediaeval Studies, 1934), 141–42 is elusive on this point.

5. See, for example, Robert Pasnau, *Thomas Aquinas on Human Nature: A Philosophical Study of Summa Theologiae Ia 75–89* (Cambridge: Cambridge University Press, 2004), 382; Joseph Owens, "Thomas Aquinas," in *Individuation in Scholasticism: The Later Middle Ages and the Counter-Reformation*, edited by Jorge J. E. Gracia (Albany: SUNY Press, 1994), 178; Robert A. O'Donnell, "Individuation: An Example of the Development in the Thought of St. Thomas Aquinas," *New Scholasticism* 1 (1959): 49–67; Kevin White, "Individuation in Aquinas's *Super Boetium De Trinitate*, Q. 4," *American Catholic Philosophical Quarterly* 4 (1995): 543–56; Brian Leftow, "Soul, Mind, and Brain," in *The Waning of Materialism*, edited by Robert C. Koons and George Bealer (New York: Oxford University Press, 2010), 395–415; Brian Leftow, "Souls Dipped in Dust," in *Soul, Body, and Survival: Essays on the Metaphysics of Human Persons* (Ithaca: Cornell University Press, 2001), 128n31; Gilson, *Thomism*, 231.

6. ST I, q. 29, a. 1.

7. Richard L. Purtill, "Disembodied Survival," *Sophia* 12, no. 2 (1973): 6.

The advantages of this interpretation are at least three. First, it spells out *what in the body* works as the actual principle of individuation: not the body as such, but the idiosyncratic dispositions of the body.[8] My contribution is simply to show that the nature of these indeterminate dimensions can be made more explicit by appealing to bodily idiosyncratic dispositions. Second, it shows that it is possible to understand the cause of individuation of the intellectual soul in a *dynamic* way: while it is true that being embodied is the cause of individuation of the soul at the beginning of life, it is also true that there are *supervenient* causes of individuation of the soul as the human being grows, notably his intellectual habits. This interpretation allows for a more comprehensive theory of individuation, one that is able to give both the body and the intellect their due. Third, this interpretation advances a clear hypothesis about the function that the *intellect* might play in individuation. The traditional interpretations usually overlook St. Thomas's opinion that individuation is realized in the human being in "a more special and perfect way" because of his rational nature.

Figuring out where St. Thomas stands about the individuation of the soul is no easy task. This is due to the fact that, as Joseph Owens remarks,[9] St. Thomas never devotes to this topic a broad discussion in its own right. This is why an interpretation of St. Thomas on this point must be not only explicative, but also heavily reconstructive. As I will point out, the different conclusions to which I come have different degrees of probability, depending on the evidence that can be extracted from the texts, and ranging from very likely—those regarding the body as the cause of individuation—to merely hypothetical—the conclusion regarding the intellect. Further, following Owens, where the letter of the text fails, I have tried to reconstruct its spirit in order to come up with a picture that, if not proved beyond any reasonable doubt by the letter of the texts, is at least philosophically cogent.[10]

8. For a recent discussion of the role of determinate and indeterminate dimensions for individuation, see Gaston G. LeNotre, "Determinate and Indeterminate Dimensions: Does Thomas Aquinas Change His Mind on Individuation?," *American Catholic Philosophical Quarterly* 94 (4): 503–546.

9. Owens, "Thomas Aquinas," 173.

10. I dare to follow Josef Pieper's insight: "an interpretation that does not reach the unspoken assumptions underlying the actual text must remain, in essence, a misinterpretation, even if on other respects the letter of the text be commented upon with considerable learning; this latter fact may, indeed, make matters worse." *The Silence of St. Thomas* (Chicago: Henry Regnery and Company, 1965), 46.

II. Two Objections: Individuated and Unique, Accidental and Substantial

The problem of the individuation of the intellectual soul in St. Thomas cannot be understood apart from that of uniqueness: what makes each soul, and hence the human being, a unique specimen in its kind. What makes me individuated is also what makes me unique, and the other way around. However, as the first objection goes, individuation is not uniqueness. I reject this objection. Part of the trouble in appreciating St. Thomas's view on individuation results from neglecting the fact that these problems are essentially united, and I cannot see what we gain in keeping them apart. The answers to the two questions go hand in hand, so that it becomes a matter of stress in speech to refer to one or the other: if we speak of individuation, we might take for granted that we are also speaking of uniqueness; and if we speak of uniqueness, we might take for granted that we are also speaking of individuation. This is true even just at the level of a purely indexical conception of individuation: 'What makes this tree *this* tree? The fact that I am pointing at *it* and not at another tree.' 'What makes this tree unique, i.e., different from all other trees?' 'At least the *unique* indexical properties belonging to the *one* tree that I am pointing at right now.' If we move to a nonindexical, more robust doctrine of individuation, the deep unity of the two questions does not change. If there is anything new (and maybe controversial) in my interpretation, it is the claim that the problem of uniqueness is a necessary constituent of individuation, so that it is impossible to understand the latter apart from the former.[11]

My interpretation is also unusual in that it states that accidents, both bodily and purely intellectual, play an essential part in individuating the soul. However, a second objection would retort that *accidents cannot individuate*. The reason is that a human being is substantially individuated, not accidentally individuated. The substance must be already somehow individuated in itself before bestowing its individuating power over its accidents. This objection is consistent with the common interpretation of the development of the idea of individuation in the Middle Ages. According to this interpretation,[12] the standard theory of individuation in the early Middle

11. As a consequence, I shall take "individuation" of the soul to cover both meanings that Brower sees in this notion, namely, the source of the "distinction" of a human being from another and the "individuality" characterizing each human being. See Brower, *Aquinas's Ontology*, 97–98.

12. See King, "The Problem of Individuation in the Middle Ages."

Ages was the one inaugurated by Boethius, according to which accidents individuate substances. My interpretation suggests that the continuity between Boethius and St. Thomas's views on individuation is stronger than is usually thought. Even though St. Thomas says in some places that "substance is individualized by itself, whereas the accidents are individualized by the subject,"[13] elsewhere he also talks about "individualizing accidents."[14] This shows in my view that the traditional opposition of St. Thomas to the early medieval view should be weakened. The objection just outlined relies, I believe, on a misinterpretation of the notion of accident. 'Accidental' means contingent, not inessential. Thus, when I say that accidents play an essential part in individuating the soul, this claim does not mean that the substance that I am is not essentially individuated; it simply means that my individuation could have been realized otherwise, therefore making me a different individual. The accidents of a substance, at least some of them, are not superficial traits; they go deep in the constitution of that substance. If Socrates had been born with a significantly different bodily temperament and physical dispositions, he would have been individuated differently, namely, he would have been a different individual.[15] I claim that for St. Thomas the *individualizing ontological force comes from the substance*, but this individualizing ontological force *would remain empty if it did not mediate itself through the accidents. In this sense, the accidents are responsible for the individuation of the substance.* This framework applies also to the case of the human being: the individualizing ontological force comes from the substantial form, i.e, intellectual soul, insofar as the soul represents the "productive" priority of the first act over the second act; but this individualizing ontological force would remain empty if it did not mediate itself through the accidents of the body (from the very beginning of life) and the intellect (once the intellect develops).[16]

13. ST I, q. 29, a. 1, co.

14. ST I, q. 3, a. 3, co.

15. St. Thomas speaks explicitly of "individualizing accidents." Cf. ST I, q. 3, a. 3; a. 6, co; q. 77, a. 6; a. 8, ad 2.

16. Mark K. Spencer, "Created Persons are Subsistent Relations: A Scholastic-Phenomenological Synthesis," *Proceedings of the American Catholic Philosophical Association* 89 (2016): 230–31, beautifully describes the importance of considering the accidents as individuating features of a substance especially when it comes to the human being: "ET [existential Thomism] and Lublin Thomism capture what is missing in these accounts with the idea that the acts and experiences a person undergoes, and especially the free acts he or she performs, are modifications to who he or she fundamentally is. Similarly, some versions of personalism such as Edith Stein's present the idea of a

Denying the role that accidents play in individuation results in the claim that contingent facts and personal history are absolutely inessential to the individuation of my person, which seems to me a weaker, less interesting, and less faithful position than the one I am ascribing to St. Thomas. Thus, accidents depend on substances for their existence and being *and* they contribute to the realization of individuating features of those substances, to the point that the substance can be said to be related to its accidents as potency is related to its actualization.[17] Intellectual habits constitute a sort of 'supervenient' cause of individuation: the accidental forms of the intellect individuate the soul in a more special and perfect way than the body alone does even though their function would be impossible if the soul were not already individuated by the body. My interpretation proposes to see individuation as the result of a *circular action* between substance and accidents: the soul, individuated by bodily idiosyncratic dispositions at the beginning of life, keeps bestowing individuation on the whole human being, including its accidents, while receiving additional individuating features from the accidents developed by the person.[18]

III. The Outline of St. Thomas's Doctrine

St. Thomas's position on the individuation of the intellectual soul can be found in DEE, cap. 5. This passage seems crucial for both what is says and for what it fails to clarify, as it allows us to realize what further questions need to be asked and what spots need to be filled in. Here's the passage:

changeable essence.... Indeed, many in recent CT [Catholic philosophical tradition on the human person] have turned to narrative and history as a proper approach to understanding the person, including phenomenologists (e.g. Richard Kearney), the Radical Orthodox (e.g., Catherine Pickstock), analytic Thomists (e.g., Eleonore Stump), and virtue ethicists (e.g., Alasdair MacIntyre). While in traditional metaphysics these approaches would have been the study of accidents, on the view that focuses on concreteness and relationality, they are foundational to any account of the human person, due to the elevated status that these acts have in an understanding of the person as concrete, dynamic existence."

17. See ST I, q. 3, a. 6, co.

18. Understanding individuation in light of this circular action between substance and accidents is not incompatible with St. Thomas's idea that God knows-loves every individual and His knowledge and love are the ultimate cause of the individual being—the "principia individui" (ST I, q. 14, a. 11, co.). My proposal supplements the theological side of the theory of individuation, in agreement with the broader principle that there is no ontological conflict, but mutual and necessary ontological clarification, between secondary causes and primary cause: God's individual and individuating idea of each being is articulated in nature according to the circular action of substance and accidents explained in this essay.

... even though the individuation of the soul depends on the body as for the occasion (*occasionaliter*) of its beginning (*quantum ad sui inchoationem*), because it acquires its individuated being only in the body of which it is the actuality, it is not necessary that the individuation ceases when the body is removed. Because the soul has an absolute being, once the soul has acquired its individuated being by having being made the form of a particular body, that being always remains individuated. This is why Avicenna says that the individuation and multiplication of souls depends on the body as regards its beginning (*quantum ad sui principium*) but not as regards its end (*quantum ad sui finem*).[19]

First, St. Thomas states that the individuation of the soul depends at first on the body (*ex corpore*). He qualifies this claim by saying that such dependency on the body concerns the individuation of the soul "at its beginning" (namely, at the beginning of human life upon creation). Such a claim already rules out the interpretation on which God creates the soul *as an individual* and *then* destines it to a proportioned body. St. Thomas's qualification that his claim concerns the individuation of the soul "as regards it beginning" seems to leave open the possibility that the human being can *develop over time* also a different, superior kind of individuality. Moreover, the use of the adverb *occasionaliter* does not imply that in the later stages of the earthly life individuation can be realized without the body. All that is said here is that the "beginning" of the individuation of the soul is caused by a certain "occasion," a certain event—the event of the soul's embodiment.

Second, the individuation of the soul "as regards its end" (*quantum ad sui finem*) is caused by "something in the soul" itself, and belongs in a special way to the soul in its own ontological order. This claim conflicts with a recent interpretation by Jeffrey Brower according to which the human soul "is not individuated in itself," in the sense that "what serves as its principle of individuation—in particular, a specific portion of matter—is wholly extrinsic to it."[20] If taken without qualification, Brower's claim seems incorrect. Elsewhere,[21] St. Thomas says that although the soul cannot obtain its individuation without the body, such individuation remains in the soul because it does not ultimately depend on the body. St. Thomas's talk of the soul's

19. References to the works of Aquinas are to *Sancti Thomae Aquinatis Opera Omnia*, http://www.corpusthomisticum.org/iopera.html and *Sancti Thomae Aquinatis Opera Omnia*, ed. Leonine Commission (Rome/Paris, 1882–). Aquinas's position is repeated throughout his work, e.g. ST I, q. 76, a. 2, ad 2.

20. Brower, *Aquinas's Ontology*, 276.

21. *In Sent. I*, dist. 8, q. 5, a. 2, ad 6.

"absolute being" in the DEE passage makes us immediately think of the fact that for him the intellectual soul is not only the "substantial form" of a body but also a "subsistent" principle, "absolute" in the sense of being "separable" from the body and irreducible to the actualization of any physical matter.

Third, the DEE passage explains that the soul gets individuated in virtue of the fact that the soul is the form of a certain body. For this reason, while the individuation "as regards its end" is first *of* the soul—because it belongs to the soul in its absolute being—and is derivatively communicated to the body that that form configures—it could not be attained if not in a body, through a body, or by configuring a body. It is important not to confuse this third point with the first: St. Thomas is not repeating that the individuation of the soul is caused by the body; rather, he is qualifying his second claim that the soul becomes individuated by something in the soul itself. More precisely, he is claiming that, whatever the individuation in the soul's "absolute being" might be, it cannot be produced without the body.

IV. "Quantum ad sui inchoationem"

What does it mean that the body is the cause of the individuation of the soul "at the beginning"? Each human body is characterized by *idiosyncratic or individual-specific features,* features that are responsible for the beginning of the individuation of the *soul* when the soul is created. More specifically, I suggest that each human organism has an idiosyncratic *sensible* or *bodily temperament.* In addition, each organism is characterized from the beginning by certain *material dispositions* that give it an idiosyncratic configuration. In my view, this is what St. Thomas means when he speaks of the "indeterminate dimensions" of the body. These idiosyncratic bodily features are what St. Thomas refers to synthetically as the "body" when he says that "the individuation of the soul depends on the body as the occasion of its beginning."[22]

In ST I-II, q. 51, a. 1, St. Thomas speaks of a different "bodily temperament" (*corporis complexio*) as characteristic of different human beings.

22. This interpretation could be challenged on the basis of an alleged change of mind that St. Thomas would have had around 1260. However, Owens expresses well the correct attitude one should have on this issue: "The historical objection that Aquinas does not mention them [the indeterminate dimensions] in the final period of his writings remains to be met in the manner of an argument from silence. Nowhere is there any hint that he is deliberately rejecting them, and there seems to be no adequate ground for showing that the relevant passages in the later works required repetition of the doctrine of undefined dimensions."

After distinguishing between a "special nature" and an "individual nature," he writes:

> . . . there is a certain natural disposition demanded by the human species, so that no man can be without it. And this disposition is natural in respect to the specific nature. But since such a disposition has a certain latitude, it happens that different grades of this disposition are becoming to different men in respect of the individual nature.

Notice that St. Thomas says that a "natural habit in respect of the individual nature" is mainly due to the "body." Then, he goes on to clarify that the dispositions determining the individual nature are the idiosyncratic realization of specific habits that are, due to their "latitude," prone to be diversified in the different members of the species. As St. Thomas explains, a habit can be "natural" for an individual "as it is nature for Socrates or Plato to be prone to sickness or inclined to health in accordance with their respective temperaments." This point is illuminated by what St. Thomas says in the same article about the "apprehensive" and "appetitive powers" present in a human being at the beginning of life. In both cases, these habits "in respect of the individual nature" are identified with some bodily dispositions. Concerning the apprehensive powers, St. Thomas writes that "in respect of the intellectual nature, a habit of knowledge is natural as to its beginning, in so far as one man, from the disposition of his organs of sense, is more apt than another to understand well, since we need the sensitive powers for the operation of the intellect." Along these lines, in relation to the appetitive powers, he explains that "on the part of the body, in respect of the individual nature, there are some appetitive habits by way of natural beginnings. For some are disposed from their own bodily temperament to chastity or meekness or such like." Thus, what causes the beginning of the individuation of the soul is the fact that the soul by configuring some matter into a human body produces a human body with an idiosyncratic bodily temperament, and it is by this bodily temperament that the soul is individuated.[23]

St Thomas's tenet that it is the body that individuates the soul has the further implication that not only the bodily temperament, but *also other material dispositions* are responsible for such individuation. St. Thomas refers to these as the "indeterminate dimensions" of an organism. An organism

23. John F. Wippel seems to overlook this point about the bodily *temperament* in his otherwise illuminating treatment of bodily individuation in *The Metaphysical Thought of Aquinas: From Finite Being to Uncreated Being* (Washington, D.C.: The Catholic University of America Press, 2000), 351–75.

can be considered either as having actual material properties (actual in the second act), which constitute what St. Thomas calls "materia signata quantitate,"[24] or as having dispositional material properties (actual only in the first act), which are the "dimensiones interminatae."[25] The bodily indeterminate dimensions understood as dispositional material properties pinpoint the singular person, say, Socrates. As St. Thomas says sometimes—and this is an enlightening qualification—these indeterminate dimensions would be part of the "definition of Socrates," if it were possible to provide such a definition.[26] They are something in between the actual material determinations that Socrates shows at some precise point in space and time and the generic property of "having a specific organism" without any further determination of *how this organism is disposed to be in the case of Socrates.* So, while the actual determinations of a certain body change continuously (e.g., the spatiotemporal determinations, including the reciprocal position of its bodily parts in different moments, the organic material of which it is constituted, the size at different stages of growth, etc.), certain dispositional properties remain more or less regular throughout that change (e.g., the dispositions that make possible that a certain organism is sexually characterized, that a certain face has always the same traits, that the hands have always the same fingerprints, etc.).[27] As Socrates grows older, the organic material constituting his body is replaced several times, but his body remains the same, not only specifically (it is always a *human* body), but also numerically (it is always *Socrates's* body) because of the idiosyncratic indeterminate dimensions constituting it.[28] Notice that, although "indeterminate" in the sense of nonactual in the second act, these properties are not indeterminate in the sense in which "prime matter" is completely void of determinations. Their indetermination simply refers to their dispositional status and is perfectly consistent with the idea that one organism has certain bodily dispositions while another organism has others.[29]

24. I have called these 'indexical properties' in part 2 above.

25. To be precise, "signatum quantitate" can be taken in two senses: as complete and as incomplete. In this latter sense, "signatum quantitate" is close to the idea of indeterminate dimension. However, the opposition between "signatum quantitate" and "dimensio interminata" is helpful here to clarify the two senses in which the matter individuating a substantial form should be understood.

26. DEE, chap. 2.

27. The soul is not only the principle of order and operation, but also that of stability and permanency. Cf. SCG II, chap. 88, no. 11.

28. Cf. SCG IV, chap. 81, no. 12.

29. See *In DT*, pars. 2, q. 4, a. 2, co. 7. It is easy to find passages in which Aquinas seems to

V. Act of Being, Body, and Individuation

Among those who claim that for St. Thomas the soul is originally individuated in itself, some take the notion of "act of being" as pivotal.[30] Their basic idea is that God creates different beings as different existential units, as it were. More explicitly, they reason that since the act of being of the human being resides chiefly in the soul and is communicated to the whole soul-body composite,[31] the true cause of individuation must reside in each act of being. According to this interpretation, the body would simply receive its individuation from the soul/act of being and would have no individuating efficacy. So, for Owens, "Whether as subsistent in God or accidental in creatures, existence is, in the order of being, the basic cause of individuation."[32] He applies this axiom to the problem of the individuation of the soul. He mainly relies on two passages: "For everything in accordance with the way it has existence has unity and individuation,"[33] and "Each being possesses its act of existing and its individuation in accordance with the same factor."[34]

But this interpretation cannot be correct. Taking these passages to mean that each human being's act of being, residing in the soul, is already individuated in itself apart from the causal action (mediation) of the body is misleading. In fact, the first claim used by Owens as evidence of his interpretation is taken from a longer passage which seems to me nothing else than a confirmation of the interpretation that I am proposing. In that text, St. Thomas claims that the individuation of the soul survives the corruption of the body, which is the second point I have mentioned in the previous section. The text reads as follows:

> That ... the souls, individuated by the individuation and the matter of the bodies, maintain their individuation even when they are separated from them, like the wax in the impression of the seal, can be understood in a correct way and in an incorrect way: if it is understood that the souls are individuated by the bodies as if the

deny that it is the indeterminate dimensions that individuate. For instance, QDV, q. 2, a. 6, ad 1 on matter.

30. See Gilson, *Thomism*, 231; White, "Individuation in Aquinas," 545; Owens, "Thomas Aquinas," see notes 22 and 25 above.

31. Cf. *In Sent. I*, d. 23, q. 1, a. 1, Solut.

32. Owens, "Thomas Aquinas," 175.

33. *Responsio ad Fr. Joannem Vercellensem de articulis XLII*, q. 108.

34. QDA, q. 1, ad 2.

bodies were the total cause of the individuation of the souls (causa totalis individuationis animarum), this claim is false; if it is understood that bodies are somehow (aliqualiter) the cause of the individuation of the souls, it is true; for everything in accordance with the way it has existence has unity and individuation. Just as the body is not the total cause of the soul ... so the body is not the total cause of the individuation of this soul ... and this [the individuation] remains in the soul also after the destruction of the body.[35]

St Thomas is far from suggesting that the body plays no role in individuation. Rather, he is saying that despite the body having some causal efficacy in individuating the soul, it is not "the total cause" of individuation. (Although the "how" of bodily causality is not explained here, the passage clearly points in the direction of the body having *some* causal efficacy in individuating the soul.[36]

VI. "Quantum ad sui finem"

What St. Thomas means by the individuation of the soul "as regards its end" poses a bigger problem. For in the DEE passage commented at the beginning, St. Thomas does not spell out what the source and nature of such ultimate and incorruptible individuation might be. This forces us to look elsewhere for a complete reconstruction of the picture. In DEE he only says that "once the soul has acquired its individuated being by having been made the form of a particular body, that being always remains individuated." I propose to take this claim at face value and interpret it in the sense of what I shall call the *minimal condition for the individuation of the soul*. According to this, *the mere fact of having been embodied*—having been created as the configuring principle of a body—is a sufficient condition for the soul to remain individuated afterwards.[37] However, this still leaves us very much in the dark concerning the *nature* of the individuation thus produced.

Some clues can be found elsewhere. In *In Sent.* I, dist. 8, q. 5, a. 2, ad. 6,

35. *Responsio ad Fr. Joannem Vercellensem de articulis XLII*, q. 108.

36. If I understand him correctly, Owens interprets the "occasionaliter" in the DEE passage (the same passage I discuss in part 2 above) as an occasional cause, or something of that sort (Owens, "Thomas Aquinas," 178): the body gives the soul the "occasion" to individuate itself, but the fundamental cause of the individuation is the act of being. However, this interpretation strips the body of any robust causal efficacy in individuating the soul.

37. Oderberg, "Hylomorphic Dualism," 95–96 and Christopher M. Brown, *Aquinas and the Ship of Theseus: Solving the Puzzles about Material Objects* (New York: Continuum, 2005), 129 propose a similar interpretation.

St. Thomas repeats literally the same ideas of the DEE passage and identifies explicitly the cause of individuation "quantum ad finem" with certain "affections or dispositions" that the soul has acquired by being embodied and explains that this is Avicenna's position. Now, what is the nature of these affections and dispositions? St. Thomas does not say explicitly, but a likely reconstruction would be as follows. When a soul is created and destined for certain material to configure a human body, the hylomorphic encounter of soul and matter produces a human body by producing the principles of the typical material powers of a human body, which will develop over time into fully formed organs and biological systems. As we have seen, for St. Thomas an organism is distinguished from another because it has from the start idiosyncratic bodily characteristics. Thus, it would not be a stretch to say that the nature of the individuating affections and dispositions of which St. Thomas speaks in *In Sent.* I, dist. 8 is *at least* that of an idiosyncratic bodily temperament and indeterminate dimensions: by being the configuring principle of a human body with idiosyncratic characteristics, *the soul itself can be said to have acquired habits*—affections and dispositions—corresponding to those idiosyncratic characteristics through its very act of configuring a matter.

As it is known, one momentous consequence of St. Thomas's idea of the intellectual soul being the only substantial form of the human being is that the soul is responsible not only for the intellectual operations but also for the bodily constitution and functioning of the person. For this reason, we might advance the hypothesis that the separate soul retains a kind of "bodily memory"—a potentiality for a body with idiosyncratic characteristics—corresponding to the body that it once configured.

St Thomas seems to point in this direction when he talks about the resurrection of the body. SCG IV, chap. 81 considers the objection that "the same man cannot rise again." He tackles this objection by stating that none of a human being's essential principles is completely annihilated after death: not the soul—since the soul is subsistent—*nor the body,* because "the matter which was subject to that form remains under the same dimensions that individualized it." But how can a body, subject as it is to corruption, not only survive death, but also maintain its idiosyncratic features? The solution relies upon a distinction of two meanings of "corporeity" (*corporeitas*) that St. Thomas distinguishes: in one sense, corporeity means the substantial form of a corporeal substance, namely, the principle turning matter into a specific body and in regard to which the substance can be said to be in its proximate genus, "body" or "animal"—with all its sensitive and nutritive powers in the latter case; in another sense, corporeity means the accidental form of a corporeal substance, namely, the principle in relation to which a substance can be said to be in the genus of quantity. It follows that "corporeity taken as meaning the substantial form in man, is nothing else but the rational soul, which requires the three dimensions in its matter, since it is the actuating principle of a body." St. Thomas concludes:

> Although corporeity [taken in the latter sense] returns to nothingness, when the body is corrupted, this cannot prevent a man from being identically the same when he rises again, since corporeity, taken in the first sense, does not return into nothing, but remains the same.[38]

If the separate soul is responsible for the bodily individuating traits that the resurrected body will have, in what does the soul's "corporeity" consist? The reasoning here is partly implicit but the minimal condition of the individuation seems to be exactly what St. Thomas is envisioning: the idea of a soul retaining an individuating bodily memory ("bodily" taken in the former sense) for certain bodily "dispositions" ("bodily" taken in the latter sense)—a potentiality for re-configuring a body with the same individuating, idiosyncratic traits of the old body—is very likely what St. Thomas is after.[39]

VII. Intellect and Individuation

However, more demanding metaphysicians might reject the minimal condition for individuation (i.e., having been embodied once + retaining a bodily memory for potential idiosyncratic bodily dispositions) as unsatisfactory. They might want to say that the individuating features of a separate soul cannot be only potential but must be *actual*. It is at this point that the *intellect* makes its appearance. For although St. Thomas's overall position, I believe, admits the minimal condition for the individuation of the soul, it nevertheless points also in the direction of the intellect playing a "supervenient" part in individuating the soul. Admittedly, this is the most specu-

38. SCG IV, chap. 81. Cf. QDV, q. 25, a. 3, ad 7.

39. This passage seems to add evidence to the "survivalist" view against the "corruptionist" view. (For a list of survivalists and corruptionists, see Patrick Toner, "Personhood and Death in St. Thomas Aquinas," *History of Philosophy Quarterly* 2 (2009), 135nn1 and 2.)

lative part of the interpretation I am proposing. Nevertheless, I shall claim that it is a view worth exploring.

If we follow this new direction, an additional interpretation of the "affections and dispositions" of *In Sent.* I, dist. 8 might be that these affections and dispositions are the habits that actualize the incorruptible "possible intellect" and make it "habitual." It would remain true that the individuation of the soul, even at this purely intellectual level, is possible only *through* the body, through the phantasms produced by the imagination, which is a material power.

An additional clue supporting this interpretation comes from the brief but crucial passage where St. Thomas connects rationality and what he calls a "more special and perfect way" of being an "individual":

> In a more special and perfect way, the particular and the individual are found in the rational substances which have dominion over their own actions; and which are not only made to act, like others; but which can act of themselves; for actions belong to singulars. Therefore, also the individuals of the rational nature have a special name even among other substances; and thus name is person.[40]

This "more special and perfect way" of realizing individuality is potential in human beings at the beginning of life and becomes actual when the intellect emerges.[41] The passage refers to the capacity for self-movement and self-actualization characteristic of a rational nature, but St. Thomas's point seems to be clear enough to allow for a broader application to the connection between intellectuality and individuation (intellectuality is in fact the source and condition for the "dominion" that a person has on her acts). As I pointed out at the beginning of the essay, most interpretations tend to neglect this claim, probably because St. Thomas's opinion with respect to the connection between individuation and intellect is only sketched. [42] Nevertheless, I think it is necessary to try to develop St. Thomas's suggestion as

40. ST I, q. 29, a. 1.

41. Cf. Montague Brown stresses how different human beings, already individuated by their souls, reach a fuller individuation by the acquisition of unrepeatable "personal" traits. He even flirts with an understanding of individuation as "self-constitution" in "Aquinas and the Individuation of the Human Person Revisited," 175. Similarly, Joseph de Finance speaks of the "personal discontinuity" among human beings; see "Le continu social et le discontinue personnel," *Gregorianum* 1 (1976): 5–38.

42. See Brower as a recent example: "although the human soul is both subsistent and individual, for Aquinas, it is not individuated in itself. That is to say, what serves as its principle of individuation – in particular, a specific portion of matter – is wholly extrinsic to it." *Aquinas's Ontology*, 276.

much as possible. The result of this speculative venture will of course remain open to doubt, but it will not be without value for understanding St. Thomas's overall project. Before St. Thomas's claim, only two interpretative directions are possible (if *interpretation* has to achieve something at all): either dismissing the claim as inessential for St. Thomas's overall view, or reconstructing its likely implications that St. Thomas left underdeveloped. As many interpreters have followed the former path, I try to follow the latter.

The overall interpretative hypothesis that I am proposing would be as follows: while the beginning of the individuation of the soul at the moment of its creation and before the emergence of the intellect is caused by the body, it is the more mature intellectual life of a person that brings that individuation to a new, more special and perfect stage, namely, the development of an intellect with characteristic habits.[43] The intellectual individuation "supervenes" upon the bodily one. And these individuating habits are not removed from the soul after the corruption of the body—and do not recede to mere potentiality—because the intellect is incorruptible.

In *In Sent.* II, d. 17, St. Thomas repeats the ideas contained in the DEE passage, but this time the primary object of his discussion is not the individuation of the soul, but that of the *intellect*: "the possible intellect is numerically different in different men, rooted in the essence of the rational soul, and is not a bodily power that would begin and end with the body."[44] This is no small qualification, as St. Thomas speaks here of the individuation of the intellect and not of the intellectual soul more generally.[45] My reason for saying this is that St. Thomas's discussion of the individuation of the intellect (what makes my intellect different from yours) has to have substantial consequences for the individuation of the soul (what makes this ensouled being that I am different from yours). Thus, d. 17 introduces something new, what I shall call the minimal condition for the individuation of the intellect. A passage from *De Unit. Intell.* chap. 5 is most helpful in clarifying this point:

43. This interpretation accords with the semantic richness (ambiguity?) of St. Thomas's claim that the body is necessary for the individuation of the soul "quantum ad sui inchoationem," which can mean "at its beginning" (namely, at the beginning of human life upon creation), but also "as far as its beginning is concerned." In the latter sense, the expression suggests something like the growth or development of the determination of individuation.

44. *In Sent. II*, d. 17, q. 2, a. 1, resp. St. Thomas is elaborating here on an Avicennean doctrine.

45. Although St. Thomas sometimes uses "intellect" to refer to the intellectual soul as a whole (ad 1, "on the division of matter, which causes diverse individuals, the multiplication of intellects also follows, that is of intellective souls"), we can exclude that this is what is meant in this passage given that St. Thomas explicitly distinguishes between "intellectual soul" and "intellect."

"the intellect is a power of the soul, which is the act of the body. In many bodies, therefore, there are many souls, and in many souls there are many intellectual powers which are called intellects."

The final picture we get of Thomas's overall position is the following. On the one hand, the already individuated but shapeless intellect individuates the intellectual species apprehended by a person, so that this person's knowledge of X is in a sense different from another person's knowledge of the same X—different as far as the existence of the forms in the intellect goes, even though not different in the representational function that those forms have: "these species or concepts are individuated by the individuation of intellects."[46] On the other hand—and this is my most speculative hypothesis—the soul receives an additional and "supervenient" individuation through the idiosyncratic configuration of intellectual habits that each intellect is.

According to this model, then, individuation implies a threefold movement. First, the individuation of the soul brought about by the body causes the (minimal) individuation of the intellect. Second, the minimally individuated intellect is the pivotal point around which the universal forms apprehended get organized into a unitary and individual-specific configuration. Finally, the individual-specific configuration that each intellect is contributes, as a supervenient cause, to the more special and perfect individuation of the soul, so that *my* soul is *this* soul not only because it has acquired dispositions to configure a body with idiosyncratic features, but also because it contains an intellect with *a* special configuration.

VIII. Conclusion

In conclusion, I suggest that for St. Thomas the "bodily memory" for idiosyncratic features present in the soul is sufficient for granting the soul indestructible individuation. And nevertheless, since St. Thomas speaks of a more special and perfect form of individuation realized in rational natures, I also think it is *necessary* to look for an additional cause of individuation. This I have identified with the special configuration of the intellect, which functions as a 'supervenient' cause of individuation. My interpretation is summarized thus:

46. *In Sent. II*, d. 17, q. 2, a. 1, ad 3. Overlooking this distinction, Anthony Kenny is left with no response to how "concepts" can individuate, see his "Body, Soul, and Intellect in Aquinas," in *From Soul to Self*, edited by James Crabbe (New York: Routledge, 1999), 45.

First, the soul's individuation is initially caused by the idiosyncratic bodily temperament and individual-specific material dispositions of the human body that the soul configures. Such individuation remains in the separate soul as the potentiality to configure again a human body with the same idiosyncratic features. Second, there is a more special and perfect way in which individuation is brought about in the human being and this involves the intellect. As the intellect emerges, we witness a midway situation in which it can be said that the cause of the more special and perfect individuation of a human being is the intellect as long as it is the immaterial power emerging from an embodied and thus already-individuated soul (individuated, however, in a less special and perfect way, even though completely). Third, once it becomes habitual, the intellect can be considered *a fortiori* the cause of the more special and perfect individuation of the soul in virtue of the characteristic configuration of its acquired habits. And fourth, since the intellect is an immaterial and incorruptible power, the disembodied soul does not lose its individuation after death not because it has the potentiality to reconstitute a body with certain idiosyncratic features (if we reject the minimal condition of individuation of the soul), or not only because of that (if we accept the minimal condition but also demand a stronger principle), but also because the soul is maintained in an individuated status by its purely intellectual habits.

TRAVIS DUMSDAY

Alexander of Hales on the Irremediable Demons

I. Introduction

THE NOTION THAT HELL will one day be empty, such that all will eventually be saved, is enjoying something of a revival within both popular Christian literature and academic theology. While universalist soteriologies and eschatologies arguably have deep roots in Church history, in latter centuries they have been associated more with schismatic movements (most famously the Unitarian Universalists) and the various brands of liberal Protestantism. Yet universalism has begun to achieve broader interest and adherence, and the past decade in particular has seen some significant new developments. Notably, it has seen a defense of the rationality and theological orthodoxy of the *hope* for universal salvation by the prominent Evangelical Rob Bell, whose bestselling book generated attention even within the mainstream media.[1] More recently has come the strident defense of the moral necessity of universalism by the well-known Eastern Orthodox theologian David Bentley Hart, aimed both at scholars and a general readership.[2] Additional recent book-length defenses of Chris-

1. Rob Bell, *Love Wins: A Book About Heaven, Hell, and the Fate of Every Person Who Ever Lived* (New York: HarperCollins, 2011). Strictly speaking the book does not advocate universalism as that term is most commonly understood; though Bell maintains that Christians should hope that all *may* be saved, he does not positively affirm that all *will* be saved, since he grants the possibility (however unlikely) that in the afterlife some sinners might forever freely opt to reject God.

2. David Bentley Hart, *That All Shall be Saved: Heaven, Hell, and Universal Salvation* (New Haven, Connecticut: Yale University Press, 2019).

tian universalism include Kronen and Reitan,[3] MacDonald,[4] Ramelli,[5] and Talbott.[6]

Others have of course replied in defense of an eternal (and eternally populated) hell; Evangelical responses written for a lay audience—and primarily targeted at Bell, whose book inspired a veritable cottage industry of rebuttals—include works by Chan and Sprinkle,[7] Galli,[8] and Jones.[9] Within the scholarly literature the most recent and extensive critique of universalism is certainly to be found in McClymond's impressive two-volume work.[10] Other arguments against universalism by Orthodox and Protestant authors may be found for instance in Farley,[11] Kvanvig,[12] and Walls.[13] There are also many worthwhile Roman Catholic defences of the reality of an eternal hell that could be cited here—e.g., Dulles,[14] Egan,[15] Grisez and

3. John Kronen and Eric Reitan, *God's Final Victory: A Comparative Philosophical Case for Universalism* (London: Bloomsbury, 2011).

4. Gregory MacDonald, *The Evangelical Universalist: The Biblical Hope that God's Love will Save us All*, 2nd ed. (Eugene, Oregon: Cascade, 2012). In the preface to this second edition of his book, the author (Robin A. Parry) notes that its first edition (published in 2005) was released under a pseudonym due to the intense opposition to universalism then prevalent within Evangelicalism. The popularity of Rob Bell's work seems to have functioned as something of a hall pass, permitting more Evangelical universalists to espouse the view openly; as MacDonald / Parry puts it: "Then along came Rob Bell's book *Love Wins*. Overnight the issue of universalism went from being an issue on the margins to being a white-hot topic that everyone wanted to have their say on." *The Evangelical Universalist*, xix.

5. Ilaria Ramelli, *A Larger Hope? Universal Salvation from Christian Beginnings to Julian of Norwich* (Eugene, Oregon: Cascade, 2019).

6. Thomas Talbott, *The Inescapable Love of God*, 2nd ed. (Eugene, Oregon: Cascade, 2014).

7. Francis Chan and Preston Sprinkle, *Erasing Hell: What God Said About Eternity, and the Things We've Made Up* (Colorado Springs, Colorado: David C. Cook, 2011).

8. Mark Galli, *God Wins: Heaven, Hell, and Why the Good News is Better than Love Wins* (Carol Stream, Illinois: Tyndale House, 2011).

9. Brian Jones, *Hell is Real (But I Hate to Admit It)* (Colorado Springs, Colorado: David C. Cook, 2011).

10. Michael McClymond, *The Devil's Redemption: An Interpretation of the Christian Debate Over Universal Salvation*, 2 vols. (Grand Rapids, Michigan: Baker Academic, 2018).

11. Lawrence Farley, *The Unquenchable Fire: The Traditional Christian Teaching About Hell* (Chesterton, Indiana: Ancient Faith Publishing, 2017).

12. Jonathan Kvanvig, *The Problem of Hell* (Oxford: Oxford University Press, 1993). Note that although Kvanvig explicitly rejects universalism (at least as that doctrine is typically understood and justified), his own positive account of damnation is quite nuanced, presenting a sort of hybrid between a more traditional model of hell and annihilationism.

13. Jerry Walls, *Hell: The Logic of Damnation* (Notre Dame, Indiana: University of Notre Dame Press, 1992), and *Heaven, Hell, and Purgatory: A Protestant View of the Cosmic Drama* (Grand Rapids, Michigan: Brazos, 2015).

14. Avery Dulles, "The Population of Hell," *First Things* 133 (2003): 36–41.

15. Harvey Egan, "Hell: The Mystery of Eternal Love and Eternal Obduracy," *Theological Studies* 75 (2014): 52–73.

Ryan,[16] Brotherton[17]—but on the whole it is safe to say that Catholic scholars have not been quite as heavily engaged in the recent universalism debates as have Protestants or Orthodox. This is perhaps because the Roman Catholic Church's unambiguous (at least to my eyes)[18] condemnation of the doctrine has left less room for active debate on the topic amongst orthodox Catholics. That said, certainly some significant Catholic figures (like von Balthasar)[19] have entertained ideas that skirt near the edges of universalism, for instance by advocating for the orthodoxy of retaining the *hope* of universal salvation (akin to Bell's position as described above); in other cases the entertaining of quasi-universalist ideas has been more creative and interesting, as in the eschatological speculations of Jacques Maritain. He tentatively entertained the idea that all the damned, including even the demons, may, in course of eons, ascend to a better station—not to the supernatural beatitude of heaven, to be sure, but at least to the permanent enjoyment of a *natural* beatitude suitable to them, in the uppermost division of hell known as limbo. Maritain's suggested picture here is not universalism, but it is a substantial departure from much traditional Roman Catholic thinking on hell (if taken up partly for the goal of trying to attain a deeper understanding of the nature and theological meaning of the heavily contested notion of limbo).[20]

The pro-universalists cited above collectively marshal an impressive array of data from historical theology, as do the anti-universalists. However, despite considerable attention given to Aquinas (a resolute opponent of universalism),[21] none engages in an extended examination of the larg-

16. Germain Grisez and Peter F. Ryan, "Hell and Hope for Salvation," *New Blackfriars* 95 (2014): 606–615.

17. Joshua Brotherton, "Universalism and Predestinarianism: A Critique of the Theological Anthropology that Undergirds Catholic Universalist Eschatology," *Theological Studies* 77 (2016): 603–626.

18. This despite ambiguous statements made by Pope Francis, such as the following from *Amoris Laetitia* no. 297: "No one can be condemned for ever, because that is not the logic of the Gospel!" Quoted in McClymond, *The Devil's Redemption* vol. 1, xx.

19. Hans Urs von Balthasar, *Dare We Hope 'That All Men Be Saved'? With a Short Discourse on Hell*, translated by David Kipp and Lothar Krauth (San Francisco, California: Ignatius Press, 1988)

20. For more on Maritain's ideas here, consult Travis Dumsday, "Maritain on Limbo and Demonic Beatitude," in *The Things that Matter: Essays on the Later Work of Jacques Maritain*, edited by Heidi Giebel (Washington, D.C.: American Maritain Association, distributed by The Catholic University of America Press, 2018), 24–40. For a relevant comparative study of von Balthasar and Maritain, see Joshua Brotherton, "Presuppositions of Balthasar's Universalist Hope and Maritain's Alternative Eschatological Proposal," *Theological Studies* 76 (2015): 718–47.

21. See for example ST Suppl. III, q. 99, aa. 1–5.

er Scholastic tradition. The early Franciscans in particular are given short shrift, with Bonaventure receiving no more than an occasional passing mention in the aforementioned popular and academic works, and his mentor Alexander of Hales being wholly overlooked. This is regrettable, insofar as the early Franciscans actually have quite a bit to say on the topic. The present short essay can be seen as an initial step towards rectifying this situation in the current universalism literature.

My focus here will be on Alexander of Hales (born sometime between 1180 and 1186, died 1245), who has a particularly interesting discussion of universalism in the third volume of his giant *Summa Theologica* (sometimes referred to as the *Summa Fratris Alexandri* or as the *Summa Halensis*).[22] There he delves into universalism's starkest (and trickiest?) test case: the issue of whether the devil and his angels are forever damned or might someday be saved. His treatment of the issue is interesting for its own sake, as he tidily synthesizes and deploys a number of earlier patristic and Anselmian points; it is also interesting historically as an indicator of the standard Franciscan line of thought on the topic at the time (his *Summa* having been intended as a theology textbook and reference guide for the Order); and, relatedly, his discussion is significant for the lines of influence that exist between his work and treatments of the same issue by his pupil Bonaventure and by later Scholastics. A perusal of Alexander's treatment of the topic can thus function as a prelude to further work on subsequent figures, and as a stepping-stone to a more comprehensive discussion of the history of demonic irremediability as a significant, if less prominent, battleground in the universalism/anti-universalism conflict.

On that lesser prominence: unsurprisingly, the above-cited literature on universalism (whether pro or anti) is mostly focused on the issue of *human* salvation. Talbott does feature some brief discussion of demonic redemption,[23] as does MacDonald[24] and von Balthasar.[25] Farley and Ramelli both repeatedly take note of patristic views on the matter, as does McClymond—appropriately enough, since he titles his work *The Devil's*

22. Note that I say 'his' while remaining cognizant of the continued uncertainties regarding just how much of the *Summa* was directly composed by Alexander. For more on the authorship issue see Christopher Cullen, "Alexander of Hales," in *A Companion to Philosophy in the Middle Ages*, edited by Jorge Garcia and Timothy Noone (Oxford: Blackwell, 2003), 104–108.

23. Talbott, *The Inescapable Love of God*, 15 and 64–66.

24. MacDonald, *The Evangelical Universalist*, 88–89, 128–32, and 188–91.

25. von Balthasar, *Dare We Hope*, 112–15.

Redemption. On the whole, however, the academic literature on the history of western angelology and demonology seems a better initial guide to historical sources and arguments on demonic redemption than the academic literature on universalism, with Russell being quite a useful entry point for mediaeval discussions specifically.[26]

Are there reasons contemporary theologians ought to take any special interest in this, even if they generally (and laudably) incline away from any interest in demonology? Consider that if demons *can* be saved, presumably that boosts our own hopes of avoiding hell, so the issues of demonic salvation and human salvation remain inherently related. On the flipside, if demons *cannot* be saved one might suppose that this fact could *also* work in our favor, in a sense; from the Roman Catholic perspective, in particular, one might think that the Church's dogmatic affirmation of an eternally populated hell can be grounded simply in the damnation of the demons. On such a scenario, although universalism could not be true in toto, it could perhaps still be true for *us*. Macdonald for instance entertains this idea, writing as follows:

> [W]hile I take it to be a datum of divine revelation that there is a hell populated by rational creatures, I don't take it as a datum of divine revelation that hell is also populated by human beings.... Whether the entirety of the biblical witness and the teaching of the Church (both historically and presently) are consistent with agnosticism about the actual human population of hell is, of course, a matter of real theological debate, which I will not enter into further here. Nevertheless, agnosticism about the human population of hell seems entirely orthodox.[27]

Macdonald's last claim there is of course controversial; nevertheless it draws out one reason why Roman Catholic theologians might today be especially interested in the issue of demonic redemption. (Writing from an Evangelical perspective, our other MacDonald (with a capital 'D') asks rhetorically: "Alternatively, if hell is required to be inhabited why need it have more than one inhabitant and why could that not be Satan?"[28])

This essay aims to provide a clear and accessible summary and assessment of the arguments laid out in the *Summa Halensis'* two principal dis-

26. Jeffrey Burton Russell, *Lucifer: The Devil in the Middle Ages* (Ithaca, New York: Cornell University Press, 1984)

27. Paul A. Macdonald, "Hell, the Problem of Evil, and the Perfection of the Universe," *American Catholic Philosophical Quarterly* 89 (2016): 603–628, with quote at 627.

28. MacDonald, *The Evangelical Universalist*, 21.

cussions of demonic irremediability, one dealing with Lucifer and the other dealing with the lesser fallen angels. Two broader aims to which that modest goal is in turn oriented: (i) to make a minor contribution to the much larger project of examining what (if anything) historical Scholastic sources on demonic irremediability might be able to contribute to today's re-energized contest over Christian universalism, and (ii) to encourage the study of Alexander amongst contemporary Thomists. Here, we should recall that Thomism is properly situated within a broader Scholastic tradition whose other schools warrant respectful attention. When we think about Thomism and tradition, that is the principal tradition which ought to come to mind.

II. Alexander of Hales' Arguments as to Why Lucifer is Rightly Hopeless

For reasons that will become clear shortly, Alexander treats of Lucifer's hypothetical redemption separately from that of the lesser fallen angels. He deals with Lucifer first, with the title of the relevant article in the *Summa* being "Whether the sin of Lucifer be Remediable or Irremediable."[29] In an arrangement fairly typical for Alexander, it is divided up as follows: he first presents us with a set of four arguments for his own favored view (which arguments he does not necessarily support in full); then eight objections to that favored view; then in an extended 'solutio' passage he gives us his own verdict (in this case that Lucifer's sin is irremediable) along with some supporting arguments he takes to be compelling, at least when taken in conjunction; and finally he goes back and answers each of the eight objections. For clarity's sake I'll adhere to that same schema in this summary. I will also have some exegetical comments and clarifications to make along the way, which I hope will prove useful.

As noted, Alexander begins by providing us with four quick reasons for the irremediability of the devil's sin. His first two points are adapted from Gregory the Great: (a) angels are created fully formed, in a sense; they are

29. "Utrum peccatum Luciferi sit remediabile vel irremediabile." My own translation, here and throughout. Alexander of Hales, *Summa Theologica*, Tomus III (Quaracchi: Collegi S. Bonaventurae, 1930), 92. The full citation information for this article on Lucifer is as follows: *Summa Theologica*, Tomus III, Inq. II, Tract. II, Sect. I, Quaest. I, Tit. I, Caput IV, Art. I (pages 92–95 in the Quarracchi critical edition). Note that unlike for Aquinas' *Summa*, amongst mediaevalists there is at present no uniform citation style for Alexander's.

mature and not in need of any further development when it comes to moral decision making (thus, the devil sinned knowingly and willingly). Relatedly, (b) whereas Lucifer and all angels (fallen or unfallen) are pure spirit, man is a composite of spirit and flesh and thus inherently more infirm (morally speaking), and by extension less culpable and therefore more redeemable; (c) whereas man sinned at the suggestion of the devil and so isn't as blameworthy as the devil, the devil sinned by his own prompting, and so is more blameworthy and less apt for redemption. Finally, (d) Alexander quotes Augustine to the effect that the devil fell from a much more exalted ("most sublime") initial condition than did man, and so while the latter is capable of redemption the former isn't. And like Gregory, Augustine also supports the idea that because the devil's sin (unlike man's) was not externally prompted, he cannot be redeemed. (As we shall see shortly, Alexander does not view all of those opening points as equally strong, and he will go on to qualify and clarify some of them in the course of presenting his own preferred defense of Lucifer's irremediability.)

Alexander then proceeds to provide eight reasons for thinking that the devil might yet be saved: (1) A just punishment fits the crime. Man is subject to eternal damnation (i.e., punishment of infinite duration) for his sin, which is a just punishment. Yet it is still a *remissible* punishment—man can justly escape damnation. Now consider the devil's just punishment, which is the same as man's: eternal damnation. Since a just punishment fits the crime, presumably the devil's crime was no worse than man's (since it merits the same punishment). That being the case, if man's sin were remissible but the devil's was not, then that would be unfair because disproportionate. And so the devil's sin must be remissible.

(2) If the claim is that Lucifer's sin cannot be forgiven because it was self-prompted rather than the product of external suggestion, whereas man's sin can be forgiven because it was prompted by the devil, then presumably the lesser fallen angels can be redeemed because their sin was in this respect analogous to man's: they were just imitating Lucifer. And yet it is typically claimed that the lesser fallen angels can't be redeemed either. So the self-prompting argument for Lucifer's irremediability doesn't work.

(3) Before he sinned the devil had greater knowledge than man, but he didn't have *infinitely* more knowledge than man. They both had merely finite knowledge. Why then should man's lesser knowledge make him apt for escape from infinite punishment, when the devil's larger (but certainly still

finite) knowledge supposedly opens *him* up for infinite punishment with no chance for redemption?

(4) The idea that man's sin is remissible because he is a weak and infirm conjunction of flesh and spirit is also faulty. For consider the possible scenario (entertained by certain heretics) that man's soul existed in a separated state before being joined with a body, and that it sinned in that immaterial antenatal state, which goes to show that conjunction with a body cannot be the relevant factor in determining whether or not a soul's sin is remissible.

(5) Lucifer was incomparably great among created beings prior to his fall, and so supposedly his sin was irremediable. But then the lesser fallen angels were obviously not incomparably great, so if falling from an incomparable height is the relevant factor determining irremediability, then the sin of the lesser fallen angels ought to be remediable. But it isn't. Consequently that argument for Lucifer's irremediability doesn't work.

(6) The devil is by nature a morally mutable being (i.e., he can switch from being good to evil and vice versa). Now, whatever is natural to a thing will continue to exist unless and until that thing itself is destroyed. But God doesn't will the destruction of angels or of any angelic nature. Consequently, so long as the devil exists he is necessarily capable of changing his moral state, and that means his sin is remissible.

(7) Alexander presents the seventh objection as follows: "Likewise, either God was able to give grace to him (the devil) after his sin or not. If He was unable to give grace to him, then He isn't omnipotent. If God was able to give grace to him, then the devil was able to receive it; and if the devil was able to receive it, he was able to have his sin remitted; and if he was able to have his sin remitted, his sin could not have been irremissible; therefore his sin wasn't irremissible."[30]

(8) Both Origen and Bernard of Clairvaux taught us that God's mercy is infinite and so can overcome the malice of any creature. Now, mercy is most greatly manifested in cancelling out the very worst sin. The very worst sin was Lucifer's. Consequently either God will forgive it, or else His mercy will not be manifested in the greatest possible manner.

Alexander then opens his Solutio with a conceptual distinction: when

30. A direct translation of the following: "(7) Item, aut Deus potuit post peccatum dare ei gratiam aut non. Si non potuit ei dare gratiam, ergo non est omnipotens. Si potuit Deus dare ei gratiam, ergo iste potuit habere; et si potuit habere, potuit ei dimitti peccatum; et si potuit ei dimitti peccatum, non fuit peccatum eius irremissibile; ergo peccatum eius fuit remissibile."

we talk of a sin's being irremissible, we might be talking about the fact that it *is* not remitted, or about the fact that it *cannot* be remitted (in the sense that there is no potential whatever for the sin to be remitted, such that not even God could remit it). Lucifer's sin is irremissible in the first sense. So that's the sense relevant here.

That meaning of 'irremissible' admits of a further distinction, between (a) a sin's not being remitted of a person who has free will but whose free will exists in the midst of an *external* condition or state whereby that person is not receptive of forgiveness, vs. (b) a sin's not being remitted of a person who has free will but whose free will exists in the midst of an *internal* condition or state whereby that person is not receptive of forgiveness. Now, postmortem man is in condition (a)—a damned human soul remains inherently able freely to receive forgiveness, its problem is simply that the afterlife is not a place in which new merit or demerit can be acquired. So the damned human soul stays damned for that reason. (After all, earning one's way out of hell, if even possible, would require as a starting point the ability to accumulate new merit and to avoid new demerit.) The devil, by contrast, is in condition (b) and so stays damned for a different reason. The devil does remain the sort of being that by nature possesses free will, however in his damned state he is unable to exercise his free will towards the good and thus towards a free reception of God's forgiveness. Lucifer's inherent freedom is exercised only in further sinful acts, acquiring ever more demerit. Why exactly does this (b) variety of irremissibility pertain to a damned angel, but not to a damned man? Alexander presents us with four reasons: (i) the devil's mind is utterly hardened against God; (ii) he is in a state of despair (in the theological sense of 'despair'); (iii) repentance entails sorrow at one's sin and some level of joy at the prospect of repentance, but the devil, far from sorrowing over his sin, revels in it; (iv) because Lucifer had such an exalted status amongst created beings (i.e., was so high up on the ontological hierarchy), his nature was such that while it was at first mutable between good and evil (prior to his sin), nevertheless once he made his choice for good or evil that free choice automatically became fixed forever. And in fact this is the case for all angels, whatever precise level of the hierarchy on which they dwell: by nature, they must freely choose one or the other moral state, whether that's good or evil, and the outcome of that choice becomes irrevocable.

By way of clarification, I take it that Alexander's fourth point there is basically this: angels have by nature a single, simple sort of moral mutability, namely an ability to choose an overarching orientation towards good or towards evil (i.e., a misdirected and disordered love of self over God). Once that choice is made, angels are then (in that respect) immutable, and in this immutability are more like God, even if they made the wrong choice. By contrast we humans, because of our lower, partly bodily being, have a more complicated, twofold sort of mutability: an ability to choose good or evil, and then, having made that choice, an ability to go back and efficaciously change our minds (at least prior to death — in hell we may change our minds but doing so can have no practical effect, since by its nature the place we're stuck in rules out the acquisition of new merit). We are both more mutable and more complex than angels, whose greater stability and simplicity render them ontologically more akin to the divine nature and so higher up than us on the ontological hierarchy. In what may initially seem a counter-intuitive claim, *angels are hopelessly damned when they fall precisely because they are ontologically superior to us,* who have hope of redemption because of our lower, doubly mutable moral status. (It is interesting that in this portion of the discussion Alexander does not yet assign a major role to divine grace in assuring angelic perseverance or demonic obstinacy. Here, the focus instead is on the kind of thing that angels are by nature.)

Alexander concludes the 'solutio' by making explicit a further distinction between two terms he has mostly been using interchangeably up to this point: 'irremissible' vs. 'irremediable.' A sin is irremissible when the sinner lacks the inner motivation to repent (such that the sin isn't remitted), and irremediable when the sinner is unable to receive remedy either through himself or through another. Humans' original sin is remediable since a man (Christ) acquired grace for us to satisfy our debt. No such remedy via a third party is available to the fallen angels, so their sin can be called both irremissible and irremediable.

Alexander proceeds to go back and reply to each of the eight previously stated objections: (1) It is true that Lucifer's sin did not exceed Adam's in terms of severity, and it is true that both of them are subject to eternal damnation as a just punishment for their sins. In that sense there is a sort of equivalence between their penalties. The alleged disproportion arises from the fact that Adam's sin is remissible but Lucifer's is not. Alexander thinks the problem with this objection is that it assumes the two punishments are relevantly commensurable, when in fact they aren't, since while there is indeed a sort of disproportion here, it is not a *quantitative* disproportion. Punishment for an irremissible sin is endless. So, while there is a sort of disproportion involved (one penalty is endless and the other is not), it is not a quantitative disproportion of the kind alleged in the objection as stated. It is the endlessness that leads to the disproportion, not any quantitative difference per se, such that the objection misses its target.

I take it that Alexander considers this morally relevant insofar as we typically make judgments about disproportionality between punishments on the basis of quantitative facts (e.g., Bob gets 5 years in prison for running a speakeasy whereas Bub gets 4 for precisely the same crime, and we cry foul because of the arbitrary quantitative disproportion). But strictly speaking the difference between an endless punishment and a punishment that has an end is not a quantitative difference: we are *not* comparing two finite punishments and saying that the severity or duration of A is much larger or smaller than B for the same offence, which is unjust. An endless punishment is in the relevant sense quantitatively incommensurable to a punishment that ends, whereas the objection presupposes commensurability, and so is off-base. At least I think that is Alexander's point here; I confess I am a bit unsure of the proper interpretation of this passage, in part because I don't see the moral force of his counter-reply. Why wouldn't the quantitatively incommensurable *but still disproportionate* irremissible penalty imposed on Lucifer be unjust when compared with Adam's remissible penalty? Perhaps the original objection should have been formulated somewhat differently, but the underlying worry remains (or so it seems to me).

(2) The second objection errs because it fails to note a relevant difference between the lesser angels' sinning by Lucifer's prompting and Adam's sinning by Lucifer's prompting: the former was by *imitation,* the latter by *suggestion.* I.e., the fallen angels saw Lucifer's rebellion and followed along by imitation. Lucifer didn't argue them into it, they simply saw and followed. By contrast, Adam never saw Lucifer sin; rather, Adam acted according to Lucifer's deceitful advice. Alexander clearly takes the imitation vs. suggestion distinction to be morally relevant, such that sinning by imitation is more blameworthy than sinning on account of someone's suggestion. The remainder of this reply consists in a supporting quote from Gregory the Great, who makes the point that the fallen angel is unable to repent because a kind of post-fall moral blindness renders it such that it is no longer motivated towards repentance by an awareness of God's observation of its own

sinful acts. (I take it that the connection between this latter, Gregorian point and the former point is that demons are no longer capable of explicit awareness of God and hence are blocked from any opportunity to imitate God rather than Satan, with this lack of opportunity to imitate God being another reason why they have no hope of emerging from their damned state.) Now, it's perhaps worth noting that it isn't immediately clear why Alexander accords such moral gravity to the "imitation" vs. "suggestion" distinction; perhaps it is because being on the receiving end of an explicit suggestion is assumed to involve a greater degree of external influence than merely witnessing something? Consider the following two cases: (a) I see someone robbing my local liquor store and with no further prompting immediately decide to go and do likewise; (b) a caring neighbor sits me down and actively tries to convince me to rob a liquor store, explaining how it will solve all my problems (no more gambling debts owed to the mob etc.), and in the end I accept his arguments and rob the store. Now, in both cases I've sinned in making the decision to rob the store. But whereas in the first case it seems obvious that I must already have harbored felonious desires (otherwise, merely seeing the act done wouldn't have pushed me to commit the same sort of crime), in the second case that is less clear. The second case involves more in the way of external prompting. And deciding to commit the crime under the influence of that greater prompting may plausibly be thought to lower my degree of blameworthiness a little, at least as compared to my decision in scenario (a). Of course, in the case Alexander is considering in this reply to objection #2, the real issue is whether the "sinning by imitation vs. sinning by suggestion" distinction could ever imply such a hefty divergence of blameworthiness that the former would entail irremediable punishment but not the latter. One might also question his idea that the angels' sin was prompted only by imitation, which has little in the way of Biblical support. At any rate, recall that the key idea being defended in Alexander's response to objection #2 is the idea that *Lucifer's* sin was wholly self-generated whereas man's was not, which allegedly can be seen as contributing to the fact that Lucifer's sin is irremediable but man's is remediable. The issue of the degree of self-generation / internal prompting only becomes relevant when the sin of the *lesser angels* is brought into the discussion.

(3) The reply to the third objection is brief: the knowledge of the angels does not exceed infinitely the knowledge of pre-lapsarian Adam, but their knowledge is importantly different in its mode. That difference in mode

of knowledge is what gives rise to the morally relevant disproportion that renders fallen angels irremediable. He backs this up with a quote from the Pseudo-Dionysius who says that for an angel to be evil is for it to be in a state of contradiction with the angel's own exalted deiform intellect (whereas for a mere soul to be evil is for it to be in a state opposed to reason, and for a body to be 'evil' is for it to be in a state opposed to the course of nature).

(4) Alexander's response to the fourth objection reasserts the idea that one of the reasons why human sin is remissible is that we have a composite body / soul nature, whereas angels' sin is graver and irremissible in part because they lack bodies and so are higher beings. As to the hypothetical heretical scenario in which the human soul pre-exists its associated body and sins in that antenatal state, Alexander simply grants that such a sin would be irremissible. So for Alexander the key here seems to be *not* whether the sin is committed by a soul / spirit / entity that happens to be inhabiting a body at the time of the sin, but whether the sin is committed by a being who belongs on a level of the ontological hierarchy that renders it *by nature* incorporeal (even if it is capable of contingently taking on a body as an accidental appendage). To Alexander's eyes, the heretical systems referenced in objection 4 are not successfully referring to human beings (things sharing our actual nature) living under a different possible scenario of embodiment; rather, these heretical systems have confused human and angelic nature, mistakenly thinking about us as if we were angels. And an angel's sin is irremissible, whether it is committed in its natural bodiless state or in a state in which it has temporarily taken on a body for instrumental purposes.[31]

(5) The reply to the fifth objection is fairly simple: the irremediability of Lucifer's sin does not arise from an alleged incomparably high ontological status, but simply from the very high degree of eminence (and incorporeality) possessed by any angel; whatever further ontological divisions existing among angels, they are all much higher up on the hierarchy than man (who is composed of body and soul), and that is the relevant point of comparison when it comes to irremediability.

(6) The important sixth objection receives the following reply from Alexander: an angel is indeed naturally morally mutable, nevertheless when an angel makes its initial choice for the good it is granted a certain immu-

31. For more on Alexander's ideas concerning that sort of angelic corporeality, see Travis Dumsday, "Alexander of Hales on Angelic Corporeality," *Heythrop Journal* 54 (2013): 360–70.

tability in the good, which reception does not contradict the angel's nature or take away its inherent freedom. The same goes for an angel that chooses evil: it receives a stability in that choice for wickedness, and that stability is compatible with its nature. In this respect the situation of the damned angel may be likened to that of the damned human soul, which remains *inherently* free even though it is no longer able to acquire merit and escape from hell. The main underlying idea behind this reply is, I think, the following: we all want to be able to affirm that good angels and the saints in heaven are stably and irrevocably members of the kingdom of God yet retain their natural freedom; they are free, yet we know for certain that by God's grace they will never sin. Now, if we want to affirm that, then we should be open to the idea that the same basic situation obtains for the damned, but in reverse: by the act of divine condemnation they are stably and irrevocably excluded from the kingdom of God yet retain their natural freedom. Consequently, Alexander's reply to objection 6 is closely connected to the issue of the freedom of those in heaven.[32]

(7) The seventh objection is somewhat related to the sixth, though the focus is now more explicitly on God's grace: surely an omnipotent God can give the grace needed for repentance to anyone He wishes, including the devil? In reply, Alexander writes: "… necessarily, God can give grace pertaining to potential virtue, however he does not agree to give the grace needed for penitence to an angel that has already been damned: for such an angel is called damned since it immutably possesses the blame for its sin. And therefore the situation differs on the part of the agent vs. the recipient: for God can give grace, but the devil is not prepared to receive it."[33] In other words, it is no mark against God's omnipotence that God does not give the grace needed for repentance to an angel that has already damned itself, since the determining limitation is not on God's side (the side of the giver of grace) but on the devil's (the side of the theoretical recipient of grace). Implicit here are the claims that God's irrevocable condemnation

32. For an accessible treatment of the later history of discussions on this, see Simon Gaine, *Will there be Free Will in Heaven? Freedom, Impeccability and Beatitude* (London: T&T Clark, 2003).

33. A direct translation of the following: "(7) Ad septimum dicendum quod, licet Deus possit dare gratiam de virtute potentiae, non tamen congruit dare gratiam ad poenitentiam angelo iam damnato: damnatus autem dicitur cum immutabiliter se habet in malo culpae. Et ideo differens est ex parte ipsius agentis et ex parte recipientis: Deus enim potest dare gratiam, sed diabolus non est paratus ad recipiendum."

of the devil's sin is just, that God will not override the devil's irrevocable choice, and that God will not forcibly change the devil's character in such a way as to render him newly open to divine grace. At this point the reader may be wondering whether the key source of the irrevocability of the devil's choice is the devil and his exalted angelic nature, or instead the external condemnation of God. So far as I can tell, Alexander's answer is: both. And he does not appear to think of these converging sources as being in tension with one another.

(8) In response to the final objection, Alexander states that God does manifest highest mercy, but in other ways; God cannot show such mercy in the manner suggested (pardoning Lucifer), since divine mercy must always be compatible with divine justice, and divine justice does not allow God to ignore the sin of those who have by their own choice turned themselves irrevocably into sinners.

There are a few points worth reflecting on before we proceed to consider (more briefly) Alexander's separate chapter on the irremediability of the lesser fallen angels. First, a minor historical observation: Alexander's discussion functions as a corrective to Hoffmann's claim that, prior to Aquinas, the Scholastics explained demonic irremediability in terms of God's decision to limit the time available for angelic acquisition of merit: "Prior to Aquinas and in Aquinas' early teaching, the obstinacy of the demons was simply explained by a divine decision to limit the period in which the angels are 'wayfarers,' that is, the period in which they could merit beatitude. When this period elapsed after their choice, the bad angels became unable to recede from their evil."[34] In support of this claim, Hoffmann cites two passages from Albertus Magnus, two from Bonaventure, and two from Aquinas' early *Sentences* commentary. Notably for our purposes, he does not cite Alexander; and as we have seen above, while a portion of Alexander's model might be described in a manner at least broadly consistent with Hoffmann's characterization, there is clearly a good deal more going on in his account than that. Indeed Hoffmann's characterization of the pre-Thomist discussions of demonic irremediability applies more to Alexander's account of *human* damnation.

Second, Alexander here betrays no doubts concerning the general fit-

34. Tobias Hoffmann, "Theories of Angelic Sin from Aquinas to Ockham," in *A Companion to Angels in Medieval Philosophy*, edited by Tobias Hoffmann (Leiden: Brill, 2012), 283–316, with quote at 306.

tingness of damnation as punishment for sin, whether of men or angels. Hell is a just penalty, and divine mercy is not obligated to get rid of it—indeed for God to do so would be to put divine mercy in conflict with divine justice. It is worth highlighting this as a point of stark contrast with much contemporary discussion of universalism, where the basic morality of eternal punishment often takes center stage. From the pro-universalist perspective, Alexander's lack of detailed engagement with the underlying moral dilemma is liable to be seen as further evidence of the obtuseness of our mediaeval forebears, vulnerable as they were to the brutalizing effects of an upbringing in a violent and oppressive feudal social structure and whatnot. From the anti-universalist perspective, by contrast, this lack of engagement might be seen as evidence of some differing but not necessarily inferior moral intuitions; perhaps the basic idea of damnation for sin seemed less reflexively objectionable to the likes of Augustine and Anselm and Alexander because they had a moral sense more finely-tuned to the true gravity of sin. Or, as Farley puts it: "When we think of eternal punishment, our first thought is, 'How could God allow this?' not, 'It is of course deserved by evil men, and even by me.' Our Liturgy may place in our mouths the confession that Christ came into the world to save sinners 'of whom I am first,' but in our hearts we no longer really believe it."[35] At any rate, those with strong leanings toward universalism (myself included) must be on our guard to try and ensure that our intuitions are being driven by reflections on the breadth and depth and efficacy of divine grace rather than by our own laxity; consideration of sources like Alexander can help remind us of this. This is also where Ramelli's perspective on the proper theological motivation for universalism is worth highlighting: "This is not a doctrine that arises from moral relaxation—as it was depicted during the Origenistic controversy—but the expectation of the total victory of God over evil, which is grounded in the inhumanation, death, and resurrection of Christ, his work as Logos-teacher and physician, and in God's 'goodness.' This goodness is not simply God's kindness or mercy, but it is God's being the absolute Good—with the relevant corollary of the ontological non-substantiality of evil, which is doomed to disappearing."[36]

Third, Alexander's work here nicely illustrates the degree to which background ontology influences mediaeval discussions of universalism.

35. Farley, *The Unquenchable Fire*, 216.
36. Ramelli, *A Larger Hope?*, 214.

An important part of Alexander's explanation for demonic irremediability is his claim that their place on the ontological hierarchy (or 'great chain of being' to use a once-fashionable label) guarantees a hopeless situation post-fall. This is in turn connected to broader debates in Western theology concerning the nature of angels; from the patristic era as late as Peter Lombard the question of whether angels were incorporeal or corporeal (even if having very different sorts of bodies than ours) remained contested, but post-Lombard the view of angels as purely incorporeal basically won out in the west, and Alexander is mostly on board with that newly solidifying consensus.[37] Obviously if he were writing from within a different ontological framework on this point, key portions of his account of Lucifer's irremediability would require rethinking.

Fourth (by way of tying the second and third points together), it is noteworthy that the vulnerability of incorporeal angels to hopeless damnation in consequence of their exalted ontological status is *not* seen by Alexander as a reason to maintain that God ought to have left that rank of the hierarchy unoccupied. Likewise the fact that the nature of the human afterlife state is such that it rules out acquisition of new merit (and so rules out escape from hell) is not seen by him as grounds for thinking that God ought to have designed that afterlife state differently. Alexander of course would have seen himself as having perfectly good Biblical grounds for maintaining that the specific design of our cosmos (physical and non-physical) is valuable and not something to be called into question by us. Alternatively, others would argue that such implications constitute evidence that the structure of the cosmos just can't be like this. E.g., 'If this Halensian cosmic scheme involves persons being subject to irremediable damnation, then God wouldn't have instantiated it. This Halensian cosmic scheme involves persons being subject to irremediable damnation. Therefore, God wouldn't have instantiated it.' Arguments of that general sort are repeatedly pressed by Hart,[38] for example. So this aspect of Alexander's case for Lucifer's irremediability

37. It is true that he, like his student Bonaventure, advocated universal hylomorphism, but the 'prime matter' of angels is sufficiently unlike the prime matter of the four elements that this does not by itself warrant accepting a claim that Alexander accepted angelic corporeality. What makes his views in this area more nuanced and original are his ideas surrounding contingent angelic embodiment (see again Dumsday, "Alexander of Hales on Angelic Corporeality," for a summary), but that is not relevant for our purposes. Note too that the 'in the West' above is deliberate; the question of angelic corporeality remains unsettled in Eastern Orthodox theology to this day.

38. Hart, *That All Shall be Saved*.

ties into larger issues concerning the axiology of the world as a whole and whether the equivalent value of this putative ontological hierarchy could have been fulfilled in some other less risky way (i.e., a way that wouldn't risk irrevocable damnation of any beings)—and if not, whether that risk was morally justifiable. Such larger axiological issues are taken up in more detail by some of Alexander's successors and are still receiving attention in the literature on universalism.[39] But from Alexander's own perspective the correct answers likely seemed obvious: Scripture tells us both that (i) Lucifer and the other demons are irremediably damned, and that (ii) in the beginning God deemed His whole creation "very good". The job of the theologian is to reconcile those two revealed propositions. One way to go about doing so is by reference to the sorts of explanations (including somewhat speculative ideas about ontological hierarchies) developed by certain Western Church Fathers, by the Pseudo-Dionysius, and by Anselm, which explanations Alexander capably synthesizes. Today we might want to dispute the Scriptural interpretations that Alexander simply takes as data, and / or dispute the ontological framework he inherited. Or we might want to update and defend them. In either case we can admire the clarity and logical rigor with which he manages the theological and philosophical hands dealt him.

III. Alexander of Hales' Arguments as to Why the Lesser Fallen Angels are Rightly Hopeless

Let us turn now to Alexander's separate chapter on the lesser fallen angels, titled "Whether the Sin of the Angels Was Irremissible."[40] It is to a considerable degree derivative on the preceding discussion of Lucifer's sin, and features extended quotes from Augustine, Gregory, and Anselm. Alexander begins by listing two arguments in favor of the lesser demons' sin being remissible, both of which take Patristic citations as their starting points: (1) Lucifer's sin is irremissible because he fell from the most exalted state, but the lesser demons didn't start off with such a high status and so their fall can be corrected. (2) Man's sin is remissible because he was led into it by Luci-

39. See Macdonald, "Hell, the Problem of Evil, and the Perfection of the Universe."

40. The full citation information is as follows: *Summa Theologica*, Tomus III, Inq. II, Tract. II, Sect. I, Quaest. I, Tit. II, Caput VII (pages 116–117 in the 1930 Quarracchi edition, with this quote at page 116).

fer's suggestion, and the same can be said of the lesser demons, so their sin ought likewise to be remissible.

He then presents five arguments in favor of their sins' irremissibility: (a) The sin of humans was lesser because we are compounds of soul and body, but the angels' sinned as pure spirits and so sinned irremissibly. (b) As John of Damascus teaches us, the fall is to an angel as death is to a man, and for man there is no more remission for sins after death. By extension there is no remission of sins for a fallen angel. (c) Anselm tells us that when faced with their initial moral choice, the now-fallen angels chose injustice. They didn't accept God's justice when they had the chance, and in consequence now they don't deserve to accept it and so don't deserve to be given another chance to accept it. So their sin is irremissible. (d) The lesser demons' sin is not only irremissible but also irremediable. Anselm tells us that redemption by another requires a biological relationship between redeemer and redeemed (hence Christ's taking on our biological human nature through the Theotokos). Angels, being pure spirit, necessarily have no such route to redemption available to them and so their sin is irremediable. (e) This point is mostly taken up with a quote from Augustine's *Enchiridion*, in which Augustine notes that some but not all angels fell, and lays out the basic idea of the angelic replacement theory of salvation history: the notion that human beings are saved in part so that we can fill up the slots in the kingdom of heaven left open by fallen angels, correcting for a problematic gap.[41] Alexander then comments on the passage, to the effect that man gets redeemed by God in part because the whole of human nature fell via Adam's fall, necessitating divine intervention to ensure that no created nature *wholly* perish. By contrast, since only a *portion* of angelic nature was lost (and since those who were lost fell entirely by their own fault, unlike Adam who was led into sin by another), there was no obligation for God to intervene to save that segment of the angelic populace that fell. In other words, because only a portion of the angels fell, those that did fall fell irremediably. This is an interesting reading of Augustine's point on Alexander's part insofar as it seems to imply that had *all* the angels fallen (and especially had they all fallen in consequence of external suggestion, like Adam did), then God would have been duty-bound to institute some sort of project of angelic redemption.

41. For an accessible account of angelic replacement theories within Western theology see Vojtech Novotny, *Cur Homo? A History of the Thesis Concerning Man as a Replacement for Fallen Angels*, translated by Paulina and Tim Morgan (Prague: Karolinum Press, 2014).

But that point seems to sit uncomfortably with the immediately preceding Anselmian argument that the non-bodily nature of angels renders any such redemption project unworkable.

The Solutio statement is brief: "To which it ought to be said that just as the sin of Lucifer was irremissible and irremediable, so was the sin of the other evil angels, as is evident from the previously stated reasons."[42]

Alexander then replies to the opening two objections: (1) "In reply to the first point, it is to be said that although the other angels did not fall from that most sublime state, nevertheless they did fall from a very sublime state in the order of intellectual creatures. For that is the state which more naturally approximated God, and so in falling from such a state they fell irremissibly."[43] (2) In reply to the second objection Alexander reiterates the distinction between a sin's being prompted by the *example* of another vs. its being prompted by the active *suggestion* of another. Adam's sin took its origin in the latter manner, and so was remissible, but the fallen angels' originated in the former manner and so was irremissible.

IV. Conclusion

I have now summarized the Halensian *Summa Theologica's* arguments on demonic irremediability, along the way clarifying some interpretive points and drawing out some implications that might not have been obvious upon first reading. While I think it safe to say that there is much of interest both theologically and historically in Alexander's discussion, when viewed in context of the contemporary universalism debate his reasoning is unlikely to move the needle in any particular direction. However, as noted in the Introduction, a knowledge of Alexander's treatment also functions as useful background to more in-depth accounts of demonic irremediability by successor Scholastics, in particular his direct pupil Bonaventure. The present study will hopefully find a place within a larger series of works on Franciscan discussions of universalism.

42. A direct translation of the following: "Ad quod dicendum quod sicut peccatum Luciferi fuit irremissibile et irremediabile, ita et peccatum aliorum angelorum malorum, sicut supra dictae ostendunt rationes."

43. A direct translation of the following: "(1) Ad id vero quod primo obicitur in contrarium, dicendum quod, licet non de sublimissimo statu alii angeli ceciderint, ceciderunt tamen de sublimi statu in ordine creaturae intellectualis. Ille enim est status qui plus naturaliter Deo approximavit, et ideo cadentes a tali statu irremissibiliter ceciderunt."

II

FROM A TABLE OF SOLID ROCK

Moral, Social, and Political Theory

FRANCIS FEINGOLD

Personalism and the Common Good

Evaluating the Maritain-De Koninck Controversy

Perhaps one of the sharpest twentieth-century debates within the Thomistic tradition was that between Jacques Maritain and Charles De Koninck. This controversy concerned the relation between the person and the common good: which comes first? Both are certainly to be loved, but which for the sake of which?

Those interested in this debate have generally awarded the victory to De Koninck.[1] The qualified defense of Maritain that I propose here is,

1. Steven Long, for example, calls De Koninck's work "the most masterful treatment of the common good in the commentatorial tradition"; see his "Fundamental Errors of the New Natural Law," *The National Catholic Bioethics Quarterly* 13 (2013): 103–31, at 117n28. For other strong endorsements of De Koninck's side of the controversy, see: Michael Waldstein, *Glory of the Logos in the Flesh: St. John Paul's Theology of the Body* (Ave Maria, Florida: Sapientia Press, 2021), 309–43; Michael Smith, *Human Dignity and the Common Good in the Aristotelian-Thomistic Tradition* (Lewiston, New York: Mellen University Press, 1995), chap. 4; Benjamin Smith, "The Meaning and Importance of Common Goods," *The Thomist* 80 (2016): 583–600; Oliva Blanchette, *The Perfection of the Universe According to Aquinas: A Teleological Cosmology* (University Park, Pennsylvania: Pennsylvania State University Press, 1992), 289–92 and 296–300 (originally a dissertation directed by De Koninck); and Sebastian Walshe, "The Primacy of the Common Good as the Root of Personal Dignity in the Doctrine of Saint Thomas Aquinas" (PhD diss., Pontificia studiorum Universitas a S. Thoma Aq. in Urbe, 2006), and "*Fidelissimus Discipulus Ejus*: Charles De Koninck's Exposition of Aquinas' Doctrine on the Common Good," *The Aquinas Review* 19 (2013–2014): 1–21 (republished in slightly revised and compressed form as "Charles De Koninck and Aquinas's Doctrine of the Common Good," in *Theology Needs Philosophy: Acting Against Reason Is Contrary to the Nature of God*, edited by Matthew L. Lamb [Washington, D.C.: The Catholic University

therefore, a somewhat contrarian analysis. To make this defense, I will proceed in the following order. First, I will examine what Maritain and De Koninck each thought was at stake in the debate. Then, second, I will seek to show that the stakes were actually lower, and the common ground greater, than either side thought. Third, I will argue that, even once the misunderstandings are cleared up, there does remain an important disagreement between them concerning the *reason* for seeking the common good: is it the dignity of the common *good* itself (De Koninck's view)? Or is it both the dignity and poverty of the *persons* who receive it (Maritain's view)? Fourth, I will critique De Koninck's account as being incompatible with the priority which Aquinas assigns to friendship-love over desire-love. Finally, I will also critique Maritain for understanding our ordering to the common good as strictly a debt of justice rather than as a form of self-transcendent love. By this analysis I hope to show how the primacy of the common good over merely private goods *for* the person may be reconciled with what I take to be the central claim of Thomistic personalism: that the *person* is a good of a radically higher dignity than any creaturely good *for* the person, including created common goods, and is therefore to be loved in a fundamentally different and higher way.[2]

---

of America Press, 2016], 267–78). Others who are gentler to Maritain but still give the edge to De Koninck include Bradley Lewis, "Personalism and Common Good: Thomistic Political Philosophy and the Turn to Subjectivity," in *Subjectivity: Ancient and Modern*, edited by R. J. Snell and Steven McGuire (Lanham, Maryland: Lexington Books, 2016), 175–96, esp. 180–91; Mary M. Keys, "Personal Dignity and the Common Good: A Twentieth Century Thomistic Dialogue," in *Catholicism, Liberalism, and Communitarianism: The Catholic Intellectual Tradition and the Moral Foundations of Democracy*, edited by Kenneth L. Grasso, Gerard V. Bradley, and Robert P. Hunt (Lanham, Maryland: Rowman and Littlefield Publishers, 1995), 173–95, at 183–86 and 191; and Gregory Froelich, "The Equivocal Status of *Bonum Commune*," *New Scholasticism* 63 (1989): 38–57 (republished in revised and expanded form as "On the Common Goods," *The Aquinas Review* 15 [2008]: 1–26).

2. For the notion of "Thomistic personalism," see, in the first place, Karol Wojtyła's article by the same name: "Thomistic Personalism," in *Person and Community: Selected Essays*, translated by Theresa Sandok, Catholic Thought from Lublin, vol. 4, edited by Andrew N. Woznicki (New York: Peter Lang, 1993), 165–75; originally published in Polish as "Personalizm tomistyczny," *Znak* 13 (1961): 664–75. Though Wojtyla does not here define "Thomistic personalism," he describes "personalism" in general as a "practical and ethical" concern "with the person as a subject and an object of activity, as a subject of rights, etc." (165) and affirms that it can be fruitfully developed using Aquinas's doctrine of the person, especially Aquinas's claim that "in the created world the person is the highest perfection" (167; see Aquinas, ST I, q. 29, a. 3); and in particular, Wojtyla recognizes personalism in Aquinas's view that love's "proper object and subject is the person," inasmuch as spiritual love is "directed in a special way toward other persons" based on an understanding of their "true worth" (172–73). For an overview of the notion and history

I. Raising the Stakes

The unusual acrimony of this debate was arguably due in part to the height of the perceived stakes. Maritain and his followers feared that prioritizing *society* over the person would reduce the person to a mere dispensable cog in a machine or cell in an organism, which in the political sphere would mean totalitarianism.[3] In totalitarianism, the parts and their well-being are *for* the exclusive good of the whole as such; but in a healthy society, Maritain thinks, the true common good of the whole is on the contrary *for* its members.[4] Pius XII had made this point vigorously in his 1943 encyclical *Mystici Corporis*:

> If we examine the relation existing between the several members and the whole body, in every physical, living body, all the different members are ultimately (*postremum*) destined to the good of the whole alone; while if we look to its ultimate usefulness (*si modo ultimum utilitatis finem inspicimus*), every moral association of men is in the end directed to the advancement of all in general and of every single member in particular [insofar as] they are persons (*utpote personae sunt*).[5]

Maritain's follower Eschmann (whose 1945 article "In Defense of Jacques Maritain" excoriating De Koninck's *On the Primacy of the Common Good Against the Personalists* made the controversy about personalism more personal[6]) calls this passage "the *Magna Charta* of the Christian doctrine of person";[7]

of "Thomistic personalism," see Thomas D. Williams, "What Is Thomistic Personalism?" *Alpha Omega* 7 (2004): 163–97, and *Who Is My Neighbor? Personalism and the Foundation of Human Rights* (Washington, D.C.: The Catholic University of America Press, 2012), chaps. 7–8. Jacques Maritain, whose view will be discussed in detail below, is perhaps the foremost representative of Thomistic personalism, which he describes as "a social philosophy centered in the dignity of the human person"; see Maritain, *The Person and the Common Good*, translated by John J. Fitzgerald (Notre Dame, Indiana: University of Notre Dame Press, 1966), 13.

3. Maritain, *Person*, 30.

4. Ibid., *Person*, 50–51; italics in original.

5. Pius XII, *Mystici Corporis* (1943): no. 61. This translation, however, curiously renders "utpote" as "for" rather than "insofar as."

6. Ignatius Eschmann, "In Defense of Jacques Maritain," *The Modern Schoolman* 22 (1945): 183–208. De Koninck had not referred to Maritain by name in his original attack on "the personalists" in *On the Primacy of the Good Against the Personalists*. However, Eschmann assumed, not unreasonably, that Maritain was the chief target since he was at the time well known for embracing the "personalist" label. Yves Simon concurred that this was at least a reasonable assumption, though not in fact entirely accurate; see Simon, "On the Common Good," *The Review of Politics* 6, no. 4 (1944): 530–33, at 532–33.

7. Eschmann, "Defense," 186. Unlike Maritain, Eschmann does not explicitly invoke the danger of totalitarianism; but his great concern with De Koninck is that he thinks De Koninck con-

Maritain himself echoes Eschmann, claiming that "this passage is truly the charter of the Christian doctrine on the person."[8]

Conversely, however, De Koninck and his followers feared that prioritizing the person over the common good would lead to radical individualism, which in the spiritual sphere would mean nothing less than the sin of the devil: "the exaltation of his personal dignity and of the good proper to his nature" over the "common good," which "was a practically personalist error."[9] Only slightly less dramatically, he holds that subordinating the common good to the private good of persons is the tyranny of individualism, and indeed fundamentally anti-person:

> A society made up of persons who love their private good above the common good, or who identify the common good with the private good, is a society, not of free men, but of tyrants. . . . Refusal of the primacy of the common good proceeds, at bottom, from the distrust and scorn of persons.[10]

Avoiding this error requires, in De Koninck's view, recognizing that "persons are willed only *for* the good of the order of the universe, the intrinsic common good that is better than the single persons who materially constitute it."[11] De Koninck thinks this claim is counterintuitive only if one forgets that "the most fundamental capacity" of the person is "that of participating in a good greater than the singular good,"[12] and that "the reasonable creature . . . draws his dignity from the end which he can and ought attain," namely "the end of the universe," which "is the good of each of them insofar as it is *their* good as a common good."[13] That is, to avoid Satanic individualism, one must find one's highest dignity in being a humble *part* of an order greater than oneself.

---

siders rational creatures as *material* parts of the universe, rather than *formal* parts—i.e., as cogs in the machine of the universe rather than as what God *primarily* intends and loves. See Eschmann, "Defense," 187–92.

8. Maritain, *Person*, 29n22.

9. Charles De Koninck, *The Primacy of the Common Good against the Personalists; The Principle of the New Order*, translated by Ralph McInerny, in *The Writings of Charles De Koninck*, vol. 2, edited by Ralph McInerny (Notre Dame, Indiana: University of Notre Dame Press, 2009; originally published 1943), 63–163, at 72–73.

10. Ibid., 80.

11. Ibid., 84; italics added.

12. Ibid., 86.

13. Ibid., 89; italics in original.

II. Lowering the Stakes

I do not believe, however, that the differences between the two views are really quite as great, or the stakes as high, as they appear. In the first place, De Koninck no less than Maritain vigorously opposes totalitarianism in the political sphere and emphasizes that any genuine common good must be a good *for* every member of the community: "Human society is made *for* man.... That is why one rightly opposes totalitarian doctrines in the name of the dignity of man."[14] Indeed, arguably De Koninck's chief purpose is precisely to prevent totalitarian philosophies from getting away with their "perversion of the common good and its primacy";[15] and he insists that "the common good is a good which is the good *of* particulars, not the good of the collectivity envisaged as a sort of singular.... If it were not the good *of* the particulars, it would not be truly common."[16] Taking the city as a super-individual and identifying the common good as this fictitious super-individual's own proper good, which might crush the individual goods of its members in its path, is, for De Koninck, the error of conflating the common good with the "*bonum alienum*"—an error which he attributes to totalitarians and personalists alike.[17] Moreover, De Koninck shares Maritain's diagnosis of totalitarianism's fundamental problem. Maritain's formulation is that "totalitarianism asserts that man is a part of political society by reason of himself as a whole and by reason of all that is in him";[18] De Koninck's formulation is that "totalitarianism identifies the formality 'man' with the formality 'citizen.'"[19]

Conversely, in the political sphere, Maritain no less than De Koninck

14. Ibid., 72; italics added. De Koninck was quite irked that Eschmann had not paid attention to this opening claim (though in fairness De Koninck's main point here was to caution against emphasizing human dignity too much); see De Koninck, "In Defence of St. Thomas," in *The Writings of Charles De Koninck*, vol. 2, 224–363, at 326–27.

15. De Koninck, *Primacy*, 73.

16. Ibid., 75; italics added. See also ibid., 101, where De Koninck opposes the totalitarian view that society is an "entity separable from its members," and especially 103, where he vigorously insists that "if the common good were the good of the city insofar as the city is a sort of individual, it would then be a particular good properly alien to the members of the society.... The city would then be like an anonymous tyrant which subjects man to itself. Man would be for the city. This good would be neither common nor the good of rational natures."

17. Ibid., 76; see also 103 and 106, and "Defence," 326. Cf. *Primacy*, 85–89, and "Defence," 223 and 306.

18. Maritain, *Person*, 72.

19. De Koninck, *Primacy*, 102.

vigorously opposes individualism. Personalism, in his view, is "opposed to both the idea of the totalitarian state and that of the sovereignty of the individual";[20] he emphasizes his desire to "separate, at the very outset, a social philosophy centered in the dignity of the human person from every social philosophy centered in the primacy of the individual and the private good,"[21] and insists that the "end of society... is neither the individual good nor the collection of the individual goods" of the citizens.[22] Moreover (unlike Eschmann[23]), Maritain affirms that the political common good is intrinsically good, a *bonum honestum*, rather than a merely instrumental *bonum utile*.[24]

And, of course, Maritain is no more a Satanist in spiritual matters than he is an individualist in politics. Like De Koninck and every good Thomist, he regarded God as the "separated *common* good": not only of the physical universe, but also "of the souls which have entered by participation into the universe of the Deity."[25] Like De Koninck, he thinks this divine common good infinitely exceeds any person's receptive capacity,[26] rather than being somehow commensurate with the person (which would be the Satanic pride De Koninck warns against). While he insists that each person attains this divine common good in "solitude," rather than in common by an *assecutio communis*[27] (a point with which De Koninck vigorously agrees[28]), he also holds that it is "the most open, most generous and most inhabited solitude," united by the "uncreated common Good, in which they all participate"[29]—certainly not a good to be desired as one's *private*, i.e., *exclusive* good.

20. Maritain, *Person*, 12.

21. Ibid., 13.

22. Ibid., 49–50.

23. See Eschmann, "Defense," 202.

24. See Maritain, *Person*, 53 and 63.

25. Ibid., 23–24; italics added. Cf. ibid., 17n7, 18, 19n9, 83, and 87–89. Even Eschmann is willing to call God a "common good" in an extended sense; unlike Maritain, however, he insists that God is not the object of beatitude or charity *as* supernatural common good. See Eschmann, "Defense," 193, 195–97, and 202–204.

26. See Maritain, *Person*, 87.

27. For emphasis on the claim that the speculative intellect's *assecutio singularis* of the speculative good surpasses the *assecutio communis* of the practical intellect's practical good, see Eschmann, "Defense," 200, relying on Aquinas, *In III Sent.*, d. 35, q. 1, a. 4, qc. 1, ad 2 and *In IV Sent.*, d. 49, q. 1, a. 1, qc. 3, ad 1. Maritain makes a similar point at *Person*, 26, relying on the same two Thomistic texts (translating *singularis assecutio* as "personal attainment" and *communem assecutionem* as "common accomplishment"). Cf. Maritain, *Person*, 21–22, 64, 80, and 83.

28. See De Koninck, *Primacy*, 97 and 100, and especially "Defence," 303–305, 311–12, and 316–21.

29. Maritain, *Person*, 22–23; cf. 81.

Even more: in both the political and spiritual spheres, Maritain agrees with De Koninck that "the good of the whole is … superior to the private good."[30] In what Maritain regards as the properly political sphere, this is because "the good human life of the multitude"—i.e., the "sociological integration" of "civic conscience," "spiritual riches," "hereditary wisdom," and the "friendship, happiness, virtue and heroism in the individual lives of its members"—is in itself greater than any individual's participation in this good, let alone his merely material possessions.[31] The same priority of the common good also applies to the broader "common good of civilization," which includes non-culture-specific goods such as the natural law, theoretical knowledge, and beauty,[32] and this in two ways: (1) inasmuch as truth in itself is greater than any mind's share of it, and (2) inasmuch as the organized body of insights of the world's great thinkers is greater than any individual contribution thereto.[33] (In the first way, the whole-part relation obtains between a good-to-be-*received* and its participants' *reception* of it; in the second way, that relation obtains between a good-to-be-*made*—a "common work"[34]—and its causes' *contributions* to it.) And this same twofold priority of the common good also holds, in Maritain's view, even in the supernatural sphere: (1) God's essence in itself is of course greater than any creature's individual vision thereof, and (2) the contribution which every individual member makes to the City of the Blessed's beauty is lesser than the ordered beauty of the City as a whole—the "collection of human goods and of the communications of created goods which derive in this whole from its union of grace with the uncreated Good." In this sense "each stone is for the city."[35]

Now, here there does remain a noteworthy (though subtle) difference between De Koninck's position and that of Maritain and Eschmann. Maritain and Eschmann hold that the second kind of priority—the priority which a good-to-be-*made* holds over its *contributing* or *constitutive* parts—subordinates rational creatures to their whole (the city or the universe) only in a certain respect: namely, if the whole is considered "from the point of view of extension" and "multiplicity" (*extensive et diffusive*),[36] that is, if the

30. Ibid., 61; cf. 59.
31. Ibid., 52–53.
32. Ibid., 62–64 (incl. n. 33) and 83.
33. See ibid., 83–84. For the first way, see p. 83; for the second, see pp. 83–84.
34. Ibid., 83.
35. Ibid., 86.
36. See ibid., 18–21 and 83–83; Eschmann, "Defense," 190–91.

whole is considered as possessing not only its own holistic-level perfection but also the constituent-level perfections of its parts. Taken *intensive et collective*—that is, as "gathered together in one single point"[37]—they hold, following Aquinas,[38] that the rational creature is *more* perfect than the whole which contains it. From this second perspective, Maritain insists that "the city is for each stone," inasmuch as the acts of the supernatural virtues belong *directly* to the stones, not to the city;[39] and in Eschmann's view at least it is this second perspective which is decisive.

For De Koninck, on the other hand, it is the first point of view (*extensive et diffusive*, where the whole comes out the winner) which is decisive; and he devotes a full 15 pages to his argument.[40] I do not think, however, that this argument does justice to Eschmann; and in particular, I think De Koninck misapplies a text of Aquinas in his effort to show that perfection pertains "absolutely" to the *extensive et diffusive* viewpoint, rather than to the *intensive et collective* viewpoint. In this text, Aquinas is arguing that the perfection of the whole universe depends upon its having *unequal* parts (some greater, some lesser): after all, we would not be improving the perfection of an animal if we replaced all its lesser parts with eyes.[41] Moreover, at least in the animal case, the whole is clearly more perfect "absolutely" than even the animal's nobler parts like eyes. But De Koninck further asserts that the animal does not possess the perfection of the eye *intensive et collective*, i.e., *qua* animal, but only *extensive et diffusive*, i.e., insofar as one of its parts possesses it; and from this he infers that "absolute" perfection corresponds to the *extensive et diffusive* viewpoint, not to the *intensive et collective* viewpoint, and hence belongs to the city and the universe rather than to the person as such.[42]

De Koninck's conclusion need not follow, however, for there is another reason for saying that the animal is more perfect "absolutely" than the eye,

37. Eschmann, "Defense," 191.

38. See Aquinas, ST I, q. 93, a. 2, ad 3.

39. Maritain, *Person*, 85–87, quoting Francisco de Vitoria, *Relectiones theologicae*, rel. 2, "De potestate Ecclesiae," §5, in Luis G. Alonso Getino, editor, *Relecciones Teológicas del Maestro Fray Francisco de Vitoria* (Madrid: La Rafa, 1933–36), 2:117.

40. See De Koninck, "Defence," 240–55; see also 311–15, in the specific context of the City of the Blessed.

41. Aquinas, ST I, q. 47, a. 2, ad 1.

42. See De Koninck, "Defence," 250–51 for his use of this text. Oliva Blanchette develops De Koninck's reading of this passage at *The Perfection of the Universe*, 296–300, explicitly taking Maritain to task at 299n32.

which is *not* based upon the animal possessing the perfection of its eyes *extensive et diffusive*. Rather, the real reason is that the animal has a higher perfection *of its own*, which belongs to it *directly*, *qua* animal (i.e., *intensive et collective*), which consists in life itself and its operations. Moreover, it is precisely the fact that the whole animal has a higher perfection *of its own* that allows it to be a substantial unity, and thus to be the fundamental subject and possessor of the perfections of each of its parts as well. So the "absolute" perfection of the animal whole vis-à-vis its parts is quite compatible with identifying "absolute" perfection with perfection taken *intensive et collective* (rather than *extensive et diffusive*, as simply subsuming the perfections which belong properly and immediately to the parts). Eschmann's and Maritain's (and Aquinas's) point is that—unlike the animal—neither the city nor the universe has a perfection *of its own*, at the holistic level, which is nobler than the perfection of their rational parts (persons); and so neither are they properly the subject nor possessor of the perfections proper to their parts.

Nonetheless, even if De Koninck is mistaken in claiming that perfection which belongs to the whole merely "*extensive et diffusive*" still belongs to it "absolutely," he is at least quite right that God's glory is *better* reflected by the whole universe, with its ordered multiplicity of rational and irrational creatures, than it is by any single rational creature, and that therefore God, even when he creates the rational creature, is still *primarily* intending the order of the universe. And here at least Maritain (though perhaps not Eschmann[43]) is in striking agreement: "Absolutely speaking, the intellectual substance is loved and willed for the order of the universe of creation *before* being loved and willed for itself." This holds even in the supernatural order where each person is "*first of all*, willed and loved... for the communication of the divine goodness which is made to the whole city of the blessed in the sense that each of its members beholds the uncreated essence according to the multiple degrees of their participation in the light of glory." Now, Maritain does restrict this statement to the intellectual substance "as individual" (i.e., as a part which radically depends on its whole); "as person," he holds that the intellectual substance is "first willed and loved for itself," not for the order of the universe. Still, Maritain asserts that we are *more* "parts" than "persons," owing to our ontological poverty, and that therefore each of us is willed first for the whole "absolutely speaking."[44]

43. See Eschmann, "Defense," 188, relying on Aquinas, SCG III, chap. 112 (also cited, but with more nuance, by Maritain at *Person*, 19n8).

44. Maritain, *Person*, 18n7; first italics added, second italics in original.

If there is so much substantive agreement, why then the continued acrimony today between De Koninck's and Maritain's followers? At least part of the difficulty is terminological, with respect to two central terms: "common good" and "personal good."

The term "common good," for De Koninck, means a good endowed with an "incommensurable communicability to many"[45]: that is, a good which is not *proportionate* to any individual recipient, but rather in which many recipients can participate on account of its "universality" and "superabundance,"[46] while itself remaining ontologically one rather than being divided up among its participants.[47] By this (certainly quite Thomistic) use of the term, an object of contemplation is no less of a "common good" than a common *project* or *work* such as, e.g., the army's extrinsic victory or intrinsic discipline. For Maritain, by contrast, the term "common good" means *primarily* the "common *work*"; indeed he frequently uses the phrases synonymously.[48] To be sure, Maritain does grant that the object of contemplation can be considered a "common good" as well; but he does not consider this to be the "strict sense" usage of the term.[49] And certainly it should be no surprise that a Thomist would subordinate a *practical* good, a "work" to be *realized* by joint effort, to the speculative good.

45. De Koninck, "Defence," 303.

46. De Koninck, *Primacy*, 75.

47. See De Koninck, *Primacy*, 96–97; "Defence," 255–59 and 288–91. De Koninck identifies the common good in this sense with the good which is common by way of causality (*commune in causando*)—e.g., the sun, which bathes the whole earth in its heat—in contrast to the good which is common merely by way of predication (*commune in praedicando*)—e.g., the warmth which every inhabitant of earth possesses thanks to the sun. This distinction between the *bonum commune in causando* and *bonum commune in praedicando* may be found in Aquinas at DV q. 7, a. 6, ad 7; *In IV Sent.* d. 49, q. 1, a. 1, qc. 1, ad 3; ST I, q. 13, a. 9; q. 39, a. 4, ad 3; II-II, q. 58, a. 6; and *Sententia super Metaphysicam*, bk. VII, lect. 13, §1571. See also Ronald McArthur, "Universal *in praedicando*, Universal *in causando*," *Laval théologique et philosophique* 18 (1962): 59–95. For the centrality of this distinction to rightly understanding the common good, see: Froelich, "The Equivocal Status of *Bonum Commune*," 43–53; Benjamin Smith, "The Meaning and Importance of Common Goods," 590–94; Waldstein, *Glory of the Logos*, 317–19; Keys, *Aquinas, Aristotle, and the Promise of the Common Good* (New York: Cambridge University Press, 2006), 193; Michael Smith, *Human Dignity and the Common Good*, 74–81 and 113–19, and "Common Advantage and Common Good," *Laval théologique et philosophique* 51 (1995): 111–25, at 121–25; and Walshe, "The Primacy of the Common Good as the Root of Personal Dignity," 13–15, 30–31, 44–48, 69–71, and 82, and "*Fidelissimus Discipulus Ejus*," 10–11.

48. See Maritain, *Person*, 65, 70, 83, 85, 93, 100, and esp. 102–103.

49. See ibid., 82–83, where he calls "truth and beauty themselves" the "common good" of the "community of minds," but a "common good only in an analogical sense," since "it is not a social good" (i.e., cooperatively achieved) but rather one "to some aspect of which each adheres in solitude." Cf. 62–63, incl. note 33.

Conversely, the term "personal good," for Maritain, means simply the kind of good to which one is ordered *qua* person—that is, *qua* rational. Thus, for Maritain, the properly personal good is the act of speculative contemplation—chiefly, the contemplation of the "whole universe of the absolute," and ultimately the "participation in the very life of God."[50] De Koninck, however, uses the term "personal good" synonymously with "private good": that is, to mean a good that is *proportionate* to its recipient, and that therefore may belong *exclusively* to that recipient.[51] Now, it is not surprising that he does so, since Eschmann too takes "common good" and "personal good" to be mutually exclusive terms.[52] But Maritain does not take "common" and "personal" as mutually exclusive; on the contrary, he holds that God is *both* the ultimate personal *and* the ultimate common good (in the broad sense).[53] Hence, in Maritain's terminology it is quite reasonable to prioritize the personal good over the common good, since the ultimate personal good (God himself) is greater than the common good in the *strict sense* (the common *work*). But to De Koninck's ears this is the blasphemy of saying that the private good (my personal share of perfection) is greater than the ultimate common good (God himself, not merely the common work).

III. The Real Stakes

There is also, however, a deeper disagreement concerning the *reason* both for loving the common good itself and for wanting one's fellow-citizens to attain it. In De Koninck's view, the reason for loving the common good is *precisely* its commonness: "Communicability is the very reason of its perfection."[54] This is because De Koninck takes it as a general principle that the nobility of any sort of cause, as such, is measured by the scope of its power; so the nobility of the final cause too should be measured by the universality or commonness of its power to draw things to itself.[55] Hence, in De

50. Ibid., 42; see also 25, 85, and esp. 88–89. Cf. Eschmann, "Defense," 197, 201–202, and 208.

51. See De Koninck, *Primacy*, 73 and 106; "Defence," 282, 296, 299, 326, 339, and 354n124.

52. See Eschmann, "Defense," 206: "A very considerable and striking part of St. Thomas' discussion of the *dictum authenticum* (a common good is better and more divine than a particular good) centers around the comparison between the *common* and the *personal* good"; italics added.

53. See Maritain, *Person*, 85–89.

54. De Koninck, *Primacy*, 75.

55. See ibid., *Primacy*, 74–75.

Koninck's view, even if there were only one person enjoying beatitude, that person's beatitude would still depend on God's "essential communic*ability* to many"; for that essential communicability just *is* his "superabundance,"[56] i.e., the fullness of his perfection.

Now, if the common good is lovable *because* of its communicability, De Koninck logically infers that it cannot be loved for what it is except *as* communicable: "We must love the universal good *as* a common good, otherwise we shall not truly love the universal good."[57] If I ignored the common good's shareability, I would not truly love or possess it at all; I would have missed the point, so to speak. And loving something *as* communicable, in turn, implies desiring that it be actually communicated. This, in De Koninck's view, is the reason for Aquinas's claim in *De caritate*, a. 2 (a central passage for De Koninck) that we should love the common good by desiring its "conservation and diffusion" to others (*ut permaneat et diffundatur*), rather than merely by desiring "to possess it" for ourselves (*ut habeatur et possideatur*): because loving the common good "for its diffusion" is the only way to love its proper goodness *at all*.[58]

Desiring the common good to be "diffused" to others, however, is just what it means to love those "others." Hence our love for the common good, far from being based in a prior love for its recipients, is itself a reason for loving those recipients. Indeed De Koninck thinks it is the primary reason, as he states in his opening thesis:

> The good of the family is better than the singular good . . . because, for each of its individual members, it is also the good of the others. That does not mean that the others are the reason for the proper loveableness of the common good. On the contrary, under this formal aspect, *the others are loveable insofar as they can participate in this common good*.[59]

56. Ibid., 97; italics added. Cf. ibid., 100.

57. De Koninck, "Defence," 269; italics added. Cf. *Primacy*, 75, 79, and esp. 83.

58. De Koninck interprets Aquinas, *De caritate*, a. 2 this way at both *Primacy*, 79–81 and "Defence," 266–67 (reiterated at 269–70). For parallel texts in Aquinas, see *In III Sent.*, d. 29, q. 1, a. 3, which also uses the language of desiring the good in the beloved to be preserved (*salvari vult in ipsa re amata*), and *De caritate*, a. 4, ad 2 (quoted by De Koninck, *Primacy*, 82 and "Defence," 264–65), where Aquinas seems to imply that the reason for sacrificing one's life for king or general is to preserve the *good* of the society, which exists primarily in its leader.

59. De Koninck, *Primacy*, 75 (and quoted at "Defence," 286); italics added. Cf. "Defence," 269 and esp. 304: "*only* because we already love God as the 'bonum commune omnium,' shall we, consequently, love this and that neighbor"; italics added.

Why, though, should we take this last step of making the common good the *primary* reason for the lovability of its recipients? Can we not love others in personal friendship, without consideration of the common good? Indeed we can. However, such individualistic friendship is, in De Koninck's view, rooted in and thus lesser than our self-love:

> If we prescind from the common good of the persons… we are left with a mere aggregate of individuals. Now, in this formal consideration, each and every one of that group could never be more than an *alter ego*, and the group itself could never be more than an aggregate … of *alter egos*. Hence, in this perspective, the whole question… becomes…: must one love oneself more than one's neighbour? There is not the slightest doubt that we must love ourselves more. . . . To love our neighbour more than ourselves would be contrary to nature, since we are more one with ourselves than with our neighbour.[60]

Thus, for De Koninck, the *only* love for neighbor that can transcend our self-love is one whose primary object and motivation is the common good, taken in its "communicability" to many.

Maritain, for his part, certainly does not give this account. On the one hand, we ought to love the common goods proper to the *personal* dimension (i.e., objects of speculative contemplation, and principally God), not because of the commonness of these goods, but rather because of their intrinsic universal fullness and absoluteness. Their commonness to many is, in his and in Eschmann's view, merely the corollary rather than the essence of this fullness, which is what perfects us and draws us to love it;[61] and in this

60. De Koninck, "Defence," 325–26; cf. 285–86 and 322.

61. See, e.g., Maritain, *Person*, 21–24, and especially Eschmann, "Defense," 195–96 and 202–204, specifically his contrast between God as *bonum universale in essendo* vs. as *bonum universale in causando*. De Koninck, in my view, misunderstands Eschmann's use of this central distinction, which he reads as a fallacious distinction between intrinsic and extrinsic *goodness*. That is, he thinks that by *bonum universale in essendo* Eschmann must have meant God's intrinsic perfection, rather than God's final causality of all things ("Defence," 273–78); and he thinks that by *bonum universale in causando* Eschmann must have meant a common good's *actual communication* to many, as opposed to its intrinsic *communicability* ("Defence," 280–85). And if that was indeed what Eschmann meant, then De Koninck would be quite right to critique him on the grounds that his *bonum universale in essendo* would not properly be "good" at all (lacking the note of perfecting others as their end), while the *bonum universale in causando* would be "good" in a purely extrinsic and accidental way (depending on an actual multitude of recipients). Rather, as De Koninck argues, any genuine good must always be good *in causando*, since the good is a final *cause*; but this "in causando" should denote intrinsic *communicability*, not actual *communication*.—But in fact De Koninck has misinterpreted Eschmann's phrase "in essendo/in causando" to modify "bonum" rather than "universale." Eschmann's actual intent, I take it, is to distinguish two kinds of *universality*, not two kinds of goodness: the intrinsic universality (*in essendo*) of possessing the

I think they are quite right. Commonness is indeed the *measure* of a final cause's power, and thus a *sign* of its excellence; but its commonness is not itself the *reason* for loving the final cause.

We ought to serve the common good in what Maritain and Eschmann call the "strict sense," on the other hand—that is, the common *work*, a practical good—in part, as we saw, because of the common work's greater perfection (speaking *extensive et diffusive*) compared to any individual contribution. The ultimate reason, however, is our concern for the persons who are the beneficiaries of that common work, and for whose sake that common work exists. That is why Maritain says that, "with respect to the eternal destiny of the soul, society"—and with it society's "common work"—"exists *for each person and is subordinated to it*."[62]

If these are the reasons for loving common goods, what are the reasons for desiring other persons to receive these common goods (either speculative or practical)? De Koninck's proposal, that loving the common good for what it is just means desiring it to be "diffused," is undermined if the reason for loving the common good itself is not precisely its commonness. Instead Maritain seems to offer two alternative reasons for seeking the common good's communication to society, corresponding to his famous distinction between our "personality" and our "individuality."[63]

As "person," each citizen is an "open and generous whole"[64] that is "capable of super-existing by way of knowledge and love,"[65] and that thus is characterized by "radical generosity" or "expansiveness in being."[66] Accordingly, as "person," each citizen is impelled to give of himself freely and in love to other persons.[67]

As "individual," by contrast, each citizen has "needs or deficiencies,"[68]

---

fullness of both perfection and perfectiveness, vs. the extrinsic universality (*in causando*) of being related to a multitude of recipients (whether possible or actual). And so taken, it is clear that it is the intrinsic universality, not the extrinsic one, that grounds our love.

62. Maritain, *Person*, 61; italics added. For the ordering of the common *good* to the person, see also ibid., 50–51, 55, 59–61, and 76–77. For the ordering of *society itself* to the person, see also ibid., 85 and 87.

63. For these two reasons, see ibid., 47–48, where Maritain addresses the question "why is it that the person, as person, seeks to live in society?" For the distinction between "person" and "individual," see ibid., 13–14 and 33–46.

64. Ibid., 59.

65. Ibid., 40.

66. Ibid., 41.

67. For Maritain's correlation of "personality" with the attributes of "love," "generosity," and "freedom," see esp. ibid., 38–42; cf. 23, 32, 44, 46–48, 59, 77, and 79.

68. Ibid., 48; cf. 47–49, 60, and 73.

and therefore is "*part* of a whole which is greater and better than its parts,"[69] insofar as the perfections which fill the part's deficiencies "depend in their very essence upon political society"[70]—a society "from which, in a certain fashion, it has received all that it is."[71] Society alone provides us with the "conditions of existence and development" by which we not only preserve our physical life but also receive the ability to "do the work of reason and virtue" through "character training, education and the cooperation of other men."[72] Accordingly, as "individuals" radically dependent on society, we are bound in justice to serve society as a whole.[73]

We find, then, the following key differences between these two motivations. As "persons," our desire for others to receive the common good is (1) an act of *love*, which (2) belongs to us as generous "wholes" and hence is (3) *free*, and (4) whose object is *other persons*.[74] As "individuals," by contrast, our desire for others to receive the common good is (1) an act of *justice*, which (2) belongs to us as needy "parts" and hence is (3) *obligatory*, and (4) whose object is the *whole community*. Both love and justice impel us to serve our fellow man, but in sharply delineated ways.[75]

In summary: for De Koninck, the fundamental reason for desiring our fellow-citizens to enjoy the common good lies in the dignity of the common *good* itself (the desire's direct object, grammatically speaking). For Maritain, however, the fundamental reason lies instead in ourselves and in society (the desire's subject and indirect object), in a twofold way: on the one hand, on account of our own "personal" generosity and the dignity of our fellow persons; on the other hand, on account of our own "individual" neediness and the corresponding fullness of the social whole.

69. Ibid., 60; italics in original. Cf. ibid., 61.

70. Ibid., 73; cf. 74–75.

71. Ibid., 69; cf. 48–49.

72. Ibid., 48–49.

73. For Maritain's correlation of our "individuality" with a duty in "justice" to sacrifice for the common good, see esp. ibid., 69–70 and 75–77; cf. 48, 65–66, and 73–74.

74. Here De Koninck would vigorously disagree: he has sharp words at *Primacy*, 105–106, for the view that the right answer to individualism is the "generosity of the person and a fraternity outside any common good." Cf. ibid., 86, and "Defence," 286.

75. Of the previously cited texts, see esp. Maritain, *Person*, 77: "The person as *person* insists on serving the community and the common good *freely*. . . . The person as *individual* is *necessarily bound*, by constraint if need be, to serve the community and the common good since it is excelled by them as the *part by the whole*." Italics added.

IV. An Objection to De Koninck

Neither Maritain's nor De Koninck's account, however, is quite satisfactory in my view. Let us take De Koninck's view first. Besides endorsing two of Maritain's and Eschmann's objections—namely, (a) that persons are nobler, absolutely speaking, than the social and cosmic order of which they are parts, and (b) that the common good is not lovable precisely on account of its commonness—I would also raise a further and more fundamental objection of my own: that by grounding love for neighbor in love for the common good, De Koninck reverses the priority of the absolute good, object of *friendship*-love, over the relative good, object of *desire*-love.

To see why this is this the case, let us turn to Aquinas's distinction between friendship-love (*amor amicitiae*) and desire-love (*amor concupiscentiae*), which is arguably at the heart of Aquinas's own personalism.[76] ST I-II, q. 26, a. 4 is the locus classicus of this distinction:

> One has desire-love (*amor concupiscentiae*) for the good which one wills for someone; one has friendship-love (*amor amicitiae*) for the one for whom one wills the good. Now, the members of this division are related as prior and posterior. For that which is loved by friendship-love is loved simply speaking and in itself (*per se*); while that which is loved by desire-love is not loved simply speaking and in itself (*secundum se*), but rather is loved for another. Just as being simply speaking is that which itself has existence, while being in a relative sense (*secundum quid*) is that which exists in another; so likewise, since good is convertible with being, good simply speaking is that which itself has goodness, while that which is the good of another (*bonum alterius*) is good in a relative sense (*secundum quid*).[77]

The central point is this: "good" in the primary sense (*simpliciter*), is always the *person*, the substance which itself has goodness, and *for whose sake* one desires the other, "relative" (*secundum quid*) good. "Good" is thus like "being," whose primary sense is that which itself has being, namely substance; accidents are merely being in a relative sense (*secundum quid*). The chief parallel texts, *In De divinis nominibus*, chap. 4, lect. 9, §404 and lect. 10, §428, make this metaphysical analogy between personal good and substantial be-

76. David Gallagher in particular identifies the friendship-love/desire-love distinction as the root of Aquinas's emphasis on the centrality of the person (though he does not use the term "personalism"). See his "Person and Ethics in Thomas Aquinas," *Acta Philosophica* 4 (1995): 51–71, esp. 56–65; "Desire for Beatitude and Love of Friendship," *Mediaeval Studies* 58 (1996): 1–47, at 2–3 and 13–18; and "The Will and Its Acts (Ia IIae, qq. 6–17)," in *The Ethics of Aquinas*, edited by Stephen J. Pope (Washington, D.C.: Georgetown University Press, 2002), 69–89, at 84–85.

77. All translations from Aquinas are my own.

ing even more strongly: for, though Aquinas in this somewhat earlier work[78] does not describe persons with the term "*bonum simpliciter*," he does say that *only* the person (*bonum substantiale*) is good in its own right (*in bonitate subsistens*). The accidental goods which we desire for persons, e.g. virtues and the activities that flow from them, are "good" not in their own right, but rather *only* insofar as they *make* the person good, just as the accident of whiteness is not a "being" (*ens*) in the sense of existing in its own right but *only* insofar as it makes its subject be white.[79]

Correspondingly, as the *Summa* text in particular makes clear, "love" in the primary sense is always friendship-love, which aims at the person. All desire-love for relative goods is itself only relative, since it is always rooted in friendship-love for the person, for whose sake we love the perfections which we wish him to possess. These two claims about the priority of friendship-love and the priority of personal goodness go hand in hand, since a thing's goodness is measured by the degree to which it is lovable for its own sake; if persons alone are loved fully for their own sake, then persons alone are "good" in the full sense.[80]

Aquinas does not discuss the common good in these passages, which we might dub the "personalist" texts. Elsewhere, however, he does say that even the created common good *par excellence*, namely the good of the universe, which we, like God, should maximally love,[81] is maximally loved precisely *in* the persons who are the "principle" of this good, and who alone are loved with friendship-love; the non-personal remainder of this good enters into

78. For the dating of the *Divine Names* commentary and of the Prima Secundae, see Jean-Pierre Torrell, *Saint Thomas Aquinas*, vol. 1, *The Person and His Work*, translated by Robert Royal (Washington, D.C.: The Catholic University of America Press, 1996), 127 and 146–47, respectively; cf. 333 and 346.

79. See Aquinas, *In De divinis nominibus*, chap. 4, lect. 9, §404 and lect. 10, §428. Cf. *In III Sent.*, d. 28, q. 1, a. 1, where Aquinas denies that it is possible to have friendship (*amicitia*) for virtues or other accidents precisely because accidents have neither existence nor goodness *per se*, as well as ST I, q. 6, a. 3, ad 3.

80. Besides ST I-II, q. 26, a. 4 and *In De divinis nominibus*, chap. 4, lect. 9, §404 and lect. 10, §428, other texts where Aquinas develops the distinction between friendship-love and desire-love and affirms friendship-love's priority include: ST I, q. 20, a. 1, ad 3; q. 60, a. 3; II-II, q. 23, a. 1; q. 25, a. 2–3; SCG I, chap. 91, esp. §757; *In II Sent.*, d. 3, q. 4, a. 1; *In III Sent.*, d. 29, q. 1, a. 3; *In IV Sent.*, d. 49, q. 1, a. 2, qc. 1, ad 3; *Super Evangelium S. Ioannis*, chap. 15, lect. 4, §2036; *Super Philipenses*, chap. 1, lect. 3, §36; *Super Romanos*, chap. 13, lect. 2, §1057; *De caritate*, a. 7 and a. 8, ad 16; *De spe*, a. 3; and *De perfectione*, chap. 14 (following the Leonine numbering; elsewhere it is sometimes listed as chap. 13).

81. For both De Koninck's and Maritain's assertion of this claim (which Aquinas frequently reiterates), see notes 11, 13, 42, and 44 above.

this maximal love only insofar as it is loved *for* persons.[82] And more broadly, it seems clear enough that the common good, as such, is an object of desire-love, since the common good is precisely what is good *for* the whole community as such;[83] and in the "personalist" texts we saw Aquinas clearly state that what is good "*for* someone" is loved with desire-love. Hence it cannot possibly be the case that we love our fellow-citizens *because* we first desire the common good's "conservation and diffusion," as De Koninck would have it,[84] since this would reverse the priority of friendship-love over desire-love. Nor does *De caritate*, a. 2, the passage on which De Koninck relies for this claim,[85] actually imply it. Aquinas says here that the good citizen desires the common good to be "preserved and diffused" not because he truly loves the common *good*, as De Koninck would have it, but rather because he truly loves the *city* (*hoc est vere amare civitatem*): friendship-love for the city comes first.

Now, De Koninck himself does not state that the common good is loved with desire-love, or that desire-love is prior to friendship-love. Indeed, he himself never explicitly makes the distinction between friendship-love and desire-love at all (though he twice quotes a long passage of the *Summa* which includes this distinction[86]), and the very words "friend" and "friendship" are scarce in his writing.[87] He does, however, insist that it is a "distinctly modern" move, traceable to Spinoza and David of Dinant, to "accord absolute priority to the subject" by identifying the primary sense of "good" ("*bonum simpliciter*") with the subject ("*ens simpliciter*"), i.e., with the end *for whom* goods are desired ("*finis cui*"), rather than with the end or perfection *which is* desired for the subject ("*finis qui*").[88]

82. See *De caritate*, a. 7, ad 5, where Aquinas gives this answer to defend his view that only persons are loved in charity with friendship-love against a De Koninck-like objection based on God's maximal love for the good of the universe, as containing all created goods within it.

83. As we saw, De Koninck himself certainly understands the common good this way, as what is perfective *of* the members of a community as such; see the texts cited above in note 16.

84. See the passages cited above in notes 54–59.

85. See p. 104 above for discussion of this text.

86. See De Koninck, "Defence," 262 and 286, both times quoting ST II-II, q. 26, a. 3 (on loving God more than self), including ad 3 where the reference to friendship-love occurs.

87. These words appear in *Primacy* and "Defence" only when De Koninck is quoting his opponents, with two exceptions: once when he calls Yves Simon a "friend" ("Defence," 209), and once to *condemn* "politicians who favor their friends precisely under the pretext of civic friendship" (*Primacy*, 99). One cannot help but wonder whether the notions of "friendship" and "common good" have much to do with each other in De Koninck's mind.

88. De Koninck, "Defence," 325. See also 254 for another instance of apparently ascribing a

De Koninck seems unaware that this allegedly "distinctly modern" view is explicitly held by Aquinas in the "personalist" texts we just cited (which he never mentions). Instead he relies on two other claims Aquinas makes which, taken together, seem to imply the opposite view: that "good," in its primary sense, means that which is good *for* the person, not the person himself.

The first claim is that the "good" is that which is *perfective* of another, specifically "as an end" (*perfectivum alterius per modum finis*). Goodness is *grounded* in and coextensive with intrinsic perfection, but is a distinct formality, since, unlike perfection, goodness (perfectiveness) explicitly denotes relation to another: the relation of final causality. Aquinas makes this claim repeatedly in DV q. 21, aa. 1–3 and 5, and at least implies it in ST I, q. 5, aa. 1 and 3.[89]

The second claim, which Aquinas makes most notably at DV q. 21, a. 5 and ST I, q. 5, a. 1, ad 1 (though De Koninck cites other texts as well),[90] is that goodness, *unlike* being, is found simply speaking (*simpliciter*) at the level of accidents, and only relatively (*secundum quid*) at the level of substance. In DV q. 21, a. 5, Aquinas offers a quite intuitive example: we do not call an unjust man "good" simply speaking. Only the virtuous person deserves the title "good" without qualification; merely possessing human nature does not suffice, since it is shared by good and bad persons alike. Moreover, the text goes on to provide a metaphysical argument for this claim: a thing's good consists in its union with its end, and this union lies chiefly in accidental being (especially activity).

From the first claim (that what is properly speaking "good" is that which is perfective *of* the person) it would seem to follow that the person himself is *not*, properly speaking, "good"—reversing the "personalist" texts' prior-

higher dignity to the perfection desired (for which De Koninck here uses the equivalent term "*finis cujus gratia*") than to the person for whom that perfection is desired (the "*finis cui*"). Cf. 221–22, where De Koninck defends the primacy of the "good that is the universe" over the person while stipulating that the universe is a "final cause" (i.e., a *finis qui*), not a "super-individual to whom" God wills goods (i.e., a *finis cui*).

89. De Koninck emphasizes this claim, using these texts, at *Primacy*, 74 (including the work's opening line) and "Defence," 220–22 and 273–81 (esp. 275).

90. At *Primacy*, 98, De Koninck quotes ST I, q. 5, a. 1, ad 1 at length. At "Defence," 273n86, De Koninck cites ST I, q. 5, a. 1, ad 1 and a. 3; *In De divinis nominibus*, chap. 4, lect. 16 (though I have been unable to locate any relevant passage in lect. 16, and believe De Koninck meant to refer instead to lect. 1); *Expositio De hebdomadibus* (probably lect. 4, §63, though De Koninck here refers not to a *lectio* but simply to a mysterious "o."); and DV q. 21, *passim*. At "Defence," 325n150, he quotes from DV q. 21 at length, specifically a. 1, ad 6, and a. 5.

itization of the good who *is* the person over the good *for* the person. The second claim seems to reverse the "personalist" texts' alignment of the good "simply speaking" with being "simply speaking"; and this reversal in turn would imply that, insofar as the person can be called "good" at all, it is not primarily as *person* (i.e., as substance) but rather as possessing that which is *perfective* of the person, namely the accidental dispositions and ensuing operations by which he attains to his extrinsic good (which is good in the proper sense, and presumably best exemplified by the common good). Taking these two claims together, it would seem to follow—with De Koninck, *contra* the "personalist" texts—that what is chiefly lovable is the object of *desire*-love, and that persons are lovable with friendship-love only secondarily insofar as they participate in some way (via accidental forms and operations) in the object of desire-love.

To resolve this tension, we must be attentive to the particular contrast Aquinas is drawing when he makes each claim. When Aquinas defines the good as "perfective of another as an end" in DV q. 21, a. 1, he is contrasting it with the other transcendentals. "Perfectiveness" separates truth and goodness from the transcendentals of "thing," "one," and "something"; adding "as an end" further distinguishes goodness from truth. But, notably, Aquinas does *not* have in mind the distinction between the good which is the object of friendship-love and that which is the object of desire-love. That distinction, along with the very word "friendship" (*amicitia*) and its cognates, is entirely absent from DV q. 21's lengthy treatment of goodness. Now this is an odd lacuna, to be sure, and perhaps it means that it was only after composing this relatively early text[91] that Aquinas came to the realization that the objects of friendship-love and desire-love must be "good" in fundamentally different senses. But, first, we should note that the term "perfective of another as an end" actually need not exclude the object of friendship-love (the beloved person). This is because by "perfective" here Aquinas means that which "measures" another and thus bears only a relation of reason to the thing measured (since his main concern is showing that goodness and truth add only beings of reason to "being," and thus are convertible with "being"); and the object of friendship-love, even more than that of desire-love, does "measure" the lover "as an end," since the beloved, in his own real existence, becomes the center of the lover's affective life and the

91. The *De veritate* significantly predates both of the "personalist" texts; for its dates see Torrell, *The Person and His Work*, 62 and 334, and cf. note 78 above.

ordering principle of the lover's desires. So the definition of goodness provided in DV q. 21 is not necessarily limited to the "relative" good *for* another, and so would not have to be abandoned to accommodate the notion of the good "simply speaking" found in the "personalist" texts. And secondly, regardless, DV q. 21 cannot be used to establish the primacy of the good *for* persons over the good that *is* the person, simply because that contrast is not even considered here.

Again, when Aquinas identifies goodness *simpliciter* with goodness on the accidental rather than the substantial level at, e.g., DV q. 21, a. 5 or ST I, q. 5, a. 1, ad 1, he is not actually contrasting the good who *is* the person with the good *for* the person. Rather, he is contrasting two kinds of intrinsic goods *for* the subject, *by which* the subject is good: substantial form, by which the subject *exists* as the kind of thing it is, and accidental forms and operations, by which the subject is *completed* and *united* to its extrinsic end. The "personalist" texts' contrast between that *by which* something is good (the good *for* the subject) and that which *is* good again is simply absent here. A cause of the interpretive difficulty is that Aquinas is using nearly the same term in two different ways in the two sets of texts. In DV q. 21, a. 5 (one of De Koninck's texts), the abstract term "bonitas substantialis" refers to a good *possessed by* the subject: the good of substantial being, which *makes* the subject good in a preliminary, basic way. In *In De divinis nominibus*, chap. 4, lect. 10, however (one of the "personalist" texts), the concrete term "bonum substantiale" refers to the substantial subject *as a whole*, taken as *already made good* by *all* his currently possessed perfections, both substantial and accidental. It is this complete subject whom we wish, out of friendship-love, to preserve and if possible increase *all* his perfections. And there is no contradiction in saying [1] that this complete subject is "good simply speaking" compared to *any* perfection we might wish for that subject (the claim of the "personalist" texts), and [2] that, *among* the perfections we wish for the subject, accidental perfections such as the exercise of virtue are "good simply speaking" compared to mere substantial existence (the claim of De Koninck's texts).

Now, it is true that that *by which* the person is good—namely, his participation in intrinsic and extrinsic "relative" goods *for* him, e.g. his humanity, wisdom, and charity—is the reason *why* the person himself is good "simply speaking," and thus *why* the person is loved "simply speaking" with friendship-love. In this sense one can accept De Koninck's claim that "person and society are not to be judged by what they *are* absolutely, but by what is their perfection, i.e., by what is their good."[92] But it does not follow that the reason *why* the person is good and loved "simply speaking" must itself be good and loved primarily (that is, with friendship-love, as Sebastian Walshe has argued[93]), any more than it follows that the substantial form (the reason *why* the substance exists "simply speaking") must itself be what exists primarily. Rather, just as the substantial form is the formal principle rather than the subject of existence,[94] so too the "relative" goods in which we participate are the formal principle rather than the subject of goodness and lovability. As Aquinas says explicitly, "Virtue or intrinsic goodness (*honestum*) is not the *final cause* on account of which the friend is loved, but rather *formally* makes him lovable. Hence it does not follow that virtue is *more lovable . . . just as it does not follow that whiteness is whiter than a white body*."[95] And the same holds of the extrinsic "relative" goods themselves in which the good person participates, including chiefly common goods. For while, for example, the goodness of philosophical truth (a common good) is the extrinsic reason for the goodness of the philosopher's wisdom, which in turn is an intrinsic reason for the philosopher's goodness "simply speaking," it is still only an indirect principle of that goodness "simply speaking," rather than its preeminent subject: supremely perfective, yet, unlike persons, still not worthy of drawing us completely out of ourselves.[96] So it remains the case, *contra* De Koninck, that what is primarily good and lovable is the person himself, and that the common good is loved for the person's sake rather than vice versa.

92. De Koninck, "Defence," 325; italics in original.

93. See Walshe, "The Primacy of the Common Good as the Root of Personal Dignity," 302–305. To my knowledge, and to his credit, Walshe is De Koninck's only supporter who seriously engages the objection based on the primacy of friendship-love. However, two texts he relies on (*In I Sent.*, d. 17, q. 1, a. 5 and the parallel *ST* I, q. 25, a. 2, cited at 303n699–700) actually explicitly contradict his claim that the perfection by which someone is worthy of friendship-love—a perfection which Walshe identifies as the common good—is itself also friendship-loved. According to those texts, that perfection is indeed loved in the same overarching *act* as the person (an act which may be called *amicitia*), but only by that overarching act's movements of *complacentia* and *amor concupiscentiae*, not its movement of *amor amicitiae*. See also *In III Sent.*, d. 28, q. 1, a. 1.

94. See, e.g., *Quodlibet* IX, q. 2, a. 2; *De potentia* q. 3, a. 8; and SCG II, chap. 54, §1292. Cf. *De ente et essentia* chap. 6 (Editio Leonina 43:379b–80a) and ST I, q. 75, a. 2, ad 1, a. 3, and a. 6.

95. Aquinas, *In III Sent.*, d. 28, q. 1, a. 1, ad 2; italics added. Cf. *De caritate*, a. 7, ad 1, and ST II-II, q. 25, a. 2.

96. For the unique "ecstasy" (*extasis*) of friendship-love for persons, see esp. ST I-II, q. 28, a. 3, and *In De divinis nominibus*, chap. 4, lect. 10, §§428–30; cf. *In II Cor.*, chap. 12, lect. 1, §447.

V. An Objection to Maritain

Nonetheless, I do not mean to hand Maritain an unqualified victory. In the first place, he himself does not directly make this appeal to the primacy of friendship-love for persons over desire-love for beneficial goods. We find hints of such an appeal, to be sure, in the very way he frames the question, in terms of *person* vis-à-vis *society*,[97] rather than De Koninck's preferred approach of weighing private *goods* against common *goods*;[98] this implies that Maritain's emphasis is on the good-for-whom, the object of friendship-love, rather than on the good-*desired*. And he does assert that only persons (not the "natures" or "qualities" by which they are lovable) are the proper objects of love.[99] But friendship-love's key distinction from, and priority over, desire-love remains absent, and with it the priority of the good "simply speaking" over the "relative" good.

More importantly, however, Maritain's account of the individual's subordination to the common good seems divorced from his account of love for other persons. A great strength of De Koninck's account is the tight bond he forges between love for others and love of the common good: in De Koninck's view, self-transcendent love of the common good is precisely the foundation of our greatest love for others. De Koninck's weakness, I have argued, is simply reversing which is the foundation and which is the effect. Conversely, Maritain's strength, in my view, is recognizing that love for other persons is foundational, rather than being founded in a prior desire-love for the common good. His weakness, however, lies in restricting this foundational love for other persons to our "personal" dimension, while restricting our duty to serve the community to our other, "individual" dimension and thus divorcing it from love.

In my view, this separation of love from civic duty is at least misleading. Moreover, by separating the part-whole relationship (which pertains to "individuality") from love (which pertains to "personality"), Maritain makes it very difficult to explain how we can *love* something more than ourselves. Certainly Aquinas himself, far from making any such separation, understands civic duty precisely as the demand of our natural *love* for the whole community; and in his view this love transcends our self-love pre-

97. See Maritain, *Person*, 11 and 85.

98. See De Koninck, *Primacy*, 103–104; "Defence," 254 and 325.

99. Maritain, *Person*, 39.

cisely because its object is our "whole," on which we radically depend as "parts."[100] After all, at least on Aquinas's terms, the person as "whole" can love nothing more intensely than himself, since the intensity of love is measured by the object's closeness to the lover.[101] Rather, in his view, one can only love an object more than oneself when one's own goodness is a "part" of the object's. We find this account most fully developed at ST I, q. 60, a. 5.[102] Aquinas here illustrates the rational creature's natural *love* for God above self with the virtuous citizen's *love* of his city above self; and he explains both instances of self-transcendent love by the principle that "something whose very being belongs to another is more and more principally *inclined* to that thing to which it belongs than to itself,"[103] or more simply that "every part naturally *loves* its whole more than itself."[104] Being a "part" here, in turn, means having goodness by participation, and being radically *dependent* on another for "the whole reason (*tota ratio*) for [one's] existence and goodness."[105] In Aquinas's view, echoing Plato[106] and Aristotle,[107] this is our relation not only to God but also (though certainly less radically) to the community. The point seems to be that the fullness of human goodness

100. De Koninck understands this connection between radical dependence and self-transcendent love very well; see his discussion of ST I, q. 60, a. 5 at *Primacy*, 98–99. However, by De Koninck's interpretation, what we depend on and therefore love self-transcendently seems to be the whole's *good* rather than the whole itself.

101. See Aquinas, ST I, q. 60, a. 4, c. and ad 2; I-II, q. 27, a. 3; II-II, q. 26, a. 4 (cf. a. 7); *In III Sent.*, d. 29, q. 1, a. 5; *De caritate*, a. 9; and *Sententia libri Ethicorum*, bk. IX, lect. 4, esp. §1812 [1166a33], and lect. 8–9, esp. §§1858–60 [1168a35–b6].

102. Besides ST I, q. 60, a. 5, other texts where Aquinas identifies civic duty with self-transcending love and grounds it in the part's radical dependence on the whole (though with less explicit emphasis on dependence) include: ST II-II, q. 26, a. 3; *Quodlibet* I, q. 4, a. 3; *In II Sent.*, d. 3, q. 4, a. 1 (though here the part-whole relation is only implicit); *In III Sent.*, d. 29, q. 1, a. 3; *De perfectione*, chap. 14; and *In De divinis nominibus*, chap. 4, lect. 9, §406, and lect. 10, §§431–32.

103. Aquinas, ST I, q. 60, a. 5.

104. Aquinas, ST I, q. 60, a. 5, ad 1.

105. Ibid. Cf. ad 2 and ad 4, where Aquinas reiterates that God is our "whole," and thus is to be naturally loved more than self, because every created goodness *depends* on God as the Universal Good. See also ST II-II, q. 26, a. 3, ad 1, where Aquinas argues that the reason why we can love only God, not individual creaturely friends, more than ourselves is because God, unlike our friends, possesses the goodness which motivates the friendship *secundum rationem totius*.

106. See Plato, *Crito* 50d–52d, where Socrates attributes his nurturing—even his birth—to the city's laws, and identifies this debt to the laws as the root of civic obligation.

107. See Aristotle, *Politics* 1.1, 1252b27–30 and 1253a19–27, where he takes each individual's radical dependence on his "complete," self-sufficient society as evidence that man is a natural part of the city. Aquinas endorses and develops Aristotle's argument at *Sententia libri Politicorum*, prol. and bk. I, chap. 1/b, §§23–25 and 30–31 [1252b27–34 and 1253a19]. Cf. ST I-II, q. 90, a. 2; q. 90, a. 3, ad 3; and *De regno*, bk. 1, chap. 2.

is found in the whole community, not in any individual, and it is thanks to the community's laws and order that each individual has received his own share of that patrimony.

Maritain certainly recognizes this radical dependence of the individual on the community;[108] what he does not seem to see is that this dependence is the basis not only for a debt of justice but also for self-transcending love. Indeed, it is not clear what place self-transcending love has in his account at all. While Maritain certainly affirms that one ought, *as* "person" or "whole," to love God more than oneself,[109] it is unclear how, in his view, such love for God is compatible with the principle that love's intensity is measured by the object's closeness to the lover, since Aquinas's own way of securing this compatibility is precisely the part-whole relation.[110] More importantly for our purposes, he seems to deny unequivocally that one loves the city more than oneself.[111] In fact, this primacy of self-love on the human level is one of the things which De Koninck finds most objectionable about personalism as he understands it.[112]

108. See notes 63 and 68–73 above.

109. See, e.g., Maritain, *Person*, 19n7 and 85–86. See also his much more thorough discussion of self-transcendent love of God in *The Sin of the Angel: An Essay on a Re-Interpretation of Some Thomistic Positions*, translated by William Rossner (Westminster, Maryland: The Newman Press, 1959), esp. 18–37, though here Maritain does not distinguish "personality" from "individuality."

110. For Aquinas's reliance on the part-whole relation as the *only* way to transcend the primacy of self-love, again see esp. ST I, q. 60, a. 5, ad 1 and II-II, q. 26, a. 3, ad 1. For Maritain's reluctance to analyze our self-transcendent love of God in terms of the part-whole relation, see *Person*, 87–88, where Maritain seems to affirm explicitly that the relation of soul to God in heaven is of whole to whole: "In relation to the object of the vision, there is no longer a question of being a part but of being identified with the Whole." Now, in his *Sin of the Angel*, Maritain does frequently reiterate Aquinas's claim that all things naturally love God more than self inasmuch as God is their "Whole" (18–22, 25–28, 30, 32, 47, 85, and 93), their "Common Good" (23, 27–28, 32, 47n9, 85, and 93), and indeed the "Principle of all good" (23–24 and 76). But (a) in these passages Maritain seems to be considering God as "Whole" and as "Principle of all good" only in the sense that God is Universal Goodness Itself—not in the sense that our own goodness radically *depends* on him and is therefore *owed* to him (which is the sense in which Maritain takes "parthood" and "individuality" in *Person*). Moreover, (b) Maritain seems to restrict love for God as "Whole," "Common Good," and "Principle of all good" to the level of *natural, necessitated* love. The *free* act of love for God, which alone is salvific, is in Maritain's view instead aimed directly at God in his *transcendence*, as *distinct from* rather than as *reflected in* his creatures; hence it is *not* primarily aimed at God as "Whole," although the natural inclination to make this free act (the "elicited love-of-nature") is so aimed (26–37 and 52–55; cf. 46–47, incl. note 9). It seems, then, that in Maritain's view love of God above self, and especially this love's *free* act, is not based on our "parthood" in the sense of our radical dependence upon God's goodness.

111. See Maritain, *Person*, 64–65 and 85–86.

112. See especially De Koninck's harsh criticism on this score of Mortimer Adler and Walter

Why did Maritain fail to see the connection between our radical dependence (i.e., our "individuality" and our resultant subordination to the whole) and love, and thus also fail to see the possibility of self-transcendent love on the human level? Three possible reasons come to mind. In the first place, he might simply have been focusing on the wrong Thomistic texts. There are many places (mostly in the context of law and justice) where Aquinas emphasizes the whole-part relation but describes it only in terms of *order* or *belonging*, not explicitly in terms of *love*. Notably, none of the texts which Maritain chooses for illustrating Aquinas's view of the common good's primacy speak of love.[113] Maritain's loveless account of the common good's (limited) primacy may thus be due in part to the limitations of the texts he is interpreting.

A second possible reason is that Maritain seems to see an opposition between love and obligation. Love, in Maritain's view, is by definition a *free* gift; obligation, by contrast, is a kind of *servitude*, an external constraint. Now, Maritain certainly does not deny that one can fulfill one's obligations with love. But if one does so, then "love, by assuming *voluntarily* that which would otherwise be *servitude, transfigures* it into liberty and a free gift."[114] In other words, Maritain thinks that love, even when it fulfills an obligation, must consider it not as an obligation but as a generous, spontaneous gift;

Farrell at *Primacy*, 129–30, and "Defence," 325n152, taking aim specifically at their "The Theory of Democracy—Part III—The End of the State: Happiness, cont.," *The Thomist* 4, no. 2 (1942): 286–354, at 321–25, 329–30 (including note 252, which De Koninck erroneously cites as note 256), and 336–37. Cf. "Defence," 267. It is perhaps worth noting that Maritain defends Adler and Farrell at *Person*, 62n33. However, Maritain is here discussing a different claim of theirs: not the primacy of self-love in the creaturely order, but rather the claim that "the natural happiness of the human being transcends in certain essential elements the political common good."

113. See esp. Maritain, *Person*, 70n8. Of the texts he cites there, two—ST II-II, q. 64, a. 2, which Maritain takes as paradigmatic, and II-II, q. 65, a. 1—describe the part-whole relation as a relation of "imperfect" to "perfect," which fits well with Maritain's view of "individuality." Another, ST I-II, q. 96, a. 4, concerns only the whole's *right to lay burdens on* its parts, on the basis of the part's total belonging to its whole. The last, ST II-II, q. 61, a. 1, deals with the whole's obligation to exercise distributive justice. See also *Person*, 28n20 and 29n21, where Maritain quotes, respectively, ST I-II, q. 113, a. 9, ad 2 and *Sententia libri Ethicorum*, bk. I, lect. 2, §29 [1094b4], which similarly do not speak of love. While Maritain elsewhere in *Person* does once mention ST I, q. 60, a. 5 and its claim that the part "*loves* the whole more than itself" (*Person*, 49n28; italics added), he mentions it only to describe the relation of bee to hive and of hand to body, which he distinguishes sharply from the attitude which persons should have toward their community (cf. the passages cited above in notes 3–4). He does discuss this article at length in his *Sin of the Angel*, but only in the context of loving God, not of loving the city, and without identifying the motive for that love as the creature's radical dependence on God, as Aquinas does.

114. Maritain, *Person*, 79; italics added. Cf. ibid., 77.

not as something due from part to whole but rather as something freely given from whole to whole. Now, Maritain is certainly right that acts of love are always "free" in the sense of being willing rather than begrudging. But this kind of freedom, it seems to me (and, I believe, to Aquinas), is entirely compatible with seeing one's response as *due* to the beloved; and so there is no need to abandon the perspective of the existentially dependent and indebted "part" in order to love the whole with the fullness of love's generosity and freedom. On the contrary, as we saw, the most generous, self-transcending love is arguably possible *only* from the perspective of the "part."

A third possible reason, and perhaps the main one, why Maritain does not see our radical dependence on the city as a motivation for self-transcendent love is his overriding concern to resist totalitarianism. As we saw in §1 and §2, neither Maritain nor De Koninck are willing to say that we should love the *city* more than ourselves for its own sake, since this would seem to make the city into a fictitious super-individual of its own, akin to a hive or a living body, whose good would therefore be "alien" to its individual citizens—sometimes coinciding with their good, but also sometimes inimical to it, and never ordered to it.[115] De Koninck's strategy for avoiding this totalitarian outcome, as we have seen, is simply to resist casting the question in terms of the priority of different objects of *friendship*-love ("city" above "self"), and to formulate it instead in terms of the priority of objects of *desire*-love ("common good" above "private good").[116] And as we have seen, this strategy comes at the cost of denying friendship-love's priority over desire-love. Maritain's strategy, conversely, is to keep the focus on the objects of *friendship*-love ("city" and "self"), but to demote both the city and its common good by confining the city's priority to the level of our indebted "individuality," thus excluding it from the level of our free and loving "personality." And as we have seen, this strategy too comes at a significant cost, here of divorcing our service to the common good from self-transcendent love.

Aquinas himself, however, seems to resort to neither strategy. While,

115. For Maritain's preoccupation with totalitarianism, see above, notes 3–4, 5, and 8; for De Koninck's, see notes 14–19.

116. See the passages cited above in notes 88 and 98; see esp. "Defence," 325: "From such a point of view [that is, the "distinctly modern" approach of giving "absolute priority to the subject"], the problem of person and society quite naturally becomes the question: is the person better than society? instead of: is the proper good of the person better than his common good? When the problem itself has been so distorted, what can be expected in the solution?"

like De Koninck, he frequently does speak of preferring the whole's *good* (e.g. at ST II-II, q. 26, a. 3), he also seems quite comfortable with the general principle that the part simply loves the *whole* more than itself, without qualification,[117] which would seem to imply that the *person* loves the *city* more than himself with friendship-love. Is Aquinas being careless here? Or does he fall into the totalitarian trap after all, elevating the city into a hive-like super-individual?

It seems to me that one need impute neither failing to Aquinas: one can indeed have friendship-love for a community as such, for its own sake, without taking it as a super-individual with its own good separate from that of its members. The reason why Maritain thinks one cannot is that, in my view, he gives too much independent reality to the "whole community" over and above the persons who compose it: he takes it as a faceless structure of which persons, though "irreplaceable" in themselves, are merely "replaceable" components.[118] A community so understood would indeed be wholly ordered *to* persons, and certainly should not be loved more than oneself for its own sake. If, however, the "community" is understood in a more personalist way, as simply the persons themselves considered as sharing the formality of citizenship, then friendship-love for this community as such simply means friendship-love for each community member, but motivated precisely by the goodness of this shared formality.

Normally, such friendship-love is not self-transcendent. However, in the special case unique to a "perfect society," where my own human goodness radically depends on the civic goodness of my fellow community members (without which I, and likewise the family that raised me, would have been uncivilized and short-lived brutes), this friendship-love does transcend self-love. Now, since no individual fellow-citizen possesses this civic goodness in full, and since I do not radically depend on any individual fellow-citizen alone, this dependence does not imply that I love any *individual* fellow-citizen more than myself. Rather, what I love more than my-

117. Aquinas lays down the principle that parts love their wholes more than themselves at ST I, q. 60, a. 5, ad 1; *Quodlibet* I, q. 4, a. 3; and *In De divinis nominibus*, chap. 4, lect. 9, §406 and lect. 10, §§431–32. He lays down the same principle in terms of "order" or "belonging" rather than "love" at ST I-II, q. 90, a. 2; q. 96, a. 4; II-II, q. 58, a. 5; q. 64, a. 2; and q. 65, a. 1.

118. Maritain, *Person*, 75. Maritain goes on to identify the reason for society's impersonal character as the fact that "the relations which make up the structure of society concern, as such, only *justice*, which is essentially impersonal because it is measured on things, and does not make acceptance of persons." Ibid., 75–76; italics in original.

self is all my fellow-citizens taken jointly, since the civic goodness on which my own goodness radically depends is found as a whole only in the whole community. This differs notably from ordinary friendships where there is no relation of radical dependence, since in these friendships the goodness motivating my (non-self-transcendent) love is found in each friend individually. The fact that the object of self-transcendent friendship-love is all the citizens taken together is reflected in the resultant inclination to self-sacrifice. Civic love as such does not impel the citizen to lay down his life for an individual fellow-citizen (though other friendship, or charity, may so impel him, as may love of his own soul[119]). It does, however, impel him to make the ultimate sacrifice for the sake of the whole community, or even for any part of the community large enough that the civic goodness specifying his love may be found wholly or at least in root in that part—which in Aquinas's view would include even the ruler taken alone, since the goodness of the whole community depends on the ruler's vision.[120]

By my reading of Aquinas's account, then, the "city" is still individual persons united by a common formality, not a super-individual. Hence, *pace* both Maritain and De Koninck, the "city" may be the object of a self-transcendent friendship-love, on the basis of a part-whole relationship, without falling into totalitarianism. I take De Koninck's central insight to be the holistic nature of the civic goodness shared by all the citizens; what he missed, in my view, is that the object of our primary love is not this goodness in the abstract but rather the persons who jointly possess it. We thus need neither follow De Koninck in insisting that we love persons because we desire the common good's "diffusion" rather than vice versa, nor follow Maritain in demoting the citizen's subordination to the city to the side of his needy "individuality."

VI. Conclusion

On the one hand, we have seen that there is more common ground between Maritain and De Koninck than perhaps meets the eye. Both oppose totalitarianism and individualism; both insist that the common good must be the good *of persons*; and both regard God as the supreme extrinsic com-

119. Aquinas, ST II-II q. 26, a. 4 ad 2; a. 5 ad 3; *De perfectione*, chap. 16; *Super Evangelium S. Ioannis*, chap. 15, lect. 2, §2009.

120. See esp. Aquinas, *De caritate*, a. 4, ad 2.

mon good, and the intrinsic order of the universe as the thing "first intended" by God in creating. Moreover, many of the differences between them may be traced either to differing use of key terms (e.g, "common good" and "personal good") or to differing emphasis (e.g., opposing individualism vs. opposing totalitarianism).

On the other hand, however, they do differ importantly on the *reason* why we ought to prioritize serving the common good. Maritain identifies our "individuality" (that is, our radical dependence on our community) as the basis for our obligation to serve the community as something above us, while identifying our "personality" (that is, our spiritual nature's generosity) as the basis for freely loving the community as something which we transcend. De Koninck, by contrast, holds that both our love for the community and our obligation to serve its common good are based on our prior love for and ordering to the common good itself, which is *ipso facto* greater than any private good and which can only be loved adequately by desiring it to be received by a whole community.

I argued that De Koninck commits the more fundamental mistake, and departure from Aquinas's thought, by prioritizing goods *for* persons over persons themselves and desire-love over friendship-love. To defend the priority of the person, I examined key Thomistic texts of which De Koninck seems unaware, and sought to show that De Koninck misinterprets other texts that he thinks subordinate the person to the good for the person. Restoring the person to his central place in rightly ordered love has been this essay's chief aim. Nonetheless, I also argued that Maritain too makes an important mistake by restricting our ordering to the community to our imperfect, needy side, since this divorces obligation from love in our service to the community, and moreover renders self-transcendent love impossible on the creaturely level.

The solution, I argued, is essentially to be more personalist than Maritain himself. I understand the "community" as not merely a structure *for* persons but as the actual persons themselves, on whose jointly possessed civic goodness we radically depend. If the community is so understood, we will owe it not only service as "individuals" but self-transcendent love as "persons." The primacy of the common good is thus safeguarded, in a twofold way: not only the claim that merely private goods are lesser than genuine common goods, on which both De Koninck and Maritain agree, but also, *pace* Maritain, the claim that the citizen is ordered to the city precisely as a free, generous, loving person. Yet, *pace* De Koninck, the common good's primacy so understood does not negate but rather presumes the personalist principle: "person" signifies that which is most perfect in all of nature (*persona significat id quod est perfectissimum in tota natura*; ST I, q. 29, a. 3), and that therefore the person is to be loved in a more fundamental way than any good *for* the person—even the common good.

CHRISTOPHER L. RAGUSA

The Right Rights

Whose Aquinas? Which Natural Law?

I. Introduction

HISTORICALLY, THERE HAVE BEEN two main narratives surrounding the idea of rights. Both narratives hold that "rights language" is a post-medieval concept. The first narrative is that rights are a true insight into the human condition and the law of nature and nature's God. It finds expression in the American Declaration of Independence and John Courtney Murray's *We Hold These Truths,* and among Thomists is perhaps most famously represented by Jacques Maritain's *Man and the State.* Such a narrative generally sees rights as stemming from the law of nature, with Murray and Maritain arguing that natural law reasoning is the only context in which rights properly make sense. For them this insight was the "proper achievement—a great achievement indeed—of the XVIII Century . . . to bring out in full light the *rights* of man as also required by natural law" in tandem with man's obligations.[1] The second narrative concerning rights is one that it is decidedly negative. Rights, it claims, are irredeemably individualistic as set out by their modern inventors—Ockham, Hobbes, or Locke—and as modern fictions, they should be rejected.[2]

1. Jacques Maritain, *Man and the State* (Chicago, Illinois: The University of Chicago, 1958), 94; italics in original.

2. Michel Villey perhaps most famously and influentially identified William of Ockham and his nominalist philosophy as the origin of the modern natural rights discourse. See for instance, "La genèse du droit subjectif chez Guillaume d'Occam," *Archives de philosophie du droit* 9 (1964): 97–127. Leo Strauss identifies Hobbes (followed shortly thereafter by Locke) as the originator of rights language in *Natural Right and History* (Chicago, Illinois: The University of Chicago Press, 1971), 165–66.

The modern exemplar of this narrative to whom most look is Alasdair MacIntyre and his memorable pronouncement, "for the truth is plain: there are no such rights, and belief in them is one with the belief in witches and unicorns."[3] On this view, rights are an invention by the Enlightenment in its failed project to find a shared secular morality and politics apart from any acknowledgment of a teleological view of human nature.[4] As such this second narrative advocates abandoning rights discourse in favor of traditional discourse concerning justice and the virtues.[5] However, although both narratives disagree on whether rights discourse is fundamentally positive or negative, they agree that the idea of rights was first invented or recognized in the Enlightenment or at least after the high Middle Ages.

More recently, it is precisely the point on which these two narratives are agreed—that rights are a modern invention—that has been contested. The idea of rights was not invented suddenly but rather developed or grew over time. In fact, it seems that it was the late scholastics at the School of Salamanca in the 1500s who were the first to pull all of the necessary ideas together to articulate what is now referred to as 'natural human rights.'[6] However, the concept of a *right* certainly preceded even the School of Salamanca. Brian Tierney argues persuasively in *The Idea of Natural Rights* that the medieval, humanistic jurisprudence of the canonists first shows a real engagement with the concept of a *right* expressed as a liberty or power that one held.[7] Drawing upon Gratian's *Decretum* (c. 1140) and its compilation

3. Alasdair MacIntyre, *After Virtue: A Study in Moral Theory* (Notre Dame, Indiana: University of Notre Dame Press, 2003), 69.

4. Ibid., 51–55, 66–70.

5. While this is certainly MacIntyre's position, it can be found without much effort in popular articles by others. Such an opinion can be seen recently in "The Ignoble Lie" in *First Things* in which Patrick Deneen argues that at the heart of modern ills is the individualism latent in liberalism, which finds its expression in the enshrining of rights language at the center of public debate. He advocates using language of justice and injustice. See Patrick J. Deneen, "The Ignoble Lie," *First Things* 282 (April 2018): 27–32. Such a discussion of justice and injustice would be seen by the first narrative on rights as complemented by rights language, not replaced by it. Focusing on both obligation and right enables one to speak of both the agent and the recipient, respectively, concerning actions in a just relationship.

6. See David M. Lantigua, "The Image of God, Christian Rights Talk, and the School of Salamanca," *Journal of Law and Religion* 31, no. 1 (2016): 19–41. However, Lantigua prefers the language of "human natural rights," pgs 35–36. See also Joseph Capizzi, "The Catholic Who Invented Human Rights: Francisco de Vitoria and Human Rights," *The Thomistic Institute*, Tulane University, New Orleans, Jan 31, 2018. https://soundcloud.com/thomisticinstitute/dr-joseph-capizzi-the-catholic-who-invented-human-rights-francisco-de-vitoria-and-human-rights.

7. Brian Tierney, *The Idea of Natural Rights: Studies on Natural Rights, Natural Law, and Church Law 1159–1625* (Grand Rapids, Michigan: Eerdmans, 2001), 54–61.

of Roman law, papal pronouncements, and the writings of the saints, the medieval canonists wrote a body of glosses reflecting a real understanding not only of claim rights (*ius ad rem*) but also active rights (*ius in re*), distinctions that would continue to be in use at least until the seventeenth century in Suarez's writings.[8] Key to this understanding was the word '*ius*' as synonymous with the idea of a *right* and its frequent association with other concepts such as *potestas, libertas, facultas,* and *dominium.*

Tierney argues that this concept of a *right,* which he calls "subjective right," eventually moves from the canonists and legal sources to theologians in both their theological and political reflection, not as a kind of necessary growth but as a real development nonetheless. There is, he says,

> a degree of continuity in the development of the idea of human rights.... Evidently the whole modern cornucopia of rights and rights theories could not have emerged from the middle ages or indeed from the Enlightenment.... [However] when one looks at the whole tradition there may be a temptation to understand it in terms of some timeworn metaphor like that of a great oak tree that grows from a tiny acorn. But this would be misleading. It suggests that the growth and present flourishing of a doctrine of human rights was something inevitable, programmed so to speak into the culture of the West. But what we actually find when we look at the history of the doctrine is a series of unforeseen contingent circumstances in which the ideas of self-dominion and natural rights were deployed for different purposes and used to defend a variety of causes.[9]

Tierney does hold that there is a real development within the history of rights discourse, but it is not a Hegelian march of history and dialectic. Rather, rights language is influenced by its thinkers and by the contingent events of history, for example, by its incorporation into the American founding documents or its use in the response to the totalitarianism of the twentieth century.

8. Ibid., 57–58.

9. Brian Tierney, "Dominion of Self and Natural Rights Before Locke and After," in *Transformations in Medieval and Early-Modern Rights Discourse,* edited by Virpi Makinen and Petter Korkman (Netherlands: Springer, 2006), 198–99. Tierney is careful to guard against a kind of Hegelian march when discussing the history of the concept of rights. As he does here concerning rights, Tierney also uses a similar example of an acorn growing into an oak to discuss "permissive natural law" and the incorrect understandings of historical development in his book *Liberty and Law: The Idea of Permissive Natural law, 1100–1800* (Washington, D.C.: The Catholic University of America Press, 2014), ix–x. As I will show later in the essay, it is not surprising that Tierney's discussion of rights and permissive natural law would use similar examples since he views the concepts as intimately connected.

However, in his historical analysis of rights discourse, Tierney claims again and again that "Aquinas himself did not develop a doctrine of natural rights"[10] and "the attribution of a definition of *ius* as a subjective right to Aquinas [is] quite mistaken; Aquinas taught no such doctrine."[11] Indeed, according to Tierney, "Aquinas did not choose to assimilate such ideas into his Christian-Aristotelian synthesis."[12] Such repeated statements are historically *curious* given that Tierney traces the initial development of a real articulation of 'rights' to the early medieval canonists, recognizes that Aquinas is familiar with these canonistic sources, and realizes that later thinkers—such as those at the Salamanca School—look to the writings of St. Thomas Aquinas as they develop an account of natural human rights. [13] Accordingly, I intend to show that, contra Tierney's claim, St. Thomas uses the term '*ius*' to refer to not only *objective right* or "what is fair" but also to a *subjective right* or a right possessed by a person. This usage of the term '*ius*' roughly parallels the modern sense of "a right" and is not only used by Aquinas in political examples but also is connected to terms such as 'faculty' or 'power' as well as 'authority' or *dominium*. St. Thomas does have an understanding of subjective or personal rights and this understanding is evident when one properly recognizes how Aquinas views justice and man's participation in God's providential governance. To show this, I will first examine Tierney's own understanding of rights and how it connects to his understanding of "permissive natural law." In the following sections I will examine St. Thomas's understanding of natural law and his understanding of man's participatory authority. Finally, I will look at how St. Thomas himself speaks of *ius*

10. Tierney, "Dominion and Rights," 179–80. In this position, Tierney seems to have been influenced by Villey's own arguments. Tierney seems to hold that Villey overstates his case in claims that St. Thomas was ignorant of any sense of subjective right but is correct in holding that Aquinas recaptured the older Roman and Aristotelian objective understanding of right or "what is fair" as the object of justice. Tierney, *Idea of Natural Rights*, 22–23, 257–58. Cf. Villey, "La genèse du droit subjectif," 103, 111 n.1., 120.

11. Tierney, *Idea of Natural Rights*, 69.

12. Ibid., 45.

13. Jean Porter also points out the oddity of affirming that the canonists had a concept of subjective right, affirming that Aquinas knows and is influenced by the canonistic sources, and then denying that Aquinas has any concept of such a right. "When we examine the relevant texts, we find that Aquinas very often does say that individuals can claim certain liberties and immunities on the basis of some natural right.... He [Aquinas] does not have a theory of rights, but neither do the scholastic jurists of the time, and his appeals to what someone can claim by right are reminiscent of their views. If they can be said to have a notion of subjective natural rights, the same can be said of Aquinas himself." Jean Porter, "Justice, Equality, And Natural Rights Claims: A Reconsideration of Aquinas's Conception of Right," *Journal of Law and Religion* 30, no. 3 (2015): 448.

both generally and in specific examples. Within this final section I will also analyze Porter's and Finnis's different responses to Tierney's articulation of natural law and rights in Aquinas and will show that their approaches are insufficient. I will argue that it is St. Thomas's understanding of natural law as fundamentally participatory that explains not only why he does not need to appeal to an account of permissive natural law, as the medieval canonists did, to ground man's authority (dominion) and agency but also how he speaks of subjective rights in a way that closely matches our modern sense of personal rights. Furthermore, it is Aquinas's participatory account of natural law and his understanding of "one's right" (*suum ius*) as the object of particular justice that truly allows for the ongoing incorporation of the best of rights discourse today, including the necessary and complimentary role that rights and the common good both play in considerations of justice, without having to assert a sphere of radical autonomy or individualism to make sense of one's rights and authority.

II. Brian Tierney: Rights and Permissive Natural Law

There seem to be few modern authors whose work give Brian Tierney more material for discussion than that of the French twentieth-century philosopher Michel Villey. Villey, reports Tierney, held that the modern understanding of rights "is rooted in the nominalist philosophy of the fourteenth century, and it first saw the light of day in the work of William of Ockham."[14] In Villey's view, this nominalism and its radical individualism allows for a turn to the subject in modern philosophy and thereby is the only fertile ground from which natural rights could arise, especially in the work of Kant.[15] However, although Tierney rejects Villey's historical account—that modern subjective rights first appeared from Ockham's nominalism—and articulates a history of rights language that is much more continuous, referencing moments when even the Roman jurist Gaius seems to use the word '*ius*' in a subjective fashion,[16] Tierney remains greatly influenced by Villey and adopts much of the substance of Villey's approach.

The substantive similarity arises from Tierney's acceptance of Villey's

14. Tierney, *Idea of Natural Rights*, 14.
15. Ibid., 10.
16. Ibid., 17

distinction between "objective right" and "a subjective right." Objective right or objective *ius* means "an objectively right relationship" or "what is fair," and this *classical* usage, hold Villey and Tierney, was restored by St. Thomas Aquinas and lost again by Ockham and the nominalists.[17] Conversely, a subjective right or subjective *ius* is a kind of power or faculty possessed by an individual person in a just relationship.[18] It is this sense of *ius* as a subjective right which they claim is the modern and more recent sense of the term. Crucially, these two meanings for Villey and Tierney are mutually exclusive.[19] In Villey's understanding, nominalism is the necessary precondition for the modern sense of subjective right since it provides the necessary understanding of man as autonomous individual. Tierney, as will be further discussed later, makes a similar move as Villey, connecting the idea of subjective right to a conception of autonomy, except through his notion of permissive natural law rather than nominalism.

For Tierney, subjective rights seem to inhere in the person as such.[20] This position is evident when Tierney discusses John Finnis's reading of rights in St. Thomas and repeatedly declares that such subjective rights are foreign to the mind of Aquinas.[21] Defining his idea, Tierney writes that a subjective "right implies also a sphere of personal autonomy within which an agent is not obliged to act but is free to determine his or her own course

17. Ibid., 22–23.

18. Ibid., 16, 20, 23, 28. The subjective sense of right is often times associated with a moral power or faculty that an individual subject has in justice. "Le droit ... signifie cette notion beaucoup plus étroite: le pouvoir qu'on a sur un bien. Pouvoir nettement spécifié: il diffère la simple *licence*" Villey, "La genèse du droit subjectif," 117. Italics in original. Villey refers to this usage of 'right' as a kind of subjective power as a distortion of its original meaning of 'the right' or 'the fair' as an objective state.

19. John Finnis similarly observes this unity between Villey and Tierney but discusses it much more forcefully. "[T]hough he [Tierney] has been an effective critic of Villey's historical analyses, he now seems gripped by Villey's *non sequitur* (if objective then not subjective)." John Finnis "Aquinas on *Ius* and Hart on Rights: A Response to Tierney," *The Review of Politics* 64, no. 3 (2002): 409. However, for Tierney, as I will show later, one can have both "objective" and "subjective" senses of right if one has what Tierney outlines as "permissive natural law." Accordingly, for all those who do not have such a "permissive" understanding of natural law, such as Aquinas, these senses are mutually exclusive.

20. Tierney, *Idea of Natural Rights*, 20.

21. Brian Tierney, "Natural Law and Natural Rights Old Problems and Recent Approaches," *The Review of Politics* 64, no. 3 (2002): 392. "Aquinas's definition did not have any reference to other persons' rights." As I will show further on, this statement is not strictly true since when Aquinas discusses and defines the relationship between 'right' and 'just,' Aquinas follows the canonists and consistently refers to justice as "rendering another *his right* [*suum ius*]" or simply "what is *his* [*quod suum est*]." See ST II-II, qq. 57–58.

of action ... Accordingly, ... a right [defines] 'a realm of sovereignty or of relatively completely free choice.' But this kind of right," Tierney notes, "cannot readily be derived from Aquinas's natural law teaching."[22] For Tierney, rights are only possible in the context of a negative sense of freedom, when one is not hindered or commanded. Rights belong to an individual as sovereign in a situation, when one is free to act but not obliged. Tierney is undoubtedly correct to say that such a concept of freedom from obligation or freedom as a realm of complete sovereignty is foreign to the mind of St. Thomas, but, as will be seen later, this is not the only way in which one can have authority or freedom and therefore is not the only possible way to ground rights had by a subject.

Like Villey before him, Tierney sees Aquinas as restoring an older objective understanding of *ius*.[23] Tierney, in union with his preference for an interpretation of objective right over and to the exclusion of "subjective" also sees Thomas as rejecting a sphere of autonomy in "permissive natural law," especially as the canonists used the concept. Concerning this law, Tierney notes that the canonists (and Roman jurists) understood "law [to consist] of precepts, prohibitions, permissions, and counsels."[24] The Decretists appealed to the permissive aspect of natural law to explain how creation, which was destined for the good of all of humanity, could be divided up and owned or claimed with property rights.

> [F]rom the twelfth century to the age of Hobbes and Locke and beyond, the idea of permissive natural law was persistently invoked as a ground of natural right, especially the right to property. In this way of thinking natural law defined an area of human autonomy and free choice but not a state of total license. The permissions of the law of nature were bounded by the commands and prohibitions of that same law. With-

22. Tierney, "Natural Law and Natural Rights," 395.

23. Tierney, *Idea of Natural Rights*, 257. "... faithful Thomists, did not teach a doctrine of subjective natural rights but adhered faithfully to the objective sense of *ius* defined by Aquinas.... Aquinas did not teach any doctrine of subjective natural rights." "Villey argued that Aquinas ... restore[d] for a time the objective, classical meaning of *ius* (a meaning that would be lost again by Ockham and the nominalists)." Ibid., 23.

24. Tierney, *Permissive Natural Law*, 16; Tierney, "Natural Law and Natural Rights," 400. Here one might point out that St. Thomas too views the law as having this four-fold division. Aquinas introduces ST I-II, q. 92 by noting that the second article of the question will be concerned with "whether the effects of law are to command, to forbid, to permit, and to punish, as the Jurist states?" St. Thomas then goes on to answer the question in the affirmative, quoting St. Isidore of Seville. St. Thomas is quoting the same passage from Isidore that Gratian's *Decretum* quotes on this topic of law. This is obvious when comparing *Decretum Gratiani*, dist. 3, c. 4 to ST I-II q. 92, a. 2.

in this framework of natural law thinking the rights derived from permissive natural law were entitled to the respect of others and likewise a right-holder was held not to violate others' rights.[25]

In certain areas of permissiveness, the law was not absent and it did not leave a vacuum for unfettered license, asserts Tierney; rather, it allowed for a *defined* realm of human freedom or choice between several different actions.[26] Thus on Tierney's account, natural subjective rights require a sphere of autonomy in which one is sovereign and free to act or not act and permissive natural law is the concept that creates such a sovereign, autonomous space for man.

However, although this idea of permissive natural law was widespread, St. Thomas did not put it to much use. Tierney notes that St. Thomas does have certain permissions within the law, such as the toleration of the rites of unbelievers in the *Summa Theologiae* II-II, q. 10, a. 11, but overall St. Thomas avoids using permissive natural law language. Although St. Thomas is concerned with both human freedom and the law, he does not make use of the concept of permissive natural law and so does not define a sphere of autonomy or circumscribed zone of freedom for man, and this is important. Aquinas does not view law and freedom as in tension in a way that requires their resolution through a category of permissive natural law. Rather, Aquinas is concerned with right relationship and discerning the right application of the precepts of the natural law in our lives. Accordingly, Tierney concludes that Aquinas holds objective *ius* in a way that excludes a subjective *ius*, which would have as its precondition some autonomous sphere of authority in permissive natural law.[27] The fact that Aquinas did not choose "to assimilate the concept of permissive natural law into his system of thought even though the idea was widespread in other works of law and philosophy ... helps explain why neither [he nor others who lacked this concept] developed a meaningful concept of natural rights."[28] For Tierney, permissive

25. Tierney, "Natural Law and Natural Rights," 401.

26. Ibid., 45. Italics added. It must be pointed out, however, that an absence of law or command does not itself equal or confer a right.

27. Ibid., 395. "[R]ight implies also a sphere of personal autonomy within which an agent is not obliged to act but is free to determine his or her own course of action."

28. Ibid., 406. We can see just how central this idea of permissive natural law is for Tierney when he also claims that the only reason Francisco de Vitoria was able to derive a subjective understanding of rights from "Aquinas's objective definition of *ius*" was because "Vitoria used the idea of permissive law" (402). It seems that Tierney's argument is almost syllogistic: Major premise: All subjective rights theories require a sphere of autonomy as some form of expression

natural law as a sphere of autonomy and sovereignty of the individual is a necessary intellectual concept for the development of rights language from the objective to a subjective sense.

III. St. Thomas Aquinas: Right and Just

Having examined Brian Tierney's understanding of St. Thomas, I have shown that Tierney conceives of the rise of subjective rights theories as intimately and necessarily linked to conceptions of permissive natural law, which constitutes a sphere of autonomy and individual sovereignty. Tierney's opinion is akin to that of Michel Villey with the exception that Villey looks to nominalism as providing the sphere of autonomy needed for subjective rights. However, I would also like to briefly note a few other interpretations of St. Thomas as I move toward an examination of Aquinas's work. Although they argue against Tierney in their own ways, Jean Porter and John Finnis both use the distinction between objective and subjective right. However, they do so to argue that St. Thomas does articulate what are recognizably subjective rights. Porter's argument is unique because she claims that although St. Thomas "does not develop a theory of rights as such,... his remarks on rights claims presuppose certain views about the normative significance of human nature.... [H]is analysis of the scope and limits of obedience depends explicitly on the claim that all are equal in some fundamental respects. This natural equality is correlated with a 'zone of autonomy.'"[29] Similarly, Porter also argues that "the fundamental human inclinations are *permissive*."[30] Porter does think that individual rights need

of 'permissive natural law.' Minor premise: St. Thomas does not deploy a concept of 'permissive natural law.' Conclusion: Therefore, St. Thomas does not have an understanding of subjective rights but only objective rights.

29. Jean Porter, "Justice, Equality, And Natural Rights Claims," 455. Porter's article is quite good but she cedes too much to Tierney on this point, namely the zone of autonomy.

30. Jean Porter, *The Recovery of Virtue: The Relevance of Aquinas for Christian Ethics* (Louisville, Kentucky: John Knox Press, 1990), 143–44. Italics added. Tierney refers to this above quote from Jean Porter to argue that St. Thomas also held man's freedom in the midst of the law (Tierney, *Permissive Natural Law*, 80). Porter does make other statements similar to Tierney's regarding the permissiveness of natural law in *The Recovery of Virtue*. "For in fact, Aquinas holds that it is always moral to act *in accordance with* the inclinations, so long as one does so in a rationally appropriate way.... In other words, insofar as they do function as a direct basis for moral norms, the inclinations are fundamentally permissive in their effect. Only secondarily do they serve to ground prohibitions. Moreover, one's pursuit of the fundamental inclinations cannot licitly be impeded by other persons'. No one can legitimately compel another either to marry or to remain celibate, for example (II-II 104.5). Because they mark out what is fundamental to human life, the inclinations indicate

a sphere of autonomy and that St. Thomas does in fact have such a sphere of autonomy or "immunity."[31] John Finnis, like Porter, argues that Aquinas does have a concept of individual rights or a subjective sense of *ius*; however, Finnis does not speak much of an autonomous sphere of moral sovereignty. Rather, Finnis holds that "every element essential to the modern concept of human rights" is present in St. Thomas, which does not include widespread "autonomous choice."[32]

It seems then that with Tierney and some of his critics there is a kind of spectrum of opinions on St. Thomas's view of rights: (1) that of John Finnis—that St. Thomas Aquinas has a conception of individual rights but no sphere of autonomy; (2) that of Brian Tierney—that Aquinas has no conception of individual rights and no sphere of autonomy; and (3) that of Jean Porter—that St. Thomas has a conception of both individual rights and a sphere of autonomy.[33] Accordingly, I now turn to examine St. Thomas Aquinas on his own terms—especially his understanding of natural law, man's authority under it, and the way Aquinas conceives of *ius* or right. As I will show, Aquinas does speak of subjective rights but this is because he views man as a participative authority, not an autonomous or sovereign one.

1. Natural Law and Participative Authority. To properly understand the natural law for St. Thomas one must first understand that it is real law. Natural law is not called 'law' in an honorific or metaphorical sense. Rather, natural law truly commands and governs for Aquinas. St. Thomas shows this in the *Prima Secundae* of the *Summa Theologiae*, when before discuss-

the parameters of individual freedom ..." (93). Italics in original. Furthermore, Porter eventually comes to use this exact example of marriage and celibacy to justify her own finding of a "zone of autonomy" in Aquinas's thought similar to that of Tierney. Cf. Porter, "Justice, Equality, And Natural Rights Claims," 454–55. While one may perhaps speak of a vague "zone of autonomy" from the state or from others—which seems to be Porter's desire—properly for man there can be no such "zone of autonomy" in the natural law from God's governance, as Tierney wants to assert. For St. Thomas, if there is a real negation—such as a denial of the authority of the body politic concerning one's marriage or choice of celibacy— and not merely a privation, it is because of some other fundamental positive, such as is the case in man's fundamental orientation to God. Man is not left alone or "autonomous." Rather, as St. Thomas notes, "Man is not ordained to the body politic, according to all that he is and has; and so it does not follow that every action of his acquires merit or demerit in relation to the body politic. But all that man is, and can, and has, must be referred to God." ST I-II, q. 21, a. 4, ad 3. There can be no "zone of autonomy" from God or from His law for the creature, rather the creature *participates in* God's providential governance.

31. Porter, "Justice, Equality, And Natural Rights Claims," 453–55.

32. John Finnis, "Aquinas on *Ius*," 409–410.

33. There is obviously a fourth option here: that St. Thomas has a sphere of autonomy like permissive natural law but only an objective rights theory and no individual subjective rights; however, it has few, if any, defenders.

ing natural law he first discusses what all laws have in common. All laws command or forbid, are connected to reason—in a special way the practical reason—and seek the common good as their end.[34] They are made by one who has care for the common good and properly made known and enacted.[35] Natural law is a law in this sense and is discussed alongside eternal law, through which God truly governs the universe, and human law, through which man truly governs society.[36] God governs creation through his divine providence and such governance "has the nature of a law."[37] As such, it is crucial to understand how natural law is in accord with eternal law.

Russell Hittinger forcefully points out that for St. Thomas "natural law is never (and [he emphasizes] *never*) defined in terms of what is first in the (human) mind or first in nature."[38] Instead, the natural law—in itself—must be understood as our participation in divine providence and God's governance. The natural law is not in itself the order of nature nor does it consist in atomistic, incommensurable basic goods discerned by practical reason. Rather, "the natural law is nothing else than the rational creature's participation of the eternal law."[39] Undoubtedly the natural law is discovered through nature and grasped by individuals in the practical intellect; however, the natural law is for St. Thomas "nothing but" the participation by man of the eternal law. St. Thomas specifies this participation by noting that "to the natural law belongs everything to which a man is inclined according to his nature. Now each thing is inclined naturally to an operation that is suitable to it according to its form.... Wherefore, since the rational soul is the proper form of man, there is in every man a natural inclination to act according to reason: and this is to act according to virtue. Consequently, considered

34. ST I-II q. 90, aa. 1–2. Any English translation with the Latin supplied in the footnote is my own; otherwise, I will be quoting from the *Summa Theologica*, translated by the English Dominican Province, 5 vols. (New York: Benziger Bros., 1947–48). The Latin is from the *Leonine Edition* of the *Summa Theologiae* available at http://archive.org/stream/operaomniaiussui08thom#page/n7/mode/2up.

35. ST I-II, q. 90, aa. 3–4.

36. ST I-II, q. 91.

37. ST I-II, q. 91, a. 1.

38. Russell Hittinger, *The First Grace: Rediscovering the Natural Law in a Post-Christian World* (Wilmington, Delaware: ISI Books, 2003), 9. Italics in original. Russell Hittinger notes well that when St. Thomas initially defines natural law and is inclined to give a definition in subsequent discussions, he always appeals to the causal understanding that natural law is a participation in the eternal law. Natural law may be discovered through the inclinations or commanded through human practical reason, but these are not the law itself.

39. ST I-II, q. 91, a. 2.

thus, all acts of virtue are prescribed by the natural law."[40] Virtue ethics is not separate from the natural law but rather within the context of natural law. The life of virtue is how man participates in the eternal law.

However, one can misunderstand the mind of St. Thomas if one stops with the statement that the natural law—man's participation of the eternal law—is to act according to virtue. One must understand the role of the practical reason and of natural inclinations. I will start with the latter first: natural inclinations. It is easy for modern readers to misread St. Thomas on the inclinations. Aquinas does not mean affective inclinations, feelings, emotions, or desires. Rather, St. Thomas holds that "since all things subject to Divine providence are ruled and measured by the eternal law, . . . it is evident that all things participate someway in the eternal law, in so far as, namely, from its being imprinted on them, they derive their respective inclinations to their proper acts and ends." [41] These are inclinations of the nature to its proper ends and its proper actions. These are not merely affective inclinations but the way a nature inclines to its fulfillment and end, namely to virtue. One may *feel* dis-inclined to eat and drink temperately or to live justly but this does not change the fact that—by our very nature's orientation to our end—we flourish and are truly happiest in such actions of justice and temperance. This ordination or inclination of the nature is for St. Thomas one way we are governed by the eternal law and divine providence. We are ordered in our very nature to our happiness and fulfillment.

40. ST I-II, q. 94, a.3.

41. ST I-II, q. 91, a. 2. "cum omnia quae divinae providentiae subduntur, a lege aeterna regulentur et mensurentur, . . . manifestum est quod omnia participant aliqualiter legem aeternam, inquantum scilicet ex impressione eius habent inclinationes in proprios actus et fines." Although "participation" features heavily in this essay, a full account of St. Thomas's metaphysics of participation and the way it permeates his theory of law and virtue is beyond the scope of this article; however, the recognition that St. Thomas's participation theory extends to his moral theology is nonetheless crucial. For those who recognize the importance of participation in the metaphysical thought of St. Thomas see John Wippel, *The Metaphysical Thought of St. Thomas Aquinas: From Finite Being to Uncreated Being* (Washington, D.C.: The Catholic University Press, 2000); W. Norris Clarke, SJ, "The Meaning of Participation in St. Thomas" in *Exploration In Metaphysics: Being—God—Person* (Notre Dame: University of Notre Dame Press, 1994), 89–101; ———, "The Limitation of Act by Potency: Aristotelianism or Neoplatonism?" *New Scholasticism* 26 (1952): 167–94; ———, "The Platonic Heritage of Thomism," *Review of* Metaphysics 8, no. 1 (1954): 105–124 and many others. After the initial presentation of this paper at the Maritain Conference in 2020, I completed a fuller and more extensive analysis of Aquinas's metaphysics of participation and its important implications for properly understanding Thomistic natural law, acquired virtue, and infused virtue—especially charity. For more see Christopher L. Ragusa, Jr., "'Partakers of the Divine Nature' (2 Peter 1:4): The Role of Participation in St. Thomas Aquinas's Moral Theology" (PhD diss., The Catholic University of America, 2023).

However, these natural inclinations should not be understood as providing literal commands for every single action of our lives. Rather, they are limited in a certain respect and we need the guidance of practical reason and its virtue: prudence. While the inclinations of lower creatures seem to correspond one-to-one to their objects, "the rational powers, which are proper to man, are not determinate to one particular action, but are inclined indifferently to many: and they are determinate to acts by means of habits"; these habits Aquinas notes are the virtues.[42] The inclinations must be further determined or specified through rationally building up right habit, namely virtue. We participate in our formation to our proper end under the natural law through our formation in virtue.[43] In this way the commands of virtue are nothing less than a participative authority in the natural law itself.

Furthermore, St. Thomas notes that man's participation in divine providence is not only through his natural or essential inclinations but also in a special way through his practical reason: "Now… the rational creature is subject to divine providence in the most excellent way, in as much as it is a participant in providence, by being provident both for itself and for others. From which it is participating in the Eternal Reason, through which it has a natural inclination to its proper act and end: and this participation of the eternal law in the rational creature is called the natural law."[44] Man is provident and actively participates in the eternal law and governance of God. Man does this through the practical intellect—especially the virtue of prudence—and applies the natural law to the particular situation, discerning the virtuous actions. The first principle of practical reason is simultaneously the first precept of the natural law—do good and avoid evil.[45] All other precepts of the natural law are founded on this first one such that the practical reason—using these

42. ST I-II, q. 55, a. 1.

43. Jean Porter similarly points out that our inclinations "are indeterminate in a way that the inclinations of nonrational creatures are not. They can be expressed in ways that undermine the agent's attainment of her good, as well as in ways that promote the agent's true good. If the inclinations are to function in such a way as to promote the agents true good, they must be directed by the appropriate dispositions toward action—and that is precisely what the virtues are." Jean Porter, *Nature As Reason: A Thomistic Theory of the Natural Law* (Grand Rapids, Michigan: Eerdman's, 2005), 176. We participate in our own formation in the natural law. As ST I-II, q. 91, a. 2 notes, through our proper acts of virtue guided by reason we participate in the eternal law.

44. ST I-II, q. 91, a. 2. "Inter cetera autem rationalis creatura excellentiori quodam modo divinae providentiae subiacet, inquantum et ipsa fit providentiae particeps, sibi ipsi et aliis providens. Unde et in ipsa participatur ratio aeterna, per quam habet naturalem inclinationem ad debitum actum et finem. Et talis participatio legis aeternae in rationali creatura lex naturalis dicitur."

45. ST I-II, q. 94, a. 2.

precepts—commands with the participative authority of the natural law. For this reason, St. Thomas notes that the proper act of prudence is to command the means to one's end, i.e. to command the virtues.[46] In this way, man applies the natural law to his life, and forms himself in it through the virtues. The authority of the practical reason—indeed prudence itself—is a participation in the natural law. Furthermore, by means of prudence's command, all the other cardinal virtues participate the natural law as well.[47]

As mentioned above, prudence, as the virtue of the practical intellect, commands the particular virtues with the authority of the natural law. In this way, through reason man rules and commands even himself.[48] "Every man, for as much as he is rational, participates in ruling according to the judgment of reason."[49] Through this same faculty of reason through which man participates in the eternal law and judges and commands with the participative authority of the natural law, man, as free and rational, is called a master [*dominus*] of his own actions.[50] Man has authority and dominion over himself; however, this does not create a defined "realm of sovereignty" or of "immunity" in the natural law. As master of his own actions, man governs himself and moves himself for an end—which for the will and the practical reason is "to do good and avoid evil."[51] He is still governed by the natural law which commands virtue. Yet, he applies and discerns the law in the particulars and contingencies. The rational creature receives the law—in the first principle of practical reason and in the inclinations of his very

46. ST II-II, q. 47, aa. 6 and 8.

47. ST I-II 61, a. 4.

48. ST II-II, q. 47, aa. 8, 9, and 12.

49. ST II-II, q. 47, 12. "... quilibet homo, inquantum est rationalis, participat aliquid de regimine secundum arbitrium rationis ..."

50. ST I-II, q. 1, a. 1. "Differt autem homo ab aliis irrationalibus creaturis in hoc, quod est suorum actuum dominus ... Est autem homo dominus suorum actuum per rationem et coluntatem." David Lantigua in "Image of God, Christian Rights Talk, and the School of Salamanca" argues that the concepts of human *dominium* or authority and mastery for St. Thomas proved crucial for the later Spanish scholasticism of the School of Salamanca. Vitoria especially "appealed to Aquinas's teaching on the image of God in order to identify the ontological and moral basis upon which the possession of things, and political self-rule, could be asserted legally—that a human person as *dominus actionem* or owner of his act" (31). The Salamanca scholastics thus deployed St. Thomas's understandings of rights due to another in justice in reference to the Amerindians. These same Amerindians were understood as having true authority over themselves and in politics in virtue of being made in the image of God and therefore having *dominium*. As true masters of themselves and their land, they had certain rights in justice. "[I]t was this theological anthropological view [concerning the image of God] that enabled them [the School of Salamanca] to generate a discourse concerning *human* natural rights" (33). Italics in original.

51. ST I-II, q. 91, a. 2.

nature to its end—and governs and rules according to it. Man does not operate within some "autonomous sphere" in the natural law that is somehow outside of the duties of justice. Rather, as a participative authority, he is a ruled ruler and his intellect a measured measurer.[52]

Given this discussion of St. Thomas's understanding of natural law and man's participative authority within it, I return to Tierney's idea of permissive natural law as "natural law [that] defined an area of human autonomy and free choice but not a state of total license."[53] To search for an area of human autonomy in the natural law, even if it were bounded or defined by certain commands, would seem on St. Thomas's account to be fruitless—at best—and fundamentally misguided, at worst. As noted above, for St. Thomas the natural law is nothing but man's participation of the eternal law of God, by which He providentially governs creation.[54] To look for permissive natural law or "'a realm of sovereignty or of relatively completely free choice'"[55] on this account would be to look for an area in our lives which was not subject to divine providence, where we were somehow left *alone*.[56] It would be looking for the "state of nature" in the midst of "the garden." Finding a sphere of autonomy in the natural law would be tantamount to the claim that either God does not govern or only governs in a deistic, metaphorical sense. Man participates in God's governance through his inclinations and his practical reason. He is a steward who participates in the authority of another, not an autonomous authority or even a circumscribed sovereign. Similarly, since "all acts of virtue are prescribed by the natural law"[57] such a search for an area of human autonomy in the law or a realm of sovereignty in the natural law would be to look for an area seemingly not under the purview of virtue as living out our end as grasped by the practical reason.[58] Such a search would be meaningless, if not

52. Martin Rhonheimer, *Natural Law and Practical Reason: A Thomist View of Moral Autonomy*, translated by Gerald Malsbary (New York: Fordham University Press, 2000), 244.

53. Tierney, "Natural Law and Natural Rights," 401.

54. ST I-II, q. 91, a. 2.

55. Brian Tierney, "Natural Law and Natural Rights," 395.

56. Indeed, it would be impossible: "Where can I go from your spirit? / From your presence, where can I flee? / If I ascend to the heavens, you are there; / if I lie down in Sheol, there you are. / If I take the wings of dawn/ and dwell beyond the sea, / Even there your hand guides me, / your right hand holds me fast." Psalm 139: 7–10.

57. ST I-II, q. 94, a.3.

58. ST I, q. 79, a. 12; II-II, q. 47, a. 6, ad 1–2. The rational creature judges according to the first precept of practical reason—to do good and avoid evil—and all the precepts drawn from it. To look for a "sphere" or "realm of sovereignty" within the natural law—within man's participation in

sinful.[59] Such a conception of God's governance and "area" or "zone" for man's freedom views God's governance and law as a competitor with man's freedom, which is not the vision of St. Thomas.[60] The natural law, grasped and applied by the practical intellect, enables man to rationally participate in his own formation as true master (*dominus*) as well as makes him truly free to choose to participate in the good. In all this, man is fundamentally a participatory authority and not an autonomous one. Man needs no sphere of autonomous authority for the whole of the natural law is the domain of man's participative authority as true master (*dominus*) of his actions.

2. *Right and Justice under the Law*. Given this understanding of St. Thomas's conception of natural law and man's authority and freedom within it, I now turn to St. Thomas's handling of *ius* or "right." Accordingly, I will examine the way St. Thomas defines *ius*, its relationship to justice and the common good, and the way that St. Thomas uses the word in several examples in other parts of the *Summa Theologiae*. For Aquinas, who quotes St. Isidore of Seville approvingly, "'*ius* is so called because it is fair [*iustum*].' Now the fair [*iustum*] is the object of justice ... Therefore, *ius* is the object of justice."[61] As the object of justice, *ius* seems to be roughly equivalent to "right"

---

the eternal law—regardless of how circumscribed would seem then to remove man's participation and thereby remove at the very least the principles and standard by which the practical reason judges. It would destroy man's ability to reason practically, on Aquinas's account.

59. One might worry about the search for such an area of sovereignty from virtue, as human flourishing, or from the participation in the eternal law. "Were [human moral] autonomy to imply a denial of the participation of the practical reason in the wisdom of the divine Creator and Lawgiver, or were it to suggest a freedom which creates moral norms, on the basis of historical contingencies or the diversity of societies and cultures, this sort of alleged autonomy would contradict the Church's teaching on the truth about man. It would be the death of true freedom: 'But of the tree of the knowledge of good and evil you shall not eat, for in the day that you eat of it you shall die' (Gen. 2:17)." Pope St. John Paul II, *Veritatis Splendor*, Vatican Translation, (Boston: Pauline Books and Media, 2003), no. 40, p. 56.

60. Indeed, the view of eternal and natural laws as competitors to man's freedom and authority is not the mind of St. Thomas, as if God and creatures could ever be in competition. Such a view has more in common with Thomas Hobbes than Thomas Aquinas. When speaking about natural law, Hobbes asserts that "right, consisteth in liberty to do, or to forbeare; whereas law, determineth, and bindeth to one of them: so that law, and right, differ as much, as obligation, and liberty; which in one and the same matter are inconsistent." Thomas Hobbes, *Leviathan*, edited by C.B. Macpherson (New York: Penguin Putnam, 1985), part 1, chap. 14, p. 189.

61. ST II-II, q. 57, a. 1. "ius dictum est quia est iustum. Sed iustum est objectum iustitiae... Ergo ius est objectum iustitiae." Here Aquinas is quoting the same line of Isidore as Gratian does. See *Decretum Gratiani*, dist. 1, c. 2. I will from time to time note when St. Thomas is quoting from Gratian's *Decretum* or from a source that is important to Gratian, though my references will in no way be exhaustive. It is important to note such quotes though even if only in passing. As Jean Porter excellently points out, St. Thomas does not have a unified "theory of rights, but neither do

in the sense of "right relation" or perhaps "*the* right" instead of "*a* right." However, Aquinas also notes that in a just relationship people must "render to each one his right [*suum ius*]."[62] It is important to note that even from the outset St. Thomas connects *ius* with *suum*. The right is what is another's; it is *theirs* in justice. While in the above definition of the object of justice St. Thomas undoubtedly means *ius* in an objective sense of right relation or another's due, even here at the outset St. Thomas quickly adds the understanding of *ius* as *claimed* or *belonging* to someone (*suum ius*).

Similarly, St. Thomas distinguishes *ius* from *lex* in ST II-II, q. 57, a.1, ad 2. He quotes St. Isidore again to note this difference.[63] Law must be written or transcribed in some way but this is not the case for the right (*ius*) or what is due another. Rather for St. Thomas, law (*lex*) is an expression of the right (*ius*). For this reason, St. Thomas notes that *ius* or the right is what "is adjusted to another or commensurate with another person."[64] Aquinas continues with similar statements throughout ST II-II, q. 57, noting that this adjustment and rendering to another their due creates an equality between the two parties. In fact, although the first definition of *ius* as the object of justice seems the more commonly quoted by Tierney and others, St. Thomas more frequently uses this above definition, referring to the right as what is "commensurate with another person." One then can see why justice (*iustitia*) and the right (*ius*) are so closely aligned. To be just one must give another what is their right or due proportionate and commensurable to them. The relationality of justice is necessarily presupposed in St. Thomas's understanding of a person's *ius* or what they are rightly owed.[65] Given all this, it is unsur-

the scholastic jurists of the time, and his appeals to what someone can claim by right are reminiscent of their views. If they can be said to have a notion of subjective natural rights [as Tierney argues], the same can be said of Aquinas himself." Porter, "Justice, Equality, And Natural Rights Claims," 448.

62. ST II-II, q. 57, a. 4, ad 1. "ad iustitiam pertinet reddere ius suum unicuique, supposita tamen diversitate unius ad alterum."

63. ST II-II, q. 57, a. 1, ad 2.

64. ST II-II, q. 57, a. 3. It should be noted that although Aquinas conceptually distinguishes law (*lex*) and right (*ius*), there are some exceptions in which he seems to use '*ius*' to mean law, most especially when he is quoting someone else, like St. Isidore, or referring to another's argument. However, in context, usually it is not terribly difficult to see when Aquinas intends to use the word 'right' and not 'law,' e.g. in ST I-II, q. 58, a. 2: "Reason rules the appetitive faculty by a political command/rule, like one in charge of free citizens, who have a right [*ius*] to a certain opposition" (Ratio imperat appetitivae principatu politico, quo scilicet aliquis praeest liberis, qui habent ius in aliquo contradicendi.) Trying to translate *ius* as 'law' in this political metaphor about free individuals and what they justly *have* would simply not makes sense.

65. ST II-II, q. 57, a. 4, ad 1. "It pertains to justice to render to each one his right [*ius suum*],

prising that St. Thomas would accept the definition of the canonists that justice "is fittingly defined as the constant and perpetual will to render each one his right [*ius suum*]."[66] Thus justice is only in someone insofar as they relate rightly to another and give them *their* due or *their* right.

In this depiction of justice and "the right" or what is due to another, undoubtedly St. Thomas uses *ius* in an objective sense as what is due to someone or the right relation to them. However, it is hard to make the stark distinction Brian Tierney wishes to make between this objective sense of *ius* and the subjective sense, especially as seen in Tierney's claim that "Aquinas's own definition [of right] did not have any reference to other persons' rights."[67] In reality St. Thomas's language of justice and right lends itself to the possessive or subjective right, speaking of "another person's due" or "his right" (*suum ius*).[68] Indeed, there is such a close association between the right and the subjective possession of it that Aquinas often seems to abbreviate "rendering a person his right [*suum ius*]" simply with "rendering another his [*suum*]."[69] From the outset *ius* is identified as an individual's and something they *have*. It is *theirs*. Furthermore, so little opposition is there

the distinction between individuals still being presupposed: for if someone were to give to himself what is due [*debetur*] to him [by another], this is not properly called 'just.'" The translation is my own.

66. ST II-II, q. 58, a. 1. The title of the question is "Utrum convenientur definiatur quod iustitia est constans et perpetua voluntas ius suum unicuique tribuens." Aquinas answers that the definition of the canonists is fitting if understood properly, namely as the virtue described as an act rather than as a habit. It is interesting to note that Aquinas in some of the objections leaves out *ius* and simply refers to justice as rendering to another what is *suum*. As is noted later, from the outset *ius* is identified as an individual's and something they *have*.

67. Tierney, "Natural Law and Natural Rights," 392.

68. This expression of *suum ius* is used in ST II-II, q. 57, a. 4, ad 1 and no less than an additional four times in ST II-II, q. 58, a. 1.

69. Aquinas refers to 'rendering another what is his right (*suum ius*)' simply with the expression of giving another '*quod suum est*' in ST II-II, 57, a. 1, ob. 1 and then again no less than seventeen times in ST II-II, q. 58. These two forms of expression come from the two formulations Aquinas gives of his definition of justice as it is drawn from the Roman definition that he accepts: "the act of justice in relation to its proper matter and object is indicated with the saying 'rendering to each one his right, [*ius suum unicuique tribuens*]' because, as Isidore says (Etym.), 'a man is called just who preserves the right [*quia ius custodit*].'" ST II-II, q. 58, a. 1. This fact is brought up by John Finnis in *Aquinas: Moral, Political, and Legal Theory* (New York: Oxford University Press, 1998), 133. Finnis notes that whenever Aquinas references this definition, he uses the two formulations interchangeably: "'what is theirs {*quod suum est*}' and 'what is their right {*ius suum*}.'" Finnis holds this shorthand of Aquinas and interchange of formulations is crucial for understanding the mind of St. Thomas. Thus, when speaking about this interchange of formulation, Finnis asks "How can it be denied that, as something that belongs to the person who has it, *ius* is 'subjective'?" Finnis, "Aquinas on *Ius*," 408.

between St. Thomas's usage of objective and subjective right that not only can both senses be found in the same sentence, but Aquinas even goes so far as to draw the subjective sense *directly from* the objective: "And therefore the act of justice in comparison to its proper matter and object is indicated with the saying 'rendering to each one his right [*suum ius*],' *because* [*quia*], as Isidore says (Etym.), 'a man is called just who preserves the right [*ius custodit*].'"[70] And ultimately, this should be no surprise. Justice is dynamic. It is relational.

Given all this, it seems very clear that St. Thomas does have both an objective and a subjective sense of "right." Accordingly, there seems to be a triple way of discussing justice: (1) as the proportionate or right relation, itself, between two different individuals that establishes an equality, as The Philosopher speaks of it;[71] (2) from the relation of the agent of justice to the recipient, as giving another his due or right, as Aquinas's above definition following the canonists defines the act of virtue (as opposed to habit); and (3) from the relation of the recipient of justice to the agent, as being given his or her right. Right is the object of justice in all three above senses, and not simply in the objective meaning of right. Given how closely St. Thomas uses and understands the two senses of right, I suggest that the modern or subjective usage of right or *ius* would correspond to and be the object of justice in all three of these above senses of justice as well. It is clear how the subjective sense of *ius* could be the object of justice in (2) and (3) above: as the object or matter of the agent of justice in his relating to the recipient and the object or matter the recipient of justice can claim as *his* (*suum*) in relating to the agent. However, it is more difficult to see how in the first above sense of justice—as right or proportionate relation—the subjective sense of *ius* can be seen as its object. Nevertheless, regarding this proper proportionality and right relation, St. Thomas himself points the way by observing that that "the matter of justice is an external operation in so far as either it or the thing we use by it is made proportionate to some other person to

70. ST II-II, q. 58, a. 1. "Et ideo actus iustitiae per comparationem ad propriam materiam et obiectum tangitur cum dicitur, ius suum unicuique tribuens, quia, ut Isidorus dicit, in libro Etymol., iustus dicitur quia ius custodit." This example is crucial not only because at the outset Aquinas gives his own definition which reflects subjective right and which seems to parallel the use of *ius* that is common to other medievals, especially the canonists, but most especially because Aquinas draws the subjective sense directly from the more Roman usage of objective right as expressed by Isidore.

71. See Aristotle, *Nicomachean Ethics* 5.1, 1129a1–1130a15, and 5.3, 1131a20–30.

whom we are related by justice. Now each person's own is that which is due to him according to equality of proportion. And therefore the proper act of justice is nothing else than to render to each one what is his right."[72] Here St. Thomas concludes that the matter of justice is an act and that this act establishes a relationship of equality between two persons. This act of justice, establishing proper relation, is nothing other than rendering to another his or her right. Thus, even in the first manner of discussing justice—as being in right relation—the object and aim of this right relation, and of the act establishing this relation, is another's right, in a subjective sense. For Aquinas rights, indeed the subjective or possessive use of the word 'right' or *ius*, are of unique importance to discussions of justice. Discussions of rights are not statements about justice merely placed in a different idiom, ultimately adding nothing to an investigation of justice. Nor are rights radically individualistic, demanding a sphere of autonomy. Rather, St. Thomas views rights language as necessary for a robust and full account of justice. Rights *belong* to another and are the very *object* of justice, which is a relational virtue that creates a proportion or right relation between people.[73] In this way, it seems that it must be acknowledged, either in part or in whole, that right or *ius* in its subjective sense is what St. Thomas is speaking of when he declares that "right [*ius*] is the object of justice." [74]

Furthermore, Aquinas not only emphasizes the necessary role that considerations of a person's rights play in discussions of justice but also the role such considerations play in seeking the common good. Unlike some popular conceptions of today, St. Thomas saw no competition between the common good and the rights of the person nor did he see the discussion of the common good as completely replacing the discussion of rights. Rather, although he agrees with the canonists that justice "is fittingly defined as the

72. ST II-II, q. 58, a. 11. "materia iustitiae est operatio exterior secundum quod ipsa, vel res qua per eam utimur, proportionatur alteri personae, ad quam per iustitiam ordinamur. Hoc autem dicitur esse suum uniuscuiusque personae quod ei secundum proportionis aequalitatem debetur. Et ideo proprius actus iustitiae nihil est aliud quam reddere unicuique quod suum est." As noted in the preceding paragraph and in note 69 above, in ST II-II, q. 57 and especially in q. 58, St. Thomas develops his own shorthand and interchangeable formulations of his definition of justice in which "rendering another his right" [*suum ius*] and "giving to another what is his" [*quod suum est*] are equivalent.

73. Such an understanding of rights is indeed quite different from that of say Patrick Deneen, who asserts that "the language of rights ultimately cannot build, or even sustain, a common life." Deneen, "The Ignoble Lie," 31. By contrast, for Aquinas one's rights seem to be a necessary aspect to any discussion of particular justice.

74. ST II-II, q. 57, a. 1.

constant and perpetual will to render each one his right [*ius suum*],"[75] Aquinas makes an important observation that this definition of justice is partly deficient. It does not name the habit properly but rather names the habit by its act and thereby its object. Thus, he says of the canonists' definition that it "is a complete definition of justice, except that the act is said instead of the habit, which is specified by the act, because habit implies relation to act. And if anyone wants to reduce it to the proper form of a definition, he would say that 'justice is a habit by which a man renders to each one his right [*suum ius*] by a constant and perpetual will.'"[76] Aquinas is very clear to note that the right of another is the object of justice considered as that habit by which one, through a constant and perpetual will, takes particular acts to render another his or her right. Putting this differently, the recipient's right (*ius suum*) is the object of particular justice or particular acts of justice. This understanding is crucial to grasping the mind of Aquinas on a person's right and its relationship to the common good because St. Thomas later discusses the relationship between general justice, which is ordered to the common good as its object, and particular justice, which is ordered to a person's right. Aquinas states:

> That justice which seeks the common good is another virtue from that [justice] which is ordered to a person's private good, and for this reason the common right is distinguished from a private right.... But that justice directing man to the common good is a general virtue through its act of command because it directs all the acts of the virtues to its own end, namely to the common good. Consequently, the virtues, in so far as they are commanded by that justice, receive the name of justice.[77]

Particular justice is a lower virtue governed by and directed towards general justice and its object which is the common good, the former type of justice having as its object the person's right. In this sense, rights proper to differ-

75. ST II-II, q. 58, a. 1. The title of the question is "Utrum convenientur definiatur quod iustitia est constans et perpetua voluntas ius suum unicuique tribuens" and Aquinas answers in the affirmative.

76. ST II-II, q. 58, a. 1. "Et ideo praedicta definitio est completa definitio iustitiae, nisi quod actus ponitur pro habitu, qui per actum specificatur, habitus enim ad actum dicitur. Et si quis vellet in debitam formam definitionis reducere, posset sic dicere, quod iustitia est habitus secundum quem aliquis constanti et perpetua voluntate ius suum unicuique tribuit."

77. ST I-II, q. 60, a. 3, ad 2. "[Q]uod iustitia quae intendit bonum commune, est alia virtus a iustitia quae ordinatur ad bonum privatum alicuius, unde et ius commune distinguitur a iure privato ... Sed iustitia ordinans hominem ad bonum commune, est generalis per imperium, quia omnes actus virtutum ordinat ad finem suum, scilicet ad bonum commune. Virtus autem secundum quod a tali iustitia imperatur, etiam iustitiae nomen accipit."

ent persons are integral to and ordered to considerations of the common good, of which they are an aspect, just as considerations of particular justice would be an aspect of and governed by larger considerations of general justice. Indeed, one would not really understand general justice at all if one also did not understand the ways that it governs particular acts of justice. So too, one does not understand the common good if one does not simultaneously grasp the rights of individuals and the way they are ordered to the common good. General justice, furthermore, is not, on Aquinas's account, merely the aggregate consideration of all particular rights, but rather general justice is the rendering of the common good (*bonum commune*), a rendering which governs considerations of particular justice. Just as it would be incorrect to say that general justice is the aggregate of considerations of particular justice, likewise it would miss the mark to say that the common good is the mere aggregate of all individuals' rights. For Aquinas, rights language does not replace discussions of the common good and neither do discussions of the common good replace the discussion of rendering another their right (*suum ius*). Both the concept of the common good and of one's right are integral to the discussion of justice and, because of the governing role of general justice over particular justice, neither concept is fully understood without some discussion of the other.

3. *Aquinas's Analysis and Specific Examples of Rights.* Up to this point, I have noted not only the relationship that right (*ius*) has to justice and to the common good but also pointed out the way that St. Thomas's own subjective usage of the word "*ius*" does parallel the modern language of personal rights insofar as Aquinas regularly observes that this subjective *ius* or right as one's due is something one *has,* a fact which Tierney himself notes.[78] However, Tierney dismisses these subjective usages in Aquinas's works as "unreflective."[79] Such a response to St. Thomas's own discussion of *ius* seems shortsighted, especially in light of the way Aquinas intentionally deploys the concept of right in political metaphors and in the analysis of certain moral powers belonging to human persons. Aquinas's examples and his use of "right" in the analysis of other aspects of his thought confirm the interpretation that St. Thomas does understand *ius* in a subjective sense

78. Tierney, "Natural Law and Natural Rights," 392.

79. See Tierney, "Natural Law and Natural Rights," 392n12. Tierney makes this claim most strongly in *The Idea of Natural Rights,* 23 but also repeats it in "Author's Rejoinder" *The Review of Politics* 64, no. 3 (2002): 416–17.

and, indeed, reveal the very sense that Tierney and Villey look for concerning subjective right, namely, a concept of *ius* explicitly linked to a 'faculty' (*facultas*) or 'moral power' (*potestas*) and which belongs to individual persons.[80] To show this I will briefly look at three examples: Aquinas's political analogy for the relationship between reason and the passions, his discussion of man's dominion over creation, and his discussion of the rights and authority of parents over their children.

Perhaps the starkest example of St. Thomas's use of "right" concerns the governing or seemingly political relationship between reason—through the virtues, especially prudence—and the passions. St. Thomas notes in ST I-II, q. 58, a. 2 that, concerning the limbs of the body, the soul rules "the limbs by a despotic command, as a master rules his servant, who does not *have a right* [*non habet ius*] of opposition."[81] Following Aristotle's own example, St. Thomas uses a political metaphor concerning how the soul rules the body; however, he adds by way of explanation the expression "to have a right," or more specifically to "not have" one, in order to spell out the Philosopher's point. In contrast with the limbs, St. Thomas also notes that commanding reason rules the passions like a political authority—like "one in charge of free citizens, who *have* a right [*ius*] to some opposition."[82] Here St. Thomas is not "unreflectively" borrowing or slipping into the usage of the canonists, as Tierney claims.[83] Aquinas is very intentionally explaining Aristotle's political analogies through the way some individuals have a right to oppose the way they are being led, and this is used to speak about the way reason governs and commands the appetites. Accordingly, in his political metaphors St. Thomas is using *ius* or right in a way that is *very* similar to modern expressions of a person "having a right." Furthermore, he even closely connects having rights with freedom in a society, in a relationship between ruler and ruled. Indeed, in Aquinas's political analogy, "right" could almost be substituted by the word "power," "will," or "faculty" by which free citizens can be said to have a certain right or moral "power" of opposition. In fact,

80. Tierney, *The Idea of Natural Rights*, 28, 54–58; Villey, "La genèse du droit subjectif," 100–102, 117, 120.

81. ST I-II, q. 58, a. 2. "... anima regit corpus despotico principatu, idest sicut dominus servum, qui ius contradicendi non habet." Italics added.

82. ST I-II, q. 58, a. 2. "... ratio imperat appetitivae principatu politico, quo scilicet aliquis praeest liberis, qui habent ius in aliquo contradicendi." Italics added. Aquinas, following Aristotle, consistently describes the relationship between commanding reason and the passions with a political metaphor. Reason rules the passions not as a tyrant or a despot but with a political rule.

83. Tierney, "Author's Rejoinder," 416–17.

Aquinas speaks exactly this way when using this same political metaphor in another area. In ST I-II q. 56, a. 4, ad 3, Aquinas characterizes the kind of oppositional power that the irascible and concupiscible powers have regarding reason as a kind of *will* that can oppose in a manner that parallels free citizens.[84] These political examples intentionally unite concepts of right (*ius*), freedom, and a moral power or faculty, namely the will, even outside of the explicit questions on justice and right in order to explain a point Aristotle makes about reason and the passions. They hardly seem unreflective.[85]

The closeness in the concepts of a power (*potestas*), faculty (*facultas*), and right (*ius*) can also be seen in Aquinas's own discussions of property and dominion (*dominium*) in ST II-II, q. 66. Initially, Aquinas discusses man's natural dominion as a "power of using" (*potestas utendi*) and also "managing" (*dispensandi*) things.[86] He further discusses the power of acquiring/appropriating property. The human person has this power of using, proper to human dominion, by nature, Aquinas notes in this question, because of the faculties of intellect and will, which are the hallmarks of the image and likeness of God in us.[87] In a further article within this very same question, Aquinas substitutes "right" for "power," using the phrase "have the right of possessing" (*haberet ius possidendi*) where exclusively before he had used phrases such as "power of possessing or governing" (*potestas procurandi*) or "power of using" (*potestas utendi*).[88] Furthermore, although in ST II-II, q. 66 Aquinas usually describes "dominion" as a "power" and notes

84. ST I-II, q. 56, a. 4, ad 3. "Sed irascibilis et concupiscibilis non ad nutum obediunt rationi, sed habent proprios motus suos, quibus interdum rationi repugnant, unde in eodem libro philosophus dicit quod ratio regit irascibilem et concupiscibilem principatu politico, quo scilicet reguntur liberi, qui habent in aliquibus propriam voluntatem." In this connection of 'freedom,' power/will, and 'right,' Aquinas seems very much in line with the canonistic understanding of 'right.' Cf. Tierney, *The Idea of Natural Rights*, 54–60. Tierney notes that Gratian himself also connected the concepts of *libertas* and *potestas* to that of '*ius*.' See Tierney, *The Idea of Natural Rights*, 57. Indeed, he even notes that glossators paraphrased some of Innocent III's work by describing right or '*ius*' as a "free power." St. Thomas's own usage seems very much in line with theirs. If the canonists had an understanding of 'subjective' rights, as Tierney rightly claims, then it seems one must hold that Aquinas does too.

85. For other similar examples of how St. Thomas uses '*ius*' even outside of the explicit questions on right and justice, see John Finnis, *Aquinas: Moral, Political, and Legal Theory* (New York: Oxford University Press, 1998), 133–34 and especially footnotes 10 and 12.

86. ST II-II, q. 66, aa. 1–2. This can be seen especially in a.1, ad.1 when Aquinas discusses human dominion as the power of using (*potestem utendi*). Aquinas later refers to dominion/the power to use things as the power to procure, govern, manage, appropriate or dispense in ST II-II, q. 66, a. 2.

87. ST II-II, q. 66, a. 1.

88. ST II-II, q. 66, a. 5, ad 2.

that man has this "dominion" because of the faculties of intellect and will, earlier in ST II-II, q. 62, a. 1, ad 2 Aquinas prefers the phrase "right of dominion" (*ius dominii*).[89] Aquinas is not "unreflectively" using his terms; rather, he is explaining why persons have certain moral powers or rights and why these rights or powers are properly called *theirs*, namely because they have a certain authority and are true masters of their actions on account of the faculties of intellect and will. This closeness in the thought of St. Thomas between a moral power and a right because of the underlying natural faculties of intellect and will is the very usage that Villey and Tierney are looking for regarding an articulation of subjective rights.[90] Indeed, with his articulation of the *ius dominii*, this is probably the closest that Aquinas gets to discussing what today we would call a "universal human right."[91]

A final example, one which is brought up by Jean Porter, where St. Thomas's affirmation of rights seems to parallel the modern usage is his dis-

89. Tierney explicitly claims this reference to '*ius dominii*' is one of Aquinas's 'unreflective usages' of right or *ius*, in his *Idea of Natural Rights*, 23. However, as I show, Aquinas's usage of '*ius*' or right in this 'subjective' way is not 'unreflective' or unintentional and should not be dismissed or glossed over out of hand but rather should be examined seriously.

90. Tierney, *The Idea of Natural Rights*, 28, 54–58; Villey, "La genèse du droit subjectif," 100–102, 117, 120. Given this, it seems then that it must also be concluded that, contra Tierney, de Vitoria can be said to be faithfully developing St. Thomas's thought—and not simply smuggling in Gerson or Summenheart or "misinterpret[ing]" Aquinas by connecting 'power,' 'faculty,' and 'right,' as Tierney claims—since it is to these very passages that Vitoria looks in his own articulation of natural rights. See Tierney, *Idea of Natural Rights*, 69, 256–63. De Vitoria, for instance, draws the foundation of his argument in *de Indiis* q. 1, a. 1 from some of these very passages from St. Thomas regarding dominion and ownership. Indeed, he argues that the Amerindians have the right of dominion/authority and right of ownership as true masters [*domini*] by reason of their human nature and the fact that all are by nature in the image and likeness of God, having the faculties of intellect and will. Given the above understanding of St. Thomas, it is clear that de Vitoria does no violence to St. Thomas's thought in applying it to the Amerindians and their situation, but instead he seems quite faithful in his reading, so long as one does not obstinately hold that Aquinas *never* uses or thinks of anything but the objective sense of *ius*.

91. Although Aquinas has a concept of subjective right that seems to match what modern speakers mean by a right and although he calls dominion (*dominium*) a right proper to individuals because of the faculties of reason and will, he does not explicitly develop a concept for or speak of a group of rights which modern speakers would recognize as "universal human rights." Such rights belonging to the human person, as such, were first articulated and applied to concrete situations by the Salamanca theologians who used Aquinas's theological anthropology and understanding of dominium "to generate a discourse concerning *human* natural rights." David Lantigua, "Image of God, Christian Rights Talk, and the School of Salamanca", 33. Italics in original. See Francisco de Vitoria, "On the American Indians," in *Political Writings*, ed. Anthony Pagden and Jeremy Lawrence (Cambridge: Cambridge University Press, 1991), 231–92. Nonetheless, as was shown by the Salamanca theologians, such a theory of universal human rights would not be at odds with Aquinas's views on the '*ius suum*' and dominion.

cussion of whether Jewish children can be baptized against their parents' wishes. Aquinas argues that not only would such a practice be against the universal practice of the Church, but that this would be contrary to justice since the parents "would lose the right [*ius*] of parental authority or governance over their children as soon as they became Catholic."[92] Again, he notes that it would be contrary to natural justice to baptize a child who is before the age of reason against the wishes of their parents because "by natural right [*de iure naturali*] ... he is under the care of his parents."[93] This passage from St. Thomas could easily be read in the sense of objective right or what is objectively fair and due according to justice as setting up duties rather than in the sense of a subjective right that one has; however, Porter argues that St. Thomas's understanding only makes sense if the individuals *have* a right they can claim. "After all, Aquinas says that it would be contrary to natural justice to baptize the child of unwilling parents, implying that these parents, as individuals, are asserting a claim to raise their child as they see fit. The general considerations that Aquinas sets out are only salient because these individuals are asserting a claim, as individuals, pertaining to the upbringing of this specific child."[94] This claim, Porter notes, is grounded in natural right generally and takes the form of a specific claim.

Accordingly, it can be seen that St. Thomas does, in fact, have both an objective and a subjective meaning of *ius* or right and, as Jean Porter notes, that "these are not [mutually] exclusive options."[95] From the outset of Aquinas's articulation of natural right and justice, *ius* does have subjective and, indeed, possessive usages as one's right in justice. As John Finnis argues, "the Tierney-Villey characterization of *iustum* (and also of *ius*) as 'the right thing or state of affairs that justice [seeks] to achieve' omits an essential element in Aquinas's conception: one cannot properly think of *ius* without

92. ST II-II, q. 10, a. 12. "Fieret autem Iudaeis iniuria si eorum filii baptizarentur eis invitis, quia amitterent ius patriae potestatis in filios iam fideles." Cited by Jean Porter, "Justice, Equality, And Natural Rights Claims," 453–4.

93. ST II-II, q. 10, a. 12. "Alia vero ratio est quia repugnat iustitiae naturali ... ita de iure naturali est quod filius, antequam habeat usum rationis, sit sub cura patris." It is proper to translate '*iure naturali*' as natural right here rather than 'natural law' because, as Aquinas's earlier distinction in ST II-II, q. 57, a. 1, ad 2 between *ius* and *lex* makes clear, law must be written or transcribed in some way but this is not the case for the right [*ius*] or what is due another. For St. Thomas, law [*lex*] is an expression of the right [*ius*]. In the above quote, Aquinas is not appealing to a written or transcribed law, even to the natural law or the Decalogue, but rather to the natural object of justice regarding the just relationship of parent to child.

94. Porter, "Justice, Equality, And Natural Rights Claims," 453.

95. Ibid., 450.

thinking of the *other* … Which *other*? The one who, as Aquinas promptly and constantly says, HAS the relevant *ius*. Thus *ius* can closely match our word 'right.'"[96] The close association of *ius* with justice for St. Thomas requires not only an objective but also a subjective aspect. In this latter aspect, St. Thomas *does* have a concept of subjective rights that a person *has* in a just relationship and which can be said to be his or hers and which is such a relationship's very object. Furthermore, this right is even spoken of at times as synonymous with a kind of moral power such as the "right of opposition" connected to freedom or as synonymous with the power of possessing, on account of an underlying faculty, namely of intellect and will, by which individuals have authority or dominion. In this sense, Aquinas develops and deploys a concept similar to the very sense that modern individuals mean by having a right.[97]

IV. Conclusion

In the final analysis, there is St. Thomas's understanding of "right," on the one hand, and permissive natural law that is so connected to the thought of Brian Tierney, on the other. In the three main interpretive options—(1) that St. Thomas Aquinas has a conception of individual rights but no sphere

96. Finnis, "Aquinas on *Ius*," 408. Italics in original.

97. At this point, it is clear (1) that Aquinas speaks of a subjective right that an individual subject *has* (*habet*) and which can be said to be his or hers (*suum*), and is even spoken of sometimes as synonymous with a kind of moral power, such as the "right of opposition" connected to freedom or as synonymous with the power of possessing and (2) that it is mistaken to try to look for a sphere of autonomous authority within the thought of Aquinas, as if the whole of the natural law were not also the domain of man's participative authority as true master (*dominus*) of his actions or as if there were a zone outside of the demands of justice and thus rights. However, if one wished to raise again the objection of Villey, Strauss, Tierney, MacIntyre or others that, even if St. Thomas's conception of subjective rights does not require a sphere of autonomous agency, the modern conception does then it must be replied that although in modern discourse, rights and autonomy are sometimes linked, this link is by no means a necessary one, as John Finnis argues. "Indeed," notes Finnis in response to Tierney's ideas, "the rights which head up modern declarations of 'subjective rights,' such as the right to life and the right not to be tortured, do not delimit a 'sphere of personal autonomy.' Nor does having such rights entail that one is free 'to exercise the right or not exercise it as he or she chooses.'" Finnis, "Aquinas on *Ius*," 409. It must be added that not only does right not entail autonomy, but autonomy, according to Finnis, does not entail rights. "Even advocates arguing in court for suicide or euthanasia make little or no attempt to claim that the autonomy they are pleading for is entailed by the logic of the modern concept of 'a right to.' Judges, lawyers, and contemporary legal theorists, thoroughly attuned to 'modern thought,' know that rights are simply not constrained within the straightjacketed conceptual structure which, Tierney, Villey, Strauss … *et al.* assert is 'the modern concept of rights.'" (409).

of autonomy, as held by John Finnis; (2) that Aquinas has neither a conception of individual rights nor a sphere of autonomy, as asserted by Tierney and Villey; and (3) that St. Thomas has a conception of both individual rights and a sphere of autonomy, as Jean Porter puts forward—it seems one must decide in favor of the first option. However, while Finnis appears to be right in fact, the reason why he is correct, namely St. Thomas's participatory understanding of natural law and virtue, does not figure into his argument. Indeed, it is this participatory account of the natural law that makes discrete "realms" or "zones of autonomy" or "spheres of moral sovereignty" unnecessary and so out of place in the thought of Aquinas while simultaneously making each person a true master (*dominus*) of his own actions in freedom. Aquinas needs no such "areas of autonomy" to solve a competition between law and freedom or to assert man's authority and thus his rights in justice. There is no such competition between the natural law and man's freedom, authority, and rights. As such, Aquinas easily unites concepts of freedom and rights of persons within a context of justice. Rights are something a person *has*, can be said to be *one's own*, and are even at times spoken of as a "right" of opposition connected with freedom or as synonymous with a kind of moral power ("power of possessing") which has its foundation in the natural faculties of human agency, namely intellect and will, and are so connected to the image of God. For Aquinas, man's authority is participative, not autonomous, and his rights relational in justice and not independent.

Furthermore, St. Thomas's own participative theory of law and right is exceedingly fertile for properly grounding modern rights discourse today, just as it was fertile ground for those Salamanca theologians like Vitoria in the 1500s.[98] At the outset of the essay, I noted Alasdair MacIntyre's now famous phrase regarding rights, that "the truth is plain: there are no such rights, and belief in them is one with the belief in witches and unicorns."[99] However, when pressed on this assertion, MacIntyre clarified that what he was critiquing in *After Virtue* were the "eighteenth century claims, wheth-

98. Indeed, it is not only the Salamanca theologians who have found St. Thomas's conception of rights a fertile ground for discussions of natural justice but also more recent magisterial teaching. Russell Hittinger notes that in *Rerum Novarum* (1891) Pope Leo XIII draws his own use of "rights language" regarding the right of association by laborers directly from St. Thomas's own thought, specifically *Contra impugnantes*. Cf. Hittinger, *The First Grace*, 274.

99. Alasdair MacIntyre, *After Virtue: A Study in Moral Theory* (Notre Dame, Indiana: University of Notre Dame Press, 2003), 69.

er American or French, that there are rights that first attach to individuals *as such* and that ascriptions of such rights can function as first and evident premises in our practical reason."[100] *These* rights, he says, are mistaken and are thus fictions. MacIntyre's main target, however, is the radical and autonomous individual in whom these rights inhere.[101] This type of individual is a fiction and thus so are the rights that he would have. In contrast, MacIntyre notes: "We need to reach conclusions about what rights human beings have or should have, but these are to be derived from quite other types of premises, from premises about the common good and about what both justice and generosity, virtues that are directed towards the common good, require in this or that particular situation."[102] Indeed, the sorts of rights that MacIntyre counsels as the ones society should seek are the very sorts of rights that are able to be discussed only through St. Thomas's participatory understanding of natural law and right. Aquinas's participatory understanding of the rights of the person necessarily excludes the possibility of the "autonomous individual" and instead draws upon the proper understanding of the relationality of justice, rights as the proper object of particular acts of justice, and, thereby, upon the proper understanding of the common good. In Aquinas's understanding, rights are not in competition with the common good but are a constitutive part of it. The common good is the object of general justice, that governing virtue which is not understood unless one grasps how it orders particular acts of justice (understood as rendering another his right) to the good of all. The common good for Aquinas, and indeed, discussions of justice at the greatest scale, cannot be had without this understanding of the subject's rights. As such, it must be asserted that Aquinas's thought on participatory natural law, objective and subjective rights, and the common good is thus the very fertile seedbed for the types of rights MacIntyre asserts are needed going forward.

100. Alasdair MacIntyre, "What Else Needs to Be Said? A Beginning, Although Only a Beginning, at Saying It," in *Revolutionary Aristotelianism: Ethics, Resistance, and Utopia*, a special issue of *Analyse & Kritik* 30 (2008): 272. Italics added.

101. Ibid., 272.

102. Ibid.

THOMAS ROURKE

Yves R. Simon, Alasdair MacIntyre, and Distributism

Justice in Exchange in the Contemporary Market Economy

I. Introduction

Yves R. Simon and Alasdair MacIntyre are Thomists convinced that fundamental and substantial injustices have embedded themselves in the modern market system, a fact that has generally been covered over by professional economists. Both saw the profit motive, disconnected from an Aristotelian-Thomistic conception of the common good, as the source of the problem. MacIntyre developed more the philosophical underpinnings of the problem, analyzing the fundamental rift between moral reasoning as found in its Aristotelian-Thomistic form as opposed to the fundamentally incompatible reasoning as found in people like Hume and Smith, which served as the justification of the modern capitalist market system. For his part, Simon was more extensive in his demonstration of how the profit motive as an end permitted the undermining of justice in exchanges, for him the locus of the moral problem of the system as it developed through the Industrial Revolution and the formation of modern, corporate capitalism. Both MacIntyre and Simon were further aware that capitalism failed morally insofar as it converted human laborers from the fullness of personhood into impersonal commodities to be bought and sold in exchange. Ultimately, for both, modern capitalism fails from the Thomist perspective because it lacks a clear concept of the common good materially considered. In the last part of the essay, we will explore ways in which distributism attempts to solve the problems without falling into the errors of statism and other violations of the principle of subsidiarity, in short, avoiding the errors of Marxism.

The entire problem of modern capitalism begins truly with the desire to possess what one lacks a good reason to desire. An incorrect relationship between reason and desire is the root of all evil for both Aristotle and Aquinas. A strong sense of justice in exchange tends to limit the tendency of human beings to acquire profit excessively. This holds so long as the value of a product is measured in terms of its use. People have a strong sense of what goods are useful for, and exchanges based on a common sense of the use value of a product tend to be just; people have a good common sense of the worth of a head of lettuce or a pair of work boots. Under normal circumstances, people do not trade away goods necessary to sustain life for trivialities. However, as Aristotle discusses in *The Politics*, there is a second and inherently more problematic kind of exchange, in which goods are exchanged primarily for their exchange value, not their use value; instead of trading a pair of shoes for some pants, I sell the shoes for money.[1] Of course, neither MacIntyre nor Simon see anything intrinsically evil in this. Indeed, Simon explicitly states that under the conditions of a normal human community, where buyers and sellers share a common sense of what counts as a good life along with common sense notions of justice and fairness, money exchanges will remain tied to a sense that their genuine use value and justice itself can be readily approximated in the exchanges which occur. Markets in small towns in the pre-industrial age largely presented no major deviations from justice and fairness.[2]

As an essential historical and philosophical note, Aquinas would permit merchants to sell a product at a higher price than they purchased it under five circumstances: (a) to compensate for expenses incurred during the trading; (b) when the buyer made the purchased object into something more valuable; (c) when the merchant had to take unusual risks to produce the good; (d) when the merchant had to pay a third party in order to complete the transaction; and (e) when changes in social circumstances made

1. Aristotle, *Politics* 1.9, 1257a. Saint Thomas follows the discussion in similar terms in *Summa Theologiae* (ST) II-II, q. 77, a. 4.

2. Yves R. Simon, *Work, Society and Culture* (New York: Fordham University Press, 1971), 121.

the object more valuable.[3] MacIntyre is clear as to the point the exceptions underline:

> It is never permissible to engage in market transactions only to make a profit or primarily to make a profit. The pursuit of profit for its own sake is unjust. The point and purpose of monetary exchange in markets is to enable us all to benefit from each other's labour, and financial gain is to be valued only for the goods for which it can be exchanged and for the needs that it thereby enables us to meet. We are to grow wealthier by becoming more productive. Increasing profit is never a sufficient reason for engaging in one kind of market transaction rather than another. [T]he acquisition of money is no more than a means to the ... acquisition of goods and that such achievement and acquisition is to serve common goods.[4]

In other words, for Aquinas, money is merely a means to acquiring goods, such goods being arranged hierarchically, with common goods taking priority over individual ones. Our desires need to be ordered in relation to the objective order of goods. To desire money itself as an end is not legitimate; a life devoted to the acquisition of money is a life of disordered desire.[5]

3. Alasdair MacIntyre, *Ethics in the Conflicts of Modernity: An Essay on Desire, Practical Reasoning, and Narrative* (Cambridge: Cambridge University Press, 2016), 90–91. Aquinas discusses the conditions under which one can sell something for more than he paid for it and justices in exchange generally in ST II-II, q. 77 aa. 1–4. Saint Thomas follows Aristotle here in distinguishing between "natural transactions" by which people fulfill genuine needs for the maintenance of life (e.g., buying food for one's family), and "commercial transactions," which are done for the purpose of making a profit. The second is rightly subject to moral scrutiny, because "it satisfies the greed for gain, which knows no limit and tends to infinity." ST II-II, q. 77, a. 4. [Notre Dame, IN: Christian Classics, 1981]. However, profit can be justified if it is used for an intrinsically good end, such as providing for one's household, helping the poor, or providing for the public good (ST II-II, q. 77, a. 4). Generally, the measure of justice in exchanges is the "equality of things" exchanged (ST II-II, q. 77, a. 1). Under certain conditions—e.g., having enhanced the value of the original product purchased, or having incurred losses related to the sale, a changed set of economic circumstances related to the sale price, or having undertaken risks in the acquisition of the product—a seller is morally permitted to raise the sale price above the price at which he originally purchased it (ST II-II, q. 77, a. 4).

4. Alasdair MacIntyre, *Ethics in the Conflicts of Modernity*, 91.

5. Ibid. As Aquinas puts it: "In whatever things good consists in a due measure, evil must of necessity ensue through excess or deficiency of that measure. Now in all things that are for an end, the good consists in a certain measure: since whatever is directed to an end must needs be commensurate with the end, as, for instance, medicine is commensurate with health, as the Philosopher observes. External goods come under the head of things useful for an end ... Hence it must needs be that man's good in their respect consists in a certain measure, in other words, that man seeks, according to a certain measure, to have external riches in so far as they are necessary for him to live in keeping with his condition of life. Wherefore it will be a sin for him to exceed this measure, by wishing to acquire or keep them immoderately. This is what is meant by avarice which is defined as immoderate love of possessing." ST II-II, q. 118, a. 1.

In order to keep the discourse here tethered to considerations of the contemporary world, it is necessary to establish that Thomism would take the further step of insisting that restraints put on the profit motive should be institutionalized. Institutionalization can only work when backed by political authority. Hence it is necessary to review the proper role of the pursuit of individual goods such as profit in relation to common goods and *the* common good, and the role of political authority with respect to both.

In the Thomist framework, private property is normally legitimate and is generally the best way to insure that goods are properly cared for. However, Thomism also grants a priority to the principle of common use. Given the moral priority Saint Thomas concedes to the necessities of life, and the right of people to access them, private property rights are strictly limited. No one has the right to accumulate unnecessary goods in the face of unmet human needs. In fact, in a time of famine, all food becomes common property.[6] Saint Thomas never developed a theory of government intervention; it is also clear that his preference would be for a way to work out tensions between individuals and the common good voluntarily. Yet, given the indubitable necessity to ensure access to necessary goods, it is legitimate to concede a role for the state under modern circumstances to ensure adequate conditions of life and work, particularly in an age characterized by such a high degree of concentration of wealth and economic centralization. Surely the Catholic Church, arguably Saint Thomas's principle modern interpreter, has always made the same conclusion.[7]

II. Yves R. Simon

Although many U.S. conservatives have long expressed a concern that appeals to the common good in economics inevitably degenerate into statist centralism and the socialism the Church clearly condemns, the criticism actually has no basis within the Thomist argument. As Yves Simon argued so compellingly, the pursuit of particular goods, as in private enterprise

6. ST II-II, q. 66, a. 7: "And that is why according to natural law goods that are held in superabundance by some people should be used for the maintenance of the poor. . . . If . . . a person is in imminent danger and cannot be helped in any other way, then a person may legitimately supply his own needs out of another's property, whether he does so secretly or flagrantly."

7. The legitimacy of state intervention from the time of the Industrial Revolution has been a given in Catholic Social teaching since its formal inception under Pope Leo XII in his 1891 encyclical, *Rerum Novarum.*

(and many other contexts), is clearly defended by Thomists. In fact, "That particular goods be properly defended by particular persons matters greatly for the common good itself."[8] There is often a confusion here whereby observers often see a tension between the assertion of the existence of a common good alongside the existence of a particular good, such that the good obtained by the pursuit of the particular good can only come about by negating the common good. Simon sorts this out by underlining that there is a difference in kind between the good of a multitude and the good of an individual. The common good of the political order is the good of a multitude, wherein there is a one and a many. The proper good of the political community is only realized with a plenitude of multiple goods pursued by the members of the community. Such plenitude only exists when particular people pursue particular goods.

Simon gives the example of the Latin scholar in an educational institution who seems not to care for other intellectual pursuits. Yet, Simon applauds him. This scholar understands that the knowledge of Latin by some members of society makes for a better society than one in which no one knows Latin, and that his role for the common good lies precisely in his particular, if not stubborn, insistence on Latin. Simon derides another kind of professor who refrains from any kind of zeal on behalf of his field in the interests of a well-rounded education. The point is not that Simon does not care for a well-rounded education; his point is that it is best achieved through particular professors with one-sided zeal for their fields. The common good exists only where there are multiple impassioned pursuits of particular goods which require single-minded dedication. Simon writes, "Common good cannot exist unless it does exist as the good of a multitude; but there is no good "of a multitude" unless particular goods are intended by particular appetites and taken care of by particular agents."[9]

An important conclusion emerges here. If private citizens should pursue a genuine plurality of particular goods, and indeed such a plenitude of goods is crucial to the common good itself, it follows that to will the common good in its material sense is not the role of private citizens as such; to will the common good materially is the specific function of political authority. To put the matter clearly, the citizen has the obligation to attend to the

8. Yves R. Simon, *Philosophy of Democratic Government* (Notre Dame, Indiana: University of Notre Dame Press, 1993), 98. Italics in original.

9. Ibid., 99.

common good formally, that is, to give up particular pursuits when legitimate authority has determined a need to put a restriction on the pursuit of them. So, the wife of a family rightly fights to keep her criminal husband out of prison for the good of the family so long as she does not break the law. Her job is to promote the good of the family. It is the job of the political authority to determine that the husband be deprived of his freedom.[10] So, we have clarified what Simon calls an essential function of political authority, that is, "the issuance and carrying out of rules expressing the requirements of the common good considered materially."[11]

Authority, then, is necessary because the primary material concern of citizens is to pursue particular goods, including economic ones. At some point, despite the perfect legitimacy of these pursuits, they end up in conflict with one another and with the common good. In nineteenth-century America, for example, it was widely perceived by people who did not consider themselves conservative, that at some point the mere size of an enterprise represented a threat to the common good. A part of the reason was that such entities were less likely to be responsible members of communities. States generally had laws which denied personal rights to corporations; they further insisted that such enterprises demonstrate a public need for their services.[12] The recognition was common that corporate pursuits could and should be properly limited by the state for the sake of the common good.

10. In *Philosophy of Democratic Government*, Simon notes that it is in Aquinas' discussion of the principles of morality at ST I-II, q. 19, a. 10, where we find "the most precise exposition ever made of the principles commanding the theory of government." Yves R. Simon, *Philosophy of Democratic Government*, (Chicago: University of Chicago Press, 1951), 40. He says this because it is in this passage where Saint Thomas discusses the matter with precision, as follows: "[R]eason may look at a thing from different points of view, in such a manner that it appears good from one and bad from another. Accordingly, that person's will is good which wants the thing in its character of being good, and that person is also good which does not want it in its character of being an evil. Thus a judge's will is good in passing a sentence ... for this is just, but another's will, for instance the criminal's wife or child, is also good in opposing the [sentence], for this is a real evil.... However, it is not right for a person to will a particular good unless he refers it to the common good as its end ... Now the end gives force and shape to willing what subserves it. Accordingly, for a particular good to be willed rightly as a particular object it should be like the matter that is willed, whereas the common and godlike good should be like the form. Since the human will is required to will this, it should therefore correspond to the divine will in the form of its willing, yet not necessarily ... in what materially it wills." ST I-II, q. 19, a. 10. Those interested in this discussion should read the entire article in the *Summa*.

11. Yves R. Simon, *A General Theory of Authority* (Notre Dame, Indiana: University of Notre Dame Press, 1980), 57.

12. The source is Jane Anne Morris, cited in Jim Hightower, *If the Gods Had Meant Us To Vote, They Would Have Given Us Candidates* (New York: Perennial, 2001), 392–95.

There is a second sense in which the particularity of a good requires authority. A good can be particular by being a common social good yet particular in that it is only part of the common good. The Department of Health and Human Services, the Department of Defense, and the Department of Education all represent common goods, but particular ones. It is, then, a further function of political authority, in its commitment to the common good materially considered, to ensure that the pursuit of particular common goods be tempered by the common good.

In conclusion, whether we consider the particularity of the goods sought by private individuals or the particularity of the multitude of common *goods*, the Thomist theory of political authority assigns a unique and special responsibility to political authority to achieve the common good materially considered. Yet, as we have seen, this responsibility of political authority is connected to the pursuit of a multitude of excellences and in no way is in competition with it. Simon writes, "Let it be emphasized ... that the theory of authority as agency ... is connected with the excellence of particularity. Insofar as the particularity involved is that of the subject, not that of the function, the theory of authority comprises a vindication of autonomy at all levels."[13]

Having worked out the relationship between particular goods and the common good, we can now briefly review Saint Thomas theory of authority and the common good, which he addresses in his discussion of law.[14] Thomas neatly summarizes this in his definition if law as "nothing else than an ordinance of reason for the common good made by the authority who has care of the community and is promulgated."[15] Previously, Aquinas demonstrated, following Aristotle, that human acts must be in accord with a highest end, and this end for all natural human activity is human happiness

13. Putting this in other words, the theory of authority is in no fundamental tension with the autonomy or freedom of the particular person. The common good among a diversity of people is a good that exists among those people. The theory of authority assumes that particular people pursue a wide variety of particular goods. As gleaned from the previous discussion of particular goods with reference to the common good, we certainly understand that the theory of authority in no way implies that all seek the same good, or in any way diminishes the proper role of self-directedness and autonomy in democratic societies. It matters for the common good that a great variety of particular goods be pursued by particular members. For a lengthier presentation of the distinction between the form and the matter of the common good, related to the theory of authority, see Thomas R. Rourke, *A Conscience as Large as the World: Yves R. Simon versus the Catholic Neoconservatives* (Lanham, Maryland: Rowman and Littlefield, 1997), 96–98.

14. ST I-II, qq. 90 and 91.

15. ST I-II, q. 90, a. 4.

or well-being.[16] A human person is in one sense a part of the larger whole, which is the political community.[17] Law deals with this proper subordination of the the human person to the broader human community. Again, following Aristotle, Saint Thomas asserts, "we call those acts legally just that tend to produce and preserve happiness and its components for the political community, according to *Politics*, being the State."[18]

III. David Hume and Adam Smith vs. Thomism

The definitive shift away from Aquinas's account of an economy as a component of the achievement of the common good can be found in the ethics of David Hume and Adam Smith. It is curious how the ethics of Hume and Smith, central to the cultural shifts that made for the rise of modern market capitalism, have been so widely ignored by commentators. Yet, it is precisely in these analyses that we most definitively see the breakaway not only from the Aristotelian-Thomist Tradition, but from the entire notion that the economic system is even ordered to a common good. Hume's ethics are reminiscent of both Bentham and Hobbes. Like Hobbes, Hume insists that the chief motive for action is to pursue pleasure and avoid pain, which are synonymous with good and evil. (Bentham holds a similar view.) Hume is clear, contrary to the entire classical tradition in ethics, that the ultimate ends of human action can never be determined by reason, "but recommend themselves entirely to the sentiments and affections of mankind, without any dependence on intellectual faculties."[19] When someone is asked to give an account of why they desire or avert themselves from various pursuits, there would be nothing to respond beyond the declaration that the pursuit brought pleasure or pain. There is no distinction between pursuits that will please us and what Aristotle and Aquinas would call genuine goods. Neither Aristotle's nor Aquinas' ethics makes sense without such a distinction. For the latter, all pursuits of goods rooted in any kind of sentiment or affection must be measured against the mandates of practical reason working toward a reasoned conception of what is good. For Hume,

16. Of course, this discussion is limited to the natural order. Ultimately, man's final end is to that supreme common good, the kingdom of heaven, which transcends the natural order.

17. Again, of course, there is a second sense by which man completely transcends the entire created order in his final end, which transcends nature. See note 16 above.

18. ST I-II, q. 90, a. 2.

19. MacIntyre, *Ethics in the Conflicts of Modernity*, 79.

a mere agreement on sentiments is sufficient for common moral standards and practical moral reasoning based on them. For Hume, it is sufficient that the moral actor measure himself against what he conceives to be the common moral sentiments of the human race.[20]

MacIntyre notes the radical newness in modern moral thinking of inviting people to think of themselves as individuals, separate from any social role, and of also inviting them to think about good and evil with no reference to social roles or any standard of good except what is provided for by an alleged agreement with the sentiments of others.[21] Hume himself clearly demonstrates the kind of moral reasoning involved here. Among the revered sentiments of mankind is esteem for riches. So universal is this esteem that any attempt to pursue a more egalitarian distribution of wealth would, according to Hume, actually deprive the poor of satisfaction. Hume assumes that the prosperity of the specific classes that were becoming rich in England in his time invited nothing but applause from all other groups, including the poor and those who were suffering a decline in their fortunes. This apparently included those who were victims of judicial terror and those who engaged in food riots![22]

It is illustrative to underline all that Hume excludes in his ethics. First, he fails to consider the possibility that the moral sentiments identified by him as belonging universally to mankind might be nothing more than the sentiments of the economically successful in eighteenth-century England. Second, he fails to consider that avarice may be, as Aristotle and Aquinas would have had it, a character vice. Insofar as avarice was a common sentiment, it would not have aroused negative judgment on Hume's part. Third, he fails to consider that humility might be a virtue. Finally, he dismisses the possibility that there might be something Aristotle and Aquinas called justice, which might question the existing order of property and wealth. Along the same lines, actual antagonisms over the content of justice might be found among landowners, peasants, merchants, craftsmen and laborers.[23] This casts serious doubts about the existence of "universal human sentiments" concerning matters of justice. In other words, Hume fails to consider Aristotle's recognition that different approaches to justice may result from different socio-economic conditions, a factor he overlooks entirely.

20. Ibid., 80–81.
21. Ibid., 82.
22. Ibid.
23. Ibid., 84.

Although Smith's *The Wealth of Nations* is normally taken to be his magnum opus, it is in his *Theory of Moral Sentiments* where we find the roots of his ethical theory that undergirds the modern market system. Although Smith makes a passing reference to the ancient moralists, his understanding of justice is fundamentally incompatible with the theories of Plato, Aristotle, and Saint Thomas. For Smith, justice is no master virtue, the telos of human nature. Rather the "perfection of human nature" is "to feel much for others and little for ourselves ... to restrain our selfish, and to indulge our benevolent affections."[24] For Smith, justice is "a negative virtue." Justice does "no real positive good," as it merely prevents actions that do "real and positive hurt to some particular person." We can often fulfill the demands of justice by "sitting still and doing nothing."[25] Like Hume, Smith grounds his moral philosophy in allegedly universal moral sentiments, not reason; moral evaluation of specific cases can only come from sentiments[26] and is unrelated to any reasonable quest for social justice. Justice is essentially limited to jurisprudence for Smith, so individual moral reasoning has no essential role to play in determining the content of justice.

What role, then, would there be for moral reasoning in such a society? Clearly, the notion of justice as a transcendent standard to measure the social order is excluded. In a thorough repudiation of the Aristotelian and Thomist traditions, Smith holds that moral reasoning instructs us to accept social conditions and practices that are contrary to our moral sentiments and reason. Smith concedes that the love of wealth and the respect we tend to give to it "is the great and universal cause of the corruption of moral sentiments." Nonetheless, despite having acknowledged this disposition as the prime corruptor of human nature, Smith contends that such corruption should be conceded as the basis of civil order. Smith writes, "Upon this disposition of mankind to go along with all the passions of the rich and the powerful, is founded the distinction of ranks, and the order of society."[27] Smith's conception of nature permits the divergence between our moral sentiments and the social order. We prefer to see good men prosper and evil men fail, but "the natural course of things offers results in the op-

24. Smith, *The Theory of Moral Sentiments,* Glasgow Edition, edited by D. D. Rafael and D. D. Macfie (Indianapolis, Indiana: Liberty Fund, 1982), 25.

25. Ibid., 79–80, 82.

26. Ibid., 339–40.

27. Adam Smith, quoted in Thomas R. Rourke, *A Conscience as Large as the World,* 40.

posite.... Violence and artifice prevail over sincerity and justice."[28] Nature imposes a deception on us when it prompts us to pursue wealth and avoid poverty, because wealth does not necessarily lead to happiness. Nonetheless, nature's deception and the ensuing corruption of moral sentiments is a positive thing for Smith, as it motivates us to work hard and produce wealth. This deception leads to the buildup of wealth and all we associate with civilization.

Here we can insert the keystone to Smith's economic theory, the "invisible hand." The pursuit of self-interest, which Smith's convoluted ethics comes out justifying, actually leads to an increase in the wealth of nations, even though no actor, including political authority, actually intends the common good materially considered. Nor do we need to concern ourselves with the distribution of wealth.[29] Yves Simon characterizes economic liberalism's commitment to this belief as follows:

> [Liberalism] assumes that chance occurrences are controlled from within in such a way as to produce the greatest good of the greatest number. The ambiguous Deity which achieves this control is generally referenced under the name of Nature or Providence. Adam Smith calls it an "invisible hand." It is closely related to the "luck" which renders the gambler deaf to the warnings inferred from the calculus of probabilities. It is a principle of order which, strangely enough, dwells inside chance.[30]

As Joseph Cropsey has noted, Smith does concede that the reconciliation between individual and common interests is accompanied by what Smith terms moral irregularities. The invisible hand that promotes the greatest prosperity does in fact lead to the division of labor which "stultifies the working classes [and] turns economic life over to merchants and manufacturers prone to mischief and exaction of rents and the broader process of capital accumulation which did not help laboring classes in the short run."[31]

Smith's sense of universal human sentiments is even more suspect today than ever. Whatever lack of social advances may still beset working people in the global economy, we would all wince at what Smith has to say concerning human wretchedness: "The fortunate and the proud wonder at the

28. Smith, *The Theory of Moral Sentiments*, 169.

29. Ibid., 182–85.

30. Yves R. Simon, *The Community of the Free* (Lanham, Maryland: University Press of America, 1984), 138.

31. Joseph Cropsey, "Adam Smith," in Leo Strauss and Joseph Cropsey, *History of Political Philosophy*, 3rd ed. (Chicago: University of Chicago Press, 1987), 646–52.

insolence of human wretchedness, that it should dare present itself before them, and with the loathsome aspect of its misery presume to disturb the serenity of their happiness."[32] What this reveals starkly is how far Smith's sense of universal human sentiments is from any genuinely Christian sentiment. Further, given that Christian sentiments were common in Smith's time, we come to doubt that his understanding of the content of universal human sentiments is anything more than the sentiments of the more economically prominent sector of the English population in his own time.

Hume and Smith's moral theories prepared the way for the justification of the modern market economy. Neither Hume nor Smith would live to see the specific development of that system, particularly in its corporate form from the time of the Industrial Revolution, nor the moral irregularities that would accompany it. Yves R. Simon, on the other hand, would develop his moral critique in light of these specific developments, as they came about in the post-Industrial Revolution world. At the forefront of the difficulties would be the widespread failure of the state to preserve its independent position standing above the conflict of interests. Pius XI spoke about this in stark terms in *Quadragesimo Anno*:

> [G]rave evils ... have resulted from an intermingling and shameful confusion of the functions and duties of public authority with those of the economic sphere—such as, one of the worst, the virtual degradation of the majesty of the State, which although it ought to sit on high like a queen and supreme arbitress, free from all partiality and intent upon the one common good and justice, is become a slave, surrendered and delivered to the passions and greed of men. And as to international relations, two different streams have issued from the one fountain-head: On the one hand, economic nationalism or even economic imperialism; on the other, a no less deadly and accursed internationalism of finance or international imperialism whose country is where profit is.[33]

Simon discusses the same problem with somewhat more specificity:

> First comes the problem ... of the independence of the state. Briefly, the establishment of big financial, commercial, and industrial concerns, with strong monopolistic tendencies, puts into private hands a power, able not only to challenge the authority of the state, but also to lay hold of it and to exert a decisive influence.[34]

32. Smith, *The Theory of Moral Sentiments*, 64.
33. Pope Pius XI, *Quadragesimo Anno* (1931): no. 109.
34. Simon, *The Community of the Free*, 154–55.

Simon believed that it was unequal exchange which was the principle problem besetting modern democracy, principally because of the tendency of the relatively well off to overlook or fail to see that modern democracy had remained a concern of the privileged few.[35] In the shared Aristotelian and Thomistic vocabulary, we are talking about violations of commutative justice.[36] He saw three principal ways that unequal exchange had become institutionalized in the twentieth century.[37] The first of these is illusory services. The root of this problem goes to the very roots of the modern market system. It comes about because work produces wealth for exchange rather than use, which gets us back to the very origins of commercial activity as discussed by Aristotle in *The Politics*. [38] When production is simple and local, the disassociation between production for use and production for profit is not necessarily a problem, as previously discussed.[39] However, with modern corporate megaproduction, there is a difference in kind. The relations between buyer and seller are distant and largely abstract, with the entire system influenced by modern advertising, in a context where profit is clearly center-stage and there are millions to be made or lost depending on how the market goes; the relationship between service and profit of work is clearly obscured.

35. Yves R. Simon, *Philosophy of Democratic Government*, 248.

36. All agree that the discussion of commutative justice goes back to Aristotle's *Nicomachean Ethics*. Here Aristotle distinguishes between distributive justice, which concerns the proportional distribution of goods from the common good to the particular components of society, and commutative justice, which concerns the reciprocal dealings between individuals in their voluntary transactions, or justice in exchanges between members of the community. See Aristotle, *Nicomachean Ethics* 5.2, 1130b; 5.5, 1133b. Saint Thomas furthered the discussion in ST II-II, q. 61, a. 4. The concept made its way down through the ages because of its centrality in Catholic thought. In particular, it is one of the bases of Catholic Social Teaching. See *Compendium of the Social Doctrine of the Church*, no. 201.

37. It is important to clarify here the relationship between Simon's critiques of what he considers unequal exchanges and Saint Thomas' treatment. Saint Thomas discusses justice and injustice in exchanges in ST II-II q. 77, aa.1–4. Clearly, Saint Thomas's discussion is limited to the pre-capitalist world he inhabited. Simon considers patterns of exchange specific to the post-Industrial era. Nonetheless, it is entirely fair to consider Simon's discussion of unequal exchange "Thomist." The bottom line for Saint Thomas is that exchanges are considered a part of commutative justice, wherein "the paramount consideration . . . is the equality of things" (ST II-II, q. 77, a. 1). Hence any species of exchange wherein the value of goods transacted are unequal would be for Saint Thomas a violation of commutative justice (unless there were mitigating factors of the kind discussed earlier). Therefore, the following discussion of unequal exchange is fundamentally Thomist in orientation.

38. See note 1 above. The following discussion is taken from Yves R. Simon, *Work, Society, and Culture*, edited by Vukan Kuic (New York: Fordham University Press, 1971), 119–26.

39. See note 2 above.

Many times, there is a growing gap between actual service and profit of work. To take a contemporary example, consider the relationship between service and profit of work in the financial industry in the years leading up to the financial meltdown of 2008. We know now that the industry created new financial instruments the value of which were underwritten by billions of dollars of home mortgages sold under dubious circumstances, as in the infamous "ninja loans" (no income, no job, no assets). Ultimately, these financial instruments were deemed worthless. They were, however, for quite some time bought and sold on international markets, backed by so-called collateral debt obligations, which included all of the worthless loans. The point is that billions of dollars of profit were made for what a reasonable person would have to call no service at all. Thorstein Veblen recognized the problem:

> The vital point of production with [the businessman] is the rendibility of the output, its controvertibility into money values, not its serviceability for the needs of mankind. A modicum of serviceability, for one purpose or another, the output must have if it is to be saleable. But it does not follow that the highest serviceability gives the largest gains to the businessman in terms of money, nor does it follow that the output in all cases need have other than a fictitious serviceability.[40]

Simon makes the further point that illusory service has no place in the theory of the market economy. Economists, Simon writes, like to be very empirical and study the market itself. Yet, Simon insists that everyone knows that, recognized or not, illusory services exist. There is a body of law to prevent fraud. But the problem clearly does not end with illegal services. Simon would have us consider the impact of modern advertising, which encourages people to purchase cars, homes, and consumer articles beyond what they need and can afford. To deny the existence of illusory services is ultimately to assert that every desire corresponds to a genuine human need, which no one really believes.

The problem goes back to the fundamental assumption of ethical neutrality in modern economics. Simon denies the facile claim that modern economics, as its proponents often claim, is free from value judgments. Ultimately, if economics is to be considered to be a humanistic discipline to be exercised for the good of society, economics cannot properly be separated from a philosophically defensible concept of the good for human beings. Simon concludes forcefully:

40. Thorstein Veblen, quoted in Simon, *Work, Society, and Culture*, 121.

we can never be convinced that the concept of genuine service of work, as distinguished from mere satisfaction of just any desire, is not relevant from the point of view of a science that deals specifically with wealth.[41]

Related to illusory services are what Simon refers to as "one-way exchanges," wherein "wealth leaks out of society."[42] Here Simon draws on Aristotle's discussion of exchanges. Strictly speaking, for Aristotle, a commercial exchange occurs when a real commodity plays an intermediate role between two sums of money, as when someone purchases a commodity merely to sell the same product later at a higher price, without producing any additional value in between. If a man purchases property merely to sell it at a higher price, this is a properly commercial transaction.[43] A striking example of this is seen in boom real estate markets. There is no strict violation of commutative justice so long as such exchanges occur in a context wherein the rules governing exchanges have been deemed to be the best workable. Nevertheless, commutative justice demands a better way to compute the value of things. This would be a higher interpretation of commutative justice. Simon believes that the "cost price" would be a better approximation of the just price. Although Simon does not discuss the concept at length, he does note that the socialist tradition is to be credited for its vision of an order which would "guarantee the full reality of the processes of exchange and keep all wealth within society."[44]

The next example of an unequal exchange is probably the one most recognized: the exploitation of human labor.[45] In order to appreciate Simon's argument we must first understand that it arises for him in the context of illusory services and the impacts of the institutionalization of such services in the modern market economy. For Simon, the existence of illusory services contributes to the alienation of the working class. During the Depression, farmers who raised and sold pigs made less than those who butchered them to keep them off the market. In Brazil, coffee was used to provide for locomotives. Serviceable activities became illusory as the products were left to rot or used for extraneous purposes. Simon contends that it was properly the experience of real destitution existing in the context where wealth

41. Ibid., 126.

42. Simon, *Community of the Free*, 160–65.

43. Again, see note 1 above.

44. Simon, *Community of the Free*, 165.

45. The following draws on Simon, *Work, Society, and Culture*, 126–33.

was plentiful that did more to shape the twentieth century than even the Russian Revolution. Real people were left unemployed, the workbench was depleted, but there were plenty of idle machines and unmet human needs.

Excessive production dissolves the moral connection between service and profit of work. This does not itself mean that the worker is exploited. Unequal exchange enters whenever the worker is forced by circumstances to accept whatever wage is offered. If the working man is in a situation wherein he cannot afford to turn down whatever is offered, the result most of the time will be exploitation. The worker will not be paid a wage corresponding to his contribution because the employer can and does get away with it. It is a kind of involuntary tribute extracted from the worker; it is a form of servitude. This is why Simon insisted, as said earlier, that unequal exchange was the central problem that democracy had to deal with in the post-Industrial Revolution era.[46] Simon cites twentieth-century developments, such as the International Labor Organization Charter, wherein it became increasingly recognized that labor was not simply to be considered a factor of production or a commodity.[47] When we consider that the U.S. economy produces an abundance of low-wage, no benefit jobs, that health care costs bankrupt many, and that growing inequality which includes abundant poverty, we still have reason to believe that exploitation of labor remains a real moral concern.

A consideration of actual historical conditions is here helpful. MacIntyre notes, following Marx, that the actual generation of a capitalist working class was contingent on some surrounding circumstances. It required a class of people unable to meet their needs in traditional ways such as farming the land they lived on, either as tenants or as sharers in customary rights to common lands, or as farmers of their own land. The proliferation of large numbers of vulnerable people of this kind meant that they would have to compete with one another. Corresponding to this, there had to be a class of people who owned the land, tools, machines, and raw materials, who could hire these workers out. The key point to be made concerning the wages corresponding to this social divide is that the workers were not paid an amount equal to what they produced. This was the source of the profits that supported the extraordinary rates of growth in productivity characteristic of the Industrial Revolution.[48]

46. See note 27 above.

47. Simon, *Work, Society, and Culture*, 132.

48. MacIntyre, *Ethics in the Conflicts of Modernity*, 97.

For MacIntyre, those whose labor power became an undercompensated commodity did not generally recognize themselves as commodities to be exchanged for money. The political and social reality of contract became determinant here. The relationship of exchange between owner and worker was in fact as Simon described it: exploitation. It was exploitation because the wage did not correspond to the wealth produced; it was exploitation because the worker was not free to decline the wage and survive. The freedom was all on the side of the owner. According to MacIntyre, however, the political interpretation of control was always an exchange among equals. It was the fiction of legal equality that disguised the reality of exploitation. As capitalism became the dominant form of production, this way of thinking about oneself and one's relationship with others as equals, became the dominant mode of social and moral thought. Clearly, however, over time much of the working class would come to see the reality of unequal exchange. The Industrial Revolution had the impact of underlining the degree of exploitation involved.

IV. The Distributist Critique

In the context of the Industrial Revolution, a new critique emerged on the Catholic side, one which would target simultaneously both Marxism and the dominant economic order. This critique would come from the revival of Thomism occasioned by Leo XIII and the developments leading to the formulation of modern Catholic social teaching.[49] The new criticism being developed in the Catholic milieu was in fact secular, in the sense that it was addressed to all reasonable people of good will willing to think about what could reasonably be conceived to be a good social order in the emerging context of the Industrial Revolution and the new, industrial capitalist

49. On August 4, 1979, Leo XIII issued the landmark encyclical, *Aeterni Patris*, which was his call for a renewal of Thomism as the specific answer to a variety of modern threats. Among the influences of the famous encyclical was the generation of a new generation of scholars, often called neo-Thomists, who advanced Thomism in a variety of ways. Simon himself was a participant in this great movement. Along with Jacques Maritain, he specifically developed Thomism's political philosophy, demonstrating its compatibility with democracy, at the same time showing that democracy needs to depend on its roots in classical philosophy not to degenerate into anarchy and authoritarianism. Leo XIII writes: "We exhort you, venerable brethren, in all earnestness to restore the golden wisdom of St. Thomas, and to spread it far and wide for the defense and beauty of the Catholic faith, for the good of society, and for the advantage of all the sciences.... Let carefully selected teachers endeavor to implant the doctrine of Thomas Aquinas in the minds of students, and set forth clearly his solidity and excellence over others. Let the universities already founded or to be founded by you illustrate and defend this doctrine, and use it for the refutation of prevailing errors" Pope Leo XIII, *Aeterni Patris* (1879): no. 31.

system. Their claims were rooted in a reasoned interpretation of the human good, justice, and the best way to create and direct civic institutions. Drawing as it did on Thomism, the critique emphasized that the individual good was to be sought precisely in the context of the pursuit of common goods ordered to a comprehensive sense of *the* common good. These common goods are many in the modern context, where there are increasingly a myriad of social, political, and economic goods to be shared. Again, in the absence of a clear sense of the common good, we would simply have individuals pursuing individual goods in the absence of an understanding of justice in the Thomist sense of the term and a corresponding lack of clear commitments to relations with others with whom we should be living a shared commitment to the good life.

At the most basic level, justice requires a living wage to support the worker and his family, safe working conditions, adequate time for rest, participation in family and community activities. Unfortunately, under the influence of liberal economic doctrines, such as Social Darwinism, such conditions were generally unavailable in the earlier stages of the Industrial Revolution. MacIntyre cites Cardinal Manning's support for East London dockworkers in 1889, in the broader context of supporting organized labor. Manning was clear in his rejection of industrial capitalism in the form it was in, his strident language echoed in Leo XIII's famous characterization of life for workers as a "yoke little better than slavery itself." [50] This critique would be central to the criticism of industrial capitalism as well as to the sense of what would be needed to control it. In the face of the extremes of individualism and decisions made under the profit motive the Church would continue to proclaim the existence of common goods and the solidarity needed to transform the system. The political developments emerging out of the critique would include support for better wages, benefits, safer working conditions and social insurance. Nonetheless, the larger problems of the

50. MacIntyre, *Ethics in the Conflict of Modernity*, 107. Pope Leo XII, *Rerum Novarum* (1891): no. 3. Leo XIII played an indispensable role in what I am here calling the Catholic critique of the Industrial Revolution and the corporate capitalist system that emerged from it. The Industrial Revolution had already been underway for some decades at the time Leo XIII decided to address it specifically in an encyclical. *Rerum Novarum* was the landmark papal encyclical that launched Catholic Social Teaching as a formal and systematic body of thought. Leo attempted to carve out a principled critique of the thinking behind the Industrial Revolution that distinguished it from the Marxist critique. Subsequent contributions to Catholic Social Teaching were often published in memory of *Rerum Novarum*. After many encyclicals over the next 120 years, the Church finally authorized in 2004 *The Compendium of the Social Doctrine of the Church*.

system remained intact. Here the potential collaboration between socialist movements, now dominated by Marxists, fell apart.

The Marxists sought a solution in the centralization of power in the state, whereas the state would exercise a greater concentration of ownership and power than existed even by the bourgeoisie under industrial capitalism. This was due to the deeper anthropological flaw in Marxism that overemphasized man as an economic animal, in a frankly materialist conception of life. Marxists could never see beyond social class as the source of all the social evils. The Catholic critique, on the other hand, understood the dangers flowing from the materialist conception of politics. By the 1920s it had become clear to a wide variety of people that the Catholic critique was valid.[51]

Distributism developed in the Catholic world precisely because of these considerations. The problem with the economic order was deeper than what the Marxists had limited themselves to seeing. The Distributists understood that the problem was not as simple as the exploitation of the working class, although they agreed that such was the case. The problem was situated in a much larger-scale perversion of desire and the impact this had on the conception of what a good life is. Human beings are rational agents who pursue genuinely common goods in concert with others of their kind. As Simon put it, this implies a real "communion-in-immanent-action," for Simon a criterion of a genuine common good, which includes "in addition to immanent acts relative to the same object, my knowing that the others know and desire the same object and want it to be effected by the action of our community."[52] Such intentionality must include the local level, since this is the context where most people live, work, and desire. Multiple human pursuits are necessary to achieve the common good, and at all levels, political, economic, social, and cultural. The radical distinction between workers and owners must be eliminated through cooperative enterprises and employee stock ownership plans. A wide variety of specific pursuits come to mind to preserve and promote common goods at all levels: communal land trusts to maintain affordable housing; political provisions for capital to be accountable to the localities where it is invested; the reservation of airwaves to non-commercial programming; ending monopolistic control over patent and copyright laws; reawakening the older American tradition demanding that corporations serve a public good; changing laws

51. MacIntyre, *Ethics in the Conflicts of Modernity*, 107–108.
52. Simon, *Philosophy of Democratic Government*, 65.

that consistently place investor profits over concerns of workers and the environment.[53] Preservation of local forms of economy and culture would be paramount. The point is that concentration of ownership and the larger, destructive influence of the profit motive need to be offset on all sides by what Catholic social thought will come to call "solidarity" in pursuit of a wide variety of human goods which otherwise tend to get lost under the one-sidedness of the profit motive.[54]

Ultimately, there were two critiques of modern industrial capitalism. They overlapped in some respects, but ultimately were separated by a difference-in-kind. The Marxist critique focused narrowly on the economic problem, which it sought to solve through class struggle. It assumed that class was *the* source of the modern social problems. The Catholic critique focused on the centralization of power and ownership in the political and economic spheres, which made the exploitation problem intractable. The solution was in a decentralization of power and ownership, the principle of subsidiarity,[55] and the growth of diverse centers of production. Moreover, in order to combat modern materialism, there was a further need for a plethora of other, non-economic goods to be pursued in the political, social and cultural arenas, wherein all could make their contribution. The Marxists, on the other hand, were indifferent to the related problems of centralization and materialism. In addition, through their negation of original sin, they assumed that there would be no problem with the centralization of authority without any checks being placed on the state, as government was going to be in the hands of an allegedly morally pure class. History taught otherwise. It remains for the Catholic critique to grow and become politically viable. Why it has not will be the subject of another essay.

53. For these and other solidaristic practices see www.solidarity-party.org/about-us-platform.

54. MacIntyre, *Ethics in the Conflicts of Modernity*, 108.

55. The principle of subsidiarity is a distinctly Catholic contribution to political and economic thought. It is a response to the specific and widespread tendency for the modern state, in its attempt to institute regulations for the common good, to swallow up or control society's smaller and voluntary groupings. At its worst, as in the former Soviet Union, the state becomes the only entity that citizens belong to, with every other institution squashed by the tendencies toward centralization and uniformity. It was originally stated by Pius XI in *Quadragesimo Anno* in 1931. Pius XI wrote: "Just as it is gravely wrong to take from individuals what they can accomplish by their own initiative and industry and give it to the community, so also it is an injustice and at the same time a grave evil and disturbance of right order to assign to a greater and higher association what lesser and subordinate organizations can do. For every social activity ought of its very nature to furnish help to the members of the body social, and never destroy and absorb them." Pope Pius XI, *Quadragesimo Anno* (1931): no. 79.

III

THE SOUND OF MIGHTY WATERS

MacIntyre on Desire For the Good

MARK MOES

God and the Good

MacIntyre, Ur-Platonism, and the Retrospective Rational Vindication of Trinitarian Theism

THIS ESSAY FIRST EXPOUNDS Alasdair MacIntyre's view of the way in which Plato and Aristotle are to be understood as co-founders of a single developing philosophical tradition of theistic thought and practice rather than as representatives of utterly rival and incompatible points of view. I include a summary of MacIntyre's doctrine that all rational enquiry—whether it is in the natural sciences, in philosophy, in theology—is tradition-dependent, and that the rational vindication of any theoretical account provided in the course of any such enquiry is always a retrospectively constructed history of the struggles and successes of that account during its development. The next two parts of the essay draw on the work of Lloyd Gerson in order to corroborate and to expand upon MacIntyre's view of the relation between Plato and Aristotle. Gerson contends not only that Aristotle was a Platonist who differed with his master only over matters of detail, but also that the entire Platonic/Aristotelian tradition of theistic philosophy, from Plato to Plotinus and beyond, is aptly termed "Ur-Platonism". These two parts of the essay also sketch the way in which philosophical theology during the millennium from Socrates to Proclus underwent a complex history of struggles and successes until it finally came, in Plotinus and Proclus, to a maturity that was not without residual problems. The final section of the essay reflects upon how specifically Christian Trinitarian conceptions derived from revelation complemented and completed classical philosophical theism, by dissolving some metaphysical problems left over from the classical theistic tradition and by providing an improved account of the relationship between the Goodness of God and the human good. Taken as a whole this essay can be read as a sketch for a retrospective rational vindication of Christian Trinitarian theism.

I. MacIntyre on the Form of the Good: From Plato to Aristotle

In a 1990 paper entitled "The Form of the Good, Tradition, and Enquiry,"[1] Alasdair MacIntyre notes that most recent attempts to re-introduce Platonic or Aristotelian theses into the debates of contemporary moral philosophy have isolated these theses from their original metaphysical and theological settings. MacIntyre complains that such isolation has little to do with philosophy itself but is socially and psychologically determined within the framework of the modern nation-state. He calls for engagement in an alternative anti-modern form of philosophical enquiry which will allow us to reckon with the particular arguments and theses of Plato and Aristotle in such a way that in particular the connections between their metaphysical theologies and their conceptions of the human good are preserved. He hopes we may thereby encounter Plato and Aristotle not exclusively in terms dictated by the contemporary condition of philosophy, but rather in terms which leave open the possibility that it is modern atheistic modes of thought which need to be put in question rather than the theological modes of Plato and Aristotle. He contends that such an alternative standpoint vis-à-vis Plato and Aristotle is furnished by the conception of a philosophical[2] tradition,[3] according to which philosophy is essentially historical in the form of its enquiry.

1. Alasdair MacIntyre, "The Form of the Good, Tradition, and Enquiry," in *Value and Understanding: Essays for Peter Winch*, edited by Raymond Gaita (London: Routledge, 1990) 242–62.

2. By "philosophical" he means, as a Thomistic thinker, "concerning ultimate issues discoverable by human reasoning unaided by revelation."

3. MacIntyre published an interview in 1991, the year after he published "The Form of the Good, Tradition, and Enquiry," an interview conducted for the journal *Cogito* by Gordon Reddiford and William Watts Miller, first published as "An Interview With Alasdair MacIntyre" in *Cogito* 5, no. 2 (1991): 67–73. In the interview MacIntyre says the concept of tradition is important in his thinking for three reasons: *First,* concepts are embodied in and draw their lives from forms of social practice (as Wittgenstein saw), and how a concept is used has to be located in terms of the activities and norms of some form of established practice. But any practice of any

From this standpoint, Plato and Aristotle belong to a single developing theological tradition, and the standards by which good theorizing is to be judged in them and in their successors are set by the question of whether or not thinkers are able to carry further or to transcend the limitations of the best work of their predecessors. In a 1984 paper "The Relationship of Philosophy to its Past,"[4] MacIntyre remarked that it was in carrying further and transcending the limitations of pre-Socratic philosophy that Plato constituted and founded philosophical enquiry and set the standards by reference to which in the end all subsequent enquiry has to be judged. He also remarked that it was only insofar as Aristotle continued and improved in some ways upon Plato's work that most of Aristotle's own theses and arguments can be adequately understood and evaluated.

In "The Form of the Good, Tradition, and Enquiry," MacIntyre chided Peter Winch for understanding the philosophies of Plato and Aristotle as constituting rival, alternative, and incompatible points of view. Winch had maintained that Aristotle simply rejected the Platonic "Form of the Good" because as some kind of "separate Form" it was irrelevant to any conception of the human *telos* able to provide action-guiding knowledge. Against this view MacIntyre argued that Plato's conception of the Form of the Good in the *Republic* was more complex than Winch realized, and that Aristotle argued against one aspect of Plato's conception of the Form of the Good in order to sustain and develop other aspects of that conception. MacIntyre rejected the view that for Plato the Form of the Good was just an ordinary, but higher-order, Form that stood to other forms in a way analogous to that in which those other forms stood to particulars. Instead MacIntyre maintained that the conception of the Form of the Good was, like much else in

---

importance has a history of development. Modes of evaluation, judgment, and action have to be handed on from one generation to another. *Second,* one prerequisite for the kind of social life in which rational discussion of both ends and means is possible is a shared ability to ask and answer together such questions as "What is our common inheritance?" and "What in it is open to criticism and requires remaking?" Answers constitute some conception of a common good which can provide an alternative to the mindless conservatism of hierarchies of established power and to the fragmentation caused by conflicts among group interests and individual preferences. *Third,* rational inquiry in general is itself always tradition-dependent. The vindication of any contemporary natural science, for example, is the *history* of that science, the retrospectively constructed history of a prospectively oriented tradition of inquiry, within which the development of the standards by which incoherence and resourcelessness are judged itself has a history.

4. Alasdair MacIntyre, "The Relationship of Philosophy to its Past," in *Philosophy in History*, edited by Richard Rorty, J. B. Schneewind, and Quentin Skinner (Cambridge: Cambridge University Press, 1984), 31–48.

the *Republic,* intentionally paradoxical. One of the dialogue's central paradoxes, on MacIntyre's interpretation, was that those being introduced to the theory of Forms by Socrates lacked the capacity to understand the metaphysical complexities of what they were being told. And the person who like Glaucon could not as yet use dialectical reasoning adequately did "not know the Good or any other good, but if he laid hold of some image of it, he did so by *doxa,* not by *episteme,* and was dreaming and sleeping away his life" (534c).[5]

Not only was the conception of the Form of the Good paradoxical, but it had many functions in Plato's thought, according to MacIntyre. For example, it was posited to explain the unity underlying the multiplicity of goods of every kind, to provide an unconditional first principle by appeal to which the tasks of rational justification of an account of justice (or of any good) could be brought to completion; and provided a justification in practical reasoning for judging which *particular* actions or experiences or states of affairs were good. At 517c Socrates said the Form of the Good is the source in the visible world of light and of the source of light. For Plato's Socrates the Form of the Good escaped definition in any final way and was not identifiable with any range of particular types of good. Plato's conception was complex and mysterious.

MacIntyre theorized that Aristotle, participating in a set of inquiries he shared with Plato, argued against one aspect of Plato's conception of the good in order to sustain and develop other aspects of Plato's conception. Aristotle was careful to distinguish: (i) the good which is that towards which all things, human and nonhuman alike, direct themselves; (ii) the specifically human good, which must be a mode of life fitted to the rational contemplative and political nature of human beings; (iii) the large variety of *types* of good discerned by human beings, and; (iv) the *particular* goods that are identified correctly or erroneously by particular agents on particular occasions. In the course of his enquiries Aristotle discovered first that, though the concept of *eidos* was indispensable, the various discussions of forms in

5. In a paper written 17 years later, Macintyre contends that Plato's dramatic intention in having Socrates introduce the similes of the Sun, Line, and Cave is to introduce an elaborate *aporia*: that it is apparently impossible, if the theory of Forms is true, of coming to learn that it is true only by means of a series of arguments. "Yet Another Way to Read the *Republic*?" *Proceedings of the Boston Area Colloquium in Ancient Philosophy* 23 (2007) 205–223. MacIntyre suggests a reading according to which the discussions of mimetic poetry in Book X are meant in part to resolve the *aporia* by giving a cognitive account of poetic imagery.

the Platonic dialogues had not solved all Plato's problems, and secondly that when he had supplied his own account of the variety of human goods and of the Good, integrating into it Plato's explorations, one central problem remained that neither he nor Plato had solved. Aristotle recognized that the kind of unity involved in the multiplicity of goods was not that of membership in one and the same genus or species; he saw that 'good' was an analogous term. But more importantly he also recognized that though it may be that the underlying unity of all goods is that of "something existing separately and independently," nevertheless it is not obvious that such a good can by itself explain what the good is which is to be done or attained by human beings (NE 1.6, 1096b31–35). Aristotle recognized the puzzling character of the relationship between the divine goodness and the human good.

Aristotle did not dismiss Plato's Form of the Good out of hand, said MacIntyre, but rather only held that it does not yet supply the kind of philosophical account of the unity of the notion of goodness which is needed. In Aristotle's mature metaphysical enquiries, the Form of the Good reappeared in a new guise as the Unmoved Mover, but still as "something existing separately and independently." There is a much-discussed problem of the relationship between the conception of the *telos* of human life as the *eudaimonia* of a whole life in which the political virtues are achieved advanced in the first book of the *Nicomachean Ethics,* and that of the *telos* of human life as the contemplation of the unchanging and divine in the tenth book of that work. Aristotle had stated more adequately than Plato the relationship of the human mind to various finite goods and to the Good, but the nature of the goodness of the final object of contemplation, whether understood as the Form of the Good or as the Unmoved Mover, remained for Aristotle both in itself and in its effects very obscure.

When large and unsolved problems are discovered within a philosophical system, there are two ways of responding, remarks MacIntyre. One is to regard the presence of such problems as a symptom of the defectiveness of the system (the response of the seventeenth- and eighteenth-century rationalists and empiricists to Aristotle's system). A different response is to understand the fertile generation of such problems as a virtue, rather than a vice, a virtue in that it opens up the possibility for some new systematic statement of philosophical arguments and theses which will both preserve from its predecessor whatever has so far withstood the objections posed by dialectical questioning, and yet also integrate new conceptual resources into that inheritance. In this way, the earlier system generates its successor precisely by providing it with a problematic, a set of issues and difficulties in terms of which the philosophical achievement of the successor can be initially evaluated. This is the relationship, maintained MacIntyre, in which the work of Socrates stood to that of Plato, and Plato's dialogues stood to Aristotle's treatises.

Progress within a philosophical tradition may on occasion consist in the reformulation of a problem in such a way as to preserve all the elements of the problem, rather than to arrive at a premature and misguided solution by discarding one of its elements. So it was with the problem of the relationship of the supreme Good, existing separately from, and independently of, the contingent cosmos, to the variety of goods pursued for the sake of this and that particular end which compose the good life for human beings. If this problem is made to go away by treating one or the other of these as having exclusive title in an account of goodness, the consequences can be brutal. Somehow the theory of the good must integrate the transcendent Good and the goods attainable in this world into a teleology that concerns this world and its destiny. Otherwise one is left, at one extreme, with a dualism between a transcendent Good and a meaningless world of flux, or, at the other extreme, with something like a consumer capitalism concerned only with this world.

II. Gerson on Ur-Platonism as the Background of the Platonic Tradition

MacIntyre's contention that Plato and Aristotle belong to a single ongoing philosophical tradition, at the center of which is Plato's God, is corroborated and supplemented by Lloyd Gerson. Gerson argues that Aristotle was a Platonist at all stages of his career and that Aristotle's work was a carrying forward of Plato's project in areas of physical theory and cognitional theory. Gerson points out that one of Aristotle's greatest contributions to the Platonic project was his development of that concept of *dunamis* (potency or power) that plays an important role in Plato's theology in the *Sophist*. Gerson even maintains that the entire tradition of theistic philosophy from Plato to Plotinus and beyond has a kind of unity that makes it appropriate to label the set of basic principles constituting that tradition *Ur-Platonism*. In a trilogy of erudite scholarly works—including *Aristotle and Other Platonists,*

From Plato to Platonism, and *Platonism and Naturalism*—Gerson has presented an illuminating vision of the unity of the history of philosophy from the pre-Socratics through Plato and Aristotle to the Middle Platonists to Plotinus and Plotinus' heirs Numenius and Proclus.[6] In this trilogy Gerson provides an insightful interpretive articulation of the theistic core of the thought developed by the best practitioners of the philosophical tradition he calls Ur-Platonism, from Plato to Proclus, before that thought got absorbed and further developed by Christian thinkers.

Gerson's conception of "Ur-Platonism" is closely related to his understanding of "Platonism." He writes: "Platonism dominated Western philosophy more or less from the time of Plato's death until the seventeenth century."[7] He reads Plato and Aristotle primarily from the standpoint of the Middle- and Neo-Platonist writers who philosophized from circa 100 B.C until the death of Proclus in 486 A.D, many of whom were students of both texts and oral traditions deriving from both Plato and Aristotle. From that standpoint he offers a schematic list of the seven elements of "Platonism."[8] (1) The universe has a systematic unity, so that particular doctrines in metaphysics, epistemology, ethics, and so on are ultimately inter-relatable within the system. (2) That unity involves an explanatory hierarchy such that all existing things are susceptible of top-down explanation, with the ultimate explanatory principle of the universe being an unqualifiedly simple reality—the One (or the Good). (3) The fundamental Platonic exhortation to the person to "become like God" entails that there is a "personal" or super-personal aspect to the One. Benevolence and providence are taken to be essential features of the divine. (4) The psychological constitutes an irreducible explanatory category. Life is not epiphenomenal or supervenient upon nonliving matter. "Soul" has a unique explanatory role in the systematic hierarchy. (5) The happiness of rational persons consists in achieving a *lost* position within the hierarchy. Normativity is an aspect of the real, and there is a normative Form of human nature deriving from the One. There is a gap in every human life between "what is" and "what ought to be." Persons are capable of virtue or vice and are somehow immortal or at least capable of immortality. (6) Like all Forms, Forms of moral and aesthetic values are

6. Lloyd Gerson, *Aristotle and Other Platonists* (Ithaca, New York: Cornell University Press, 2005); ———, *From Plato to Platonism* (Ithaca, New York: Cornell University Press, 2015); ———, *Platonism and Naturalism* (Ithaca, New York: Cornell University Press, 2020).

7. Gerson, *Platonism and Naturalism*, 198.

8. Gerson, *Aristotle and Other Platonists*, 32–34.

capable of various degrees of excellence of instantiation. All things are relatively good or bad, beautiful or ugly, etc., depending upon their excellence and upon their position within the hierarchy of being. The First Principle of all—God or the One—is at once the standard and the limit case "instance" of all the moral and aesthetic Forms (all the pure perfections). (7) Metaphysics is prior to epistemology. Knowledge can only be understood in terms of a theory of being as knowable (thus immaterial). Modes of cognition are hierarchically gradable according to the hierarchical levels of objective reality, which are their objects. The highest modes of cognition have as their objects God or the One, Forms, and immaterial beings of various sorts.

Behind Platonism, according to Gerson, lies "Ur-Platonism," which arises from the conjunction of the negations of the philosophical positions already on offer but explicitly rejected in the Platonic dialogues. The five pre-Platonic positions opposed by Ur-Platonism are materialism, mechanism, nominalism, relativism, and skepticism. Hence Ur-Platonism is the conjunction of anti-materialism, anti-mechanism, anti-nominalism, anti-relativism, and anti-skepticism. To be a Platonist, minimally, is to have a commitment to refuting the five pre-Platonic positions, as well as a commitment to discovering the most consistent, integrated, and systematic way of doing so. Plato's philosophy is perhaps the greatest single attempt to work out such a construct, but many of his successors and epigones, not least Aristotle and Plotinus, did excellent philosophical work as "Platonists" in Gerson's sense.

A few words more should be said about the five components of Ur-Platonism.[9] (1) *Anti-materialism* is the view that it is false that the only things that exist are bodies and the attributes of bodies. (2) *Anti-mechanism* is the view that the only sort of explanations available in principle to a materialist are inadequate for explaining the natural order. Whereas contemporary anti-mechanism contends that mental events have no sufficient physical causes, ancient anti-mechanism contends that not even *physical* events have sufficient physical causes. (3) *Anti-nominalism* is the view that it is false that the only things that exist are individuals, each uniquely situated in space and time. Nominalism in a general sense denies the real existence of anything other than individuals. The anti-nominalist, by contrast,

9. Gerson, *From Plato to Platonism*, 9–19.

can allow that two or more individuals can be the same in some respect and still be different and unique individuals (each instantiating a Form or property type that exists somehow independently of the individuals). Hence the anti-nominalist allows conceptual space for sameness that is not identity. (4) *Anti-relativism* is the denial of Protagoras' claim that "man is the measure of all things, of what is that it is and of what is not that it is not." Anti-relativism holds that what is true or good is determinable independently of what appears to a person or group as true or good for him or it. (5) Finally, *anti-skepticism* is the view that knowledge is possible, where knowledge is a mode of cognition wherein the real is in some way "immediately present" to the knower. In the Platonic dialogues, we learn that if either materialism or nominalism is true, skepticism follows, because the immediate presence of the real to any knower requires the existence of immaterial Form.

Ur-Platonism opposes these five philosophical positions. In the tradition of Ur-Platonism, *anti-materialism* and *anti-mechanism* are warranted in part by the constitutive role in reality of irrational numbers or limits that are immaterial and mind-dependent (that something is formally or mathematically understandable to us indicates that an Intellect has made it so). *Anti-nominalism* is warranted as a necessary condition for the possibility of knowledge and for the possibility of there being two or more individuals with a sameness that is not identity. *Anti-relativism* and *anti-skepticism* are warranted by the existence of noetic knowledge (such as mathematics), a mode of cognition wherein the real is in some way "immediately present" to the knower (more or less partially and so "fallibly"). Such immediate presence is possible only if there is Intellect that can become identical with immaterial Form.[10] These five principles constitutive of Ur-Platonism, though they each have some independent warrant, make most sense and are best warranted as part of a unified theistic account of all reality. Platonic theism provides that unified account. It adds to the five principles a recognition of the interrelatedness of all Forms, and of the explanatory need for a positively infinite intelligence that is the source and locus of all *possible* finite Forms.[11] This theistic explanatory framework provides a unified ex-

10. See Edward Feser, "Kripke, Ross, and the Immaterial Aspects of Thought," *American Catholic Philosophical Quarterly* 87, no. 1 (2013): 1–32.

11. See the discussion of the Stranger's doctrine of ultimate Being in the *Sophist* as the power that makes the cosmic whole of parts (both material and immaterial parts) the whole that it is, in my "Intimations in Plato's *Republic* of Some Doctrines of Maritain's *The Person and the Common*

planation of the five principles of Ur-Platonism and of the interrelatedness of all the Forms, while positing that the stopping point of all explanation—both of the intelligible and of the sensible realms—is a self-explanatory "un-hypothetical first principle of all" at the top of the hierarchy of reality.[12] The history of more or less partial achievements in articulating and refining "Platonic" theistic metaphysical theory from the pre-Socratics to Plotinus constitutes a pre-Christian and purely philosophical tradition.

Now I turn to the mysterious conception of the "Idea of the Good" found at the center of the *Republic*, which we saw discussed by MacIntyre. Gerson lists a number of Plato's *dicta* concerning the Idea of the Good.[13] In 504a–517c Socrates says the "greatest study" for mankind is that of the Idea of the Good (504d–505a). This entity is analogous to the Sun in its luminousness, creativity, transcendence, and visibility. It is the endpoint of all striving (505d–e). The Idea of the Good explains the existence of finite intelligences capable of knowing finite Forms, and it is the source of the existence (*einai*) and essence (*ousia*) of the intelligible Forms, even though itself "beyond essence" in rank and power (509b). The Forms are "good-like." The causal reach of the Idea of the Good extends below the Forms to the production of the sensible world formed by the Forms (517c) and so the Good is "in a certain sense cause of all things" (516c). Grasping it is necessary for knowing the nature of the Forms, that is, for knowing what the Forms are for (511b–c). The Idea of the Good is apprehensible and some account of it can be given (508e, 517b–c, 532b, 534b–d). Dialectical reasoning is the sole means of attaining knowledge of the Idea of the Good, the "un-hypothetical first principle of all" (510b, 511b, 533a–d), and dialectical knowledge of the Idea of the Good is the means to the highest human happiness (498c, 532e, 540b–c).

These passages leave no doubt that the Idea of the Good is held by Plato to be the focus of his thought, indeed the focus of his systematic phi-

Good," in *In Search of Harmony: Metaphysics and Politics*, edited by James G. Hanink (Washington, D.C.: The American Maritain Association, distributed by The Catholic University of America Press, 2019), 39–61, especially 44–48.

12. See Alasdair MacIntyre, "About What Do Contemporary Atheists and Theists Disagree?" in *Ciphers of Transcendence: Essays in Philosophy of Religion In Honour of Patrick Masterson*, edited by Fran O'Rourke (Newbridge: Irish Academic Press, 2019), 358–70. MacIntyre argues that the disagreement is not merely about whether or not to add one more being (a transcendent one) to the list of existing things but rather, more importantly, about what constitutes adequate explanation.

13. Gerson, *Platonism and Naturalism*, 120–27.

losophy as a whole, because of its unique, comprehensive, and superordinate causal scope. The philosophical puzzles raised by these descriptions of the Idea of the Good constitute part of Plato's legacy to his successors and elicit profound philosophical insights from them. Here are just three examples of Platonic questions eliciting philosophical solutions from later thinkers: (1) How can the Idea of the Good exist if it is beyond *ousia* (essence) and so has no essence? Plotinus uses a conception of pure *energiea* to characterize it, and later Aquinas uses a conception of *Ipsum Esse Subsistens*. (2) How can such a Being cause anything else, and what kinds of causation might be involved in answering that question? (3) Why cannot Forms be understood without understanding the Idea of the Good, and what does it mean for the Idea of the Good to provide knowability to the Forms? This question is well answered in Aristotle, Plotinus, and other theists by remarking that the Forms make possible and produce *integrative unity* in their participants, acting as principles of unity for their participants (in *Metaphysics* Alpha Aristotle testifies that Plato identified the Idea of the Good with "the One"). This makes the Forms Good-like because the Good itself—the limit case instance of all the pure perfections which include not only Unity but also order, truth, and beauty—is that in which any entity, Form or physical-sensible, must participate if it is to have any of these perfections, especially the integral unity that constitutes its identity in the first place. The Good gives integrated unified existence to all of its products, both Forms and sensibles. Just as the human craftsman has the idea for the thing-to-be-made within himself, so the Idea of the Good is virtually all that is ordered and intelligible in the finite forms and bodily things it produces.

This conception of the Idea of the Good as the source of all integrated unified existence—coextensive with all order, beauty, truth, or any of the pure perfections—is the metaphysical foundation for Plato's anti-relativism about values, including moral values. It performs the functions MacIntyre told us Plato's Idea of the Good was designed to perform: to explain the unity underlying the multiplicity of goods of every kind, to provide an unconditional first principle by appeal to which the tasks of rational justification of an account of justice (or of any excellence) can be brought to completion, to provide a justification in practical reasoning for judging which *particular* actions or experiences or states of affairs are good, and to account for the causal origin of the entire finite universe, seen and unseen. And it serves as a proper explanation and elucidation for all the different kinds of good that MacIntyre told us Aristotle was concerned to distinguish: the ultimate Good towards which all things direct themselves, the specifically human good of self-actualization in a unified life through the practice of *phronesis* and the other virtues in the "art of living," the large variety of *types* of good pursued by human beings in all the arts, crafts, and sciences, in the course of producing excellent artifacts, artworks, performances, services, and so on, all the *particular* goods identified by particular agents on particular occasions that are the materials from which an excellent life is constructed.

So it is no wonder that the "Idea of the Good" is central for Plato's ethics. One reason why this centrality often goes unnoticed is a widespread impression that Aristotle's critique of the Form of the Good in Book VI of his *Nichomachean Ethics* is decisive as a critique of Plato's conception of the Idea of the Good. In the first part of this essay we mentioned that Alasdair MacIntyre found it necessary to criticize Peter Winch for succumbing to this impression.[14] Aristotle's critique of the idea of goodness succeeds only as a critique of Plato's understanding of the coordinate Form of the Good, not of his conception of the superordinate Idea of the Good, that which on Aristotle's own testimony is identical to "the One."[15] And Aristotle himself folds Plato's superordinate Idea of the Good, along with Plato's Demiurge Intellect eternally cognizing all the Forms, into his conception of an Unmoved Mover which is pure Intellect and pure *Energeia*.[16] Whereas Plato's first principle is *beyond ousia*, Aristotle's is a *perfect ousia*, an eternally actual omniscient

14. See Samuel Baker, "The Metaphysics of Goodness in the Ethics of Aristotle," *Philosophical Studies* 174, no. 7 (2017): 939–56.

15. Gerson calls attention to Proclus' little-read *Commentary on Plato's Republic*, which discusses with insight the exegetical and philosophical problem of how there can be two Ideas of the Good, one that is coordinate with other Forms or *ousiai* and one that is "beyond *ousia*." Proclus distinguishes a class of Forms that name various perfections and suggests that the coordinate Form of the Good is the *genus* of these various perfections.

16. Attending to Aristotle's conception of an Unmoved Mover which is pure *Energeia* and pure Intellect eternally cognizing all the Forms or Intelligibles can go some way toward showing that Aristotle's apparent "denial of Forms separate from sensibles" does not disprove the harmony of Aristotle's philosophy with Plato's. It is often thought that Aristotle's supposedly relentless criticism of what is supposedly the centerpiece of Plato's philosophy—a "theory of separate Forms"—makes him radically depart from Plato. In "rejecting separate Forms" Aristotle was not only concerned with fashioning the idea of immanent substantial Form, but also with rejecting a conception of Forms as self-subsisting divine entities that were (1) separate from each other (Plato in the *Sophist* also rejects this idea of Forms separate from each other), (2) separate from a divine Intellect (Plato also rejects this, arguably, in the account of cosmic Nous in the *Philebus*), and separate from a first principle (Plato rejects this, arguably, in the *Parmenides*). See Gerson, *Aristotle and Other Platonists*, 20–21, 187, 209, 220–21, 278–79, and 290.

Intellect. So Aristotle, theological differences aside, shares with Plato a strong antipathy to naturalism and a strong commitment to "Platonism."

Plato's occasional treatment of the Form of the Good as a mere Form co-ordinate with other Forms is what led scholars to overlook the theistic significance of the Idea of the Good.[17] This failure elicited MacIntyre's complaint about philosophy practiced in the officially non-theistic modern nation-state and global market: that scholars will always stay clear of theism in order to escape persecution from the naturalist, pluralist, and secular humanist culture of today. Plato's transcendent Idea of the Good grounds the absoluteness of true moral norms and non-relativism about values in general. If the divine Good is really the source and norm of all good-making attributes of persons, then those attributes *in fact* make people good, regardless of the preferences or feelings people may have about them. And if the divine Good is also the source and norm of the essentially social nature of persons made to find their own good in the pursuit with others of *common goods* which can never be at the expense of the goods of others, then various kinds of greed and *pleonexia* are *objectively wrong*, regardless of the feelings and judgments people may have about them. And indeed the highest common good sought by all persons, on a post-Platonic Christian conception, is shared knowledge of the "Idea of the Good" itself, a "beatific vision." Such Platonic or post-Platonic anti-relativistic conceptions are unwelcome in a society of advanced consumer capitalism based on ruthless competition and on the value primacy of personal preferences for consumer goods, lifestyles, identities, and world-views. On a Platonic account, one identity or lifestyle or integrative life-story is better than another if and only if the integrative unity it achieves—the order, truth, and beauty of the life so integrated—more adequately reflects and instantiates aspects of the Good itself than its rival.

III. Plotinus

One of the greatest philosophers in the Platonic tradition was of course Plotinus.[18] Gerson says that Plotinus provided "a moment of powerful sys-

17. Elsewhere I defend a theistic interpretation of the Idea of the Good while allowing that Plato also occasionally refers to goodness as a coordinate Form. See my earlier cited "Intimations in Plato's *Republic* of Some Doctrines of Maritain's *The Person and the Common Good*."

18. In the next few pages about Plotinus, I am indebted not only to Gerson but also to A. H. Armstrong, *An Introduction to Ancient Philosophy* (London: Methuen and Co., 1947), chaps. 16 and 17.

tematic consolidation analogous to the role of Thomas Aquinas in the history of Christian theology."[19] Plotinus' system very obviously counters the nominalist, materialist, mechanistic, relativistic, and skeptical positions that any Platonic system must oppose. Plotinus recognized that the One cannot have any passive *dunamis*, but he nevertheless sometimes retains Plato's terminology and equates the unlimited active *dunamis* of the One with the perfect *energeia* or actuality of Aristotle.

Plotinus took the notion of pure *energeia* that Aristotle had applied to the supreme *ousia*, the Unmoved Mover, and extended its application to the One beyond *ousia*. Plotinus' God is identical with Plato's transcendent Idea of the Good, more perfect and unified than even the highest *ousia* and even more perfect and unified than any Intellect cognizing a field of finite Forms or *ousiai*. On Plotinus' account, the One's unique simplicity as containing virtually "in" itself every possible finite good but in an infinitely integrated way makes language about it problematic, for it is always misleading to attribute predicates to a reality that does not "have" attributes but "is" its attributes. Nevertheless, just as Aquinas later employs in his discourse about God both a *via negativa* and a *via eminentiae*, Plotinus supplements his own negative approach to God with a more positive approach, maintaining that finite perfections are pointers to, and lesser imitations of, the perfection(s) of their infinite source. Plotinus does not hesitate on occasion to speak "by analogy" and to say the One/Good "loves itself" or is "pure will" or "cause of itself."

The world of Forms, which provides the intelligible content of Plotinus' Second Hypostasis, the Divine Mind (which is his stand-in for Plato's Demiurge and ranks next below the One in the hierarchy of reality as he conceives it), is only an imperfect and more differentiated or dispersed imaging in multiplicity of the single Good. For Plotinus, although the Good contains virtually all that is in the finite field of Forms cognized by Nous, it has an infinite content only partially expressible in any finite field of Forms (any "possible world"). That is why he finds Aristotle's most perfect Intellect or Nous—the Unmoved Mover that is Aristotle's highest *ousia*—to be an inadequate conception of God, because the Unmoved Mover is conceived, not as the source and locus of all possible finite Forms, but only of all Forms constitutive of our actual world.[20]

19. Gerson, *Platonism and Naturalism*, 225.

20. For Plotinus the Second Hypostasis, the Divine Nous, can fully know the Good only by going beyond noetic intellection into ecstasy. Its normal intellection gives it only that pluralized

Plotinus took divine "attributes" or functions from earlier tradition—transcendence, priority to the Forms, self-contemplating intelligence, supreme unity and goodness, the creating of souls and of physical things carried out by the Demiurge in the *Timaeus*—and referred some of them to the One, some of them to his First Hypostasis, the Divine Mind or Nous, and some of them to his Second Hypostasis, the Divine "Soul." Plotinus' "Soul" is the link between the higher immaterial spiritual world and the bodily world. It has to do duty both for the operations of *Timaeus'* Demiurge (higher soul) and of *Timaeus'* World-Soul (lower soul, or "Nature"). Plotinus does not characterize human souls the way the Pythagoreans did as being imprisoned or entombed in their bodies, but he does maintain that a human soul that devotes itself selfishly to the interests of its body becomes entrapped in the atomistic particularity of the material world, isolates itself from the whole, and cuts itself off from its high destiny of reuniting with the One. The highest part of the human soul remains in the world of the Divine Nous even when it is embodied, retaining the power to connect with the Divine Nous and even to attain, if only rarely, an ecstatic union with the One that surpasses the power of human Nous.

IV. Christian Theism as a Development of Platonism: Some Improved Conceptions of Divine Perfection and of the Human Good

When the great Christian Platonists of the fourth and fifth centuries A.D., including Augustine and others, begin to work on the ideas of Plotinus in order to elucidate their own doctrine of God, they drop his conception of the Divine Hierarchy consisting of the Supreme One and of the two hypostases of Nous and Soul. Instead, these Fathers reconceive the whole of Divinity as concentrated in the One and they apply to the Trinity-in-Unity everything that Plotinus says about the divine hypostases, although occasionally they associate a particular function with a particular person of the Trinity.[21] What Plotinus says about Divine Nous they apply either to the

image of the One or the Good which is the finite field of Forms governing the finitely real physical world.

21. This way of speaking of the relation of Trinitarianism to Plotinus' theology I take from A. H. Armstrong. But it *may* get things backwards. It has been speculated that Plotinus' teacher Ammonius Sachus, once a Trinitarian Christian, may have influenced Plotinus' doctrine of the One and the two Hypostases.

divine nature shared by the three persons or to the Second Person of the Trinity. All finite and relative being outside the Godhead depends somehow on this eternal generation of the Word. The "essential productivity" that Plotinus attributed to the One's Self-love becomes associated with the eternal generation of the Second Person of the Trinity.[22] The Christian Fathers of this period also apply a good deal of what Plotinus says about the activities of his higher Soul to the external activities of the Holy Spirit. Where Plotinus had placed all divine theoretical activity in his Divine Nous, and all divine practical production and providence over the material world in his Divine Soul, Christian thinkers acknowledge that in God's creative activity *ad extra* theoretical and practical reason collapse together into the one timeless creation of a temporal world by the Three-in-One.[23]

A Trinitarian notion of God solves certain problems remaining in pre-Christian Platonist theism and offers an improved understanding of the ethical implications of the divine goodness. I will discuss several such solutions and improvements in the remainder of this essay. One problem solved by a Trinitarian notion of God has to do with making sense of how a simple One might generate a world of multiplicity. This problem is perhaps raised in sharpest form by Proclus, who was only eighteen when Augustine died. For Plato, the beginning of a solution comes in the *Sophist* where the Stranger distinguishes between a Form and the nature it has. The nature is what is shared with the Form's participants without the participants being identical with the Form. But the distinction between Form and its nature generates problems if it is applied to the absolutely simple superordinate Form of the Good or One. Presumably for the coordinate lesser Forms to participate in the One, there must be a distinction in the One between itself and its nature participated in by the lesser Forms. But, because of the One's absolute simplicity, no sense can be made of such a distinction or of the

22. Dorothy Sayers once modeled the Trinitarian relations in a quasi-Augustinian way upon the psychology of mental creativity. She compared the Father to the artist's original idea, the Son to the embodied execution of the idea in the artwork, and the Spirit to the full appreciation and comprehension of the embodied artwork. See Dorothy Sayers, *The Mind of the Maker* (New York: Harcourt Brace, 1941).

23. This shift in emphasis correlates with Aquinas' doctrine of the *primacy of practical knowledge over speculative knowledge in God* (not necessarily in man). God's creative activity is modeled by Aquinas on the relation of an artisan to his product, and human craftsmanship comes into focus as a partial participation in the divine creative activity. In this Aquinas' thought returns to Plato in order to incorporate into theology Plato's conception of ethics and politics as higher-order *crafts*.

participation of any Form in the superordinate One/Good. But if the One cannot be participated in, what explanatory role is it supposed to fill? This problem seems to provide a *reductio ad absurdum* of Plotinus' notion of *absolute simplicity*. Platonism will not work without the self-existent One that explains everything else, and this ultimate explanatory principle must be in some sense uniquely simple. Yet Plotinus' notion of absolute simplicity will not do the job. The Plotinian philosopher faces a dilemma. On the one hand, the first principle must be "absolutely simple." On the other hand, absolute simplicity seems to be impossible for that which is causally explanatory of anything else. There appears to be an irresolvable tension between the absolute simplicity of the One and its explanatory adequacy for any "many." In order to save Platonic theism, a new conception is needed of a unique ultimate explanatory principle of all else that is uniquely simple but yet has in itself the paradigm of complexity as well. But this is just what the Trinitarian doctrine of God provides. It teaches that the source of all finite reality is a unique divine nature fully shared by three unique divine persons. The one "nature" by definition does not have the kind of *absolute* simplicity that makes sharing it or participating in it impossible.

A second problem solved by Trinitarian theology is Plotinus' problem about whether God's production of the two hypostases, and through them of the finite world, occurs with *necessity* or not. Another way to conceive of this problem has to do with whether or not God is absolutely *self-sufficient*, whether or not the divine life of love and knowledge is complete and self-contained and in primacy over God's external activity of Creation. Plotinus argues in *Enneads* 6.8 that the Good (the One) is essentially an activity of self-loving. Recalling Plato's doctrine that the Good is an overflowing treasury of goodness, he says the self-loving of the Good is "essentially productive." This nicely explains why the soul who achieves spiritual union with the Good (the One) is able to achieve true virtue that "bears fruit." Yet this doctrine of "essential productivity" makes it seem that Plotinus' Good *must* generate the finite world.[24] But in a Trinitarian context, the eternal generation of the Word by the Father, together with the spiration of the Holy Spirit, can be taken as such perfect expressions of the productive overflowing self-loving power of the Father that the theoretical need to conceive of God's creation of the finite universe as necessary is removed. For

24. But there are other interpretations possible for the Platonist. See Lloyd Gerson, "Plotinus' Metaphysics: Creation or Emanation?" *Review of Metaphysics* 46 (March 1993): 559–74.

the Christians, unlike Plotinus, creation is not an automatic reflex emanation of the Self-loving One. The Divine Productivity is perfectly expressed in the Eternal Son even apart from the creation of the finite temporal world. Creation and Redemption are, analogously speaking, *freely willed* by the persons of the Trinity in order to *share as a gift* the Trinitarian life with finite persons.

At this point it will be useful to expand upon how the conceptions of Creation and Redemption are interrelated in Christian theology as two aspects of God's free agency. Christian thinkers did not see in Plato any definitive account of why the highest reality should ever produce anything distinct from itself. Although they found congenial Plato's notion of a Form of the Good naturally diffusing itself in a non-jealous manner, they also thought they saw in Plato residual Parmenidean elements, according to which the highest reality, because changeless, cannot *act* as finite persons do.[25] On the other hand, Jewish and Christian thinkers found in Aristotle a conception of God as "pure activity" that was compatible with the doctrine of creation, but also found Aristotle struggling to formulate any account of how that God is any sort of *efficient cause* of the universe, and contending that God can only be described as engaged in the highest activity of thinking, and that directed only to Himself, so that it would be unworthy of God to pay attention to any being lower than Himself let alone consciously and voluntarily to create a finite universe. Plotinus improved upon Aristotle to the extent that he spoke of the generation of the cosmos as a result of the "self-love" of the One. However, he at least seems to have ended up describing the finite world as a *necessary* consequence of the divine nature. Therefore, his philosophical theology remained, like Aristotle's, in danger of collapsing back into a pantheism. Neither Aristotle's nor Plotinus' theology clearly rules out some sort of *quasi-pantheism* according to which the world is a necessary side-effect of God's self-contemplation or self-love (or, as later in Spinoza and Hegel,[26] a stage in God's necessary self-unfolding), and a "part" of the divine nature but not the "external" result of a free creative act, and so not really distinct from the divine. Nor does either rule out some sort of Parmenidean acosmism, according to which the world is not real and

25. Or so claims Patrick Madigan. See Patrick Madigan, SJ, *Christian Revelation and the Completion of the Aristotelian Revolution* (Lanham, Maryland: University Press of America, 1988).

26. Both Spinoza and Hegel provide non-Christian conceptions of salvation combined with pantheistic metaphysics. For Spinoza, salvation consists in intelligent resignation to the truth that God is impersonal.

so does not need explanation (echoed in some forms of Hinduism). For if the world is in some way independent of God and not merely a necessary consequence of His nature, then its existence cannot be explained by God's nature or form, but demands an independent "personal" act on God's part to explain its existence. Plotinus demurs from admitting a free creation of the world by God, even though he does articulate a notion of self-earned "salvation" and of the return of the soul to God.

What an elucidation of the doctrine of Creation required was some account of divine agency, some account of why God would bring into existence a world distinct from Himself, an account in accord with the divine perfection insisted upon by the theistic tradition from Socrates to Plotinus. (Many pagan thinkers held that attributing personal agency to God was simply relapsing into mytho-anthropomorphism.) What was needed was some conception that would allow God to know and to interact with finite things beside Himself without thereby slighting the divine perfection or the divine simplicity. What emerged in the Christian theistic tradition was the view that Creation only makes sense if it is joined to or embedded within a wider context of "salvation" (in the Johannine tradition of "friendship with God"). The efficient causation or production of the world from and by a perfectly intelligent and self-sufficient God only made sense if it was conceived to be an expression of the Divine Will to display, to manifest, and to share various degrees and kinds of his perfection with intelligent created persons equipped to appreciate and to participate in that perfection through a kind of loving friendship with God. Creation, Revelation, and Salvation demand personal initiative on God's part, an initiative that constitutes a condescension absolutely scandalous to pure Aristotelianism or to Plotinian Neoplatonism. God takes no personal initiative toward humanity in either Aristotle or Plotinus. Pagan resistance to the specifically Christian doctrine of Creation centered on the idea that any attribution to God of a will to share himself in friendship with finite human (and super-human) intelligent beings was not just anthropomorphic but scandalously beneath the divine dignity.

In Book 8 of the *Nichomachean Ethics,* Aristotle explicitly says in his discussion of friendship between unequals that God and men cannot be friends (1159a), in part because God could get nothing from this relationship that would be commensurate with His greatness. Aquinas will later attempt to preserve Aristotle's and Plotinus' doctrines of the divine perfection by saying that God necessarily is aware of His own perfection, in its actual simplicity, *qua* exemplar of all the finite possibilities by which his goodness might be expressed, and of all the personal perspectives from which it may be appreciated (as by friends). God wills into existence finite things as partial mirrors of His own goodness and as potential *sharers* in that goodness in a way compatible with the divine perfection as understood by Aristotle and Plotinus. But, Aquinas says, the world is not willed from necessity, since God's perfect goodness subsists completely and independently of created things. God's will to share and to communicate His perfection with creatures is a free and non-necessitating motive for Creation entirely compatible with the divine perfection, especially so in light of the Trinitarian doctrine according to which the Divine Perfection is constituted by three Persons already sharing a divine nature with each other. God's sharing Himself with rational creatures, for Aquinas, makes possible a friendship involving the mutual love and communication between persons, thereby overcoming and to some extent transforming Aristotle's doctrine of friendship in a way that accommodates a friendship between unequals.

The Trinitarian conception of God, especially as it is bound up with the Incarnation of the Second Person, also makes for at least three important improvements upon Plotinus' ethical thought. This is highly relevant in light of MacIntyre's original contention that perhaps the main problem Plato and Aristotle confronted in their philosophies was the problem of the relationship between the divine goodness and the human good. The first improvement is this. The Trinitarian God who is also the Supreme Good is the ultimate paradigm for the ethical notion that the essence of rational personhood is to share a common good with other persons, the common good in the case of the Trinity being the divine nature itself. Trinitarianism strongly emphasizes the social nature of the human good. Plotinus' ethics, on the other hand, is, unlike Aristotle's, somewhat individualistic. It is true that he recognizes that a person who devotes himself inordinately to the interests of the body becomes a competitor with others for zero-sum goods, and to that extent he condemns a kind of greedy individualism. Yet when he discusses the spiritual quest, he says that the foolish and the wicked who undergo bodily suffering in this world only get what they deserve, and they have no right to expect good men to lay aside their own lives and come to help them. The sage exerts his or her own desire for God in an individualistic quest for Enlightenment. There is no "communion of the saints" in

Plotinus' thought. The Christian view, on the other hand, is that salvation is communal, cannot be had without the saving work of the Incarnation and the aid of the Church Christ founded; that the merits of some can be transferred to others who cry out in spiritual need, and that persons can pray to God for aid and can ask adepts or saints to intercede for them to God on behalf of their spiritual needs.

Secondly, the eternal generation of the Word and the eternal spiration of the Spirit provide divine paradigms for the great goodness of embodiment, biological generation (the Trinity is often used as a model for the relations between human parents and their children), and of embodied craftsmanship. In a recent papal teaching about sexual relations, the human body is conceived in part as a means for the communication of love and knowledge from one person to another, and in Jacques Maritain's *Creative Intuition in Art and Poetry* the making of embodied art is a primary way of glorifying God and participating in the "eternal productivity" of the Second Person.[27] In Christian thought the body and the material world are very good, means for communicating with others in intelligent love, for participating in the divine goodness through arts, crafts, and sciences. But matter and the body are not properly respected in Plotinus' ethics. The practice of virtue for Plotinus is a means to spiritual ascent. Plotinus' morality, as we noticed earlier, possesses a sharply otherworldly Pythagorean tendency or tenor which regards embodiment as an evil, a tendency to which Plato himself never succumbed. Plotinus seems to regard embodiment as a natural but regrettable necessity. But in Christianity God unites himself with a human body in the Incarnation, and part of the meaning of that event is that the human body possesses enough goodness that it is apt for such a union.

The doctrine of the Incarnation of God in Christ opens the way for yet a third improvement upon Plotinus' ethical-spiritual thought. For Plotinus shares with many Greek thinkers the view that the philosopher could and must purify his life, act virtuously, know the truth, and ascend to the threshold of union with God by his own strength and effort and without any special divine help.[28] Saints Paul and Augustine, and after them all Christian teachers, teach to the contrary that human beings are spiritual-

27. See also note 23 above.

28. Perhaps Plato avoided this fault to some extent, since at *Republic* 6, 492e–494a he makes Socrates say: "if anyone is saved and becomes what he ought to be under our present constitutions, he has been saved—you might rightly say—by a divine dispensation (*theia moira*)." The translation is from *Plato "Republic,"* translated by G. M. A. Grube, revised by C. D. C. Reeve.

ly helpless without "sanctifying grace." Plotinus holds out little hope for the non-philosophical person who cannot ascend by the power of his own spirit to the higher world. Augustine, on the other hand, puzzled about how Plotinus' "One" (or Aristotle's "thought thinking itself") might be conceived as going out to rescue mankind by "speaking" a divine "Word" within the world through patterned historical events. He puzzled over how it might be possible for a transcendent, immaterial, bodiless God to nevertheless "speak" in the world and so to offer succor and aid to mankind. Unlike Neo-Platonism, Hinduism, or Buddhism, Scripture depicts the ascent to God not only as an ascetic individual effort but also as assisted by divine grace and by the love of God revealed in history.

We are finally in position to restate and to summarize the argument of this essay. We began by noting Alasdair MacIntyre's call for an anti-modern form of philosophical enquiry which would allow us to reckon with the works of Plato and Aristotle and Plotinus as systematic wholes so that they could be seen as contributions to a single developing and historically interconnected tradition of theistic thought, so that in particular the connections between their metaphysical theologies and their conceptions of the human good would be preserved. MacIntyre contended that such enquiry requires us to articulate a conception of a philosophical tradition, according to which philosophy, just like science, is essentially historical in the form of its enquiry. MacIntyre maintained that in any developing theological tradition of enquiry, just as in any developing scientific tradition of enquiry, the standards by which good theorizing is to be judged in any enquirer or group of enquirers are set by the question of whether or not that enquirer or group is able to carry further and to transcend the limitations of the best work of predecessors. MacIntyre's jeremiad against the modern "Cartesian" abandonment of tradition in inquiry contends that *all* rational enquiry is always tradition-dependent. Just as the vindication of any contemporary natural science is the history of that science, the retrospectively constructed history of the struggles and successes and transformations of that science, so the vindication of any philosophical theology is the retrospectively constructed history of the struggles and successes and transformations of that philosophical theology.

With this view of tradition in enquiry as a guide, we offered in the second two sections of this essay a sketch of Lloyd Gerson's erudite trilogy on Ur-Platonism and the history of Platonism from Plato through Aristotle and

Plotinus to Proclus. This sketch showed that philosophical theology during this millennium of development underwent a number of struggles and successes and transformations until it came to a sort of maturity in the *Enneads* of Plotinus. Finally, in the fourth and last section of the essay, we noted five ways in which Christian Trinitarian theology not only solved some metaphysical problems of, and to some extent transformed, the pre-Christian purely philosophical tradition of theism, but also showed how Trinitarian thought gives us an improved account of the relationship between the divine goodness and the human good. I suggested by implication the way in which the "water" of pre-Christian theistic philosophy gets transformed into the "wine" of revealed Trinitarian theology, even while that philosophy retains its value and its autonomy from divine special revelation concerning salvation.[29]

29. If philosophy is not given its autonomy from theology, it succumbs to the intellectual danger labeled "theologism" by Gilson in *The Unity of Philosophical Experience*. A philosophy of God is presupposed in any rational claim to a special revelation complementing it. Without philosophy, theology becomes fideistic.

KELSEY TUNING

MacIntyre and Meno

After Virtue vs. a Socratic Objection

I. Introduction

ALASDAIR MACINTYRE AND SOCRATES' interlocutor Meno seem to share a problem. Each defines virtue in relation to achieving goods, making both definitions appear prey for Socrates' objection, "Shall we not add to this *justly and not unjustly*?"[1] Socrates delivers this critique when Meno defines virtue as the ability to rule over people[2] and as the power of securing good things.[3] He thinks these definitions fail because we must supplement them with the virtue justice, and a definition cannot include what it defines. Centuries later, in *After Virtue,* MacIntyre defines virtue in three interrelated tiers: the qualities that allow man to obtain goods internal to practices,[4] that aid his quest for the good life,[5] and that sustain traditions.[6]

At first glance, this seems prey for Socrates' historic objection: must we not, after all, obtain the goods internal to practices, pursue the good life, and sustain traditions justly and not unjustly? Yet, as I will attempt to show, that is not the case. MacIntyre's definition withstands Socrates' objection

1. Plato, *Meno,* in *Five Dialogues,* translated by G. M. A. Grube, 2nd edition (Indianapolis, Indiana: Hackett Publishing Company, 2002), 73d.

2. *Meno,* 73d–74a.

3. *Meno,* 78b–79e.

4. Alasdair MacIntyre, *After Virtue: A Study in Moral Theory,* 3rd edition (Notre Dame, Indiana: University of Notre Dame Press, 2007), 191.

5. Ibid., 219.

6. Ibid., 223.

because it is rooted in internal goods. Meno's definitions, conversely, are based on external goods. By their very nature, internal goods cannot be obtained unjustly, since doing so makes them vanish.

After providing some general background information on MacIntyre's relationship to Plato, Aristotle, and Thomas Aquinas, I begin to defend my thesis by examining the most fundamental part of MacIntyre's account of the virtues: the goods internal to practices. My aim is to show that, for MacIntyre, practice's internal goods are intrinsically linked to virtues like justice, so justice never has to be superimposed on his definition from the outside. In doing so, I also address ambiguities about evil practices, the precise distinction between internal and external goods, and the definition of practices, with an eye to showing these do not threaten my thesis. Then I defend the second two tiers of MacIntyre's interrelated definition, the good life and traditions. My goal is not to unequivocally defend MacIntyre's account, but simply to show that Socrates' objection does not overturn it.

II. MacIntyre's Virtue Theory Compared to Plato's, Aristotle's, and Aquinas's

MacIntyre's theory falls within the Aristotelian family of virtue ethics, but his approach is different. He defines virtues in relation to their genealogy, maintaining that virtues arise through participation in practices, which in turn are situated within narrative quests for the good life and traditions. In other words, participating in disciplines like games and arts causes one to develop virtues like justice, temperance, courage, etc. This differs from Aristotle and Aquinas, who define virtues based on overarching theories of human nature and focus more on their structure and psychology. Of course, it also differs from Plato, who famously fails to define virtue in the *Meno*.

Regarding Plato specifically, MacIntyre's approach at the surface seems to share similarity with Plato's craftsman analogy. In the *Republic*, Plato compares the virtue of justice to practical skills (*technē*), saying that just as "medicine does not consider what is advantageous for medicine, but for the body" and "horse breeding does not consider what is advantageous for horse breeding, but for horses" justice ought to benefit its subject, the ruled, rather than the rulers.[7] Plato seeks to illumine aspects of virtue by comparing it to practical skills. At first, this seems similar to MacIntyre's account of

7. Plato, *Republic*, translated by C. D. C. Reeve (Indianapolis, Indiana: Hackett, 2004), 342b–e.

virtues arising from practices. Plato even insinuates that crafts have internal goods, e.g. bodies and horses, that are perverted through undue pursuit of external goods, e.g. wages.[8] Yet Plato never addresses MacIntyre's central question. Plato *compares* virtue to practical skills. Of course, whether virtues are or are analogous to skills is an interesting question, taken up by authors such as Julia Annas and Matthew Stitcher.[9] But this is not MacIntyre's question. Rather, MacIntyre focuses on virtues *arising through* practical skills, which Plato never addresses. Thus, Plato's craftsman analogy is not directly comparable to MacIntyre's account of virtues arising through practices—although it is fascinating that they describe crafts and practices in such similar ways.

Comparing MacIntyre in *After Virtue* to Aristotle and Aquinas is more complicated. To start with, like Plato, Aristotle compares virtues to practical skills, saying that just as "men become builders by building and lyre-players by playing the lyre; so too we become just by doing just acts, temperate by doing temperate acts, brave by doing brave acts."[10] MacIntyre talks past Aristotle here in the same way he talks past Plato, namely, by treating virtue as *arising from* practical skills rather than possibly *being* or *being like* practical skills. But a more serious difference exists between MacIntyre in *After Virtue* and Aristotle—one which also applies to Aquinas. This is that for both Aristotle and Aquinas, virtue is based on nature. For Aquinas, this is developed into a full account of natural law: "Wherefore according to the order of natural inclinations, is the order of the precepts of the natural law."[11] In *After Virtue*, MacIntyre opposes this. He famously rejects Aristotle's "metaphysical biology," the grounding of teleology in human nature, despite then considering himself an Aristotelian.[12] Due in part to this, MacIntyre also contends with Aquinas's theoretical rather than empirical virtue theory and rejects Aquinas's unity of the virtues and lack of tragic conflict.[13] These issues demonstrate significant differences between MacIntyre, Aristotle, and Aquinas.

8. *Republic*, 346a–347a.

9. See Julia Annas, *Intelligent Virtue* (Oxford: Oxford University Press, 2011) and Matt Stichter, *The Skillfulness of Virtue: Improving Our Moral and Epistemic Lives* (New York: Cambridge University Press, 2018).

10. Aristotle, *Nichomachean Ethics*, in *The Basic Works of Aristotle*, edited and translated by Richard McKeon (New York: The Modern Library, 2001), 2.1, 1103a36–1103b1.

11. Thomas Aquinas, *Summa Theologiae*, translated by the Fathers of the English Dominican Province (New Advent, 2017), I-II, q. 94, a. 2. Available at: https://www.newadvent.org/summa/

12. MacIntyre, *After Virtue*, 162.

13. See ibid., 178–80.

However, in the introduction to *After Virtue*'s third edition, MacIntyre states that he had unwittingly presupposed something like Aquinas's good in *After Virtue*. Thus, he realizes that his "conception of human beings as virtuous or vicious needed not only a metaphysical, but also a biological grounding, although not an especially Aristotelian one" and that it "is only because human beings have an end towards which they are directed by reason of their specific nature, that practices, traditions, and the like are able to function as they do."[14] Since penning *After Virtue*, MacIntyre has embraced Thomism. It seems he now believes that an alternative metaphysical biology supports his central theses in *After Virtue*.[15]

Thus, MacIntyre's virtue theory holds similarities to those of Plato, Aristotle, and Aquinas, but has its own unique flavor.

III. The Internal/External Goods Distinction

The distinction between MacIntyre's and Meno's definitions rests on their respective focus on internal and external goods.[16] "Internal" and "external" refer to MacIntyre's description of goods intrinsic and extrinsic to practices. "Practice" means a "coherent and complex form of socially established cooperative human activity" allowing one to achieve goods internal to it by attempting to achieve its appropriate standards of excellence, and by which "human conceptions of the ends and goods involved, are systematically extended."[17] Practices span a wide range of disciplines. They include games, architecture, farming, the sciences, and sustaining communities, among many others. Goods internal to practices are only achievable through their practices.[18] In the case of the practice of chess, for instance,

14. Ibid., xi.

15. Thomas D'Andrea's commentary is a good resource for further information on the relationship between MacIntyre, Aquinas, and Aristotle. See Thomas D'Andrea, *Tradition, Rationality, and Virtue: The Thought of Alasdair MacIntyre* (New York: Routledge Taylor and Francis Group, 2006).

16. I assume the internal/external goods distinction is legitimate. Some thinkers, such as David Miller and Paul Hager, have expressed doubts that it is workable: see David Miller, "Virtues, Practices, and Justice," in *After MacIntyre: Critical Perspectives on the Work of Alasdair MacIntyre*, edited by John Horton and Susan Mendus (Cambridge: Polity Press, 1994) and Paul Hager, "Refurbishing MacIntyre's Account of Practice," *Journal of Philosophy of Education* 45, no. 3 (2011): 545–61. I address some of their concerns below. Their criticisms are worth considering, but I do not think they threaten my thesis.

17. MacIntyre, *After Virtue*, 187.

18. Ibid., 188.

internal goods might include "the achievement of a certain highly particular kind of analytical skill, strategic imagination and competitive intensity."[19] To be clear, internal goods are not goods existing subjectively inside a person, like pleasure. They are internal in the sense of being internal to a practice, not internal to a person. In fact, by definition, internal goods must benefit the whole community.[20] Sometimes the communal benefit is direct, notably in the practice of sustaining communities, and sometimes indirect, as when the community benefits from containing established members. Yet it is always there. Conversely, external goods are "contingently attached… by the accidents of social circumstance," the classic examples being money, power, and status.[21] These external goods are not essentially linked to the practice and can always be sought through other means. This distinction allows MacIntyre's definition to stand firm while Meno's collapses.

IV. Meno's Definition—Based on External Goods

Meno's definition is defeated because it is based on external goods. When Meno first declares that virtue is "to be able to rule over people,"[22] his definition seeks the external good of power. Meno intends to say that a good ruler necessarily possesses virtues enabling him to rule justly. But instead of aiming his definition at a good internal to ruling justly, perhaps the well-being of the state, he aims it at power, an external good pursuable through alternate means. Needless to say, we can pursue power through unjust means, e.g. poisoning our competitors. Thus, Socrates rightly insists that virtue be defined not merely as the ability to rule people, but the ability to rule people justly.[23] At this point, however, Meno's definition dissolves, having included what it hoped to define. Because Meno bases virtue on a good achievable without virtue, his definition fails to define virtue. The same thing happens with Meno's next definition, "to desire beautiful things and have the power to acquire them"[24] or "the power of securing good things."[25] Even more than the previous, this definition aims at external

19. Ibid.
20. Ibid., 190–91.
21. Ibid., 188.
22. *Meno*, 73d.
23. Ibid.
24. *Meno*, 77b.
25. *Meno*, 78b–c.

goods, examples including health, wealth, gold, silver, honors, and offices in the city.[26] Obviously, we can pursue these unjustly: stealing produce to preserve our health, cheating business transactions to get gold and silver, using bribery to gain city offices. Hence, Socrates' same objection applies. Indeed, all definitions focusing on external goods fail, because external goods can always be obtained unjustly. Meno's foundation is thus crippled. But MacIntyre's is not.

V. MacIntyre's Definition—Based on Internal Goods

MacIntyre's definition is based on internal goods, which can only be sought justly. In fact, as MacIntyre intends, justice and the other virtues are defined in relation to these internal goods. His definition comprises three interrelated tiers: the practices, the good life, and traditions. I will now examine each in turn, showing that together they have the resources to deflect Socrates' objection through their foundation in internal goods. I will also address some ambiguities regarding practices and internal goods that may at first glance appear to inhibit MacIntyre's ability to avoid Socrates' objection.

1. *The First Tier of MacIntyre's Account: The Practices.* The first and most fundamental tier of MacIntyre's threefold definition is the practices, which declares, "A virtue is an acquired human quality the possession and exercise of which tends to enable us to achieve those goods which are internal to practices and the lack of which effectively prevents of us from achieving any such goods."[27] As aforementioned, a practice is a coherent, complex, cooperative activity whereby participants strive to achieve standards of excellence and consequently achieve its internal goods.[28] Examples include activities like chess, painting, biology, and breadmaking. By MacIntyre's account, the qualities we need to seek goods internal to a practice are the virtues. For example, sport practices necessitate qualities like justice, honesty, temperance, and courage. Since these qualities help us achieve goods internal to the sport, and in doing so define the relationship between the seekers, they become virtues.[29]

26. *Meno*, 78c.
27. MacIntyre, *After Virtue*, 191.
28. Ibid., 187.
29. See ibid., 191–92.

MacIntyre's definition withstands Socrates' objection through its foundation in these internal goods. The goods internal to practices are impossible to attain without justice and many other virtues; we need not supplement his definition with justice from the outside, as we must with Meno's. In other words, since internal goods can only be achieved justly, unlike external goods which can be achieved justly or unjustly, there is no need to add the qualification Plato insists on in the *Meno*. MacIntyre's example of a child offered money to win chess may be helpful.[30] Should the child successfully cheat at chess, he will obtain the external good of money. But will the child have the satisfaction of winning a fair game? Will he have sharpened his analytical abilities? Certainly not—using unjust means dissolves these and other goods internal to the practice. Hence, we need not supplement MacIntyre's definition with justice, because justice arises in and through the definition. MacIntyre's definition deflects Socrates' attack.

2. *Ambiguities Concerning MacIntyre's Account of Practices.* Now, MacIntyre's account does lend itself to several ambiguities. Although it is outside the scope of this essay to address these in detail, it would be beneficial to mention them briefly to show they do not impede his account's ability to withstand Socrates' objection.

One frequent confusion concerns the possibility of evil practices.[31] Should evil practices exist, then it would seem there must also be "evil virtues," requiring an external justice to eliminate. Consequently, MacIntyre's account would fall entirely prey to Socrates' objection. Yet MacIntyre himself addresses this criticism in two parts.[32] First, he doubts there are evil practices; he does not think, for instance, that "either torture or sado-masochistic sexuality answer to the description of a practice which [his] account of the virtues employs."[33] His commentator Christopher Lutz expounds this as follows: "Practices are forms of activity that draw people together into shared

30. See ibid., 188.

31. See ibid., 199–200.

32. I here expound MacIntyre's approach in *After Virtue.* Christopher Stephen Lutz has since pointed out that this problem with evil practices follows directly upon MacIntyre's prior rejection of the unity of the virtues; see for instance Christopher Stephen Lutz, *Reading Alasdair MacIntyre's "After Virtue"* (New York: Continuum International Publishing Group, 2012) and Christopher Stephen Lutz, *Tradition in the Ethics of Alasdair MacIntyre: Relativism, Thomism, and Philosophy* (New York: Lexington Books, 2004). If this is the case, then MacIntyre's later reversal of his stance on the unity of the virtues in *Whose Justice? Which Rationality?* could solve the problem concerning evil practices and virtues. Naturally, an examination of the unity of the virtues is beyond the scope of this essay.

33. MacIntyre, *After Virtue*, 200.

enterprises that help to develop the character of the agents involved, as those same agents contribute to the development of the practice. It is difficult to imagine base or injurious practices that could contribute to social life in these ways."[34] Rebecca Gordon picks up this line of thinking regarding torture, arguing that according to MacIntyre's conception it can only be considered what she calls a "false" practice, with false goods and thus false virtues.[35] But most thinkers, including MacIntyre himself, prefer to defend his account primarily with reference to the broader moral framework in which practices are embedded, namely, the good life and traditions. In brief, practices are embedded in an overall preconception of what it means to live a good life, which in turn is defined by an overarching cultural tradition.[36] This means that bad practices, and their corresponding "virtues," are eliminated if they do not fit the overarching view of the good of man—all of which, of course, are claims MacIntyre extensively defends.[37] "[W]ithout an overrid-

34. Lutz, *Reading Alasdair MacIntyre's "After Virtue,"* 165.

35. See Rebecca Gordon, *Mainstreaming Torture: Ethical Approaches in the Post-9/11 United States* (New York: Oxford University Press, 2014); Christopher Einolf, "The Ethics and Politics of Torture," dual review of *Talking About Torture: How Political Discourse Shapes the Debate*, by Jared Del Rosso and *Mainstreaming Torture: Ethical Approaches in the Post-9/11 United States* by Rebecca Gordon. *Public Administrations Review* 20, no. 20 (2016): 1–4.

36. Many scholars accuse MacIntyre of falling into relativism because he defines virtues in relation to traditions. This could also be grounds for thinking he fails to escape Socrates' objection. MacIntyre here uses an Aristotelian functional concept of the good for man, sometimes also called the old natural law approach. But MacIntyre also wants to maintain that our concept of what is functional for man, i.e. what our *telos* is or what contributes to our flourishing, is defined in terms of a cultural tradition. For a more detailed discussion, see David Lorenzo, "A. MacIntyre: Person, Community and Tradition Against Individualism," *Ramon Llull Journal of Applied Ethics*, no. 11 (2020): 85–115. MacIntyre defines virtue in relation to traditions in part because he rejects Aristotle's "metaphysical biology"—the idea that teleology is grounded in our nature. MacIntyre, however, does not consider his view relativistic. My own interpretation of him in *After Virtue* is that he sees the practices, the good life, and traditions as three interrelated facets of the definition of virtue that provide checks and balances on one another, so that anything falling through the cracks on one level is corrected by the others. Thus, the good life and traditions eliminate the possibility of evil practices, but the internal goods and interpersonal nature of the practices also prevents the existence of truly evil traditions and conceptions of the good life. MacIntyre also holds that traditions can be corrected by other traditions; see his postscript to the second edition of *After Virtue*. Naturally, it is beyond the scope of this essay to examine whether MacIntyre's account ultimately remains relativist. If we assume he is successful against relativism, he certainly escapes Socrates' objection. If we do not, then Socrates' objection gains traction—yet perhaps not enough traction, for even a relativist account could provide a definition of justice, based on goods internal to the relative tradition, albeit not a universal one. In any event, MacIntyre's later acceptance of Aristotle's metaphysical biology erases this issue entirely.

37. It is of course beyond the scope of this essay for me to also defend these claims; see the second half of *After Virtue* for MacIntyre's defense. I said at the beginning that my goal in this

ing conception of the *telos* of a whole human life," he states, "our conception of certain individual virtues has to remain partial and incomplete."[38] Or, as J. B. Schneewind explains, "MacIntyre himself points out that virtue at [the practice] stage is not adequate to constitute the whole moral life.... Not all practices are morally acceptable: some should be abandoned or drastically altered.... To resolve these problems we must construct a way of seeing the good for a whole individual life."[39] With this approach, we can see that MacIntyre's account has the resources to eliminate "evil virtues" arising from evil practices, and so does not need an external definition of justice superimposed. Thus, the (illusory) possibility of evil practices does not affect his ability to withstand Socrates' objection.

Another serious issue is the finer distinction between internal and external goods. MacIntyre focuses his account on games, which, as critic Paul Hager point outs out following David Miller, are "self-contained"—existing only for the achievement and contemplation of internal goods.[40] But games are not the best representative sample, since many practices aim at least partially at an external good through their internal constitution, in addition to internal goods. This means that rather than having "morally dubious" external goods attached from the outside like money, power, and status—not to indicate that these are inherently dubious, but MacIntyre often invokes their dubious connotations—practices can pursue wholesome external goods as part of their inner structure.[41] Take fishing, for instance, Hager's example.[42] Fishing has its internal goods—refined skill, joy of the water, etc.—but it also exists to produce food, an external good. Moreover, producing food hardly seems morally dubious. Scientific pursuits follow a similar model: certainly, chemistry has internal goods, like wonder or the thrill of discovery, but it also exists to increase our chemical technology to better our communities. MacIntyre claims it is institutions that make practices concerned with external goods, including these.[43] But it seems improbable

essay was not to unequivocally defend MacIntyre's account, but to show that Socrates' objection against it cannot hold.

38. MacIntyre, *After Virtue*, 202.

39. J. B. Schneewind, "Virtue, Narrative, and Community: MacIntyre and Morality," *The Journal of Philosophy* 79, no. 11 (1982): 656.

40. Paul Hager, "Refurbishing MacIntyre's Account of Practice," *Journal of Philosophy of Education* 45, no. 3 (2011): 548.

41. See ibid, 552–56.

42. See ibid., 552 and 554.

43. Alasdair MacIntyre, "A Partial Response to My Critics," in *After MacIntyre: Critical Per-*

that only institutions make fishing interested in producing food or sciences interested in technological advancement.[44] Hager solves this problem by arguing that practices need to be defined through the appropriate balance of internal and external goods rather than by internal goods alone.[45] He may be correct. Yet in relation to withstanding Socrates' objection, it is enough to affirm that practices *at least* have internal goods, whatever other external goods they may rightly pursue. No activity that exists solely for the sake of external goods, after all, seems to be a practice. Indeed, should fishing become exclusively about production, it would lose its status as a practice; likewise, if science became exclusively about technology. Thus, whatever the position these intrinsic external goods hold, practices still need to foster virtues through the achievement of internal goods, which can only be done justly. Consequently, despite this ambiguity, MacIntyre's account still resides fundamentally in internal goods, and as such evades Socrates' attack.

A third ambiguity concerns which activities count as practices, what Hager calls scope issues.[46] MacIntyre himself lists several criteria: complexity, a collaborative nature, the internal goods objective, standards of excellence, and a history.[47] Yet these leave much to be desired. In particular, "complexity" and "history" are too vague to adequately discern what counts as a practice. Regarding complexity, while there are many intuitive cases of activities too simple to be considered practices, a lot of gray area also exists. Hager subdivides farming as an example.[48] Is farming as a whole a practice, or must it be divided into, say, livestock farming and vegetable farming? What about the various kinds of livestock and the various kinds of plants that can be farmed, which, as anyone of experience will tell us, are quite complex on their own? It is unclear. History is likewise vague. In fact, it is even uncertain why a practice needs a history at all. Thought experiments can easily concoct activities that meet all other criteria for a practice, and it is unclear why they are not practices. For example, if a group of friends develops a complex, collaborative strategy game with standards of excellence and internal goods, and they are totally devoted to this game, play it all the

spectives on the Work of Alasdair MacIntyre, by John Horton and Susan Mendus (Cambridge: Polity Press, 1994), 284–86.

44. Hager, "Refurbishing MacIntyre's Account of Practice," 549.

45. Ibid., 554.

46. Ibid., 548, 550–52.

47. See MacIntyre, *After Virtue,* 187, 193–94.

48. Hager, "Refurbishing MacIntyre's Account of Practice," 551.

time, and—as I would venture to say—consequently develop virtues like diligence, patience, justice, etc., is this game a practice? MacIntyre would say no for its lack of a history. But when it comes to philosophically defending this claim, it becomes entirely unclear why the history matters, or at least at what point an activity has enough history. The simple length of time is a decidedly unsatisfactory answer. Perhaps we chase the train of thought to the point of asking whether "history" has to do with social or cultural importance. But then what constitutes a culture? If one close-knit group of friends practically had their own subculture and were very devoted to this game, what would prevent them from fostering virtues and achieving internal goods through their participation in it? No clear answer exists. I have received a couple suggestions in this regard.[49] Perhaps, to have a history, a practice needs to become independent of those who created it, taking on a life of its own, so to speak, which in practical terms means at least its first generation of creators needs to die off. One could also venture to defend MacIntyre in this area by saying that he is simply describing how, in real life, virtue grows, and is unconcerned with obscure thought experiments. Rather than asking precisely when an activity has enough of a history to become a practice, he observes that all activities we recognize as practices have histories, so it must be necessary in some way. He may even say that trying to pinpoint when an activity has enough history to become a practice is to engage in the continuum fallacy. Thus, although it is unclear what constitutes a practice, it seems clear enough that there are nonetheless many practices, that these practices have internal goods that are achieved through virtues, and that this setup escapes Socrates' objection. We do not need to know precisely how practices come to exist to know that the ones that do exist necessitate justice through their orientation to internal goods. Thus, with these confusions clarified, we see all the more that MacIntyre's conception of virtue—while perhaps not perfect—does have the resources to sidestep Socrates' critique of Meno.

3. *The Second Tier of MacIntyre's Account: The Good Life.* The second facet of MacIntyre's definition withstands Socrates' objection for the same reason. In his second tier, MacIntyre posits the conception of virtues begun in the practices is partially completed by qualities that help man quest for the good life in story-like fashion. These qualities, or virtues, "sustain us in the

49. I received these suggestions from Ronald Klingler and Dr. Brandon Dahm, respectively.

relevant kind of quest for the good, by enabling us to overcome the harms, dangers, temptations, and distractions which we encounter, and which will furnish us with increasing self-knowledge and increasing knowledge of the good."[50] Once again, the question becomes, Can man quest for the good life unjustly? For several reasons, he cannot. First, questing for the good life entails the practices, and the practices require the virtues. Second, according to MacIntyre, questing for the good life largely means figuring out what the good life is,[51] and history demonstrates that serious seekers rarely arrive at answers lacking some version of virtue—justice in particular is rarely contested. Finally, and most importantly, the good life for man involves all men seeking the good life, and this puts men in a relation with other men, a relation which MacIntyre already examined in the context of the practices, and determined necessitated the virtues. In a sense, therefore, we can view questing for the good life as one massive practice, which MacIntyre later calls a tradition.[52] To obtain goods internal to this practice, the goods of pursing the good life, we need the virtues for the same reason we need them in all other practices, to define the relationship between the seekers. For these reasons, the second part of MacIntyre's definition also withstands Socrates' objection.

4. *The Third Tier of MacIntyre's Account: Traditions.* The third part of MacIntyre's definition cannot resist Socrates' objection on its own, but does so easily with aid from the former two. It posits the virtues as qualities sustaining "those traditions which provide both the practices and individual lives with their necessary historical context. Lack of justice, lack of truthfulness, lack of courage, lack of the relevant intellectual virtues—these corrupt traditions."[53] Traditions help define the goods which constitute the practices and the good life.[54] Now, unlike the previous, this part of MacIntyre's definition cannot bear Socrates' objection alone. This is because sustaining a tradition—expanding, purifying, and prolonging it—seeks an external good. Sustaining traditions may entail internal goods, as well, but its simplest aim is external. To assure ourselves of this, notice we can sustain traditions unjustly, e.g. by massacring those who oppose the tradition. Yet, as aforementioned, MacIntyre's theory is holistic, and sustaining tradi-

50. MacIntyre, *After Virtue,* 219.
51. Ibid.
52. See ibid., 220–23.
53. Ibid., 223.
54. Ibid., 222.

tions is its very last tier. Thus, while the traditions are important for fleshing out aspects of his theory, we should not be surprised if they rely on their foundation for support. On their own, traditions cannot withstand Socrates' objection, but strengthened on either side by the other regiments of MacIntyre's holistic account—the practices and the good life—they easily manage the assault.

VI. Conclusion

Thus, MacIntyre's threefold definition of virtue deflects Socrates' objection because it is based on internal goods. These goods can only be pursued justly; attempting to gain them unjustly sabotages them. Consequently, Socrates' objection cannot compromise MacIntyre's definition like it does Meno's, which is based on external goods. A definition based on external goods needs justice imposed externally because external goods can be achieved unjustly. This obviously destroys the definition because a definition of virtue cannot include a virtue. On the other hand, a definition based on internal goods can only be sought justly. Every virtue is inside the definition as it should be: no virtue must be added externally. MacIntyre's definition clearly meets this standard. As we have seen, the practices aim primarily at internal goods. Questing for the good life can be seen as one massive practice that similarly aims at internal goods. Finally, although sustaining traditions seeks an external good, it does not compromise MacIntyre's definition because traditions must be sustained in light of the practices and the good life. Therefore, despite defining virtue in similar ways, MacIntyre's and Meno's definitions are not of equal strength. Meno's buckles under Socrates' objection, but MacIntyre's, strengthened from within through internal goods, survives the attack of the ancient thinker.

IV

THE CASCADE'S RYHME

Twentieth-Century Thomism

CHRISTOPHER LUTZ

Thomistic Aristotelianism vs. Moral Alienation

A Response to Bernard Williams

I. Preface

BERNARD WILLIAMS WAS NOT an Aristotelian, much less a Thomist. On his own terms, he was not even a moral philosopher; he rejected moral philosophy in general. Nonetheless, Alasdair MacIntyre suggests that Williams' rejection of moral philosophy raises questions that can help us, as Thomistic-Aristotelians, to appreciate the peculiar value of Thomistic moral teaching.[1] Williams accuses moral philosophy of alienating the agent; an agent is alienated from his actions, in William's sense, when he cannot recognize or pursue his own ends because he has been coopted by another or by social structures to support ends that are not his own or to do things contrary to his own interests.[2] Responding to Williams's complaint demands that we frame the questions of moral philosophy in a way that may seem unusual for some of our contemporaries but may bring new light to some of the issues. This essay will proceed in three parts: first, an overview of MacIntyre's theory of the rationality of traditions, second, an introduction to Williams' complaint against moral philosophy as a way of framing certain questions concerning the virtues, and third, a MacIntyrean Thomist's reply to Williams and to those questions about the virtues.

1. Alasdair MacIntyre, *Ethics in the Conflicts of Modernity: An Essay on Desire, Practical Reasoning, and Narrative* (Cambridge: Cambridge University Press, 2016), §§3.10–3.11, pp. 150–65.
2. This definition is my own.

II. MacIntyre on the Rationality of Traditions

MacIntyre teaches that the human pursuit of knowledge is hemmed in by human limitations. We seek tradition-transcendent truth, but as long as we seek the truth by merely human means, our enquiries will be influenced, and may be limited, or even stymied, by the forms of rationality that govern our pursuit of that truth.[3] For MacIntyre, a "rationality" is a set of intellectual resources that we use to interpret and judge our experience. The rationalities we each took into the world as young adults were shaped by our families and teachers. The methods by which we apprehend and interpret phenomena, the criteria we employ when we weigh evidence, and the principles we follow when we make judgments are all informed, conditioned, and limited by our own individual educations in our native traditions of enquiry.[4] Thus for MacIntyre, at the outset of one's quest for knowledge, one's rationality is "tradition-constituted."[5]

In most cases, most of the time, owing to an absence of conflicting evidence, or to intellectual complacency, or perhaps to ideological fervor, a person's rationality remains tradition-constituted. In some cases, however, *some* people *may* recognize phenomena that they cannot explain or cannot assimilate, so that they lose confidence in their understanding of the world; they suffer an "epistemological crisis."[6] When someone's apparently workable solution to an epistemological crisis is taken up by others and becomes part of the tradition, we say that the rationality of the person who solved the problem has become "tradition-constitutive."[7]

MacIntyre's account of "the rationality of traditions"[8] allows that the tradition-constitutive use of reason can go well or badly. When it goes well, improvements to our form of rationality may open new ways of examining

3. See Alasdair MacIntyre, "The End of Ideology and the End of the End of Ideology," in *Against the Self-Images of the Age* (London: Gerald Duckworth & Co., 1971; reprinted, University of Notre Dame Press, 1978), 3–11; hereafter cited as ASIA. See also Alasdair MacIntyre, *Whose Justice? Which Rationality?* (Notre Dame, Indiana: University of Notre Dame Press, 1988), 9.

4. See MacIntyre, "The Rationality of Traditions," in *Whose Justice? Which Rationality?*, 349–69.

5. Ibid., 354, 360.

6. See "Epistemological Crises, Dramatic Narrative, and the Philosophy of Science," in Alasdair C. MacIntyre, *The Tasks of Philosophy: Selected Essays Volume I*, (Cambridge, UK: Cambridge University Press, 2006), 3–23.

7. See MacIntyre, *Whose Justice? Which Rationality?*, 354–55.

8. See MacIntyre, "The Rationality of Traditions," in *Whose Justice? Which Rationality?*, 349–69.

and understanding our world, helping us to grasp and comprehend phenomena more adequately. When it goes badly, a plausible solution that distorts our understanding may be celebrated an advance in the tradition even as it causes us to misunderstand the phenomena in question and misinterpret our predecessors.[9]

MacIntyre defends the rationality of traditions as an alternative to Enlightenment notions of universal reason, which he rejects. All people engage in enquiry through the rationality of some tradition.[10] The tradition in question is not Thomism or Aristotelianism; it is the culture—whatever culture—that informs the rational judgment of any particular person.[11] Everyone has a tradition; the only question is whether one acknowledges one's tradition and engages it critically.

A would-be Descartes may say that he has rejected his tradition and that he is starting from scratch to reexamine all questions from the neutral standpoint of a rationality that does not depend on any tradition; but any such claim is self-deceiving.[12] Questions about how to examine the world, what counts as a pertinent question, what counts as good evidence, and what counts as a good argument, are all answered for us initially by our teachers and communities. To reject tradition and engage in enquiry is only to pretend that one's native tradition does not shape and condition one's thinking and theorizing.[13]

The rationality of traditions maps a middle way between Enlightenment universal reason on one side and post-modernism on the other. It is a middle way that justifies the search for truth even as it acknowledges the obstacles in that search. MacIntyre explains: "I don't think that cultural difference has the last word, for I am, after all, an Aristotelian. But I do think that cultural difference ought to have the first word."[14] Rational enquiry is possible, but it is always enquiry within the rationality of a tradition.

9. See Alasdair MacIntyre, *After Virtue* (University of Notre Dame Press, 1981, 1984, 2007), 3–4; see also, Christopher S. Lutz, "Tradition as a Fragile Practice," Special Issue on the Philosophy of Alasdair MacIntyre, *American Catholic Philosophical Quarterly* 88, no. 3 (fall 2014): 619–40.

10. See MacIntyre, *Whose Justice? Which Rationality?*, 350.

11. See Christopher S. Lutz, "Narrative and the Rationality of Traditions," *Acta Philosophica: Rivista internazionale di filosophia*, Special issue: *MacIntyre at 90: Critically Reading Virtue, Flourishing, and Narrative within Traditions*, edited by Marta Rocchi e Robert A. Gahl, Jr., 28, no. 2 (2019): 205–224.

12. See MacIntyre, *The Tasks of Philosophy*, 8–9.

13. See ibid., 9; see also comment on Kant's trust in his parents in MacIntyre, *After Virtue*, 44.

14. Alasdair MacIntyre and Thomas D Pearson, "*Kinesis* Interview with Alasdair MacIntyre," *Kinesis*, 20, no. 2 (1994): 34–47. Reprinted in *Kinesis* 23, no. 1 (1996): 49–50.

The title of the 2020 meeting of the American Maritain Association, *Whose Thomism? Which Tradition?* (where this essay was originally presented as a paper) invites us to examine our tradition in light of MacIntyre's theory of rationality. In doing so, we bring a new tool to the critical task that Pope Leo XIII prescribed in his encyclical letter, *Aeterni Patris*;[15] for MacIntyre's theory helps us to understand how the Thomistic renewal has been complicated by the native rationalities of those working on the project.[16] MacIntyre's account of the rationality of traditions suggests that controversies over interpretations of traditional teachings and texts may benefit from interventions that bring a new perspective to the question. I want to turn to one of those controversies now, to see how the ideas of Bernard Williams might illuminate a debate among some contemporary Thomists about the infused moral virtues.

III. Reframing Questions about the Virtues with the help of Bernard Williams

1. *A Thomistic Debate about the Infused Moral Virtues.* In *Whose Justice? Which Rationality?*, MacIntyre reported that for St. Thomas, "justice cannot flourish, cannot indeed, so it turns out, even exist as a natural virtue, unless and insofar as it is informed by the supernatural virtue of *caritas*."[17] Thomas Osborne notes that MacIntyre's position follows that of Jacques Maritain and John of Saint Thomas,[18] but others questioned MacIntyre's reading of Aquinas. Bonnie Kent accused MacIntyre of "moral provincialism," which she summarized as the doctrine, "Only those with the 'correct' theological commitments can have true moral virtues."[19] Brian Shanley replied with

15. Pope Leo XIII, *Aeterni Patris* (1879): no. 31.

16. See Alasdair MacIntyre, "Too Many Thomisms?" in *Three Rival Versions of Moral Enquiry: Encylopaedia, Genealogy, and Tradition*, Gifford Lectures delivered in the University of Edinburgh in 1988 (Notre Dame, Indiana: University of Notre Dame Press, 1990), 58–81; see also "From *Aeterni Patris* to *Fides et Ratio*" in *God, Philosophy, Universities: A Selective History of the Catholic Intellectual Tradition*, a Sheed & Ward Book (Lanham, Maryland: Rowman & Littlefield Publishers), 151–63.

17. MacIntyre, *Whose Justice? Which Rationality?*, 205. Compare to ST II-II, q. 23, a. 7.

18. Thomas M. Osborne, Jr., "Perfect and Imperfect Virtues in Aquinas," *The Thomist* 71 (2007): 39–64.

19. Bonnie Kent, "Moral Provincialism," *Religious Studies* 30 (1994): 269. Kent argues that St. Thomas rejected St. Augustine's teaching that there can be no true virtue without faith and repeated this argument in "Golden Age Revisited: Scholastic Ethics" in Bonnie Kent, *Virtues of the*

"Aquinas on Pagan Virtues," agreeing with Kent that MacIntyre "has misread Aquinas on the reality of genuine virtue apart from charity."[20] Thomas Osborne responded to Kent and Shanley in defense of St. Thomas's Augustinian view of grace.[21] Angela McKay Knobel joined the conflict in 2005, taking a stand against Reginald Garrigou-Legrange and Jacques Maritain, as well as Thomas Osborne.[22] As the debate between McKay Knoble and Osborne developed, McKay Knoble came to formulate its central issue in this way: "The only coherent subject of debate is whether the pagan can perform any genuinely good actions at all."[23] That controversy continues. In what follows, I want to take MacIntyre's advice to let a voice outside the mainstream of Thomistic academic culture present the issue in a different way.

2. *Bernard Williams vs. Alienation in Moral Philosophy*. Like other English philosophers of the mid-twentieth century, including Philippa Foot,[24] Peter Geach,[25] Elizabeth Anscombe,[26] and Alasdair MacIntyre,[27] Williams ques-

---

Will (Washington, D. C.: The Catholic University of American Press, 1995), 19–34. T. H. Irwin rejected Kent's interpretation of Augustine and of the differences between Augustine and Aquinas in footnotes in "Splendid Vices? Augustine For and Against Pagan Virtues," *Medieval Philosophy and Theology* 8 (1999): 106n4, and 121n53.

20. Brian J. Shanley, OP, "Aquinas on Pagan Virtue," *The Thomist* 63, no. 4 (October 1999): 554.

21. Thomas M. Osborne, Jr., "The Augustinianism of Thomas Aquinas's Moral Theory," *The Thomist* 67, no. 2 (April 2003): 279–305.

22. Angela McKay, "Prudence and Acquired Moral Virtue," *The Thomist* 69, no. 4 (October 2005): 535–55.

23. Angela McKay Knoble, "Aquinas and the Pagan Virtues," *International Philosophical Quarterly* 51, no. 3, issue 203 (September 2011): 340 and 354.

24. Philippa Foot, "A Philosopher's Defense of Morality," *Philosophy* 27, no. 103 (October 1952): 311–28; Philippa Foot, "Moral Arguments" *Mind* 67, no. 268 (October 1958): 502–513; Philippa Foot, "Moral Beliefs" *Proceedings of the Aristotelian Society*, New Series, vol. 59 (1958–59): 83–104; and Philippa Foot, "Goodness and Choice" *Aristotelian Society Supplementary Volume* 35 (1961): 45–60.

25. Peter Geach, "Good and Evil," *Analysis* 17, no. 2 (December 1956): 33–42; Peter Geach, "Ascriptivism" *Philosophical Review* 69, no. 2 (1960): 221–25; and Peter Geach, "Assertion" *Philosophical Review* 74, no. 4 (1965): 449–65.

26. Elizabeth Anscombe, *Intention* (Oxford: Basil Blackwell, 1957; reprinted, Cambridge, Massachusetts: Harvard University Press, 2000); and "Modern Moral Philosophy," *Philosophy* 33, no. 124 (January 1958): 1–19

27. Alasdair MacIntyre, "What Philosophy is Not," *Philosophy* 32, no. 123 (October 1957): 325–35; reprinted in *Against the Self-Images of the Age*, 96–108; Alasdair MacIntyre "Hume on Is and Ought," *Philosophical Review* 68, no. 4 (October 1959): 451–68; also reprinted in *Against the Self-Images of the Age*, 109–124; Alasdair MacIntyre, "Notes from the Moral Wilderness I," *New Reasoner* 7 (Winter 1958–9): 90–100; reprinted in *The MacIntyre Reader* (Notre Dame: University of Notre Dame Press, 1998) 31–40; also reprinted in Paul Blackledge and Neil Davidson, eds., *Alasdair MacIntyre's Engagement with Marxism* (Leiden: Brill Academic Publishers, 2005; paper-

tioned contemporary philosophers' treatments of the relationship between morality and the motives for human action. Williams introduced his critique of modern moral philosophy in his 1965 lecture, "Morality and the Emotions" [28] and developed it through other publications in the decades that followed. I will draw a rough summary of his critique from the 1965 lecture and from his 1973 "Critique of Utilitarianism."[29] Williams argues that moral philosophy should be rejected as morally alienating, because it undermines practical reasoning by encouraging people to act against their own good.

3. *Morality and the Emotions (1965)*. In "Morality and the Emotions," Williams criticizes the separation of reason from emotion in Kantian moral philosophy. After acknowledging the inadequacy of emotivism as a theory of the meaning of moral utterances,[30] Williams asked what might be learned from emotivism nonetheless: "My aim," he writes, "will not be to reconstruct emotivism, but to steal from it; not to rebuild the pagan temple, but to put its ruins to a holier purpose."[31]

To this end, Williams examines the effects of insincerity upon the significance of six kinds of speech-acts.[32] Insincerity does not change the meaning of (1) a greeting, (2) a command, or (3) an objective judgment grading or commending the merits of a thing; these speech-acts mean what they say, whether they are sincere or not. (4) Promising implicates the emotions to some extent, but an insincere promise remains a promise. When we consider (5) speech-acts expressing intention or belief, however, insincerity changes what the speech-act signifies.[33] Insincere expressions of intention and belief express neither intention nor belief, and it is not clear what they do express. A speech-act that (6) expresses emotions is simply unintelligi-

back edition. Chicago: Haymarket Books, 2009), 45–57; Alasdair MacIntyre, "Notes from the Moral Wilderness II," *New Reasoner* 8 (Spring 1959), 89–98; Reprinted in *The MacIntyre Reader*, 41–49; also reprinted in *Alasdair MacIntyre's Engagement with Marxism*, 57–68.

28. Bernard Williams, "Morality and the Emotions," Inaugural Lecture at Bedford College, London (1965), in J. Casey ed., *Morality and Moral Reasoning* (London: Methuen, 1971), reprinted in Bernard Williams, *Problems of the Self: Philosophical Papers 1956–1972* (Cambridge: Cambridge University Press, 1973), 207–229.

29. Bernard Williams, "A Critique of Utilitarianism," in *Utilitarianism: For and Against*, with J. J. C. Smart (Cambridge: Cambridge University Press, 1973), 77–150.

30. Williams, "Morality and the Emotions," 207–209.

31. Ibid., 209.

32. Williams credits his teacher, Austin, for bringing attention to speech-acts.

33. Williams cites Peter Geach's description of "bad" as an *alienans* adjective; see Peter Geach, "Good and Evil," 33.

ble if it is insincere; "he is not expressing his feelings if his words are insincere."[34]

For Williams, the problem with Kantian moral philosophy is that it treats moral judgments only as examples of "(2) and (3): the giving of orders, and grading, commending, etc.," while overlooking, if not denying, the role of the speaker's beliefs, intentions, and desires in those orders and assessments. Emotivism, the moral theory of A. J. Ayer and C. L. Stevenson, was a false theory of the meaning of moral judgments, but it did teach something valuable that modern moral philosophy had overlooked: A speaker's beliefs and emotions are not separable from the meaning of that person's moral speech-acts. This is the part of the "ruins" of emotivism that Williams puts "to a holier purpose."

Williams's study of moral speech-acts draws attention to the subjective side of moral commands and judgments, namely, the "moral disposition" of the one who commands or judges. In the Catholic intellectual tradition, we could say that Williams holds that actions should conform to conscience when he speaks of acting sincerely and with moral integrity. Williams observes that Kant divides "the moral man," who acts only out of respect for moral principle, from another kind of person, who does good things from inclination.[35] Kant honors the moral man, claiming that his actions alone have moral worth, but from William's perspective Kant honors him precisely because those actions are insincere. Williams asks whether any of us would want to receive help from someone who helped us against his inclinations, only out of respect for moral duty. Would we not prefer the human gesture of kindness from someone who wanted to help us? An honest answer threatens Kantian ethics:

> Either the recipient *ought* to prefer the ministrations of the moral man to the human gesture, which seems a mildly insane requirement; or, alternatively, if it be admitted that it is perfectly proper and rational of the recipient to have the preference that he has, the value of moral men becomes an open question, and we can reasonably entertain the proposal that we should not seek to produce moral men, or very many of them, but rather those . . . who make the human gesture.[36]

34. Williams, "Morality and the Emotions," 216.

35. See Immanuel Kant, *Groundwork of the Metaphysics of Morals*, revised edition, translated by Mary Gregor and Jens Timmermann (Cambridge: Cambridge University Press, 2012), 7–8 (4:392); 13–17 (4:397–402).

36. Williams, "Morality and the Emotions," 227.

Williams concludes that we should promote "the capacity for creative emotional response,"[37] rather than Kantian moralism.

4. *A Critique of Utilitarianism* (1973). Williams develops and expands his criticism of moral philosophy in his 1973 essay, "A Critique of Utilitarianism." Where Kantianism threatens moral sincerity by dividing judgment from emotional response, utilitarianism alienates the agent from his feelings and actions by demanding compliance with a moral criterion that may dictate actions against the agent's interests.

Williams questions whether a generalized pursuit of the greatest happiness of the greatest number could leave room for unusual and, strictly speaking, unnecessary pursuits so important to so many people's happiness:

> Utilitarianism would do well then to acknowledge the evident fact that among the things that make people happy is not only making other people happy, but being taken up or involved in any of a vast range of projects, or … commitments. One can be committed to such things as a person, a cause, an institution, a career, one's own genius, or the pursuit of danger.[38]

These private pursuits could be judged to violate the principle of utility by wasting time and resources that should be shared with everyone. Hence, it seems that Utilitarianism leaves little room for many pursuits that make individual human lives richer.[39]

Williams considers what it would mean to demand that a person with a healthy, well-rounded, richly developed character make utilitarianism the sole measure of morality in his life:

> It is to alienate him in a real sense from his actions and from the source of his action in his own convictions. It is to make him into a channel between the input of everyone's projects, including his own, and an output of optimific [sic.] decision; but this is to neglect the extent to which his actions and his decisions have to be seen as the actions and decisions which flow from the projects and attitudes with which he is most closely identified. It is thus, in the most literal sense, an attack on his integrity.[40]

Williams argues that by dividing the agent from his feelings and his goals, utilitarianism attacks the moral integrity of the agent in much the same way that Kantianism does.

37. Ibid., 229.

38. Williams, "A Critique of Utilitarianism," 112.

39. Susan Wolf argues similarly in "Moral Saints," *The Journal of Philosophy* 79, no. 8 (August 1982): 419–39.

40. Williams, "A Critique of Utilitarianism," 116–17.

5. *William's response to alienation, and MacIntyre's critique.* Alasdair MacIntyre commends Williams' critique of moral alienation in modern ethics in his 2016 book *Ethics in the Conflicts of Modernity,* but MacIntyre finds Williams's response inadequate. Williams argues that we should correct moral alienation by following our own convictions. What Williams proposes, however, is, in the terms of the Catholic tradition, like demanding that people follow conscience without forming it. Anscombe criticized Joseph Butler for taking a similar position: "Butler exalts conscience, but appears ignorant that a man's conscience may tell him to do the vilest things."[41] For MacIntyre, the solution Williams proposes is unworkable, because it leaves the agent alone to face the practical questions of life and because it insulates the shortcomings of the agent's practical rationality—his cultural prejudices, poor judgment, and failures of discipline—from critique and correction.

The Catholic tradition defines conscience as the act of applying knowledge to a particular choice;[42] it follows that the wisdom of our judgments of conscience is limited by our knowledge of the relevant issues. We cannot improve that knowledge if we isolate ourselves from the judgment of others. The alienation that Williams finds in modern morality cannot be overcome by turning to oneself, but only by learning how to recognize and pursue what is truly desirable and choice-worthy, and for that we need friends. MacIntyre has written repeatedly, throughout his career, on the importance of friends both for correction in practical matters and for guidance in the formation of good habits of judgment and action.[43]

Williams has the right problem. Alienation destroys rational human agency. A morality that tells me what I ought to do, not for the sake of any practical good that I could want, but only because it is my duty to do so, leaves me with no internal compass to guide my actions, except for habits of obedience.[44]

What kind of moral scheme can overcome the alienation Williams observes in modern morality, and support the integrity of the moral agent, while also forming the agent's conscience? It will be a scheme that sets aside

41. Anscombe, "Modern Moral Philosophy," 2.

42. See Aquinas, ST I, q. 79, a. 13; and I-II, q. 19, a. 5. See also, Sancti Alphonsi Mariae de Ligurio, *Theologia Moralis,* edition nova, Leonardi Gaude, ed. (Graz, Austria: Akademische Druk- U. Verlangsanstalt, 1954), book 1, treatise 1, chapter 1, article 2.

43. See, for example, MacIntyre, *Dependent Rational Animals,* 97, 99–118; ———, *Ethics in the Conflicts of Modernity,* 52, 56.

44. See Geach, "Good and Evil," 40; we will return to this later.

"moral reasoning" about duties and obligations to focus instead on "practical reasoning" about means to ends. Peter Geach made this point in "Good and Evil":

> We must allow … that the question, 'Why should I?' or 'Why shouldn't I?' is a reasonable question, which calls for an answer, not for abusive remarks about the wickedness of asking; and I think that the only relevant answer is an appeal to something the questioner *wants*.[45]

This shift to practical reasoning may lead us to Aristotle and St. Thomas. For Aristotle and St. Thomas the virtuous man is precisely the person who finds his duty in making what Williams called "the human gesture," motivated by justice, charity, and friendship, who makes the other's good his own.

6. *A MacIntyrean Thomist's Reply to Williams: Thomistic Aristotelianism vs Alienation.* Unlike modern moral philosophers who defined happiness as subjective pleasure and theorized moral obligation in opposition to it, St. Thomas Aquinas, following Aristotle, defines happiness objectively and places the pursuit of that happiness at the center of his moral teaching. For St. Thomas, moral teaching is a partnership between an examination of the ends of human life and a study of the means to attain it. The desire to attain identified ends demands that we discover effective means including the moral virtues, while working out the means may illuminate the ends more adequately making us more prudent. If we are fortunate, our study of morals may help us to recognize the demands of our relationships with God and neighbor, and to acknowledge various duties and obligations toward them, but we begin with practical reasoning, not moral reasoning, with ends, not with rules. The goal of this study is not theoretical knowledge of duties and obligations; it is moral excellence, virtue, practical wisdom, the ability to recognize and do what is good and best.

7. *Thomas Aquinas on Wisdom, Teleology, Law, Prudence, and Sin.* An agent is alienated from his actions when he cannot recognize or pursue his own ends because he has been coopted by another or by social structures to support ends that are not his own or to do things contrary to his own interests. An account of human action that would overcome alienation for everyone must help all agents to recognize and pursue their own good. The good in question cannot be an essentially moral or obligational good and it cannot be imposed in any sense. Rather, it must be, in Geach's words, "some-

45. Ibid., 39; italics in original.

thing the questioner wants";[46] it must be an essentially appetible good that satisfies the needs of the agent, a good that will bring the agent's desires to rest. Excellence in human agency consists in recognizing that good and pursuing it as a goal.

Like Aristotle, St. Thomas approaches moral teaching through questions about practical reasoning, but unlike Aristotle, St. Thomas teaches that every human being is capable of happiness, because everyone can desire it:

> Happiness is the attainment of the Perfect Good. Whoever is capable of the Perfect Good can attain happiness. Now, that man is capable of the Perfect Good, is proved both because his intellect can apprehend the universal and perfect good, and because his will can desire it.[47]

For St. Thomas, our desire for perfect happiness, that is, our desire to see God, implies that the perfect happiness of the beatific vision is possible for us; for,

> if we suppose that that the created intellect could never see God, it would either never attain to beatitude, or its beatitude would consist in something else beside God; which is opposed to the faith.... But if the intellect of the rational creature could not reach so far as the first cause of things, the natural desire would remain void.[48]

Happiness, for St. Thomas, depends on charity: "he who possesses the more charity, will see God the more perfectly, and will be the more beatified."[49] The problem for the Thomistic Aristotelian, then, is to learn how to live a life of charity.

Our secular colleagues may object that St. Thomas alienates every agent by subjecting everyone to a religious ideology. That, of course, is a matter of perspective; there is no small difference between an atheistic rationality and a theistic one.[50] To the extent that we share St. Thomas's form of rationality we can read the *Summa Theologiae* as a study of that remark from

46. Ibid.

47. Thomas Aquinas, *Summa Theologica*, translated by Fathers of the English Dominican Province, revised 1920 (New York: Benziger Bros., 1948; reprinted, Westminster, Maryland: Chistian Classics, 1981). ST I-II, q. 5, a. 1.

48. ST I, q. 12, a. 1.

49. ST I, q. 12, a. 6; See also ST I-II, q. 5, a. 2.

50. Theism of any kind opposes the "antitheological beliefs" of atheists (MacIntyre, *The Tasks of Philosophy*, 22), and thus conflicts with the presuppositions of their form of rationality. Thus, theism can only appear as an ideology to those caught up in that form of rationality. See Alasdair MacIntyre, "On Being a Theistic Philosopher in a Secular Culture," *Proceedings of the American Catholic Philosophical Association* 84 (2010): 23–32.

the opening prayer of St. Augustine's *Confessions,* "You have made us for yourself, and our heart is restless until it rests in you."[51] From a perspective where freedom is understood as submission to truth,[52] and "true self-love consists in directing oneself toward God,"[53] what St. Thomas offers is a path to liberation, practical wisdom, freedom from alienation, and the renewal of human agency, for all people.

8. *Wisdom.* Saint Thomas Aquinas does not alienate the agent from his desires, because St. Thomas observes action as a motion toward appetible goods, and because he takes the rationality of human actions to be measured by their effectiveness in procuring true goods. He holds that wisdom is the measure of action, not only for human acts, but even for divine acts. This point appears obliquely in various places.[54] But he argues it forcefully in *De Veritate,* when he denies that the demands of justice depend only on the divine will:

> the first thing upon which the essential character of all justice depends is the wisdom of the divine intellect, which constitutes things in their due proportion both to one another and to their cause. In this proportion the essential character of created justice consists. But to say that justice depends simply upon the will is to say that the divine will does not proceed according to the order of wisdom, and that is blasphemous.[55]

St. Thomas rejects what later authors would call "divine command theory;" for him, wisdom is the measure of action, even in God.

In the human agent, wisdom is more problematic. When St. Thomas describes the moral life in the *Summa Theologiae,* he maintains Aristotle's insistence on the central role of desire in virtuous action. But from the first article of the *Summa Theologiae,* St. Thomas argues that philosophy is insufficient to guide human life "because man is directed to God, as to an end that surpasses the grasp of his reason."[56] We cannot pursue what we cannot recognize; thus, we need revealed theology to live wisely and to reach our

51. Augustine, *Confessions,* 1, 1.

52. "Our freedom is this: to submit to this truth, which is our God Who set us free from death—that is from the state of sin." Augustine, *On the Free Choice of the Will,* translated by Anna S. Benjamin and L. H. Hackstaff, Library of Liberal Arts (New York: Macmillan, 1964) book 2, chap. 13, para.143.

53. ST I-II, q. 100, a. 5, ad 1.

54. See ST I-II, q. 21, a. 1, ad 2; see also Thomas Aquinas, *De potentia,* q. 3, a. 15, third argument.

55. DV q. 23, a. 6.

56. ST I, q. 1, a. 1, co.

human goal. In his treatments of teleology, law, and virtue, St. Thomas argues that revealed truth is crucial to the perfection of human agency.

St. Thomas holds that we need revelation for anthropological reasons; Jacques Maritain defends this point in his *Essay on Christian Philosophy*.[57] "Man is not in a state of pure nature, he is fallen and redeemed. Consequently, ethics, in the widest sense of the word . . . is not a purely philosophic discipline. Of itself it has to do with theology, either to become integrated with or at least subalternated to theology."[58] "Here is a philosophy which must of necessity be a superelevated philosophy, a philosophy subalternated to theology, if it is not to misrepresent and scientifically distort its object."[59] Thomistic philosophers cannot ignore St. Thomas's position on the need for revelation without distorting his moral teaching.

9. *Teleology*. According to St. Thomas, "every agent acts for an end under the aspect of good,"[60] where "good" is taken to mean "appetible" or desirable;[61] "appetible" is taken, in turn, to mean perfective or fulfilling of the agent.[62] To act is to try to get something that one takes to be fulfilling, completing, or perfecting. The human will, the rational appetite, is constituted to desire the good,[63] namely *felicitas* or *beatitudo*, St. Thomas's words for Aristotle's *eudaimonia*; all three of these terms are translated into English as "happiness." In everything we do, we are trying to attain *beatitudo*. The problem for us is that we are constituted for a kind of *beatitudo* that we cannot recognize by our natural powers, and thus we cannot apprehend, much less pursue that end without divine assistance.[64] For the human agent, perfected practical wisdom consists in directing all of one's actions to nothing less than the end of *beatitudo, felicitas, or happiness*.[65]

10. *The Twofold Human Good?* St. Thomas allows that "man's happiness

57. Jacques Maritain, *An Essay on Christian Philosophy*, translated by Edward H. Flannery (New York: Philosophical Library, 1955), 38–43, 61–100

58. Ibid., 39.

59. Ibid., 40.

60.ST I-II, q. 94, a. 2, co. See also St. Thomas Aquinas, *Summa Contra Gentiles* (book III, chaps 1–113) in Anton Pegis, translator, *Basic Writings of Saint Thomas Aquinas* (New York: Random House, 1945; reprinted, Indianapolis: Hackett, 1997) book III, chap. 3; See also, ST I, q. 82, a. 1; ST I-II, q. 8, a. 1; q. 9, aa. 1 and 2.

61.ST I, q. 5, a. 1, co.

62.ST I, q. 5, a. 5, co.

63.ST I, q. 82, a. 1.

64.ST I, q. 1; and I-II, q. 91, a. 4, esp. ad 1.

65.ST I-II, q. 1, a. 6.

is twofold."[66] There is an "imperfect happiness" that we can seek by our own powers.[67] "[T]he light of natural reason can direct the intention in respect of a connatural good."[68] But imperfect happiness is not the goal of human action. For St. Thomas, supernatural *beatitudo* alone can bring our desire to rest.[69] Inasmuch as St. Thomas holds that "the will is out of order when it loves more the lesser good," and finds that this "disorder of the will" is a cause of sin,[70] and affirms St. Augustine's teaching that "sin is nothing else than to neglect eternal things and to seek after temporal things,"[71] it seems that we should regard earthly, imperfect happiness with caution, for it may stand as a tempting alternative to our ultimate end, as a distraction from our real goal.[72] We will return to this point in our treatment of law.

11. *Law.* Law, for St. Thomas, exists to direct human agents to the good.[73] He defines law as "nothing else than an ordinance of reason for the common good, made by him who has care of the community and promulgated."[74] Law is first and foremost "an ordinance of reason" not a command of the will.[75] It must be promulgated by competent authority—it is not a law until it is commanded by an act of the will—but that command is not a law unless it orders action rationally to the common good.[76]

St. Thomas presents the natural law in two ways in the *Summa Theologiae*. In his discussion of the divine law, St. Thomas says that all of the moral precepts of the Old Law belong to the natural law.[77] In an objection he observes, "the first and principal precepts of the law are, *Thou shalt love the Lord thy God*, and, *Thou shalt love they neighbor*," and he cites the Gospel of Matthew.[78] In reply to that objection, he writes,

66. ST I-II, q. 62, a. 1.

67. ST I-II, q. 5, a. 5.

68. ST II-II, q. 10, a. 4, ad 2. See also Irwin, "Splendid Vices? Augustine For and Against Pagan Virtues," 123n56.

69. See SCG III, chap. 37; ST I-II, q. 3, a. 8.

70. ST I-II, q. 78, a. 1.

71. ST I-II, q. 71, a. 6, arg. 3; see also ad 3.

72. Denis J. M. Bradley emphasizes the unity of the human telos in his book, *Aquinas on the Twofold Human Good: Reason and Revelation in Aquinas's Moral Science* (Washington, D.C.: The Catholic University of America Press, 1997).

73. ST I-II, q. 90, prologue.

74. ST I-II, q. 90, a. 4.

75. ST I-II, q. 90, a. 1.

76. ST I-II, q. 91, a. 2; ST I-II, q. 96, a. 4.

77. ST I-II, q. 100, a. 1.

78. ST I-II, q. 100, a. 3, arg. 1.

Those two principles are the first general principles of the natural law, and are self-evident to human reason, either through nature or through faith. Wherefore all the precepts of the Decalogue are referred to these, as conclusions to general principles."[79]

Does this mean that everyone should be expected to know the Ten Commandments without difficulty? No. A few articles later he writes:

The precepts of the Decalogue can be reduced to the precepts of charity. Now there was need for man to receive a precept about loving God and his neighbor, because in this respect the natural law had become obscured on account of sin.[80]

In these passages, it appears that the natural law should be a set of rules, known propositionally, reducible to the precepts of charity, the universal rational knowledge of which may be obscured by sin. Yet this is not St. Thomas's primary way of presenting the natural law.

Earlier, when St. Thomas introduced the natural law,[81] and when he examined it,[82] he argued that the natural law in us accounts for our inclinations toward our proper act and end: "the rational creature . . . has a share of the Eternal Reason, whereby it has a natural inclination to its proper act and end: and this participation of the eternal law in the rational creature is called the natural law."[83] Here he finds the natural law in us manifested in our natural inclinations to good things and in our avoidance of evil things:

this is the first precept of law, that good is to be done and pursued and evil is to be avoided. All other precepts of the natural law are based on this: so that whatever the practical reason naturally apprehends as man's good (or evil) belongs to the precepts of the natural law as something to be done or avoided.[84]

St. Thomas next surveys our natural inclinations and lists some natural law obligations that follow from them.[85] From our inclination to preserve our own being there follows an obligation to "whatever is a means of preserving human life and of warding off its obstacles." From those inclinations that we share with other animals there follow obligations concerning "sexual

79. ST I-II, q. 100, a. 3, ad 1

80. ST I-II, q. 100, a. 5, ad 1; see also ST I-II, q. 94, a. 4.

81. ST I-II, q. 91, a. 2.

82. ST I-II, q. 94.

83. ST I-II, q. 91, a. 2.

84. ST I-II, q. 94, a. 2.

85. This derivation of the precepts of the natural law from natural inclinations follows the method of Cicero in *De officiis* I, chap. 4, nos. 11–14.

intercourse, the education of offspring, and so forth." Our specifically human, rational powers give rise to "a natural inclination to know the truth about God and to live in society," from which follow obligations "to shun ignorance, to avoid offending those among whom one has to live, and other such things."[86] In each of these cases, our awareness of the natural law in us follows from our inclinations to certain goods, as a rational recognition of what it takes to pursue those goods.

St. Thomas's remarks about the reduction of the natural law to the precepts of charity in the later question concerning the precepts of the Decalogue do not conflict with his remarks here defining the natural law in terms of natural inclination. We have a natural inclination to live in society, thus we recognize living in society as a good that is worthy of pursuit. When St. Thomas discusses the precepts of the Decalogue in q. 100, a. 5, he treats the Ten Commandments precisely as directives to pursue the good of life in society more effectively:

> Now in order that any man may dwell aright in a community, two things are required: the first is that he behave well to the head of the community; the other is that he behave well to those who are his fellows and partners in the community. It is therefore necessary that the divine law should contain in the first place, precepts ordering man in his relations to God; and in the second place, other precepts ordering man in his relationships to other men who are his neighbors and live with him under God.[87]

The precepts of the Decalogue belong to the natural law because they show us more clearly how to pursue goods that we desire by nature. In short, in the objective order of things, St. Thomas's identity between right reason and eternal law leaves no place for the kind of divorce between desire and morality that Williams sees as a threat to moral integrity; there is no place here for the kind of alienation that Williams condemns.

12. *The Virtues.* Following Aristotle, St. Thomas holds that moral virtues can be acquired by habituation.[88] To explain the limits of acquired virtue, St. Thomas introduces a division of the virtues into four levels, taken from Macrobius,[89] who had taken it from Plotinus[90] and Plato[91]:

86. ST I-II, q. 94, a. 2.
87. ST I-II, q. 100, a. 5.
88. ST I-II, q. 63, a. 2; see Aristotle, *Nicomachean Ethics* (NE), 2.1.
89. The quotation comes from Macrobius, *Commentary on the Dream of Scipio*, 1.
90. Macrobius cites Plotinus, *Ennead* 1.2, chapters 2–3.
91. See Plato, *Phaedo*, 81b–83c.

Macrobius says: Plotinus, together with Plato foremost among teachers of philosophy, says: "The four kinds of virtue are fourfold. In the first place there are social virtues; secondly, there are perfecting virtues; thirdly, there are perfect virtues; and fourthly, there are exemplar virtues."[92]

The natural or acquired virtues are at best the "social virtues;"[93] they are virtues only in the lowest and most limited sense. Natural prudence, for example, cannot apprehend the *summum bonum*, thus "The good that [acquired prudence] takes for its end is not the common end of all human life, but of some particular affair."[94] St. Thomas holds that acquired virtues help us to behave well only "in respect of human affairs."[95] People need different virtues to "behave well in respect of their being *fellow-citizens with the saints, and of the household of God*."[96] For this higher pursuit we need the virtues of those "who are on their way and tending toward divine similitude."[97] Yet we cannot acquire these "perfecting virtues"[98] through habituation.[99]

Saint Thomas's account of the virtues crosses a kind of border in ST I-II, q. 61, a. 5, at the end of his statement on the social virtues when he says "It is in this sense that we have been speaking of these virtues up to now."[100] At this point, he begins again with a brief description of the perfecting virtues and perfect virtues through which the saints attain to the divine similitude. In the questions that follow this passage, he examines the three theological virtues, which are caused only by divine infusion,[101] and their connection to the four infused moral virtues that accompany the theological virtue of *caritas*.[102]

These seven infused virtues transform both our understanding of our *telos* and our desire for it, and thus enable us to pursue the *summum bonum*.

92. ST I-II, q. 61, a. 5.

93. "Social" translates "*politicae*"; other translations call these "political virtues."

94. ST II-II, q. 47, a. 13. I take it that "true but imperfect prudence" must be acquired prudence.

95. ST I-II, q. 21, a. 5; see also, q. 63, a. 4.

96. ST I-II, q. 63, a. 4.; in the italicized phrase St. Thomas quotes Ephesians 2:19.

97. ST I-II, q. 61, a. 5.

98. Ibid.

99. ST I-II, q. 63, a. 3.

100. Dividing the acquired virtues from the infused virtues at the break between political and perfecting virtues may be controversial. In my judgment, because St. Thomas holds that perfecting and perfect virtues enable a person to tend toward divine similitude, the notion that these virtues could be acquired by habituation, rather than infused with charity, seems Pelagian.

101. ST I-II, q. 63, a. 3.

102. ST I-II, q. 63, a. 4; q. 65, a. 3.

Faith perfects the intellect to hold the articles of faith.[103] Hope perfects the will "to tend to that end as something attainable."[104] Charity perfects the will by transforming it into its end.[105] Charity disposes a person well toward the ultimate end,[106] and makes it possible to exercise perfect prudence, which "takes counsel, judges, and commands aright in respect of the good end of man's whole life."[107] This transformation is substantial. "All the moral virtues are infused together with charity."[108] These virtues that fit us for life in the household of God "differ in species" from the acquired virtues.[109]

For the Thomist, the problem of alienation is the problem Augustine identified in the opening prayer of the *Confessions*, "You have made us for yourself, and our heart is restless until it rests in you."[110] For St. Thomas, the life of true practical wisdom is impossible unless we know what we are, and what we are for, and are able to pursue our true end effectively. The alienation that disables that pursuit is the consequence of sin; the liberation we seek is life with God; nothing less will satisfy us.

13. *St. Thomas closes the Euthyphro dilemma: Sin Violates Right Reason and Eternal Law.* St. Thomas defends the Augustinian definition of sin as "a word, deed, or desire contrary to eternal law"[111]; he does so against an objection that sin should be defined instead as a violation of right reason. Does God command things because of right reason, or does right reason follow upon divine will? The first option suggests ethical naturalism; the second option constitutes divine command theory. In his reply to this objection, Aquinas treats the difference as a matter of perspective: "The theologian considers sin chiefly as an offense against God; and the moral philosopher, as something contrary to reason."[112] For St. Thomas the difference is merely a matter of perspective and terminology, for *the eternal law is identical with divine wisdom*; the same divine knowledge that is the cause of things[113] is

103. ST I-II, q. 62, a. 3.

104. Ibid.

105. Ibid.

106. See ST I-II, q. 23, a. 6.

107. ST II-II, q. 47, a. 13.

108. ST I-II, q. 65, a. 3.

109. ST I-II, q. 63, a. 4.

110. Augustine, *Confessions*, 1

111. Thomas Aquinas, ST I-II, q. 71, a. 6, arg. 1. He had already used this quote as the *sed contra* in both I-II, q. 19, a. 4 and q. 21, a. 1.

112. Thomas Aquinas, ST I-II, q. 71, a. 6, ad 5.

113. ST I, q. 14, a. 8.

also the measure of right reason in action that directs all things to their proper acts and ends.[114] With that, this version of the Euthyphro dilemma is resolved. Right reason is not distinct from, much less prior to eternal law; rather, right reason is identical to eternal law. St. Thomas's approach avoids ethical naturalism as well as voluntarism and divine command theory.

IV. Ockham Reopens the Euthyphro Dilemma with Divine Command Ethics

In the decades that followed Aquinas's death, however, the Euthyphro dilemma would reemerge in new versions. The shift in the meaning of freedom that Servais Pinckaers characterizes as the abandonment of "freedom for excellence" in favor of "freedom of indifference,"[115] changed the questions that Christian scholars asked about divine knowledge, divine will, and creation. The work of William of Ockham serves as a good marker for this shift, although Heiko Oberman's work on the history of the Reformation has provided ample evidence that the Nominalist movement was far more varied and widespread than many commentators had acknowledged and therefore that it cannot be reduced to Ockham's influence.[116] Ockham defended the freedom of God by abandoning the eternal law. Ockham acknowledged "right reason" as the basis for natural moral knowledge, but unlike St. Thomas, Ockham taught that both right reason and divine law followed only upon arbitrary divine command.[117] In short, Ockham took up the position that St. Thomas had condemned as "blasphemous."[118]

The rise of nominalist theology in Western Christian thought brought about a very subtle change in the relationships between human desire, wisdom, obligation, and obedience. The focus of morality moved from obedience as formation in wisdom to obedience as an end in itself. It is this shift that, in Bernard Williams's terms, alienates the agent from his feelings and

114. ST I-II, q. 91, a. 1, and q. 93.

115. See Servais Pinckaers, *The Sources of Christian Ethics*, translated by Sr. Mary Thomas Noble, OP (Washington, D.C.: The Catholic University of America Press, 1995), 242, 327–78.

116. Heiko Oberman, "Some Notes on the Theology of Nominalism: With Attention to Its Relation to the Renaissance," *The Harvard Theological Review* 53, no. 1 (January 1960): 47–76; ------, *The Harvest of Medieval Theology: Gabriel Biel and Late Medieval Nominalism*. The Robert Troup Paine prize-treatise, 1962, rev. ed. (Grand Rapids, Michigan: W.B. Eerdmans, 1967); ------, *Dawn of the Reformation* (Edinburgh: T. & T. Clark, 1986).

117. Osborne, "William of Ockham as a Divine Command Theorist," 17.

118. See above at note 55.

actions; for a morality of obligation imposes its law against the desires of its subjects. We could follow the history of this turn by looking at the ways that Renaissance and early modern Catholic moral theologians of the manualist tradition treated teleology, law, the virtues, conscience, and obedience. A careful examination of this part of our history would fill many volumes; but it is possible to trace some of the main lines of the bigger picture by comparing St. Thomas Aquinas on a few key points to St. Alphonsus Liguori, the eighteenth-century founder of the Redemptorists,[119] Doctor of the Church, Father of Modern Moral Theology, and Bishop of Sant'Agata dè Goti.[120] St. Alphonsus's importance relates to his way of understanding obedience to the moral law, so we will begin by considering the shift that created the problem that Alphonsus addressed.

1. *Ockham vs. Aristotle: Obedience displaces Boulesis.* Free and deliberate human actions aim at some goal or *telos*.[121] According to Aristotle, human action moves through distinct stages, beginning with *boulesis* or "wish" for some end, through deliberation about the means to that end, ending in choice, which brings the action about.[122] In *Nicomachean Ethics*, book 3, chapter 4, Aristotle addresses a question that determines whether morality can be tied to the desires—the wishes—of the agent:

> That *wish* is for the end has already been stated; some think it is for *the good*, others for the *apparent good*. Now those who say that *the good* is the object of wish must admit in consequence that that which the man who does not choose aright wishes for is not an object of wish (for if it is to be so, it must also be good; but it may well have been bad); while those who say the *apparent good* is the object of wish must admit that there is no natural object of wish, but only what seems good to each man. Now different things appear good to different people, and, if it so happens, even contrary things.[123]

Either alternative would make the rational investigation of practical reasoning impossible. The first option is untenable. If we say that everyone wishes

119. Congregation of the Most Holy Redeemer, *Congregatio Sanctissimi Redemtoris*, abbreviated C.Ss.R.

120. For a brief but insightful biography of St. Alphonsus, see Joseph Oppitz, CSsR, *Autumn Memoirs of St. Alphonsus Liguori* (Liguori, Missouri: Liguori Publications, 1986). For a more extensive examination of his life, see Theodule Rey-Mermet, CSsR, *Alphonsus Liguori, Tireless Worker for the Most Abandoned*, translated by Jehanne-Marie Marchesi from the second French edition [of *Le Saint Du Siecle Des Lumieres* (Paris: New Cite, 1987)] (Brooklyn, New York: New City Press, 1989).

121. See Aristotle, NE 1.1, 1094a1–10.

122. NE 3.2, 1111b25–29.

123. NE 3.4, 1113a 15–23; italics on "wish" in original, other italics added.

for the true good, we make the role of wish in wicked human actions unintelligible. But that connection is really quite simple; as Anscombe said, "the primitive sign of wanting is *trying to get*."[124] People who try to get bad things want bad things; the crimes of the Nazis and the Soviets were not accidents. The claim that everyone seeks true goods is falsified by human experience. The second option eliminates the *summum bonum*. If different people simply want different things, then no true goal measures human action.

Aristotle resolves this dilemma by distinguishing the ways that good and bad agents apprehend the good:

> If these consequences are unpleasing, are we to say that absolutely and in truth *the good* is the object of wish, but for each person the *apparent good*; that that which is in truth an object of wish is an object of wish for the good man, while any chance thing may be so to the bad man.[125]

We wish for happiness generally by nature, but we wish for happiness in some specific form according to our own rationality: our culture, opinions, and moral character. Thus the problem for moral philosophy is to distinguish true goods from apparent goods and to gain habits of judgment and action that enable good rational choices. This arrangement, which St. Thomas maintains,[126] makes desire for the objective human *telos* the driving force for human action.

William of Ockham's account of freedom makes Aristotle's solution to the problem of *boulesis* irrelevant in two ways. First, by making the divine command prior to right reason, Ockham has shifted the meaning of good and evil from primarily prudential categories to primarily moral ones. Ockham makes obedience to divine commands the only moral good to be chosen by the will.

Second, Ockham denies that human agents have a natural desire for the good. Osborne summarizes: "The will is not determined to the agent's own good, or indeed to any good. It is distinct from a natural active principle because it is free and contingent."[127] Freedom of the will, for Ockham, consists

124. Anscombe, *Intention*, §36, 68; italics in original.

125. NE 3.4, 1113a23–26.

126. Aristotle's *boulesis* ("wish" in Ross's translation), becomes *voluntas* (will) in ST I-II, qq. 8–9. Cf. Osborne, *Human Action in Thomas Aquinas, John Duns Scotus, & William of Ockham*, 113–32; See also ST I-II, q. 5, a. 8.

127. Thomas M. Osborne, Jr., "William of Ockham on the Freedom of the Will and Happiness," *American Catholic Philosophical Quarterly* 86, no. 3 (2012): 435–56, at 438.

in the ability to choose between contraries; moral choices, for Ockham, are not prudential choices between better and worse goods; they are choices between obedience and disobedience. This change in emphasis allows Ockham to take the position that the human agent can choose evil qua evil: "the will is able to will a bad thing that is neither really nor apparently good; and able to will against a good thing that is neither really nor apparently bad."[128] In these two ways, Ockham reduces morality to obedience and makes the agent's desires and goals superfluous to morality, hence his moral teachings alienate the human agent from his desires and actions.

Ockham emphasizes the separation of obedience from desire in his argument that God could command a person to hate him:

> every will can conform itself to a divine command. But God can command that the created will hate him, therefore the created will can do this. Moreover, everything that can be right on earth can be right in heaven. But hating God can be right on earth, for instance if it is commanded by God, therefore [it can be right] in heaven.[129]

What could be the motive to obey a command to hate God? Rational desire for the ultimate good has been displaced by cold conformity of the will to an imposed moral obligation. Obedience takes the place of *boulesis*.

Obligation and obedience to moral law became the entire focus of Western Christian morality. In the Catholic Church, renaissance and modern manuals of moral theology provided catalogues of opinions—often conflicting opinions—about the requirements of the moral law, prefaced with treatises on the psychology of obedience or "conscience," and on the proper method of weighing conflicting opinions on moral issues.

Careful treatment on the topic of conscience was particularly important in the manuals. The emphasis on obedience to objective moral law raised the specter of accidental disobedience to laws that one had failed to notice. "Scrupulosity," a paralyzing fear of accidental infractions against the moral law, became a common disorder among morally serious Catholics and remained so until Vatican II.[130] In moral theology, the most important achieve-

128. "... voluntas potest velle malum quod nec est bonum realiter nec apparenter; et potest nolle bonum quod nec est malum realiter nec apparenter." Ockham, Q.V., qu. 8 (OTh 8, 443); quoted in Osborne, "William of Ockham on the Freedom of the Will and Happiness," 442.

129. Rep. 4, q. 16 (OTh, vol. 7, 352). Quoted in Thomas Osborne, "Ockham as a Divine Command Theorist," *Religious Studies* 12, no. 1 (March 2005); Latin at 21n54.

130. Books on the treatment of scruples or scrupulosity were published regularly through the mid-1960s. For example: Frederick William Faber, *Scruples* (Baltimore: J. Murphy, 1893); Sylvester Jenks and Roger Hudleston. *The Blind Obedience of an Humble Penitent: The Best Cure for*

ments of Alphonsus Liguori, who struggled with scrupulosity throughout his life, were to formulate the teaching on conscience in a way that could foreclose scrupulous conclusions, and to establish a method of weighing the opinions catalogued in his manual that reduced the alienating tendencies of its underlying voluntarism. How does Alphonsus differ from Thomas?

V. St. Alphonsus Liguori vs. St. Thomas Aquinas on Inculpable Ignorance

In the *Summa Theologiae*, St. Thomas Aquinas examines the question of inculpable ignorance[131] and draws two conclusions. First, although we are bound to shun ignorance and form our consciences as well as we can, when a person is faced with the need to choose, one is always bound to follow the subjective rational assessment of one's conscience. In answer to the question "whether the erring conscience binds" St. Thomas concludes, "every will at variance with reason, whether right or erring, is always evil" inasmuch as to will against reason, against the judgment of one's conscience, is to choose what one takes to be evil.[132] Second, St. Thomas concludes that the invincibly ignorant agent who performs a materially evil behavior is not culpable for it; the behavior is simply involuntary[133] and is therefore neither morally evil nor morally good.[134]

When St. Alphonsus treated the same questions in his *Theologia Moralis*, he drew a different conclusion. Like St. Thomas, St. Alphonsus taught that we have a duty to form our conscience, that the erring conscience binds, and that an invincibly ignorant person who performs a materially evil behavior does not sin; but Alphonsus, citing his contemporaries, goes further: "Not merely does the person who acts with an invincibly erroneous conscience not sin, but *more probably even gains merit*, as Fr. Fulgetius Cuniliati[135] and others correctly think."[136] Why the difference?

Scruples, Orchard Books. Extra Series, 2 (New York: Benziger, 1926); Vincent M. O'Flaherty, *How to Cure Scruples* (Milwaukee: Bruce Publishing Co., 1966); Malachy Gerard Carroll, editor, *The Treatment of Scruples* (Techny, Illinois: Divine Word Publications, 1964).

131. ST I-II, q. 6, a. 8; q. 19, aa. 5–6; q. 76.

132. ST I-II, q. 16, a. 5.

133. ST I-II, q. 19, a. 6; q. 76, aa. 2–3.

134. ST I-II, q. 19, a. 6.

135. Fulgenzio Cuniliati, OP (1685–1759) was a Venetian Dominican moral theologian.

136. Alphonsus Liguori, "The Treatise on Conscience" [*Theologia Moralis*, Book I, Treatise I], in *Conscience: Writings from Moral Theology by Saint Alphonsus*, translated by Raphael Gallageher,

The difference between Thomas and Alphonsus follows from the differences between the morality of practical reasoning and the morality of obligation. Alphonsus's Redemptorist translator observes, "Alphonsus accepts the legal nature of moral theology as it was understood after the Council of Trent (1545–1563). Law was the undisputed matrix."[137] Nevertheless Alphonsus recognizes the dangers inherent in obligational morality and strives to mitigate them.

For St. Thomas, *an act is good if it is wise.* A foolish, materially evil behavior that follows upon a person's ignorance violates right reason objectively, even if it is not subjectively blameworthy. For St. Alphonsus, however, *an act is good if it is obedient*; thus an act performed in a spirit of obedience is good—even if that action is objectively foolish or materially evil—provided the agent cannot be faulted for his ignorance[138]:

> In order to call some action good, or at least not imperfect, it is sufficient that the action be guided by the directive of reason and prudence. Therefore, in acting, provided the person does so prudently, one undoubtedly ought to be rewarded in view of the good purpose for which the action is performed.[139]

Alphonsus's treatment of "prudence" here is clearly different from Thomas's; it reflects the kind of change that Pinckaers finds in Ockham: "Practical reason and prudence were, then, simply intermediaries between law and free will. Their function was to transmit precepts and obligations."[140] For Alphonsus, "the goodness or evil of human actions becomes known exactly in the way that conscience understands it."[141] So to follow conscience is to obey the law as one knows it; hence it is to act prudently and thus meritoriously—even if one's judgment about the moral obligations imposed by the law is faulty.

CSsR. (Liguori, Missouri: Liguori Press, 2019), 12 (article 6), italics in original. See also St. Alphonsus Liguori, *Theologia Moralis: Moral Theology,* translated by Ryan Grant, 2 vols. (Post Falls, Idaho: Mediatrix Press, 2017), vol. 1, 26 (book 1, treatise 1, article 6). Redemptorist theologians place greater confidence in the Gallagher translation.

137. Raphael Gallagher, CSsR, *Conscience,* xvii.

138. Alphonsus, like Thomas Aquinas, insists that there is a moral obligation to form one's conscience by learning to the best of one's ability what the moral law requires. Conscience, for Alphonsus, is a judgment about the moral obligations imposed by the moral law in some concrete, particular situation. It is one's best efforts to judge that situation according to an objective law; it is subjective only insofar as one is bound to make such a judgment according to one's own rationality.

139. Alphonsus Liguori, *Theologia Moralis,* translated by Gallagher, book 1, treatise 1, chapter 1, article 6, p. 12.

140. Pinckaers, *The Sources of Christian Ethics,* 250.

141. Liguori, *Theologia Moralis,* book 1, treatise 1, chapter 1, article 1, p. 9.

The fact that Alphonsus Liguori is not cited as much today as he once was may obscure his importance to the Catholic moral tradition in the modern period, but he was no marginal figure; he is called "the Father of Modern Moral Theology." After his death in 1787, the religious community he founded, the Redemptorists, grew to be one of the largest in the world. St. Alphonsus was named a Doctor of the Church in 1871 by Pope Pius IX, and by 1900, his authority in moral theology was comparable to that of St. Thomas Aquinas. Alphonsus became important because he understood the difficulties entailed by the modern Church's morality of obligation and worked to reshape the doctrine of conscience to mitigate those problems.[142]

VI. Conclusion

The differences between these two great doctors of the Church, St. Thomas Aquinas and St. Alphonsus Liguori, give only the barest indications of the broader changes wrought by the Nominalist movement on the rationalities of the moral traditions of the Catholic Church and of Western Europe more generally. A closer study of that history is beyond the scope of this essay. What matters for us, and what these differences do indicate, is that a voluntarist morality of obligation became entrenched in Catholic moral teaching and changed the rationality of our tradition in a way that obscures the role of practical reasoning at the heart of Thomas's teleological morality.

Modern obligational morality shapes an understanding of obedience that tends to alienate the human agent from her or his actions and desires in the manner criticized by Bernard Williams. Consequently, the questions Bernard Williams raises about alienation in secular modern moral philosophy can help us to recognize similar difficulties in modern Christian morality and help us to question some unacknowledged presuppositions of our modern tradition. MacIntyre's theory of the rationality of traditions, paired with his Thomistic-Aristotelianism, offer Catholic moralists a valuable perspective to reassess Thomistic ethics on its own terms, and to retool their presentation of Catholic moral teaching to speak more intelligibly to an individualistic, secularizing, and morally alienated contemporary culture.

142. See Christopher Stephen Lutz, "Subjectivity, Conscience, and Culpability: The Phenomenon of Narrative Ground in the Catholic Intellectual Tradition(s)," *The Journal of Communication and Religion* 40, no 3 (Fall 2017): 28–48.

JAMES G. HANINK

Anscombe, Causality, and the Play of Creation

I. Introducing a Causal Provocation

On the recent centenary of Elizabeth Anscombe's birth, philosophers celebrated her work at The Catholic University of America and Harvard, as well as at conferences in Greece and Italy. There's much to celebrate *and* much to contest. Her daughter, Mary Geach, notes that Anscombe gives us plenty with which to argue. Indeed, when it came to argument she "was always ready for a bout."[1]

A prime example of this zest for debate is her Inaugural Lecture at Cambridge (1971), titled "Causality and Determination."[2] The subject reflects a long-term pre-occupation. Later Anscombe was to say, "My first strenuous interest in philosophy was in the topic of causality."[3] The distinguished Thomist Stephen L. Brock, some three decades later, judged her inaugural lecture "brilliant." [4] Few would deny that it is provocative.[5] At the lecture's

1. Mary Geach, "Introduction," in *Human Life, Action and Ethics: Essays by G. E. M. Anscombe*, edited by Mary Geach and Luke Gormally. St Andrews Studies in Philosophy and Public Affairs. (Exeter: Imprint Academic, 2005), xxi.

2. G. E. M. Anscombe, "Causality and Determination." Inaugural Lecture, Cambridge University 1971; in *Metaphysics and the Philosophy of Mind*, vol. 2 of *The Collected Philosophical Papers of G. E. M. Anscombe* (Oxford: Basil Blackwell, 1981), 133–47.

3. Ibid., vii.

4. Stephen L. Brock, "Causality and Necessity in Thomas Aquinas," *Questio*, 2 (2002): 217–40.

5. For a sampler of the discussion, see Ted Honderich, *A Theory of Determinism: The Mind, Neuroscience, and Life-Hopes* (Oxford: Oxford University Press, 1988), especially chap. 1; Thomas M. Osborne Jr., "Rethinking Anscombe on Causation," in *American Catholic Philosophical Quarterly* 81, no. 1 (2007): 89–107; and P. Godfrey Smith, "Causal Realism," in the *Oxford Hand-*

outset, she chides Aristotle, Spinoza, Hobbes, Hume, Kant, Mill, and Russell for their dogmatic slumbers with regard to causality and necessity. How is it, in her view, that these luminaries go so very wrong? They do so in that they have misconstrued the relation, or absence thereof, between causality and necessity. As a consequence, they have helped fashion "a cast of mind which is characteristic of our whole culture."[6]

It is in particular the case of Hume, on Anscombe's reading, that merits close scrutiny. Having shown that causes do not logically entail the events they bring about, he set out to explain why we still suppose that there must be a necessary connection between them.[7] But he was presumptuous to do so. What if we hesitate to suppose that there is any such necessary connection? Indeed, that is the very question that sets the stage for the five-point agenda of this essay. The first task is to set forth Anscombe's view of causality. The second is to identify some related themes in Wittgenstein and Newman. The third step is to take stock of some Thomist objections to Anscombe's position and then suggest ways that her friends might address them. The fourth step is to consider some implications of her view for any affirmation of causal necessity. My fifth and final task is to sketch an unabashedly theological way to open up a space for her view.

Let us begin, then, with Anscombe's view of causality. She thinks that we easily lose sight of what causality is chiefly about. "[C]ausality," for her, "consists in the derivativeness of an effect from its cause."[8] However many forms causality takes, its core is neither necessity nor universality; it is rather this *derivativeness*. And what sorts of causality are on offer? Holding an unwarranted pride of place, there is the causality that builds in necessity. Formally put, it is the "*necessitating cause* C of a given kind of effect E such that it is not possible (on the occasion) that C should occur and should not cause E, given that there is nothing that prevents an E from occurring."[9] For example—one taken from distant youth—if the ball hits the window with sufficient force, nothing having prevented it, then the window breaks.

Alternatively, there is also such a thing as a "non-necessitating cause."

book of Causation, edited by Christopher Hitchcock and Helen Beebee (Oxford: Oxford University Press, 2009).

6. Anscombe, "Causality and Determination," 133.

7. Anscombe makes this point elsewhere. See Anscombe, "Times, Beginnings and Causes," in *Metaphysics and the Philosophy of Mind*, 150–152.

8. Anscombe, "Causality and Determination," 136.

9. Ibid., 144.

Such a cause "can fail of its effect without the intervention of anything to frustrate it."[10] Anscombe borrows an example from the physicist Richard Feynman: "a bomb is connected with a Geiger counter, so that it will go off if the Geiger counter registers a certain reading."[11] Note: it's not yet determined whether the instrument, located near radioactive material, will register the reading. (As it happens, Feynman also hit upon the idea of "quantum supremacy" and its *sequelae.*)[12] In light of such a possibility, we cannot dismiss *indeterminism*. It is simply, she writes, "the thesis that not all physical effects are necessitated by their causes."[13]

Anscombe's account of causality, which allows for both stochastic and determinist forms, has a number of distinctive features. She is a *singularist* in that on her view particular causes produce particular events, for example, the ball's striking the window caused it to break. She is also a *realist* in that she claims that we perceive causation. Realist examples are commonplace. We "cut" and "paste," we "break" and "mend," we "pass" and "punt." In each case we visibly cause visible effects. For her, causal *relata* are best understood as general expressions.[14] Causation, moreover, is intensional[15] in that what we take ourselves to be causing is relative to some description.[16] Even so, we carry on with our ordinary activities without attending to specific causal laws. Indeed, Anscombe suggests that we might well wonder whether "knowledge of causes is possible" even without "any satisfactory grasp of what is involved in causation."[17] In any case, she sees no need to cast about

10. Ibid.

11. Ibid.

12. "Quantum Supremacy" might lead to a new wave of examples. A single extremely small object can behave like two separate objects. This allows scientists to construct quantum bits and a quantum computer. See Arute, F., Arya, K., Babbush, R., *et al.*, "Quantum supremacy using a programmable superconducting processor," in *Nature* 574 (2019): 505–510.

13. Anscombe, "Causality and Determination," 145.

14. Ibid., 144.

15. If causation is an intensional relation, one might take causation to be relative to descriptions of their relata. Thus causal relations have the form: *c* causes *e* relative to *D*, where *D* is an ordered pair of descriptions (for *c* and for *e*). See Jonathan Schaffer, "The Metaphysics of Causation", *The Stanford Encyclopedia of Philosophy* (Fall 2016), edited by Edward N. Zalta, URL = <https://plato.stanford.edu/archives/fall2016/entries/causation-metaphysics/>.

16. For a discussion of these points, see Johannes Roessler, "Perceptual Causality, Counterfactuals, and Special Causal Concepts," in *Understanding Counterfactuals and Causation: Issues in Philosophy and Psychology*, edited by Christoph Hoerl and Teresa McCormack (Oxford: Oxford University Press, 2011), 75–76.

17. Anscombe, "Causality and Determination," 136.

for "some train of minute physical events" to stand ready "as the regular correlate" of our everyday actions.[18]

A final and intriguing element of Anscombe's analysis of causality is her introduction of the concept of the "physical haphazard."[19] Some events happen that are neither determined nor absurd. They are neither predictable nor totally unexpected. Feynman's example suggests that the bomb's exploding, if it does, is "mere hap." Of great significance for us, she thinks both that physical indeterminism is an insufficient basis for human freedom and yet "physical haphazard" could well be "the only physical correlate of human freedom of action."[20] With this tantalizing note, we now have a workable sketch of Anscombe's view of causality.

II. Some Related Themes from Wittgenstein and Newman

Second, there comes the question of links between her view and themes in Wittgenstein and Newman. For Anscombe—and this hints at Wittgenstein's influence—we can imagine that the word "cause" could be added to a language that is already rich in particular and special causal concepts.[21] Broadly stated, the lived priority of our ways of acting over their theoretical grounding is central in Wittgenstein's later work. In this vein, he quotes Goethe's Faust: "In the beginning was the deed."[22] And why so? Because he wants to remind us of this priority of action over theory in the very order of things. Thus he observes: "The character of the belief in the uniformity of nature can perhaps be seen most clearly in the case in which what is expected is something we fear. Nothing could induce me to put my hand into a flame—even though it is *only in the past* that I have burnt myself."[23] On his view, induction, and theories thereof, come long after the fact. In a like vein, Anscombe points out that absent exact predictability, any theory of causal *pre*determination is dependent on what has already happened.[24]

18. Ibid., 146.

19. Ibid., 145–46.

20. Ibid., 146.

21. Ibid., 137.

22. Ludwig Wittgenstein, *On Certainty*, edited by G. E. M. Anscombe and G. H. von Wright, translated by Denis Paul and G. E. M. Anscombe (New York: Harper & Row, 1972), 51.

23. Ludwig Wittgenstein, *Philosophical Investigations*, §472. Revised 4th edition by P. M. S. Hacker and Joachim Schulte (Oxford: Wiley-Blackwell, 2009).

24. Anscombe, "Causality and Determination," 141–42.

John Henry Newman, scholars note, was a strong impetus for Wittgenstein's *On Certainty*.[25] Newman's approach to causality clearly breaks with the empiricism of his day.[26] On inspection, he has much in common with Anscombe. Like her, he is both a singularist and a realist. Both these commitments are at work in his treatment of a pivotal first principle that he examines in his *Grammar of Assent*: "Nothing happens without a cause."[27] It is this principle, as he sees it, that ranges from the ordinary and every day all the way to the sweeping enterprise of natural science.

For Newman we directly experience, in our daily lives, the power to act intelligently and for a purpose, and therein we experience our own agency.[28] This experience, moreover, is compatible with the familiar experience of being acted upon by another agent. In contrast, we have no direct experience of merely physical phenomena as active causes. But just here analogy comes into play. Discovering efficient causality in our own experience, we then extend causality to the world around us.[29] In this way, we come to recognize an order in nature. This order reflects the regular succession of antecedents and consequents, and it leads us to propose a network of physical laws. These laws are only probabilistic generalizations.[30] Neither experience nor reason affirms their necessary uniformity.[31] Anscombe puts the point bluntly. With regard to Humeans, she remarks "if you take a case of cause and effect, and relevantly describe the cause A and the effect B, and then construct a universal proposition, 'Always, given an A, a B follows,' you usually won't get anything true."[32]

In any case, no such descriptive physical law is a cause in the sense of agent causality. "By the doctrine of causation," Newman writes, "I mean the

25. See Wolfgang Kienzler, "Wittgenstein and John Henry Newman on Certainty," *Grazer Philosophische Studien* 71 (2006), 117–38. Ian Ker notes their shared interests in *The Achievement of John Henry Newman* (London: Harper Collins, 1990), 71.

26. For a helpful background discussion, see H. R. Klocker, SJ, "Newman and Causality," *Heythrop Journal* 6, no. 2 (1965): 160–70.

27. Newman, *Essay in Aid of a Grammar of Assent*, edited by I. T. Ker (Oxford: Oxford University Press, 1985), 49.

28. Ker points out that Newman's first principles are matters of "presumption" to which we assent as conclusions or abstractions from particular experiences. See *Grammar of Assent*, xiv.

29. For support for this analogy, see W. Norris Clarke, SJ, *The One and the Many: A Contemporary Thomistic Metaphysics* (Notre Dame, Indiana: University of Notre Dame Press, 2001), 189. Whether Clarke finds inspiration in Newman is unclear.

30. Newman, *Grammar of Assent*, 51.

31. Ibid., 52.

32. Anscombe, "Causality and Determination," 138.

... first principle, that all things come of effective will."[33] Indeed, he continues, "A law is not a cause, but a fact [and] when we come to the question of cause, then ... we have no experience of any cause but Will."[34] There is, to be sure, a further and provocative question. Newman affirms that "If, then, I must answer the question, 'What is to alter the order of nature?' I reply, 'That which willed it';—That which willed it, can unwill it; and the invariableness of law depends on the unchangeableness of that Will."[35] In answering the question as he does, Newman advances from a personalist view of causality to the reality of an Absolute Person. With this turn to the person, he also encourages us to move from an unchallenged causal necessity to the role of freedom in causality.

III. Thomistic Challenges: Aquinas and Maritain

We come next to the third point on the agenda: objections that Thomists raise to Anscombe's account of causality. To consider this point, let us look first to the Common Doctor. In doing so, I will draw on Stephen Brock, here as elsewhere an exemplary guide.

Thomas affirms free choice and moral responsibility. Yet he is a determinist with regard to physical events. As Brock notes, he does not recognize non-necessitating causes, much less Anscombe's "mere hap."[36] Thomas, moreover, repeatedly links causality and necessity. In his *Commentary on Aristotle's Metaphysics,* he remarks that "a cause is that on which something else follows of necessity."[37] He also denies that a cause can be indifferent with regard to its effect.[38] Absent a specific cause, an act lacks a determinate end. Nonetheless, sometimes a cause only has its effect "for the most part." Such a cause is contingent rather than necessary due to an impediment of some sort. By way of contrast, as Brock comments, Anscombe's interest is in effects that come about even though their causes do not meet with impediments.[39]

33. Newman, *Grammar of Assent,* 51.

34. Ibid., 52.

35. Ibid., 53.

36. Brock, "Causality and Necessity," in *Questio* 2 (2002): 218 and 231.

37. Book 5, lect. 1, §749, in *Commentary on Aristotle's "Metaphysics"*, translated by John P. Rowan (Notre Dame, Indiana: Dumb Ox Books, 1995), 277.

38. Brock, "Causality and Necessity," 220.

39. Ibid., 222.

Still, neither Thomas nor Anscombe think that chance can be a cause. As a coincidence, a "concursus," a chance does not have internal unity. As such, a chance cannot necessitate anything. A pair of examples come to mind. Aristotle instances a man who eats spicy food, steps out for something to drink, and upon doing so dies at the hands of thugs.[40] Coincidence sets the stage for his death, but the thugs kill him. Fast-very-much-forward, if you will, to Albert Camus's *The Stranger*.[41] Coincidence sets the stage for the Arab's death as he walks along a beach; but it is Meursault, the protagonist, who kills him.

Thomas, nonetheless, teaches that God brings it about that there are coincidences. As Brock explains, God "causes the common nature of being itself, and all its modes" which "include the necessary and the contingent."[42] Thus, he continues, "Thomas reconciles God's infallible efficacy with contingency in things."[43]

In reviewing Thomas's determinism in the physical order, we need to distinguish between *absolute* and *conditional* necessity. Whatever something has of its own nature it has with absolute necessity. But what something has due to something other than its own nature, say as the result of an impediment, belongs to it with conditional necessity. Thus Brock specifies that "[f]or Thomas, if the effect of a given cause is necessary *simpliciter* and not contingent, then no other cause, free or otherwise, could intervene."[44]

Nonetheless, in considering human agency, Anscombe would ask how physical natures, supposing them to have an absolute necessity, comport with the freedom of will and moral responsibility. Some think that matter itself has a "margin of indetermination" and "undetermined potency" that, as Brock reports, "allows for failures that cannot be traced to any determinant or set of determinants ... even accidental ones."[45] If this is so, perhaps natural causes can *underdetermine* their effects. In that case, they would be non-necessitating causes.

Brock, however, rejects this move. Such causal failures, if rightly ana-

40. Aristotle, *Metaphysics*, 6.3, 1027a29–1027b11. From *The Basic Works of Aristotle*, translated by W. D. Ross, edited by Richard McKeon (New York: Random House, 1941).

41. Albert Camus, *The Stranger*, translated by Matthew Ward (New York: Vintage International, 1989).

42. Brock, "Causality and Necessity," 229.

43. Ibid.

44. Ibid., 230.

45. Ibid., 233.

lyzed, have their own positive causes. In contrast, the role any material privation plays is negative, and so it only opens the way for the intervention of an impediment. Thus, he finds that "the imperfect determination of an agent's matter by its form explains ... only the possibility of its being impeded.... [T]he margin of indetermination is not a sufficient condition for failure."[46] Thus Brock concludes that for Thomas "the order of physical causes, in itself, is deterministic."[47]

To support this verdict, he refers us to a passage in Thomas's account of sin:

> [T]hat which naturally is and ought to be in a thing, is never lacking except on account of some impeding cause. And accordingly ... evil, which consists in a certain privation, has a deficient cause, or an accidental efficient cause. Now every accidental cause is reducible to a direct cause (ST I-II, q. 75, a. 1).[48]

Very well; but once again we might wonder how it is that we are able to move from the determined physical order to the nature of our own free agency, in that it manifestly interacts with the physical order.

By nature we are rational. We are self-governing, and our deliberate choices direct our actions. Thomas gives the example of a fellow who sees his journey as a worthy but not compelling end, and who considers whether to walk or to ride a horse (ST I, q, 19, a. 3). Neither the object of the act nor the means of achieving it are irresistible. To be sure, God causes us to act, whether to walk or to ride. Yet we act freely and in accord with our nature. As Thomas writes: "[F]rom contingent causes, effects follow contingently. Since, therefore, the will is an active principle ... having an indifferent relation to many things, God so moves it, that He does not determine it of necessity to one thing, but its movement remains contingent ... except in those things to which it is moved naturally" (ST I-II, q. 11, a. 4). For Thomas, then, God's providence ranges over both the deterministic physical order and the free order of human choice.

I accept Brock's exegesis and find his final comment a welcome challenge. Noting Anscombe's call for deeper reflection, especially on interference and prevention in causality, he observes: "Surely this makes it all the more a pity that we can only guess what she might have made of Thomas

46. Ibid., 235.

47. Ibid., 236.

48. All translations from the *Summa Theologica* are from the five volume edition of the English Dominicans (New York: Benziger Brothers, 1947).

Aquinas's treatment."[49] For her part, Anscombe *was* familiar with Thomas's view of causality, as Brock would later acknowledge.[50] Indeed, she appeals to it in challenging Hume's thesis that the proposition "Every beginning of existence has a cause" is not logically necessary.[51]

Doubtless, moreover, she would encourage us to engage our own Thomism. So it is that I want to raise, and here only that, three lines of inquiry. These inquiries might well lead us to think more about the end of an action, about just what counts as a privation that occasions an impediment to a cause, and about how both the end of an action and a supposed privation depend on the nature of their subject.

The first line of inquiry is this: might not an action have a determinate, yet not singular, end? Every agent, rational or irrational, acts for an end. Thomas, moreover, teaches that "the first of all causes is the final cause" (ST I-II, q. 1, a. 2). Yet might not *C* cause *E* where *E* proves to be a *range* of particular expressions?[52] Note: the range in question is a specific range; it is not just any range. In this case, the causal pattern continues to reflect the function of the final cause. For example, a sub-atomic event might cause an effect that itself has a range of instances. Or Mt. Everest might this very day cause an effect on its climbers that gives rise to a range of responses. And might not the healing of ten lepers, *mysterium tremendens*, effect a result that finds expression in another range of responses?

The second line of inquiry is this: might not the indeterminacy of matter, which allows for a privation, also be the basis for a capacity? Why not see the margin of indeterminacy as positively contributing to the richness of range causality? We do, after all, recognize that the indeterminate potential of matter allows both corruptibility and transformation. The limited matter of a human being at the morula stage of embryonic development disallows its exercise of intelligence, yet it enables that same human being to devel-

49. Brock, "Causality and Necessity," 240.

50. Stephen L. Bock, "G. E. M. Anscombe and Thomas Aquinas on Necessity and Contradiction in Temporal Events," in *Analytical Thomism: Traditions in Dialogue*, edited by Craig Paterson and Mathew S. Pugh (New York: Ashgate, 2006), 282–302.

51. G. E. M. Anscombe, "Times, Beginnings and Causes," 152–53.

52. Arthur Holly Compton, winner of the Nobel Prize in Physics for demonstrating the particle nature of electromagnetic radiation, held a range causality view. He writes: "A set of known physical conditions is not adequate to specify precisely what a forthcoming event will be. These conditions, insofar as they can be known, define instead a range of possible events from among which some particular event will occur." See his *The Cosmos of Arthur Holly Compton*, edited by Marjorie Johnston (New York: Alfred A. Knopf, 1967).

op from a cluster of several cells to, say, identical triplets doing molecular biology! There is, as well, a striking theological role for *materia dimensiva*. Thomas suggests that the *materia dimensiva* of the body at death is the *materia dimensiva* of the resurrected body (ST Suppl., q. 79, a. 1, *ad*. 3).[53]

The third line of inquiry is this: does not the end of an act, and what counts as a privation, depend on the nature of the subject in consideration? God, indeed, creates and sustains that nature. What follows? It seems that God might create the nature of a given subject so that the end of one of its acts is either a single particular or a range of particulars. God might also create the indeterminacy of a subject's matter so that in one case it is the basis of a privation, say a rigidity, and in another case the basis of a capacity, say a fluidity. In every case, all Creation reflects God's grandeur.

With these lines of inquiry introduced, and only that, I now turn to Jacques Maritain's account of causality and necessity. It suggests further Thomist concerns about Anscombe's causal provocation. In his *Degrees of Knowledge*, he links the ideal type of science with necessity.[54] Such a science, he writes, is "a knowledge in which, under the compulsion of evidence, the mind points out in things their reason for being," that is, how they "are founded in being and intelligibility."[55] There is in such a science "*Cognitio certa per causas* ... a knowledge so rooted as to be necessarily true."[56]

Even so, contingency remains. Without opening the way for "hap," Maritain does remark that "the existential positing of things is not implied in their nature, and amongst them there are encounters which are themselves not nature, the necessity for which is not prescribed in any nature. Existing reality is therefore composed of *nature* and *adventure*."[57] He adds, with reference to Thomas, that "it is only 'according to the intelligible constituents of universal natures' that the necessities known by science apply to singular things."[58]

Maritain was a student of the new physics and the sciences that follow its model. They are far from the ideal classical type. Empiriological sci-

53. For another example: Thomas argues that in the Eucharist the accidents of the bread and wine adhere in *materia dimensiva* (ST III, q. 77, a. 2).

54. Jacques Maritain, *The Degrees of Knowledge*, translated from the fourth French edition by Gerald B. Phelan (New York: Charles Scribner's Sons, 1959).

55. Ibid., 23.

56. Ibid., 23. See also ibid., 136.

57. Ibid., 26; italics in original.

58. Ibid., 27. His appeal is to Thomas's *In Perihermeneias*, bk. 1, chap. 9, lect. 13, §6.

ence, as he terms it, brings with it different sorts of causality, including an "empirio-ontological"[59] notion of causality and a "pure empiriological"[60] causality that underscores "phenomenal co-determination."[61] As science crosses the sub-atomic level, explanation in terms of causal determinism is no longer in play.[62]

In his later *Preface to Metaphysics*, Maritain offers a fuller metaphysics of causality. [63] First comes the principle of sufficient reason, "*Everything which is, to the extent to which it is, possesses a sufficient reason for its being.*"[64] It is broader than the principle of causality, which states, as Norris Clarke puts it, that whatever "does not contain the sufficient reason for its own existence within itself requires a cause."[65] In accounting for causality, Maritain avoids a merely psychological grounding, for example, "the muscular effort producing a particular effect and felt by us when we exert it."[66] No doubt he would fault Newman's appeal to personal experience, but at some point we must address just how it is that we come to enunciate first principles. How do we come to grasp the concepts therein?

Nonetheless, in the context of the first principles of theoretical reason, Maritain understands the principle of causality to affirm that "everything which exists or happens contingently or mingled with potency has a cause, in accordance with the requirements of being or unity."[67] We are to grasp causality in terms of potency and act. Potency does not reduce itself to act, and thus causality requires that which is in act to engage a receptive potency in order to realize its effect. This interplay of act and potency tells us that "[b]being an agent is itself an inclination to communicate a good," and that it leads to a shared perfecting of both agent and patient.[68] Maritain

59. Maritain uses this neologism to refer to cause "as a phenomenon to which another phenomenon is linked in a necessarily universal concatenation in which a 'law' of the world is expressed." *The Degrees of Knowledge*, 150.

60. This second neologism refers to cause "as the spatio-temporal conditions of a phenomenon, or the constellation of observable determinations to which a phenomenon is linked." *The Degrees of Knowledge*, 150.

61. Ibid., 150.

62. Ibid., 152.

63. Jacques Maritain, *A Preface to Metaphysics* (New York: Mentor Omega Books), 1962.

64. Ibid., 98. In the same place he offers an alternative: "*Whatever is, is intelligibly determined; whatever is, has that whereby it is.*"

65. Clarke, *The One and the Many*, 21.

66. Maritain, *A Preface to Metaphysics*, 126.

67. Ibid., 138.

68. Ibid., 129.

recognizes and underscores the intrinsic generosity of being.[69] In a sense the agent becomes present in the patient. Moreover, if "the created universe were not *open* to the action ... of subsistent Intellect and Love," there could be no causal production whatsoever.[70] To be sure, especially in considering the First Cause, Maritain reminds us that we need to keep in mind "that the notion of cause, like that of being, is essentially analogous."[71]

For Maritain causality is dynamic. Yet one might wonder whether his account suggests any way for friends of Anscombe to develop her sense of causality. At this point I want to mention, and no more, a pair of considerations that might be useful. The first is that causality ultimately depends on the First Cause and on the receptivity of what is caused to that which actuates its potentiality. The second is that causality is a dimension of the intelligible. Causal explanation helps us articulate the intelligibility of what is caused.

IV. Meeting the Thomist Challenge

We come now to the fourth step on our agenda, as stated earlier. How might a friend of Anscombe begin to meet the Thomistic challenges which she faces? Let's consider a few points in aid of a reply to that question. First, there is the need for humility. Our intellect is ordered to truth. As Maritain writes, "There is a nuptial relationship between mind and reality."[72] But we cannot fully grasp ontological truth, that is, the full intelligibility of being. We are both self-transcending and limited. Nonetheless, metaphysics can lead to a deeper appreciation of that which remains a mystery.[73]

A second point, already noted, is that the concept of cause is analogous. Its predecessor is the Greek "*aitia*," a legal term that means "whoever or whatever is responsible for something happening or coming to be."[74] Broadly construed, that which is caused might not be predictable. As far as we can tell, it might even be the upshot of spontaneous self-determination.[75]

A third point is that an efficient cause finds its focus in a corresponding

69. Jacques Maritain, *Existence and the Existent: An Essay on Christian Existentialism*, translated by Lewis Galantiere and Gerald B. Phelan (Garden City, New York: Image Books), 89–90.

70. Maritain, *A Preface to Metaphysics*, 129–30.

71. Ibid., 132.

72. Maritain, *The Degrees of Knowledge*, 40.

73. On this first point see Clarke, *The One and the Many*, 21–22.

74. Ibid., 188.

75. Ibid., 196.

final cause. Efficient causality is always directed to an end. That directive or final cause "perdures" in the act of causal production. As Norris Clarke puts it, "The final cause resides, therefore, in the efficient cause but as focused toward its future effect-to-be-produced."[76] It seems to follow that insofar as God is the overarching final cause of created natures, and as such is their final end, created natures might well reflect something of God's freedom in their own causal activities. The Common Doctor tells us that because of God's goodness "the dignity of causality is imparted even to creatures" (ST q. 22, a. 3.).

With these points in mind, I propose a pair of arguments. Perhaps they will loosen the bond between causality and necessity, the very bond that Anscombe disputed. Together they form a sort of analogical argument linking the sources of meaning with the sources of intelligibility. The first argument considers the relation between meaning and verifiability.

On the Sources of Meaning

P1 Many statements are cognitively meaningful.

P2 Cognitively meaningful statements are often empirically verifiable.

P3 But some cognitively meaningful statements are not empirically verifiable.

P4 One such statement is the *verifiability principle* which states that all meaningful statements are analytic or empirically verifiable, even though it is itself neither.

C Therefore, cognitive meaningfulness has more than one basis.

Note that this argument by no means suggests that cognitive meaningfulness is arbitrary. In propositional form, cognitive meaningfulness has both syntactic and semantic requirements. While we are free to say what we want, what we say must make minimal sense if we are to say anything that is true or false.

The second argument considers the relation between intelligibility and necessity.

76. Ibid., 201.

Intelligibility and Necessity

P1 All events are at least partly intelligible.

P2 The intelligibility of events requires that they have some grounding.

P3 That events are causally necessitated suffices to provide their grounding.

P4 But not all events are causally necessitated, for example, our doing philosophy together.

C The intelligibility of events has more than one grounding.

Note that this argument is compatible with causal necessitation as the ground of many or even most events. Moreover, to limit causal necessitation is not to admit radical incoherence; derivation still requires an account even if it is not necessitating.

Reflection, however, suggests that we distinguish between (a) a strict causal necessity and (b) a broader range causality. In the case of (a), a cause or combination of contributory causes brings about a specific effect, whereas in the case of (b), a cause or combination of contributory causes brings about a range of effects. Range causality is an alternative to either mere chance or strict necessity. Here a pair of examples comes to mind. In a game of pool, absent impediments, the cue ball's striking the eight ball just as it does causally necessitates the sinking of the eight ball in a side pocket, absent an impediment. In contrast, the player's directing the cue stick "just so" calls into play a range of personal powers, both intellectual and physical. The player's action opens the way for a broader range causality.

We daily experience personal powers and capacities, and we take both animate and inanimate beings to have distinctive powers and dispositions. Indeed, we come to know the nature of a being through its powers, and it is through their exercise that an entity realizes its potential. We can, in addition, speak of an *ontology of powers* and formulate an account of *dispositional causality*.[77] We can appeal to a dispositional modality that comes into play between necessity and contingency.[78] Moreover, our very familiarity with dispositional causality suggests that it is conceptually more basic than strict

77. For recent work in this area, see *Powers and Capacities in Philosophy: The New Aristotelianism*, edited by Ruth Groff and John Greco (New York and London: Routledge, 2013).

78. Rani Lill Anjum and Stephen Mumford, "Dispositional Modality," in *Lebenswelt und Wissenschaft, Deutsches Jahrbuch Philosophie 2*, edited by C. F. Gethmann. (Hamburg: Meiner Verlag, 2011), 380–94.

causal necessity. If it is, John Henry Newman's powers-based and personalist account of causality and order, noted earlier, seems even more cogent.

In exploring range causality we can readily link it with probability. Thus we might say, "It's likely that Minnesota Fats will clear the table." Bookies will vie to set the odds of his winning the tournament. And physicists, not just pool sharks, ponder probabilities. Doubtless, many abound at the sub-atomic level of the constitution of Mr. Minnesota's cue stick. Today even non-physicists are talking about the probability-based and now celebrated "quantum supremacy" of Artificial Intelligence research.

Quantum probabilities, to be sure, present problems.[79] Einstein's "God does not play dice" expresses his resistance to them.[80] In any case and at any level, a frequentist probabilistic analysis, if only because it is inherently obscure, is not entirely hospitable to Anscombe's venture. In the epistemological very long run, every sample we produce is a small sample. Our probability analysis is as epistemically limited as we ourselves are. Most of what is long past is not accessible to us; and however expansive the future proves to be, it is not now accessible to us.

More promising is the role of probability seen as a propensity of a physical situation to yield a certain kind of outcome.[81] Here we can mention Karl Popper's view of metaphysical probability. It is especially significant in that Popper, perhaps best known for his *Conjectures and Refutations* (1963), is a commanding figure of twentieth-century analytical philosophy of science. Peter Lukan, a scholar of twentieth-century theories of probability, explains that for Popper "[p]ropensities are inherent in situations and bridge ... the modern gap between subject and object as they mirror the entanglement of a knowing subject with the world."[82] He cites Popper's view that "[c]hanging propensities are objective processes, and they have nothing to do with

79. In discussing quantum randomness, Mark Spencer offers a Thomistic alternative. See his "Quantum Randomness, Hylomorphism, and Classical Theism," *The Journal of Analytic Theology* 4 (May 2016): 13.

80. Albert Einstein, "Letter to Max Born (4 December 1926)," in *The Born-Einstein Letters*, translated by Irene Born (New York: Walker and Company, 1971). Later, in a 1945 letter to the physicist Paul Epstein, he was to write: "God tirelessly plays dice under laws which he has himself prescribed." See Mindy Weisberger, *LiveScience*, June 12, 2019. "'God Plays Dice with the Universe,' Einstein Writes in Letter About His Qualms with Quantum Theory." Live Science is a major popular science website.

81. Peter Lukan, "Probability and Metaphysics," *Interdisciplinary Description of Complex Systems* 16, no. 4 (2018): 571–72.

82. Ibid., 572.

our lack of knowledge."[83] Moreover, Popper proposes a kind of teleology. As he observes: "It is not kicks from the back, from the past, that impel us but the attraction, the lure of the future and its competing possibilities that attract us, that entice us. This is what keeps life—and, indeed, the world—unfolding."[84]

Suppose that we grant that there is a metaphysical probability that correlates with a metaphysical indeterminacy. Might we do so at least for now? To be sure, everything is what it is. But everything is in relation, and what is might in some respects be indeterminate. After all, Thomists see indeterminate prime matter as a metaphysically indispensable explanatory principle. If we proceed with the supposition proposed, still another question comes to mind. Why is there this probability and indeterminacy in the reality that we never fully grasp? How we answer this question might even return us to Elizabeth Anscombe's "hap."

V. Creator and Creation at Play

We come now to the fifth and final task on the agenda. Suppose that we see causality and necessity in the context of the principle of sufficient reason and the intelligibility of being. Suppose, as well, that intelligibility allows for metaphysical indeterminacy. There awaits us, if we move through reason to Revelation, an infinitely personal context and its freedom. Scripture invites a fresh causal provocation. Let's revisit the opening lines of the "Last Gospel" of the Extraordinary Rite. "In the beginning was the Word; and the Word was with God; and the Word was God. He was in the beginning with God. All things were made through him, and without him nothing was made. What was made in him was life. And that life was the light of men."[85] So it is, we learn, that the *Logos* brought everything into an intelligible existence. So it is, we discover, that the *Logos* sources the dynamic of derivation that structures causality.

And what does creation tell us about causality and necessity? It introduces, as Hugo Rahner notes, the great metaphysical truth that for God "[t]he creation of the world and of man, though a divinely meaningful act,

83. Karl Popper, *A World of Propensities* (Bristol: Thoemmes Press, 1995), 18.

84. Ibid., 20–21.

85. The translation is from Thomas Aquinas, *Commentary on the Gospel of John*, 3 vols. translated by Fabian Larcher, OP, and James A. Weisheipl, OP (Washington, D.C: The Catholic University of America Press, 2010).

was by no means a necessary one."[86] With the developing patristic tradition, we see in this freedom a kind of play. In doing so, to be sure, we proceed apophatically. Yet God's play opens the way for our own play. As Rahner writes, "a cosmic game is played before God, extending from the round of the stars and atoms to the gravely beautiful play of the spirit of man."[87] Creation is intelligible, yet its order welcomes an ontological freedom. "So we find, not a closed cosmic system inexorably obeying its own laws, but an order directed by the Logos after the manner of a graceful game," and, Rahner continues, "this concept of the playing God makes transparent all the bright things of his world and indeed all happenings, whatsoever their kind."[88] Fittingly, he calls our attention to St. Gregory Nazianzen's lines: "For the Logos on high plays, / stirring the whole cosmos back and forth, as he wills, / into shapes of every kind."[89]

The Incarnation deepens the wonder of creation and its lesson of freedom. Consider again Rahner's startling language.

> This tremendous outpour, a happening in which the human mingles with the divine, has been called by me a game—and in this I have followed some of the most illustrious of Christian mystics—because there is … nothing here of compulsion or calculation … there is an ever better reason for calling this a game than for applying that term to the creation, for in this game of grace Christ has actually become the playmate of man.[90]

Here we might contrast today's fierce demand for a calculating autonomy with the words of St. Therese of Lisieux. She asks to serve Jesus as "a toy … such as a child might … leave lying in a corner or press to his heart if he feels that way about it."[91] Doubtless The Little Flower was familiar with the text from Proverbs (8:27–31). Here Wisdom, like a child at play, was God's delight when He "marked out the foundations of the earth."

In the light of creation and the Incarnation, and believing that grace builds on nature, we can better see the role of play in our own lives. Experi-

86. Hugo Rahner, SJ, *Man at Play*, translated by Brian Battershaw and Edward Quinn (Providence, Rhode Island: Cluny Media, 2019), 16.

87. Ibid., 16–17.

88. Ibid., 20.

89. Gregory Nazianzen, *Carmina*, I, 2, 2, vv. 589–90 (PG 37:624a *et seq.*), as cited by Hugo Rahner, SJ, *Man at Play*, 34.

90. Rahner, *Man at Play*, 61–62.

91. Therese of Lisieux, *Autobiography of a Saint*, translated by Ronald Knox (London: Fount, An Imprint of HarperCollins reprint, 1958), 171.

ence suggests that it is a basic good of the human person. We can, to be sure, buy entertainment. We can buy political influence. We cannot, however, buy genuine play. For such play is a core constituent of human flourishing. We share in play, of course. Yet the spirit of play is within those who share it. It is for itself.

And there is more. There is a theological insight that encourages philosophers to look beyond both arbitrary chance and relentless necessity: all creation gives glory to God. It does so with a beauty that saves the world and, indeed, the cosmos. Despite Hume's skeptical strictures, perhaps a hundred million miracles *are* happening every day. Einstein's restrictive search was for a determinist and material theory of everything. So be it. Yet God is at play—surely not with dice—but with the cosmos itself.

As for the metaphysics of first principles, we can deepen our grasp of their source and implications. Joseph Ratzinger comments that in some respects "[t]he intellectual approach of modern physics may offer us more help ... than the Aristotelian philosophy was able to give," having in mind specifically the "need to think in 'complementaries.'"[92] John Paul II, the philosopher and saint, recognizes our desire to learn the full truth about reality; he realizes that the contemplation of the universe gives rise to an abiding wonder. In our search for understanding, we grasp what he terms "a core of philosophical insight within the history of thought as a whole."[93]

What is it, then, that we find in this core? The Philosopher Pope asks us to find our direction with "the principles of non-contradiction, finality and causality" together with "the concept of the person as a free and intelligent subject, with the capacity to know God, truth, and goodness."[94] The principle of non-contradiction is one of logic. The principles of finality and causality are principles of metaphysics. The final end of this creation is a new creation.

In this new creation, the human person finds a share in God's life. Finality, or the final cause, is the cause of all causes.[95] It is the derivation of all derivations. As such, it shapes every efficient cause in accord with the nature

92. Joseph Ratzinger, *Introduction to Christianity*, translated by Burns and Oates (San Francisco, California: Ignatius Press, 2004), 174.

93. Pope John Paul II, *Fides et Ratio* (1998): no. 4.

94. Ibid..

95. Aquinas writes in §782 of his *Commentary on Aristotle's "Metaphysics"* that "even though the end is the last thing to come into being in some cases, it is always prior in causality. Hence it is called the cause of causes, because it is the cause of the causality of all causes."

of that efficient cause. There is, indeed, a hierarchy of being that forms with measured spontaneity a cosmic dance before the Creator. Recall King David and think of today's Hasidim. Ours is a creation wherein "There lives the dearest freshness deep down things," and here we dare play and dance before the Lord.[96]

A final word on Elizabeth Anscombe. I began by outlining her scrutiny of the bond between causality and necessity. Perhaps I can end by suggesting where it might lead us. Her introduction of the Anglo-Saxon "hap," about which *she* wished to say more, might be just a philosopher's inkling. It might be, though, an inkling of the final freedom and happiness which even now enchant us.

96. Gerard Manley Hopkins, "God's Grandeur," in *Gerard Manley Hopkins*, edited by Catherine Phillips (Oxford: Oxford University Press, 1986), 128.

ALICE M. RAMOS

Truth and Contexts of Intelligibility in MacIntyre's Early Work

I. Introduction

THERE WAS A TIME WHEN Alasdair MacIntyre's Thomistic turn and his commitment to Thomism was perhaps not all that clear.[1] John Haldane once suggested that MacIntyre's trilogy from *After Virtue* to *Whose Justice? Which Rationality?*, followed by *Three Rival Versions of Moral Enquiry*, needed to be a tetralogy, that the fourth volume should contain a clearer statement of what distinctive ideas the Thomistic tradition might be able to contribute, together with a development of metaphysical claims, and that such a volume might be titled *The Truth of Thomism* or *The Requirements of Thomism*.[2] MacIntyre's 1991 Aquinas lecture at Marquette University, entitled *First Principles, Final Ends and Contemporary Philosophical Problems,* did in fact show more clearly his commitment to the Thomistic tradition, being therefore the answer as it were to Haldane's suggestion, and that moreover what MacIntyre has to say in this lecture

1. In an email to me (April 18, 2021), Professor MacIntyre remarked that he tends to think of himself as a Thomistic Aristotelian or a Neo-Aristotelian rather than as a Thomist; nonetheless I do think one can speak of a Thomistic turn in MacIntyre's thought and work, even if according to him Thomism can only adequately respond to present-day rejections of its principal positions in what may seem to be un-Thomistic ways. See his *First Principles, Final Ends and Contemporary Philosophical Issues* (Milwaukee: Marquette University Press, 1990), 2.

2. John Haldane, "MacIntyre's Thomist Revival: What Next?" in *After MacIntyre*, edited by John Horton and Susan Mendus (Notre Dame, Indiana: University of Notre Dame Press, 1994), 92.

about the truth in Thomism is already, to a certain degree, foreshadowed in his earlier writings. To show this foreshadowing, I would like to consider the importance of contexts in MacIntyre and to see how these contexts are either a means to truth and intelligibility or a movement away from these.

The importance of contexts in MacIntyre's work is undeniable: it is by means of a context that a concept, a text, a practice is made intelligible. When a concept is deprived of its original context, it becomes arbitrary and rationally indefensible. A good example of this is the anthropologist Mary Douglas's account of the taboo rules of Deuteronomy as presupposing a cosmology and a taxonomy of a certain kind. Once the initial context—the background of beliefs—of the taboo rules is lost, abandoned, or forgotten, then they appear as a set of arbitrary prohibitions.[3] According to MacIntyre, any theory of taboo rules that makes them intelligible without reference to their history is a false theory.[4] In a similar manner, the notions of good, right, and the obligatory are seen by MacIntyre as survivals of contexts which few, if any, thinkers have the ability to distinguish in order to help us make sense out of our unintelligible moral situation, or our cultural and moral crisis. Contemporary philosophers, who are unable to recognize the different aspects of the past from which the present is composed, fail to understand both themselves and our cultural crisis. If, however, one is able to engage, as MacIntyre does, in a history of enquiry, one is then able to place concepts or practices within certain contexts or traditions, within their original context of philosophical and theological systems, and thus ascertain whether or not these contexts permit an adequate formulation of timeless truths concerning natural kinds, essential properties, and the teleological ordering of things and persons.[5] The point of the history of enquiry is then to move toward perfected understanding.

In MacIntyre's estimation, both Aristotle and Aquinas teach us that enquiry begins to move toward the *telos* of understanding "from the dialectical interrogation of our disputing predecessors, from the identification of what truth it was that each of them had discerned and into what errors each had been led by the limitations of their different standpoints."[6] The history of

3. Alasdair MacIntyre, "A Crisis in Moral Philosophy: Why is the Search for the Foundations of Ethics so Frustrating?" in *The Roots of Ethics*, edited by Daniel Callahan and H. Tristram Engelhardt Jr. (New York: Plenum Press, 1976), 11.

4. Ibid., 13.

5. MacIntyre, "A Reply to My Critics," in *After MacIntyre*, 300.

6. Ibid., 301.

enquiry thus becomes the story of our approach to truth, or of our distancing ourselves from it.

II. The Christian Context in Ethics: Secularization and a Deviant Christian Tradition[7]

In this essay I will now consider a number of contexts in moral, epistemological, and scientific enquiry. Due to the importance which MacIntyre has given to the relationship between theism, or more specifically, Christianity, and morality, I will begin first with what I term the Christian context in ethics. The notions of context and intelligibility are recurring notions within MacIntyre's work, and it is fair to say that Elizabeth Anscombe has influenced him in the use of these notions and in the direction of his moral enquiry.

In an essay which dates from 1958, entitled "Modern Moral Philosophy," Anscombe contends that the notion of a "law conception of ethics" is derived exclusively from Christianity. Anscombe argues that the very terminology of "law," "duty," "norms," and "obligations" belongs to Christian premises, and that an ethics which makes use of such terminology without the theological and metaphysical contexts which it supposes cannot be understood. Hume's importance for the Enlightenment project of morality lies in his discovery of an ethics which had already been evacuated of its theistic content and thus rendered contextless and unintelligible. For Anscombe a concept had survived outside the context that made it really intelligible. Anscombe says that it was not that Protestants denied the existence

7. In this section I will speak of a deviant Christian tradition and also of a Scholastic tradition that is not Thomistic. Cf. MacIntyre's words on "tradition": "A living tradition then is an historically extended, socially embodied argument, and an argument precisely in part about the goods which constitute that tradition. Within a tradition the pursuit of goods extends through generations, sometimes through many generations. Hence the individual's search for his or her good is generally and characteristically conducted within a context defined by those traditions of which the individual's life is a part, and this is true both of those goods which are internal to practices and of the goods of a single life." Alasdair MacIntyre, *After Virtue*, 2nd ed. (Notre Dame, Indiana: University of Notre Dame Press, 1981), 222. See also Jeffrey L. Nicholas's succinct definition: "For MacIntyre a tradition is an argument extended through time in which certain fundamental agreements are defined and redefined both by those inside the tradition and in communication with those outside of it. Reason refers to the standards of justification and exemplars of reasoning within a tradition." *Reason, Tradition, and the Good: MacIntyre's Tradition-Constituted Reason and Frankfurt School Critical Theory* (Notre Dame, Indiana: University of Notre Dame Press, 2012), 98.

of divine law; their doctrine held that the law was given to show the human person's incapacity to obey it, and this was the case for both the prescriptions of the Torah, as well as for the requirements of natural divine law.[8] Now even though Anscombe recognized the lack of an adequate context and content for a morality of obligation—for a Divine Law ethics—she was, nevertheless, not suggesting that it be completely abandoned. According to Anscombe, since "pure prescriptive deontology only makes sense on the assumption that there is a transcendent legislative authority—God or (perhaps) Cosmic Order," if one does not believe this, then "one should abandon that kind of moral thinking."[9] Anscombe thus reasoned that moral theorists should return to the classical emphasis on an ethics of virtue, which underlines the excellence of actions rather than rules. She thus set the stage for the work of Alasdair MacIntyre.

This does not mean, however, that MacIntyre ceases to be interested in the Christian context of moral law, in that moral scheme of Christianity according to which the law which God utters to us is in harmony with the nature that He created in us and with the ends which that nature pursues.[10] In MacIntyre's moral enquiry, he will come to recognize that an Aristotelian virtue ethics, an Aristotelian moral psychology, and a Christian view of the moral law are adequately synthesized in Thomistic ethics.[11] The point, however, is not to enter into this aspect of MacIntyre's moral enquiry here, but rather to concentrate on how the Christian context, through secularization and through its deviation from the Thomistic, Roman Catholic tradition, ceases to be an adequate context for an objective or realist ethics and thus paves the way for Kantian ethics and for Enlightenment morality. Devoid of the teleological framework of human nature, this project was bound to fail.

The claim that certain types of Christianity were responsible for the loss of the context which a prescriptive deontology needed is explored by MacIntyre in a number of his writings. Before entering briefly into this aspect of MacIntyre's work, I would like to insist on the importance of religion in his intellectual and what might be called religious itinerary. In MacIntyre's book *Marxism and Christianity*, he sees traditional religion as providing

8. Anscombe, "Modern Moral Philosophy," *Philosophy* 33, no. 124 (1958): 6.

9. Ibid.

10. MacIntyre, "How Moral Agents Became Ghosts," *Synthèse* 53, no. 2 (1982): 305.

11. See my article "Tradition as Bearer of Reason in Alasdair MacIntyre's Moral Enquiry," in *Freedom, Virtue, and the Common Good*, edited by Curtis L. Hancock and Anthony O. Simon (Notre Dame, Indiana: University of Notre Dame Press, 1995), 179–93.

"an interpretation of human existence by means of which men may situate themselves in the world and direct their actions to ends that transcend those offered by their immediate situation."[12] As he sees it, religion can have a transforming function insofar as it offers a context whereby individuals are able to understand themselves independently of their social position or identity. "It is in contrast between what society tells a man he is and what religion tells him he is that he is able to find grounds both for criticizing the *status quo* and for believing that it is possible for him to act with others in changing it. For the most part lacking a religious perspective, the members of modern industrial societies have also mostly lacked any alternative framework of beliefs which would enable them to criticize and transform society."[13]

According to MacIntyre, when traditional religion no longer provides man with an effective vision of the world, then secular doctrines of man and society are elaborated, having the scope and functions of religion; one such doctrine is Marxism which, in MacIntyre's view, inherited some of the functions of Christianity, for it has been paradoxically considered an atheistic religion.[14] As MacIntyre notes, Marxism results from the development of the philosophies of Hegel and Feuerbach which are in part secular versions of the Christian religion.[15] Now an interesting point which MacIntyre brings up at the end of *Marxism and Christianity* is that Christianity has been secularized not only from without but also from within; by this I mean not only by philosophers such as Hegel and Feuerbach, but also by Christian theologians themselves. In an attempt to make Christianity understandable, as it were, to the secular man, these theologians have so impoverished the content of this religion that it can no longer carry out its original transforming function. Christianity then cannot provide man with the context or framework necessary to interpret human existence, for it has lost appreciable content.[16] MacIntyre thus points out that not only has Christianity been the victim of secularization, but that Christianity, especially Protestant Christianity, has itself been "a powerful secularizing agent."[17]

12. Alasdair MacIntyre, *Marxism and Christianity* (Notre Dame, Indiana: University of Notre Dame Press, 1968), 2.

13. Ibid., 4.

14. Ibid., 5.

15. Ibid., 6.

16. Ibid., 142–43.

17. MacIntyre, "Is Understanding Religion Compatible with Believing?" in *Rationality*, edited by Bryan R. Wilson (New York: Harper & Row, 1970), 76.

In his essay "Is Understanding Religion Compatible with Believing?" MacIntyre considers how Christian beliefs and concepts were held to be true and intelligible in the past, and how in the present they have become for many obscure and unacceptable. He notes that the transition from medieval belief to modern skepticism has to do with the intelligibility of Christian concepts and beliefs in one social context as opposed to their unintelligibility in another context. Although it is true that the apparent internal incoherencies in Christian concepts did not go unnoticed in the Middle Ages, it is nonetheless true that these incoherencies were an incentive to enquiry rather than a ground for disbelief, for skepticism, and for the abandonment of Christianity, as they often become for contemporary man. MacIntyre points once again to secularization as making incomprehensible in our times what was once intelligible in a given social context: "[T]he apparent incoherence of Christian concepts was to be taken to be tolerable (and treated as apparent and not real) because the concepts were part of a set of concepts which were indispensable to the forms of description used in social and intellectual life. It is the secularization of our forms of description, constituting part of the secularization of our life, [which] has left the contradictions high and dry."[18] MacIntyre gives as an example of this secularization the replacement of a physics which requires a Prime Mover by a physics which does not. In this area of scientific enquiry, descriptions which have any connection with the concept of God are thus dispensed with.

This process of secularization has been welcomed by some Christian theologians such as Paul Tillich, who sees it as a passage from heteronomous reason to autonomous reason. But, as MacIntyre points out, "The counterpart to secularization is that the specific character of religion becomes clearer at the cost of diminishing its content."[19] Religious utterances are taken to be unique, with a logic of their own. As a result, contradiction and incoherence are easily tolerated, through the use of concepts such as "the absurd" (Kierkegaard), "paradox" (Barth), or "mystery" (Marcel). According to MacIntyre, religion becomes logically invulnerable, but at the cost of emptiness, and the peculiar invulnerability which belongs to Christianity is "as a form of belief which has lost the social context which once made it comprehensible."[20]

18. Ibid., 74.
19. Ibid.
20. Ibid., 76.

Here it is interesting to note MacIntyre's recurring emphasis on how theologians themselves have evacuated Christianity of its content. In *Secularization and Moral Change*, MacIntyre refers to Tillich as one of those contemporary theologians who has, as it were, decontextualized Christianity: for Tillich, theism can no longer consider the metaphysics of scholastic Catholicism as a "live intellectual option."[21] The metaphysical framework for the concept of God has been replaced in Tillich by a psychological context. God is characterized in psychological terms, as simply a name given to human concern. And so MacIntyre considers that "Tillich's theism is merely a familiar form of atheism baptized with a new name."[22] As MacIntyre says, "When Feuerbach explained that he did not believe in the God of orthodoxy because God could at best only be a name for man's ultimate concerns, he was not regarded by theologians as being a particularly subtle defender of the Christian religion. In fact, the evacuation of the notion of God of its substantial content through definition seems the only possible outcome of the Tillichian (or Robinsonian) enterprise here."[23]

If MacIntyre also mentions Robinson (Dr. John A. Robinson, the Bishop of Woolwich, author of *Honest to God*, 1963), it is because of his importance in the area of the "new morality," and more specifically in the "new sexual morality." MacIntyre sees the new morality as a very substantial part of the new theology.[24] Robinson takes moral norms or rules out of the context which renders them intelligible; decontextualized, they are free floating and thus seem arbitrary. As MacIntyre puts it:

> Robinson officially abjures the legalistic form of morality (the traditional concept of moral law) and declares his allegiance to a morality guided by the motive of love; but he further maintains that a man who acts from this motive will necessarily abstain from sexual relations outside marriage. His conclusion can be correct only if the traditional rules are covertly reintroduced into his definition of the word 'love.' Since Robinson has rejected all traditional forms of justification for the traditional rules, however, his adhesion to the rules consequently appears arbitrary and irrational.[25]

MacIntyre recognizes that traditional Christian ethics has been replaced by an entirely vacuous ethics.

21. MacIntyre, *Secularization and Moral Change* (London: Oxford University Press, 1967), 68.

22. MacIntyre, "The Fate of Theism," in *The Religious Significance of Atheism* (New York: Columbia University Press, 1967), 27.

23. MacIntyre, *Secularization and Moral Change*, 69.

24. MacIntyre, "Atheism and Morals,"" in *The Religious Significance of Atheism*, 45.

25. Ibid., 46.

Once the prescription of particular types of actions has been separated from a morality of intentions such as that of Robinson, it is difficult to formulate such moralities in a way that they have any content at all.[26] The meaning of the concept of love, along with concepts such as duty and obligation, becomes so general that these notions become in effect "empty of specific content."[27] As MacIntyre sees it:

> The new theology ... involves a serious misreading of the Gospels. The Gospels were written against a background of the kind of morality which our society has lost. The presupposition of Jesus' injunction to have regard not to the letter of the law but to the spirit is that there does exist a well-defined set of social relations, in terms of which the traditional Jewish Commandments have meaning. Jesus is protesting against the legalism which does not in fact obey the Commandments in the humane spirit in which he takes them to have been intended. But his own concept of love has meaning only in the context of a legal morality. So Jesus can talk both of modifying and of fulfilling the law. The injunctions to have regard to the spirit and not to the letter have a sense which is quite different from the sense given to it by the latest kind of liberal Christian theology.[28]

And yet, faced with this impoverished sort of Christian moral theology, with "the existence of a whole group of theologians which have retained a theistic vocabulary but [which have] acquired an atheistic substance,"[29] the secularization of the modern world is not an accomplished fact, and there is still a nostalgia as it were for the revival of a Christian ethics, still a sense that there is something missing. Christianity has not been totally displaced; as MacIntyre says, "The inability of men to discard Christianity is part of their inability to provide any post-Christian means of understanding their situation in the world."[30]

Now the decay in the traditional attitude to moral rules is due not only to Protestantism, but also to Jansenist Catholicism. Both these versions of Christianity, which might be termed a deviant Christian tradition, present a human nature which has been radically corrupted by original sin; man's will and reason are so depraved that they cannot possibly adhere to the moral

26. MacIntyre, *Secularization and Moral Change*, 71.

27. Ibid., 72.

28. Ibid., 73–74.

29. MacIntyre, *Against the Self-Images of the Age* (Notre Dame, Indiana: University of Notre Dame Press, 1971), 20.

30. MacIntyre, *Secularization and Moral Change*, 75.

law except by the aid of grace, if even by grace.[31] It is not surprising then that justification should become a matter of faith alone. "The consequence of [the Protestant and Jansenist Catholic] view is that from any human standpoint the divine commandments do become arbitrary fiats imposed on us externally; our nature does not summon us to obey them, because we cannot recognize them as being for our good. The motives of hope of eternal reward and fear of eternal punishment then must completely replace temporal motives for morality."[32] Such a theistic context leaves man moralityless, since what is evident here is the dissociation between human nature and obligation. In addition, together with the Protestant conception of ethics, MacIntyre presents, in his *A Short History of Ethics*, the Ockhamist perspective or context on the divine commandments, a context which is in line with a scholastic tradition that is not Thomistic.

For Ockham, as for Duns Scotus, freedom is disconnected from nature, so that it is possible to speak of an extrinsicism with respect to an understanding of morality, since the objective foundation for the goodness or wrongness of things is only to be found in the legislative will of God. The value of things—their being good or bad—is not found in the things themselves, which would be, as it were, the reason for wanting or not wanting them, but rather, the reason is found in the will of God. This is, in my estimation, an extrinsic way of considering the goodness of things, and to this is also added in Duns Scotus the denigration of the natural inclination—of the natural love—of the will for the good. For Duns Scotus the will naturally tends toward that which is advantageous, because it is exclusively linked to the appetites and instinct. Thus the will is free when it acts independently of natural inclinations and tends toward what is good because it is good in itself, that is, because God wills it so.[33] Following Duns Scotus, Ockham does away with the idea of a natural inclination. It may be said that for St. Thomas the natural inclinations to being, the true, the good, and to happiness are at the very source of freedom. They form, so to speak, the will and the intellect, the union of which produces free will. We are free, then, because of these natural inclinations. On the contrary, for Ockham, the free power is capable of contrary acts and so of determining itself in one direc-

31. For a different interpretation of the Protestant position, including Luther, Calvin, and the notion of the individual, see Richard J. Mouw, *The God Who Commands* (Notre Dame, Indiana: University of Notre Dame Press, 1990), 55–75.

32. MacIntyre, "Atheism and Morals," 39.

33. Tomás Alvira, *Naturaleza y Libertad* (Pamplona: EUNSA, 1985), 141.

tion or another, rejecting then the natural inclination to happiness. Human freedom is thus more apparent for Ockham when it resists the natural inclinations.[34] The Aristotelian doctrine on the tendency of nature toward the good, which is affirmed and elaborated on by St. Thomas, becomes solely a proposition of faith in Ockham; and from a scientific point of view, finality cannot for him be attributed to nature. The way is thus paved for a purely formalistic ethics, a voluntaristic approach to morality, since obligation or duty is understood as separated from nature, as there does not exist an essentially good law, but rather only an essentially good lawgiver.[35]

Now, if we take, for example, Luther's ethics which follows Ockham's attempt to base morals on revelation, we see that for Luther, as for Ockham,

> The only true moral rules are the divine commandments; … they have no further rationale or justification than that they are the injunctions of God. To obey such moral rules cannot be to satisfy our desires; for our desires are part of the total corruption of our nature, and thus there is a natural antagonism between what we want and what God commands us to perform. Human reason and will cannot do what God commands because they are enslaved by sin; we therefore have to act against reason and against our natural will. But this we can do only by grace. We are saved not by works, for none of our works are in any way good. They are all the product of sinful desire.[36]

The theistic framework thus presented by Luther deemphasizes action, to the extent that what matters is not the action done or left undone, but rather the faith which moved the agent. Within such a framework, the merit of one action as opposed to another is no longer of any great concern. The realms of faith and reason thus become dissociated, as do the religious and the secular. As a result, certain realms of human life—political and economic activity, for example—become autonomous in their norms because they are not considered to belong to the realm of salvation and damnation and yet paradoxically, success in, let us say, the economic realm, is seen as a sign of redemption. The theistic framework seems then to provide for no more than divine arbitrariness. If a man considers himself to be one of the elect, then the only restraint to be put on his actions is external, that is, the fear of punishment. "The law of God becomes, therefore, only a standard against

34. Servais Pinckaers, OP, *The Sources of Christian Ethics*, translated from the 3rd edition and edited by Sr. Mary Thomas Noble, OP (Washington, D.C.: The Catholic University of America Press, 1995), 244–45.

35. Alvira, *Naturaleza y Libertad*, 141–42.

36. MacIntyre, *A Short History of Ethics* (New York: MacMillan, 1966), 121–22.

which we judge ourselves guilty and in need of redemption; and the commandments of God become a series of arbitrary fiats for which to demand any natural justification is at once impious and meaningless."[37]

Given Luther's Christian fideism, as opposed to Aquinas's Christian Aristotelianism, it is evident that we have here not only alternative metaphysical schemes but also different moral vocabularies. And what is particularly crucial in Luther is the emergence of the individual as "a new identity for the moral agent."[38] Without entering into the social process, in addition to the theorizing derived from theology, which is responsible for this emergence of the individual, let us briefly say that man no longer defines himself as he did in traditional societies vis-à-vis other men, whereby his obligations were to be fulfilled according to his status. "The individual [thus] no longer finds his evaluative commitments made for him, in part at least, by simply answering the question of his own social identity.... From the facts of his situation as he is able to describe them in his new social vocabulary, nothing at all follows about what he ought to do. Everything comes to depend upon his own individual choice."[39] And as we have seen above, since the individual's desires are corrupt and thus can no longer provide a criterion for his choices—or as in Aristotelian ethics, a major premise for his reasoning—the moral agent is thus considered sovereign in his choices. It was precisely this type of Protestant ethic which was inherited by Kant and other Enlightenment thinkers: an ethics evacuated of its true theistic content and context and thus unintelligible.

III. Contexts in Epistemological and Scientific Enquiry

Just as MacIntyre is interested in contexts as a means to truth and intelligibility in moral and in theological enquiry, he is also interested in the importance of contexts within what he calls epistemological crises. In an article which dates from 1977 titled "Epistemological Crises, Dramatic Narrative, and the Philosophy of Science," MacIntyre sheds further light on the notions which concern us here. He refers to the context, we might say, of a shared culture, or of shared schemata which are constitutive of and nor-

37. Ibid., 123.
38. Ibid., 124.
39. Ibid., 126.

mative for intelligible action by an individual and are also means for the individual's interpretation of the action of others. "It is these schemata which enable inferences to be made from premises about past behavior to conclusions about future behavior and present inner attitudes.... They are prescriptions for interpretation."[40] These very schemata which inform the interpretations of an individual's social life and which go unnoticed may suddenly be put in question because the individual finds that he has been led into error or deception. This is, for MacIntyre, the form of epistemological crisis encountered by ordinary agents and an example of such a crisis is found in Shakespeare's *Hamlet*. Hamlet's problem consists in not knowing which schema to believe. His problem could be formulated by the question: "What is going on here?" According to MacIntyre, "Hamlet's problems arise because the dramatic narrative of his family and of the kingdom of Denmark through which he identified his own place in society and his relationships to others has been disrupted by radical interpretative doubts. His task is to reconstitute, to rewrite that narrative, reversing his understanding of past events in the light of present responses to his probing. This probing is informed by two ideals, truth and intelligibility, and the pursuit of both is not always easily coherent."[41] In trying to reconstruct his narrative, his story, Hamlet is thus searching for intelligibility; in other words, he is trying to make sense out of his situation. For as MacIntyre puts it, "To be unable to render oneself intelligible is to risk being taken to be mad—is, if carried far enough, to be mad,"[42] a state in which obviously nothing makes sense.

In describing epistemological crises, MacIntyre makes reference not only to fictional characters; he takes up the example of Descartes, who was also plunged into an epistemological crisis. However, Descartes constitutes for MacIntyre a unique case, since Hamlet's crisis, for example, takes place against a background or context of well-founded beliefs, against schemata of interpretations which have been brought into question, while Descartes' doubt lacks any such background, so that MacIntyre calls it "a contextless doubt."[43] Descartes rejects history as a means to truth, but narrates to us his own history as the way through which the search for truth will be carried

40. MacIntyre, "Epistemological Crises," *The Monist* 60, no. 4 (1979): 453–72, reprinted in *Paradigms and Revolutions*, edited by Gary Gutting (Notre Dame, Indiana: University of Notre Dame Press, 1980), 55. I am using the Gutting edition here.

41. Ibid., 56.

42. Ibid.

43. Ibid., 59.

on.[44] Although Descartes starts by assuming that he knows nothing, such an enterprise of radical doubt is impossible since he does not put into doubt his capacity to use languages and thus to make meaningful utterances. As MacIntyre sees it in his essay "Contexts of Interpretation": "There is no way for the [thinker] to locate himself outside some tradition of interpretation; the very language he speaks and writes in is shaped by traditions that he cannot evade."[45] In addition, Descartes does not recognize the presence of a tradition, specifically the Platonic and Augustinian tradition, from which he had inherited his epistemological ideals. In contrasting the difference between Hamlet's and Descartes' epistemological crises, MacIntyre says: "For Shakespeare invites us to reflect on the crisis of the self as a crisis in the tradition which has formed the self; Descartes by his attitude to history and to fable has cut himself off from the possibility of recognizing himself; he has invented an unhistorical self-endorsed self-consciousness and tries to describe his epistemological crisis in terms of it. Small wonder that he misdescribes it."[46] To doubt all of one's beliefs without reference to any historical or autobiographical context is, according to MacIntyre, "an invitation not to philosophy, but to mental breakdown, or rather to philosophy as a means to mental breakdown."[47] Descartes did not completely undertake his project without some reference to a background or context of beliefs; had this not been the case, Descartes would not have been able to make any sense out of what he was doing; his undertaking would have remained unintelligible to himself and to others.

As MacIntyre notes, we do have some indications in the history of philosophy of the unintelligibility or, in fact, of the mental breakdown, which results from radical doubt or radical skepticism. Such is the case of Hume who wrote:

> The understanding, when it acts alone, and according to its most general principles, entirely subverts itself, and leaves not the lowest degree of evidence in any proposition, either in philosophy or common life. . . .Where am I, or what? From what causes do I derive my existence, and to what condition shall I return? Whose favor shall I court, and whose anger must I dread? What beings surround me? And on whom have I any influence? I am confronted with all these questions, and begin to fancy myself in

44. Ibid.

45. MacIntyre, "Contexts of Interpretation: Reflections on Hans Georg Gadamer's *Truth and Method*," *Boston University Journal*, 26 (1980): 173–78.

46. MacIntyre, "Epistemological Crises," 61.

47. Ibid., 63.

the most deplorable condition imaginable, environed with the deepest darkness and utterly deprived of the use of every member and faculty.[48]

It is evident then that by means of his radical skepticism, which is both contextless and contentless, Hume's epistemological project has become totally unintelligible both to himself and to others.

Now, the notions of epistemological crisis, narrative, and tradition which have been applied to Hamlet and to Descartes are also applicable to philosophy of science. Without entering here into MacIntyre's discussion of Thomas Kuhn and Imre Lakatos, let me say that just as Hamlet and Descartes are both searching for truth in the midst of each one's epistemological crisis, MacIntyre notes that there should also be a pursuit for truth in scientific theorizing; as he says, "It matters enormously that our histories should be true, just as it matters that our scientific theories make truth one of their goals."[49] However, MacIntyre asserts rather in amazement that Kuhn denies any notion of truth to natural science, although he does insist on truth in history; in his article "Epistemological Crises," MacIntyre points out that for Kuhn a scientific theory does not embody a true ontology, that scientific theory does not give us a true representative of what is really there.[50] MacIntyre is definitely at odds with Kuhn on this point, for he recognizes that "science has certainly shown us decisively that some existence-claims are false just because the entities in question are *not* really there—whatever *any* theory may say."[51]

According to MacIntyre, "What Kuhn's disregard for ontological truth neglects is the way in which the progress toward truth in different sciences is such that they have to converge. . . . Were it not for *a concern for ontological truth* the nature of our demand for a coherent and convergent relationship between all the sciences would be unintelligible."[52] It would seem then that what MacIntyre holds to in his article "Epistemological Crises" is the notion of an underlying order in the universe, which order serves as at least a regulative ideal of science. As MacIntyre puts it, "We do not need to understand this notion quite as Kant did, and our antitheological beliefs may make us uncomfortable in adopting it. But perhaps discomfort at this point

48. Ibid., 64.
49. Ibid., 71–72.
50. Ibid., 72.
51. Ibid.
52. Ibid., 72–73; italics added.

is a sign of philosophical progress."[53] It seems to me that the notion of ontological truth to which MacIntyre refers here, or the notion of an underlying order in the universe, makes reference to a context of meaning which is already present to the scientist in his enquiry, a context in which man already finds himself, which he does not create, and without which understanding and "an approach to truth" would not be possible. We might say that this context of meaning is given in the universe which, like the context of tradition, is itself a bearer of reason.

IV. Narrative History as a Means to Truth

Now only a few years after having discussed the concepts of tradition, intelligibility, and narrative within epistemological crises, MacIntyre continues to elaborate these concepts within a moral framework in his book *After Virtue*. If in the "Epistemological Crises" article Hamlet's question could be posed as "What is going on here?" or "How do I make sense out of my situation?" in *After Virtue*, the question could well be: "What am I doing?", "What am I doing this for?", "How do I make sense out of my activity?" Again, here as elsewhere, in MacIntyre's writings, the question of context is addressed, but this time in terms of setting. As MacIntyre puts it:

> We cannot characterize behavior independently of intentions, and we cannot characterize intentions independently of the settings which make those intentions intelligible both to agents themselves and to others. I use the word 'setting' here as a relatively inclusive term. A social setting may be an institution, it may be what I have called a practice, or it may be a milieu of some other human kind. But it is central to the notion of a setting as I am going to understand it that a setting has a history, a history within which the histories of individual agents not only are, but have to be situated, just because without the setting and its changes through time the history of the individual agent and his changes through time will be unintelligible.[54]

A particular action is identified by invoking two kinds of context: the agent's intentions are placed in causal and temporal order with reference to their role in his history, and they are also placed with reference to their role in the history of the setting or settings to which they belong.[55] Narrative history is thus for MacIntyre "the basic and essential genre for the characterization of

53. Ibid., 73.
54. MacIntyre, *After Virtue*, 206.
55. Ibid., 208.

human action."[56] According to MacIntyre, "Man is in his actions and practices, as well as in his fictions, essentially a story-telling animal. He is not essentially, but becomes through his history, a teller of stories that aspire to truth."[57] And to be the subject of a narrative that runs from one's birth to one's death is to be accountable for one's actions, to be open to being asked why one behaved in a particular way rather than in another, and to be able to respond with an intelligible narrative account.

We are thus the subjects of our own story, of a history that is our own and that has its own meaning; our personal identity, our self, "inhabits a character whose unity is given as the unity of a character."[58] MacIntyre's question, "In what does the unity of an individual life consist?" receives the following answer: "Its unity is the unity of a narrative embodied in a single life. To ask 'What is the good for me?' is to ask how best I might live out that unity and bring it to completion. To ask 'What is the good for man?' is to ask what all answers to the former question must have in common.... The unity of a human life is the unity of a narrative quest,"[59] a quest for the good, which is not only the final *telos* of the quest, but is also somehow found at the beginning of the quest. According to MacIntyre, "A quest is always an education both as to the character of that which is sought and in self-knowledge."[60] Therefore, "[T]he good life for man is the life spent in seeking for the good life for man, and the virtues necessary for the seeking are those which will enable us to understand what more and what else the good life for man is."[61] But as MacIntyre interestingly notes, "I am never able to seek for the good or exercise the virtues *qua* individual,"[62] for each one of us approaches his own circumstances as a bearer of a particular social identity. It is from this identity, from one's moral particularity that one moves forward in the search for the good, for the universal, for the truth.[63] For MacIntyre, "What I am ... is in key part what I inherit, a specific past that is present to some degree in my present. I find myself part of a history and that is generally to say, whether I like it or not, whether I recognize it

56. Ibid.
57. Ibid., 216.
58. Ibid., 217.
59. Ibid., 218–19.
60. Ibid., 219.
61. Ibid.
62. Ibid.
63. Ibid., 220–21.

or not, one of the bearers of a tradition."[64] The individual person's search for his or her good is thus conducted within a context defined by those traditions of which the individual's life is a part.[65] "The history of each of our own lives is generally and characteristically embedded in and made intelligible in terms of the larger and longer histories of a number of traditions."[66] Tradition here is thus seen as a context of intelligibility in which a human life is embedded and which sheds light on that life. Each individual person's life and his search for the good is found within such a context.

V. MacIntyre on Truth

Now if in *After Virtue* the answer to the question "What am I doing?" or "What am I doing that for?" can only be intelligibly made by reference to a setting, to a narrative history which itself is embedded in a tradition, and if the moral life of an individual is the quest for the good, for the final *telos*, within the context of a tradition, then it might be possible to suppose that the thinker who poses the above question in a general way, might well be asking himself through his writings what it is in effect that he is doing as a thinker, as a philosopher, and thus might very well through his enquiry be telling us in a sense his own story. This is simply a conjecture, but it seems to me that there are a number of indications in MacIntyre's writings which could very well point to a thinker who is telling his own story and getting to know himself, because as he writes, he is discovering the meaning of his activity.[67] And as MacIntyre says, "Self-knowledge lies at the end of a long enquiry into what is other than the self."[68] MacIntyre's life as a philosopher is a quest for truth, not a truth which has to be constructed but which is, as it were, there for the taking. In his article "Contexts of Interpretation," MacIntyre notes: "But suppose that method does not yield truth; suppose that it is not sophistication that we need but the right kind of naïveté; suppose that what we need to reflect upon to move towards the truth is what we already (in some sense) know; suppose that if truth is hidden, it is not because it requires searching out by some device of method, but because

64. Ibid., 221.

65. Ibid., 222.

66. Ibid.

67. An indication of this may be seen in MacIntyre's *Whose Justice? Which Rationality?* (Notre Dame, Indiana: University of Notre Dame Press, 1988), 396, where he speaks at one point of "conversion."

68. MacIntyre, "Contexts of Interpretation," 177.

it is so plainly before our eyes in our everyday activities and conversations that we cannot perceive it."[69]

And in *Whose Justice? Which Rationality?* MacIntyre again alludes to the notion of truth, when he describes mind as activity and refers to mind as engaging itself with the natural and social world, and thus becoming adequate or not adequate to its objects, presenting or not presenting adequately what is there. As MacIntyre puts it so well: "One of the great originating insights of tradition constituted enquiries is that false beliefs and false judgments represent a failure of the mind, not of its objects. It is mind which stands in need of correction. Those realities which mind encounters reveal themselves as they are, the presented, the manifest, the unhidden. So the most primitive conception of truth is of the manifestness of the objects which present themselves to mind; and it is when mind fails to re-present that manifestness that falsity, the inadequacy of mind to its objects, appears."[70] The movement of the mind to things as such is not a movement in isolation, as is the epistemological enterprise, à la Descartes, which is a first person project, in so far as I seek certitude with respect to the truth and error of my judgments or beliefs. In *First Principles, Final Ends and Contemporary Philosophical Problems*, MacIntyre recognizes the enormous difference between such an epistemological enterprise and the Aristotelian or Thomistic enterprise, since the Thomist who follows Aristotle and Aquinas, will give an account of the approach to and the achievement of knowledge from a third-person point of view. As MacIntyre says,

> My mind or rather my soul is only one among many and its own knowledge of my self *qua* soul has to be integrated into a general account of souls and their teleology. Insofar as a given soul moves successfully towards its successive intellectual goals in a teleologically ordered way, it moves towards completing itself by becoming formally identical with the objects of its knowledge, so that it is adequate to those objects, objects that are no longer external to it, but rather complete it. So the mind in finding application for its concepts refers them beyond itself and themselves to what they conceptualize.... The mind, actualized in knowledge, responds to the object as the object is and as it would be, independently of the mind's knowledge of it. The mind knows itself only in the second-order knowledge of its own operations and is known also by others in those operations.[71]

69. Ibid., 174.
70. MacIntyre, *Whose Justice? Which Rationality?*, 357.
71. MacIntyre, *First Principles, Final Ends and Contemporary Philosophical Problems*, 12–13.

MacIntyre then sees himself as one mind among many, which seeks to achieve perfected understanding, in which each movement of the mind conforms itself to its object. Because knowledge here is seen from a third-person point of view, rather than from the Cartesian first-person epistemological project, MacIntyre can count on others for support and for correction in the process from partial understanding to perfected understanding, in his life of rational enquiry, for of course MacIntyre does belong to a community of intellectuals who have influenced him throughout his intellectual itinerary.

And the mind which achieves perfected understanding does not remain within itself but rather re-presents what it understands; it presents the thing, and thus, as MacIntyre himself says, the mind refers concepts beyond itself: "The form of understanding and the form of what is understood necessarily coincide in perfected understanding."[72] Now, the goal or *telos* of perfected understanding is presupposed in partial understanding, for as MacIntyre says, "All knowledge even in the initial stages of enquiry is a partial achievement and completion of the mind, but it nonetheless points beyond itself to a more final achievement in ways that we may not as yet have grasped."[73] Unlike the radical philosophers of post-Enlightenment modernity from Nietzsche to Rorty, MacIntyre makes known the radically teleological framework of enquiry within the Aristotelian-Thomistic tradition, and it is only such a context which gives enquiry its intelligibility: "There is then an ineliminable theological dimension—theological, that is, in the sense that makes Aristotle's metaphysics a *theologia*—to enquiry conceived in an Aristotelian mode. For enquiry aspires to and is intelligible only in terms of its aspiration to finality, comprehensiveness and unity of explanation and understanding."[74] But MacIntyre does not only refer to the activity of mind and to its teleology, but also to that aspect of reality which makes possible the adequacy of mind to its objects: truth is predicable not only of judgments but also of things. As Aquinas held: "A natural thing, therefore, being constituted between two intellects, is called true with respect to its adequacy to both; with respect to its adequacy to the divine intellect it is called true insofar as it fulfills that to which it was ordered by the divine intellect.... But a thing is called true in respect of its adequacy to

72. Ibid., 28.
73. Ibid., 13.
74. Ibid., 29.

the human intellect insofar as concerning it a true estimate is generated." (*Quaestiones Disputatae De Veritate* I, 2).[75] According to MacIntyre, because we have forgotten that truth is predicable of things, attention has shifted from this truth to new theories of truth, such as the correspondence and coherence theories, and the idealization of warranted assertibility. And yet, it seems to me that only within a context such as that provided above by the Thomistic-Aristotelian tradition, can one speak of the movement of the mind toward perfected understanding, in which the form of understanding and the form of what is understood coincide, in which "what is thought and what is true are one."[76]

Now given modern and postmodern opponents to the teleological conception of enquiry which has been outlined here, one might ask if the progress toward greater enlightenment has in effect anything to do with the movement of the mind toward perfected understanding and thus toward truth. MacIntyre quotes David Lewis: "Once the menu of well-worked out theories is before us, philosophy is a matter of opinion."[77] What Lewis says here manifests clearly what philosophy has become given the modern and contemporary rejection of the teleological ordering of enquiry: that truth is the *telos* toward which the mind moves, that the mind makes progress or fails to make progress in achieving its good, which is the truth. And the mind achieves its good, when it arrives, as MacIntyre says, "at a perfected understanding of what things are essentially."[78] Finally, it may be said that MacIntyre's itinerary through various and incommensurable contexts and traditions has led him to the Thomistic-Aristotelian tradition, in which philosophy is indeed a matter of truth.[79]

75. Ibid., 32.

76. Haldane, "Reason, Truth, and Sacred History," *Proceedings of the American Catholic Philosophical Association* 68 (1994): 183.

77. MacIntyre, *First Principles*, 66.

78. MacIntyre, "Truth as a good: a reflection on *Fides et Ratio*," in *The Tasks of Philosophy*, vol. 1 of *Selected Essays* (Cambridge: Cambridge University Press, 2006), 211. See entire essay, 197–215.

79. I would like to thank Heather Erb, the volume editor, for her careful reading of this essay and for her excellent suggestions, which I have tried to incorporate but have fallen short here of the full development that these suggestions deserved.

JAMES D. CAPEHART

The Christian Philosophy of Gilson, Maritain, and St. John Paul II as Principle of Unity for a Twenty-first Century Thomism

If as many Thomists—including myself—propose that Thomism can be a principle of unity for the development of philosophy in the twentieth century and beyond, does it not require some unifying principle for itself to fulfill this mission more fruitfully? If so, what would that principle be? For much of their careers, Étienne Gilson and Jacques Maritain proposed a phrase to describe what they thought to encapsulate the key unifying principles for the general thought of the Christian Middle Ages, as found particularly but not exclusively in the thought of St. Thomas. That phrase was *Christian philosophy*. The most prominent unifying principles which they purported to have helped occasion the development of a truly *Christian* philosophy were aspects of Christian revelation and the life of grace. In his 1998 encyclical *Fides et Ratio*, Pope St. John Paul II revives this phrase, likewise calling for similar unifying and guiding principles for the undertaking of philosophy in our century.

In this essay, I will present and propose the notion of Christian philosophy as found in the thought of Étienne Gilson, Jacques Maritain, and St. John Paul II as a way for identifying a unifying form ordered toward a unifying end for a living, Thomistic philosophy. Such a Thomistic philosophy would in turn be of better service to both philosophy at large and to the theology from which it draws inspiration and nourishment.

I. The Problem of Christian Philosophy

With this in mind, let us begin with a discussion of the problem of "Christian Philosophy." How in fact is this a problem at all? Just to give a preview of the problem before getting into its history, I should note that it is the phrase itself which has proven to be most problematic. If Christianity has influenced a philosophy sufficiently enough to take on the term "Christian" as a specific difference, has it not thereby automatically become a theology? Now, the idea of the existence of Christian theology—in fact many Christian theologies—has never been a problem. Most of the intellectual works of Church writers in the Early Church and Middle Ages are in fact predominantly theological works. This reality will prompt the French Thomist Étienne Gilson to address the problem from a different angle: given the existence of numerous volumes of Christian works of theology, can one call any of their contents *philosophical*? If so, is any of this philosophical content unique to Christian thinkers? More importantly still, has this philosophical content developed precisely because of Christian theological and even cultural influence? These are really the key questions, because if the answer is yes to both, Gilson, Maritain, and others say that such philosophical content is truly deserving of the name "Christian philosophy."

Why is this of interest for us today? I cannot stress enough the relevance of the problem of Christian philosophy for the current situation of Western civilization. In 1998, Pope St. John Paul II promulgated *Fides et Ratio*: *On the Relationship between Faith and Reason*. One of the great problems which this encyclical addressed (and which in fact still afflicts our own post-modern milieu) is the severing of faith and reason, and the consequent loss of confidence in the capacity of either to lead man to truth. John Paul II sought to reestablish intellectual life upon a harmonious relationship between faith and reason, and especially between theology and philosophy. In making his case, John Paul II explicitly brings up the phrase "Christian philosophy." In paragraph 75, he begins to sketch two rival notions for considering the relationship between philosophy and Christian faith. The first is one in which "there is a philosophy completely independent of the Gospel's Revelation: this is the stance adopted by philosophy as it took shape in history before the birth of the Redeemer and later in regions as yet untouched by the Gospel. We see here philosophy's valid aspiration to be an autonomous enterprise, obeying its own rules and employing the powers of reason alone."[1] Clearly, this text refers to the philosophy of the ancients but also to any philosophy that might have been worked out without ever having been influenced by the Gospel or the Christian faith as a whole.

While explaining in what ways this first kind of philosophy is legitimate, the Polish philosopher-saint juxtaposes it to a style or *way of philosophizing* which in fact he appeared to be endorsing at the threshold of the third Christian millennium. This way of philosophizing he calls *Christian philosophy*. As he says in paragraph 76:

> A second stance adopted by philosophy is often designated as Christian philosophy. In itself, the term is valid, but it should not be misunderstood: it in no way intends to suggest that there is an official philosophy of the Church, since the faith as such is not a philosophy. The term seeks rather to indicate a Christian *way of philosophizing, a philosophical speculation conceived in dynamic union with faith*. It does not therefore refer simply to a philosophy developed by Christian philosophers who have striven in their research not to contradict the faith. The term Christian philosophy includes those important developments of philosophical thinking which would not have happened without the direct or indirect contribution of Christian faith.[2]

What I refer to as Christian philosophy is precisely this *way of philosophizing* that St. John Paul II appears to endorse—again not so much a specific philosophy, but a "*way of philosophizing ... conceived in dynamic union with faith*."

With these points in mind, I would like now to turn to four key areas concerning Christian philosophy before coming back to some final comments on St. John Paul II, Gilson, Maritain, and Christian philosophy. First, I will address a brief history of the phrase from its use in the early Church to its non-use in the Middle Ages. Second, I will address Gilson's use of the phrase and how that changed under the influence of the Christian philosophy debates in France in the 1930s, followed by a treatment of Maritain's use of the phrase. Third, I will then proceed to look at how this phrase gained new life with the promulgation of *Aeterni Patris* of Pope Leo XIII in 1879 and how the re-discovery of this encyclical influenced Gilson's own developing understanding of Christian philosophy. This in turn will lead us back to a consideration of *Fides et Ratio*.

1. Pope John Paul II, *Fides et Ratio* (1998): no. 75.
2. Ibid.: no. 76; italics added.

II. Four Key Areas Concerning Christian Philosophy

It is important to note that the phrase "Christian philosophy" is not a recent invention. The earliest use of the term or terms similar to it appears in Justin Martyr (100–165 AD). Justin is of paramount importance for this discussion because he is generally regarded to be the first Christian to claim the title of philosopher, and as Gregory Sadler says, he even called himself a "Christian philosopher."[3] As Maurice Nédoncelle explains, Justin was, "the first Christian whom we know to have claimed the title of philosopher and to have declared that Christianity is a philosophy, 'the only sure and profitable one.'"[4] Similarly, we can find a form of the phrase in St. Augustine's *Contra Iulianum Pelagianum*.[5] Yet, what is signified by their usage of the term is not necessarily what is meant in current or recent parlance. Both Justin and Augustine had been on a long search for wisdom—both of them finding genuine yet still only partial truths in pagan philosophy, and doing so after much difficulty. With the acceptance of Christianity, they found the fullness of wisdom and truth through *faith*. Thus if philosophy is the search for and love of wisdom, then for Justin and Augustine, Christianity itself is philosophy par excellence.

However, that is not what John Paul II, Gilson, or Maritain mean by the phrase "Christian philosophy", nor does that meaning tie into our original two questions of (a) finding if there is a genuine philosophy present within Christian teaching, and (b) whether it exists as philosophy precisely because of Christian influence. For addressing a Christian philosophy considered under these two aspects, we must turn precisely to doctrines in such early Church thinkers where the phrase is not used and to many thinkers of the Middle Ages who never used the phrase, to discover their views on the relation between Christian revelation and philosophy. For Augustine, that interaction begins with the moment of belief. He has two famous phrases

3. See Gregory Sadler, *Reason Fulfilled by Revelation: The 1930s Christian Philosophy Debates in France* (Washington, D.C.: The Catholic University of America Press, 2011), 12.

4. Maurice Nédoncelle, *Is There a Christian Philosophy?* translated by Illtyd Trethowan (New York: Hawthorn Books, 1960), 36.

5. St. Augustine of Hippo, *Contra Iulianum Pelagianum* 4.14.72: "Obsecro te, non sit honestior philosophia Gentium, quam nostra Christiana, quae una est vera philosophia, quandoquidem studium vel amor sapientiae significatur hoc nomine." My translation—"I beg you, let not the philosophy of nations be more respectable/believable than our Christian [Philosophy], which is the true philosophy, since the study or love of wisdom is signified by this name."

concerning his vision for the relationship of faith and reason. The first is "*nisi credideritis, non intelligetis*"—"Unless you believe, you will not understand."[6] There is also the related phrase, "*Crede ut intelligas*"—"Believe that you may understand."[7] St. Anselm will modify the second phrase into the grammatical first person "*Credo ut intelligam*"—"I believe that I may understand."[8] There is also Anselm's corollary "*fides quaerens intellectum*"–"Faith seeking understanding."[9] On the matter of the relationship between Christianity and philosophy, and of faith and reason, Gilson considers Anselm and Augustine to be of like mind. In this way Gilson—at least in 1931—regarded the aforementioned phrases of Augustine and Anselm to be the "true definition of Christian philosophy," *viz.*, that Christian philosophy refers to that endeavor of a believing Christian seeking also to understand that content of the faith which he might also understand.[10]

Such an assertion does not mean that one proceeds from properly revealed premises when one engages in Christian philosophical investigation. Rather, by believing, one is opened to new pathways/topics/starting points for subsequent philosophical investigations that would not have otherwise been thought of without Christian revelation. Likewise, during this process one can rely on the corrective influence of Christian revelation when one has fallen into error and begin one's philosophical investigations anew. Two primary examples of this concern the problem of evil and the problem of the human person. The notion of *personhood* was developed in a specifically theological context. Terms from the Greek and Roman theatre were appropriated for speaking about God as Father, Son, and Spirit. Prompted

6. Augustine, *Sermon 76 on the New Testament.*

7. Augustine, *In Evangelium Ioannis Tractatus Centum Viginti Quatuor*, 29.6.

8. Anselm of Canterbury, *Proslogion*, 1

9. Ibid., Proemium.

10. Étienne Gilson, "La notion de philosophie chrétienne," Session of 21 March, *Bulletin de la Societé française de Philosophie* 31, no. 2 (1931), translated by Gregory Sadler as "The Notion of Christian Philosophy," in *Reason Fulfilled by Revelation: The 1930s Christian Philosophy Debates in France* (Washington, D.C.: The Catholic University of America Press, 2011), 138–39: "What is peculiar to the Christian is being convinced of the rational fertility of his faith and being sure that this fertility is inexhaustible. If we pay attention, that is the true meaning of St. Augustine's *credo ut intelligam* [sic] and St. Anselm's *fides quaerens intellectum*: a Christian's effort to draw some of reason's knowledge from faith in revelation. That is why these two formulas are the true definition of Christian philosophy." Note that Gilson modifies this position as he comes to identify more strongly with St. Thomas as the Christian philosopher *par excellence*. For a further treatment of this modification please see, James D. Capehart, "Gilson's Notion of *Theologism* in *The Unity of Philosophical Experience* and *Reason and Revelation in the Middle Ages*" in *Studia Gilsoniana* 8, no. 1 (January–March 2019): 11–44.

by the theological notion of Divine Personhood, Christian philosophers have taken this term of "person" and "personhood" to apply to humans.[11] It is in common parlance today and was even embraced by Immanuel Kant, who is not generally regarded to be a Christian philosopher, though he was definitely influenced by the Christian philosophical tradition in some ways including in this idea of "person".

Likewise, if we turn back again specifically to Augustine, we see him bring his Christianity to bear upon his treatment of the problem of evil. Christian revelation had taught him that matter, while corruptible, was not itself evil nor was it the source of evil. In fact, as created by God, matter was ontologically good. Any philosophical solution he gave for this problem had to respect this truth which he had received through faith. Thus, for Augustine, evil is a privation of being that should be there. Moreover, evil is parasitic on a created being which is good considered in itself. At the heart of his doctrine, then, is the fundamentally Christian connection between being and goodness.[12]

Still, there is some controversy in the phraseology of Augustine on this topic. "Unless you believe, you will not understand," seems to imply the necessity of faith in order to come to philosophical understanding. Such a necessity would indeed make the datum, formally speaking, theological. Gilson offers a way to understand how faith can influence philosophy without turning the philosophy into a theology. He does so by arguing that in any truly Christian philosophical content, there can be theological influence from what are called articles of faith—those truths about God, man, and salvation which can by nature only be known by revelation—and preambles of faith—those truths about God and man necessary for salvation but which are at least in principle knowable by unaided reason (for example, God's existence, His unicity and goodness, the existence and immortality of the soul, the validity of human knowing, the moral teachings of the Decalogue). This distinction is of utmost importance because each type

11. See Boethius, *Liber de Persona et Duabus Naturis Contra Eutychen et Nestorium*, III and IV.

12. This is not a denial of Greek influence. Often Christian revelation helps the Christian philosopher to appropriate a concept from Greek philosophy in a new way. The idea that goodness is diffusive of itself is of Platonic/Neoplatonic origins. (E.g. Plato, *Timaeus* 29e: "Let me tell you then why the creator made this world of generation. He was good, and the good can never have any jealousy of anything. And being free from jealousy, he desired that all things should be as like him as they could be.") However, that the body was no longer to be considered a prison for the soul and shares in the ontological goodness of the soul due to its status as part of creation is a fundamentally Christian turn on a concept originally received from Greek philosophy.

of revealed content will provide influence in different ways. While articles and preambles may both provide a regulative role upon philosophy, the preambles may interact more directly with one's premises, given that one is capable of providing rational grounding for them. In either case, Gilson will maintain that Christian philosophical activity (namely, philosophical activity which exists because of Christian influence) is only at most in *de facto* need of revelation prior to its formulation. Why? Once this knowledge becomes philosophically grounded, one need not use or even ought not use faith directly to engage with a non-Christian philosopher over such knowledge, though one can rightly use that open house philosophical discussion to nudge one's interlocutor toward the ultimate source of that truth as revealed.[13] Thus, while in the order of discovery (Wippel's phrase[14]) this philosophy is thoroughly Christian, it is sharable with believer and non-believer alike, at least in principle.

III. Gilson, Maritain, Christian Philosophy, and the Debates

Gilson evolved in his understanding of Christian philosophy under the influence of the debate over the question of Christian philosophy in France

13. See Étienne Gilson, *The Spirit of Mediaeval Philosophy*, translated by A. H. C. Downes (New York: Charles Scribner's Sons, 1936), cited on p. 36, but found on p. 429. "The contemporary paradox of a Christian philosophy evidently true for its defenders, and of no value in the eyes of their opponents, does not necessarily imply that its defenders are blinded by their faith; it may perhaps be explained by the fact that absence of the light of faith in the opponent leaves truth opaque where it might be transparent. This in no way authorizes the Christian philosopher to argue in the name of faith, but rather to redouble his purely rational efforts until the light thus gained leads other minds also to turn to its source and draw the same enlightenment."

14. See John F. Wippel, "Thomas Aquinas and the Problem of Christian Philosophy," in *Metaphysical Themes in Thomas Aquinas* (Washington, D. C.: The Catholic University of America Press, 1984), 23–24. While the phrase "order of discovery" is not used by Gilson, I think that the notion is helpful in understanding Gilson's doctrine. In the above cited work (a re-print and updating of his 1965 essay "Étienne Gilson and Christian Philosophy," in *Twentieth-Century Thinkers: Studies in the Work of Seventeen Modern Philosophers*, ed. John K. Ryan. [Staten Island, New York: Alba House, 1965], 59–87), Wippel presents Gilson's doctrine on Christian philosophy in an accurate and fair manner, as well as in an historical order. Upon completing that treatment, Wippel provides his reflections and critiques noting that in the *order of discovery*—that is, the actual historical state in which a philosophy was developed by a philosopher—he concedes to Gilson that historically speaking Christian belief does seem to have aided in the development of a philosophy that is characteristic to Christian thinkers. Yet, ever the disciple of Van Steenberghen, Wipple maintains that in the *order of proof* this philosophy can in no way be called "Christian," for to be philosophy at all, its premises must be rational data open to believer and non-believer alike.

in the late 1920s and 1930s. The French rationalist philosopher Emile Bréhier started the controversy in 1928 with his lecture series titled "Is there a Christian Philosophy?" He famously denied the possibility of Christian philosophy, saying that there can no more be a Christian philosophy than there can be a Christian physics or mathematics.[15] At what is generally considered the first Christian philosophy debate, held on March 21, 1931 at the *Société française de philosophie*, there was on the one side the rationalists Bréhier and his philosophical ally Léon Brunschvicg arguing against the possibility of a Christian philosophy, and on the other side the Thomists Gilson and Maritain arguing in favor of its possibility. Some other non-Thomist Christian philosophers—such as Gabriel Marcel and Maurice Blondel—will enter into the second phase of the debates. As the rationalists historically fell out of the debate, Thomists such as Pierre Mandonnet and Fernand Van Steenberghen took up the charge against Gilson and Maritain, beginning at the *Société thomiste* meeting at Juvisy in 1933. In fact, Van Steenberghen would be Gilson's foil in this debate for the rest of his life, even publishing against Gilson on this topic soon after Gilson's death in 1978.[16]

In the next phase of the evolution of Gilson's understanding of "Christian philosophy," the concept takes on the meaning of a formally rational body of knowledge developed under the influence of Christian revelation and culture in its origins. In this way, Christianity is viewed as a quasi-efficient cause of Christian philosophy. This understanding of Christian philosophy is especially seen in his landmark *The Spirit of Mediaeval Philosophy* (originally given as the Gifford Lectures at the University of Aberdeen in Scotland in 1931 to 1932). Here, he famously defines Christian philosophy as an historical reality, existing due to the beneficent influence of Christianity upon reason:

15. See Émile Bréhier, "Y at-il une philosophie chrétienne?," *Revue de métaphysique et de morale* 38, no. 2 (1931): 133–62, published in English as "Is There a Christian Philosophy?" in *Reason Fulfilled by Revelation: The 1930s Christian Philosophy Debates in France*, edited and translated by Gregory Sadler (Washington, D.C.: The Catholic University of America Press, 2011), 127: "We have seen Christianity's attempts, always vain, to fix on one of these moments in order to appropriate it, but one can no more speak of a Christian philosophy than of a Christian mathematics or a Christian physics."

16. See Fernand Van Steenberghen, "Étienne Gilson, historien de la pensée médiévale," *Revue philosophique de Louvain* 77 (1979): 496–507. He repeats almost word-for-word his long held contention that while there are Christian philosophers, there can be no Christian philosophies: "Bref, il y a des philosophes chrétiens, il ne saurait exister de philosophies chrétiennes." (497)

> Thus I call Christian, every philosophy which, although keeping the two orders formally distinct, nevertheless considers the Christian revelation as an indispensable auxiliary to reason. For whoever understands it thus, the concept does not correspond to any simple essence susceptible of abstract definition; but rather corresponds much rather to a concrete historical reality as something calling for description.[17]

From this stage forward, Gilson employs a very important distinction that he takes from Maritain, viz. the distinction between the formal order (also called the order of specification) and the order of exercise. In the formal order, philosophy and theology are considered according to their essences as distinct from each other, according to their material objects, formal objects, and the principles of their demonstrations. In this way philosophy and theology are formally speaking considered different sciences. However, in the order of exercise, where the unity is in the human person acting for ends, one's Christianity may very well influence one's use of philosophical reason. In this way Gilson's understanding of Christian philosophy is as a concrete historical reality existing in the order of exercise.[18] From the mid-1930s onward, Gilson will shift his focus from Christian philosophy as *fact* to Christian philosophy as *act*.

Furthermore, Christianity may also influence the development of Christian philosophy in the order of final causality, as a Christian often employs his theologically-nourished reason for theological ends. This distinction in turn gives rise to two modes of Christian philosophy, one of which exists when a philosophizing theologian employs Christian philosophy within his theology for the theological end of salvation (cf. the use of philosophy in medieval theological texts). Gilson does not have a precise term for it, but I call it *Christian philosophy as ancilla theologiae*. The second mode exists when a philosopher properly speaking employs Christian philosophy with a merely implicit theological end. In this second mode, Christian philosophy is thoroughly sharable with all truth-seekers, Christian and non-Christian alike. Still, Christian philosophy in this mode has undergone the efficient influence of Christianity suggesting starting points for philosophical in-

17. Gilson, *The Spirit of Mediaeval Philosophy*, 37.

18. See Étienne Gilson, "Historical Research and the Future of Scholasticism," *The Modern Schoolman* 29 (1951): 1–10. Reprinted in *A Gilson Reader*, edited by Anton Pegis (Garden City, New York: Image Books, 1957), 165. In this text, Gilson employs the notion of the *order of exercise* to defend his contention that the best mode of Christian philosophy is the theologian's use of philosophy, reminding the reader that a distinction in the formal order between philosophy and theology does not entail a "separation in the order of exercise."

vestigation,[19] and can easily be employed by the philosophizing Christian theologian when so desired. Thus, I call this mode, *Christian philosophy as amicus theologiae.*

But what is the precise content of Christian philosophy whether as *ancilla* or *amicus theologiae*? In addition to the issues of the problem of evil, and of personhood, there is also Gilson's emphasis on the transformation of metaphysics by the name of God taken from Exodus 3.14, viz., "I am Who am." God is considered as Being Itself (*Esse Ipsum Subsistens*) and His creative act is rooted in His causing the *esse* of all things. Likewise, Christianity maintains the immortality of the human soul, with regard to the notion of the human person. Thus, even in those things that the Christian philosopher might originally know by means of revelation—for example, the preambles of faith—he does not remain at knowing them by faith alone. Rather, the Christian philosophical act is that attempt to philosophically ground and establish what of it can be rationally known and shared with the non-Christian or anyone of good will.

So far, then, we have seen that in his early works Gilson provided an historical account for the defense of Christian philosophy, even if our own treatment has been largely doctrinal. From the very first Christian philosophy debate on March 21, 1931 at the *Société française de philosophie*, Maritain sat beside Gilson and provided a doctrinal defense of the notion of Christian philosophy, of which method Gilson approved highly.[20] To this

19. See Joseph Owens, *Towards a Christian Philosophy* (Washington, D.C.: The Catholic University of America Press, 1990), 25–26. In this work, Owens focuses on his own interpretation and defense of the idea of Christian philosophy. Nevertheless, Owens' presentation provides a faithful development of his mentor's teaching. How Christianity can enter into the work of a Christian philosopher without turning it into something that is not philosophical is a question which Gilson will himself address on numerous occasions. Owens maintains that Christian revelation has provided this influence through the suggestion of starting points for rational investigation. He contends that doctrines such as a temporal creation, the Trinity, the resurrection of the body, and of the real presence in the Eucharist, led to the treatment of various philosophical problems which underpinned these doctrines, such as problems of change without a subject to undergo the change, and that of relation, individuation, and substance. All of the instances that he gives are examples of philosophy that is thoroughly Christian in the order of exercise, an understanding of Christian philosophy maintained by both Gilson and Maritain. Thus, while this is a key element in Owens' own writing on Christian philosophy, it is still an important interpretive element for understanding Gilson's doctrine, and even Maritain's, as well.

20. Jacques Maritain, *De la philosophie chrétienne* (Paris: Desclée de Brouwer, 1933), 12, translated by Edward Flannery as *An Essay on Christian Philosophy* (New York: Philosophical Library, 1955), 4. All subsequent English citations and references to this work are from the Flannery edition. In footnote 1 of the preface (p. x of *An Essay on Christian Philosophy*), Maritain cites at

end Maritain distinguishes between the order of specification and the order of exercise, or otherwise said, "between the 'nature' of philosophy, or what it is in itself, and the 'state' in which it exists in real fact, historically, in the human subject, and which pertains to its concrete conditions of existence and exercise."[21] A consideration of the *nature* of anything is in fact a consideration of its essence, by means of an abstraction whereby the quiddity of the thing is considered specifically, leaving aside its individuating characteristics. Such an abstraction functions not on the order of particulars or particularities but rests squarely upon the order of essence. As Maritain explains, "Turning our gaze from existential conditions it lifts it to the order of essences; it posits a possible before our thought; in sum, it disregards the *state* to ponder the *nature*."[22]

However, Maritain draws attention to the fact that this philosophy considered as an abstract essence is not found in reality, leading the mind all too often to reify that abstract essence rather than to reconsider it within the real concrete conditions of its state: "Let us not be unmindful, however, that we are dealing here with a pure, abstract essence. It is all too easy a matter to endow such an abstraction with reality, to clothe it as such with a concrete existence. An ideological monster results; such as, in my opinion, occurred in the case both of the rationalists, and the neo-Thomists whom Mr. Gilson has called to task."[23] Thus, rather than falling into the traps of focusing merely upon the abstracted essence or nature of philosophy, Maritain builds upon Gilson's historical treatment of the actual philosophies which have existed. This in turn leads Maritain down his own second method of considering philosophy—a doctrinal consideration of philosophy in its concrete state.[24] Furthermore, for Maritain any treatment of the Christian state of

length a quotation from Gilson's *Spirit of Medieval Philosophy* in which Gilson explains how his own historical account necessarily leads into and requires a doctrinal account of Christian philosophy, thus praising Maritain's work and expressing his agreement in the process: "I may say, then, that Christian philosophy is an objectively observable reality for history alone, but that once its existence has been thus established its notion may be analyzed in itself. This ought to be done as Mr. J. Maritain has done it: I am in fact in complete agreement with him." See *L'Esprit de la Philosophie Médiévale*, vol. 2 (Paris: Vrin, 1932), 290.

21. Maritain, *Essay on Christian Philosophy*, 11–12.

22. Ibid., 12.

23. Ibid., 15–16. Such neo-Thomists are precisely those who have denied the possibility of Christian philosophy based upon the consideration of the essence or nature of philosophy, particularly those of the Louvain school but even those neo-Scholastic Thomists of the Dominican tradition such as Mandonnet.

24. "As soon as it no longer is a question of philosophy considered in itself but of the manner

philosophy must also consider the actual Christian, whose nature has been thoroughly affected by grace, which includes the elevation of reason:

> . . . the Christian believes that grace changes man's state by elevating his nature to the supernatural plane and by divulging to him things which unaided reason would be unable to grasp. He also believes that if reason is to attain without admixture of error the highest truths that are naturally within its ken it requires assistance, either from within in the form of inner strengthening or from without in the form of an offering of objective data; and he believes that such assistance has in fact become so much an established part of things under the New Law that it has ushered in a new regimen for human intelligence.[25]

Maritain will then proceed to examine the "chief components of this *Christian state* of philosophy."[26] In addition to elevating man's nature and providing data which unaided reason would not have otherwise grasped, Maritain distinguishes subjective and objective aids to nature. The objective aids refer to data which Christianity presents to the mind: "First and foremost, there are those data which by their nature belong within the field of philosophy, but which in actual fact philosophers failed to recognize explicitly, and which were placed in front rank by Christian revelation."[27] He is referring here to the preambles of faith, generally so difficult to attain and so important for salvation that they have also been revealed. Examples which Maritain gives for such data are the notions of creation and of God as subsistent being.[28]

On all these points, however, it should be noted that Maritain shows himself to be of one mind with Gilson: "we may again join Mr. Gilson to speak of *revelation begetting reason*."[29] Still, this phrase—"revelation begetting reason"—which he borrows from Gilson, carries with it its own proper distinctions as applied to both theology and philosophy. Here however, Maritain aims to show how this expression can rightly be applied to philosophy in its Christian state. Accordingly, Maritain qualifies Gilson's famous statement as referring to Christian philosophy in the following manner:

---

in which men philosophize, and of the divers philosophies which the concrete course of history has brought into existence, the consideration of the *essence* of philosophy no longer suffices; that of its *state* must be undertaken"; ibid. 17.

25. Ibid., 17–18.

26. Ibid., 18.

27. Ibid.

28. See ibid., 18–19.

29. Ibid.

When applied to philosophy the word revelation should not be deemed to refer to the whole revealed deposit but simply to those elements of the natural order that are contained therein or related thereto. The moment philosophy is advised of these elements, it scrutinizes them according to its own order, which *ascends* from experience toward things divine (whereas revelation *descends* from God).[30]

So, by the term "revelation," which he and Gilson say "begets reason," Maritain is referring to truths contained in Christian revelation which are also formally of the natural order and in that way are at least in principle capable of rational attainment, viz., the preambles of faith. Once revelation points out those truths, the Christian philosopher is able to examine them philosophically, proceeding from effect to first cause.

Expounding upon these truths of the natural order which one may regard as *de facto* though not *de iure* unattainable by the mind of the ancient philosopher prior to the aid of revelation, he offers the analogy of those things existing in shadows which are illumined by the light of day. As Maritain explains:

In short, the question at issue here is rather concerned—and this is still of paramount factual importance—with differences of clarity that are, to tell the truth, extraordinarily pronounced: what used to dwell in regions of shadow or mirage is brought forth in the full light of day. Concomitantly, with the center of irradiation thus displaced, and with regions which our naturally weak eyes find obscurest now sending forth a most vivid brightness, everything takes on a fresh hue, and every view is transfigured.[31]

Regarding the second type of objective data offered to philosophy in its Christian state, Maritain refers to philosophical objects of knowledge which become known with greater confidence after revelation.[32] For example, reason's validity is confirmed by the act of faith, which, while supra-rational,

30. Ibid., 19–20.

31. Ibid., 21. It should be noted that for Maritain, the necessity for Christianity to obtain these objects does very much appear to be a de facto necessity. As objects which he says are in "shadows", they are objects within the natural order, though quite difficult for the pagan to see. Still, once seen and explained by the Christian philosopher, the pagan need not begin to accept revealed Christian doctrines in order to benefit from the philosophical fruits of this Christian philosophy. The knowledge of God as *Ipsum Esse Subsistens* occasioned by the revelation of God's name in Exodus 3:14 is an example of just such a doctrine. The factual historical connection between this notion of God and the Biblical text which helped shed light upon it does not render it an article of faith for either Maritain or Gilson.

32. See Maritain, *Essay on Christian Philosophy*, 21.

is also "eminently reasonable."[33] The third class of data concerns the use of philosophy in connection with essentially supernatural mysteries. Here, Christian theology enlists Christian philosophy to better explain what has been revealed.[34] However, even in this service to theology, philosophy in its own right is broadened further still,[35] because specific doctrines of revelation are thoroughly supra-rational objects: "It has often been remarked that unless there had been speculation on the dogmas of the Trinity and the Incarnation, it is exceedingly unlikely that the philosophers would have come to an awareness of the metaphysical problem of the person."[36] Though Christ is true God and true man according to his two natures, he is the second *person* of the Holy Trinity. While such a formulation is theological, nevertheless, the problem and the solution influenced the development of the philosophical notion of the human being, not merely as *animal rationale*, but also as *persona*, an individual substance of rational nature, to use Boethius' definition. The creative knowledge of the Word also launches Christian philosophy into an ordered and thoroughly knowable world, and fosters an attitude, as he says, "which laid the groundwork for the flowering of the empirical sciences on the one hand and for the expansion of reflective knowledge in which modern times pride themselves on the other."[37]

Maritain then proceeds to address the other ways in which philosophy is aided in a Christian state, namely, by means of, "the subjective reinforcement which Christian philosophy is heir to in a Christian climate."[38] The first of these subjective reinforcements concerns *habitus*, that is, habits, and specifically perfective habits, viz. virtues. Maritain distinguishes human/philosophical *habitus* and theological *habitus*, as well as the pagan vs. Christian practice of philosophy: "Philosophy is a certain perfection of the intelligence. In the eyes of an Aristotle it was uppermost; whereas in St. Thomas' view, philosophy being solely natural in itself, ranks below theology, a ratio-

33. See ibid., 21–22.

34. Ibid., 22: "... in a Christian regime of thought philosophy is used by theology as an instrumental organ in the effort to elucidate these mysteries...."

35. Ibid.: "... even when [philosophy] keeps on working on its own account, its field of inquiry is thereupon considerably broadened."

36. Ibid., 23.

37. Ibid. Still, one might include such a fact also in the second category of data, because at least the ancient Greeks in the tradition of Aristotle, Archimedes, and Galen, would have viewed the world as thoroughly intelligible, capable of being unlocked by means of investigation. Revelation would have given further confidence in the rectitude of their scientific aspirations.

38. Ibid., 24–25.

nal discipline rooted in grace-given faith."[39] However, within the concrete, unified individual, these virtues interact, such that the theological virtues aid in the attainment of intellectual virtue: "Now the higher virtues succor the lowlier in the proper sphere of the latter. The virtue of faith, for example, enables the philosopher, who knows of the existence of God by purely natural means to adhere rationally to this truth with a sturdier grasp."[40] Hence, the Christian with the theological virtue of faith reaches the knowledge of God's existence through demonstration, with greater confidence. As building on and perfecting nature, grace-given faith nourishes and helps the Christian better to acquire and develop the human virtue of philosophical knowledge about the highest and most sublime causes, and especially the highest Cause.

Maritain also agrees with Gilson on the transformative power of theology on the practice of the philosophy, particularly metaphysics, in its Christian state: "And in the light of theology, metaphysical truths take on a radiance so immediate and convincing that in consequence the philosopher's labors are blest with a new facility and fruitfulness. Henceforth, in fact, metaphysics cannot assume its fullest proportions in the human mind without experiencing the attraction of theology. . . ."[41] In truth, Maritain, like Gilson, maintains that metaphysics is fundamentally altered and ennobled by this new relationship with theology and the knowledge of faith. The true Christian metaphysician seeks not to run away from revealed truth but to let it suggest the most fruitful pathways for philosophical development.

In a third way, the grace of the Christian life aids the philosopher in his very act of philosophizing by helping him cope with and overcome many of the pitfalls of original sin which would otherwise hinder his search for truth. As Maritain explains, "It would be absurd to expect the *gratia sanans* to supply for the philosophic *habitus*, or to preclude aberrations, even to the gravest kind. Yet it is certain that the more the philosopher remains faithful to grace, the more easily will he free himself of manifold futilities and opacities, which are as a mote of self-love on the eye of reason."[42] Hence, the Christian philosopher in his use of reason is all the freer from various sorts of obstacles flowing from man's fall. For example, he is liberated from the

39. Ibid., 26.
40. Ibid.
41. Ibid., 26–27.
42. Ibid., 28.

"futilities and opacities" of distraction, laziness, discouragement, self-love, to the degree he is faithful to the life of grace ordering his heart and mind toward the true ultimate end, and is bolstered by faith, hope, and love. Thus, through the life of grace, the Christian philosopher is strengthened to remain on his philosophical journey precisely by being a better Christian.

In sum, Maritain provides us with a doctrinal account of the Christian state of philosophy, of a Christian philosopher who in his *state* has been influenced both objectively and subjectively by Christian revelation and the grace-filled life of virtue. Such an account is truly complementary to Gilson's historical treatment. As we will see, both Gilson's and Maritain's accounts of Christian philosophy will influence St. John Paul II's presentation of Christian philosophy. However, one more aside will be helpful before returning to *Fides et Ratio*.

IV. *Aeterni Patris*

Pope Leo XIII's encyclical *Aeterni Patris* (1879) was much more influential in this debate than at first realized. While not containing the phrase in the text, within a year of its promulgation Leo XIII will re-name the official title of the encyclical to be *On Christian Philosophy*, and even in some places it is called *On the Restoration of Christian Philosophy*. For the next fifty years after the promulgation of the encyclical, the phrase would regain popularity, though it seems that many forgot Leo's own usage of it after a short period of time. Gilson and many Catholic scholars used the phrase without fanfare in the 1920s right up until Brehier's 1928 lectures which stirred the debates, yet no mention of Leo and *Aeterni Patris* on this controversy was given until the mid-1930s.

In this encyclical, Pope Leo encourages a return to doing theology and philosophy in the mode of the scholastics, especially returning to the thought of St. Thomas Aquinas. A key passage for the ongoing development of the notion of Christian philosophy is found in paragraph 9: "Those who join submission to the Christian faith to the study of philosophy, are those who philosophize in the best possible manner, since the splendor of the divine truths, accepted by the soul, assists the intelligence itself, from which it not only does not detract anything, but actually adds considerably to its nobility, penetration and stability."[43] Influenced by this passage, Gilson will

43. Pope Leo XIII, *Aeterni Patris* (1879): no. 9, in *The Church Speaks to the Modern World:*

redefines Christian philosophy in 1957 as "a way of philosophizing", stating, "Clearly, what Leo calls Christian philosophy cannot be reduced to the content of any single philosophy; it is neither a system nor even a doctrine. Rather, it is a way of philosophizing; namely, the attitude of those who 'to the study of philosophy unite obedience to the Christian faith.' (*Aeterni Patris*, 9) This philosophical method, or attitude—*philosophandi institutum*—is Christian philosophy itself."[44]

V. Back to St. John Paul II and *Fides et Ratio*

In a way we have come full circle back to St. John Paul II, because the very definition which he gives of Christian philosophy in *Fides et Ratio* and endorses strongly resembles Gilson's 1957 definition. As we said before, John Paul II defined it as "a Christian way of philosophizing, a philosophical speculation conceived in dynamic union with faith."[45] Furthermore, in a vein similar to that of Maritain and Gilson, John Paul II acknowledges both a subjective dimension to Christian philosophy (as the theological virtue of faith ennobles and frees the reason of the Christian philosopher to perform his task better) and an objective dimension (through the content that Christian revelation helps inspire).[46] Likewise, St. John Paul II clearly praises the theologian's use of philosophy as *ancilla theologiae*, though he does not refer to such usage as a mode of Christian philosophy. He also acknowledges philosophy's and theology's mutual enrichment, with theology enriching and ennobling the practice of philosophy, as well as the benefit that theology receives from such an ennobled handmaiden, such that both would suffer unduly cut off from each other. As he explains, "Were theologians to refuse the help of philosophy, they would run the risk of doing philosophy unwittingly and locking themselves within thought-structures poorly adapted to the understanding of faith. Were philosophers, for their

The Social Teachings of Leo XIII, edited, annotated, and with an introduction by Étienne Gilson (Garden City, New York: Image Books, 1954).

44. Étienne Gilson, "What Is Christian Philosophy," in *A Gilson Reader*, edited by Anton Pegis (Garden City, New York: Image Books, 1957), 187.

45. Pope St. John Paul II, *Fides et Ratio* (1998): no. 76. N.B. One can also compare the similarity between this definition and Gilson's definition of Christian Philosophy in his 1960 work, *The Elements of Christian Philosophy*: "...Christian philosophy is that way of philosophizing in which the Christian faith and the human intellect join forces in a common investigation of truth." Gilson, Étienne, *Elements of Christian Philosophy* (Garden City, New York: Doubleday, 1960), v.

46. *Fides et Ratio* (1998): no. 76.

part, to shun theology completely, they would be forced to master on their own the contents of Christian faith, as has been the case with some modern philosophers."[47]

Just as Gilson's and Maritain's understanding of Christian philosophy suggested, John Paul II's notion was also based upon the harmony between Christian theology and philosophy, such that neither one could fully achieve what it was meant to achieve without the aid of the other, at least in fact though not necessarily in principle. In this way, in the third Christian millennium, I believe Gilson, Maritain, and John Paul II, as well as St. Thomas himself, offer a way of doing philosophy, whether in a mode explicitly ordered toward Christian ends as *ancilla theologiae*, or in the mode of *amicus theologiae* ordered toward the sharing of a truth which is but a participation of the One who is that true end. This relationship is not just a mutual enrichment for the disciplines of philosophy and theology, but is also transformative for the agents practicing them. Thus, the issue of Christian philosophy is at the very heart of how we should do philosophy today and in the future. It answers a call deep within our hearts to look for meaning and its ultimate Cause. In this way, Christian philosophy is not just for philosophizing theologians or for professional academic philosophers. It is for anyone who seeks to answer these questions with an open heart and mind, open to wherever the truth leads. Insofar as Christianity itself positively influences how we do our philosophizing, it can be the greatest principle of unity for a robust, Christian, Thomistic philosophy in the twenty-first century.

47. Ibid., no. 77.

MATTHEW LEVERING

Integrating Neo-Thomism and Ressourcement against Modernism

Garrigou-Lagrange's Christ the Savior *as a Test Case*

IF TERTULLIAN WERE ALIVE TODAY and present with us, he might ask a question pertinent to my essay. He would not literally reprise his famous question, "What does Athens have to do with Jerusalem?" Instead, he might ask, "What does the *nouvelle théologie* have to do with neo-scholastic theology?" Indeed, the answer to this question was clear to the combatants on both sides in the mid twentieth century, as it is likewise clear to many theologians today: Nothing.

Representing the neo-scholastics, Réginald Garrigou-Lagrange published an article in 1950 that has recently been translated into English as "Where Is the New Theology Leading Us?"[1] In this article, he concludes that the "new theology" or the "*nouvelle théologie*" is leading us directly back to modernism, that is, to a Catholic version of liberal Protestantism.[2] Like-

1. See Réginald Garrigou-Lagrange, "Where Is the New Theology Leading Us?," *Josephinum Journal of Theology* 18, no. 1 (2011): 63–78.

2. Indeed, immediately after the Second Vatican Council, Catholic versions of liberal Protestantism became a major and even a dominant presence in the Catholic theological academy. For the view that Garrigou-Lagrange was right about the *nouvelle théologie*, see Jürgen Mettepenningen, *Nouvelle Théologie—New Theology: Inheritor of Modernism, Precursor of Vatican II* (London: T. & T. Clark, 2010); and, from a different perspective and with more erudition, Jon Kirwan, *An Avant-garde Theological Generation: The* Nouvelle Théologie *and the French Crisis of Modernity* (Oxford: Oxford University Press, 2018). For background to Vatican II that expands the picture

wise in 1950, Pope Pius XII's encyclical *Humani Generis* set forth concerns shared by Garrigou-Lagrange and other neo-scholastic theologians. Pope Pius identified eight major problems with the *nouvelle théologie*. Let me list them here, because they shed light on the view that neo-scholastic theology and the *nouvelle théologie* are incompatible.

1. The *nouvelle théologie* mistakenly criticizes neo-scholastic methods of apologetics and does so on the basis of a false ecumenical irenicism (§§11–12).
2. The *nouvelle théologie* mistakenly wants "to free dogma itself from terminology long established in the Church and from philosophical concepts held by Catholic teachers, to bring about a return in the explanation of Catholic doctrine to the way of speaking used in Holy Scripture and by the Fathers of the Church"; and it does this on the basis of a false ecumenical irenicism and also in hopes of expressing dogma in modern philosophical language that will be more accessible today (§§14–15).
3. Some of the "more audacious" representatives of the *nouvelle théologie* fall directly into modernism by holding that "the mysteries of faith are never expressed by truly adequate concepts but only by approximate and ever changeable notions, in which the truth is to some extent expressed, but is necessarily distorted," and by holding that these human expressions of divine truths can be "even somewhat opposed, but still equivalent" (§15).
4. The *nouvelle théologie*'s "contempt for terms and notions habitually used by scholastic theologians" threatens the stability and future of dogmatic or speculative theology (§17).
5. The *nouvelle théologie* undermines the truth about "the nature and constitution of the Church" as taught by the papal Magisterium, by arguing that all contemporary papal teachings about the Church must be interpreted by recourse to the Church Fathers, i.e. from a time *prior* to later authoritative dogmatic teaching (§18).

beyond the responses to theological liberalism/modernism and exposes the roots of the movements for biblical renewal, liturgical renewal, religious toleration (though not indifferentism), and so on, see Shaun Blanchard, *The Synod of Pistoia and Vatican II: Jansenism and the Struggle for Catholic Reform* (Oxford: Oxford University Press, 2020). See also Gerd-Rainer Horn, *The Spirit of Vatican II: Western European Progressive Catholicism in the Long Sixties* (Oxford: Oxford University Press, 2015).

6. The *nouvelle théologie* undermines the truth of Scripture by re-asserting the condemned error that inerrancy pertains only to "those parts of the Bible that treat of God or of moral and religious matters" (§22).
7. The *nouvelle théologie* undermines the truth of Scripture by arguing that beneath the "human sense of the Scriptures" is a spiritual sense that contains "the only infallible meaning" (§22), and by holding that this sense grounds a new "spiritual" or "symbolic" exegesis that overcomes the difficulties with the letter of Scripture (§23).
8. The *nouvelle théologie* mistakenly places contemporary exegesis of Scripture above "the doctrine of the Fathers and of the Teaching Church," rather than "explaining Holy Scripture according to the mind of the Church which Christ Our Lord has appointed guardian and interpreter of the whole deposit of divinely revealed truth" (§22).

These errors, Pope Pius XII concludes, have led those associated with the *nouvelle théologie* to a number of further errors on particular matters, among which are the following: the claim that human reason can only demonstrate God's existence when aided by grace; the claim that because God is love it follows that creation is necessary for God; the claim that God does not eternally and infallibly foreknow human actions; the claim that angels are not personal beings; the claim that God "cannot create intellectual beings without ordering and calling them to the beatific vision"; the claim that the Church's doctrine of original sin is untenable; the claim that the Church's understanding of Christ's satisfaction on the Cross is untenable; the claim that the doctrine of transubstantiation is based upon an erroneous notion of "substance"; the claim that the Roman Catholic Church is not one and the same as the Mystical Body of Christ; the claim that the motives of credibility are not in fact credible; the claim that there is no real need to belong to the Church in order to be saved; and the repudiation of the Church's perennial philosophy (§§25–34).

My purpose here is not to evaluate these charges or to compare them to Church documents later produced under the aegis of the *nouvelle théologie* (for example, the Magisterium of Pope Benedict XVI).[3] The point is simply to confirm that the neo-scholastic theologians, and Pope Pius XII, did not think highly of the *nouvelle théologie*, to say the least. What then did the pre-conciliar *nouvelle théologie* think about the neo-scholastics?[4]

3. I think that some of the concerns were proven accurate with regard to some representatives of the *nouvelle théologie*, while some of the concerns were either overblown or mistaken.

4. For background to differences among the French and German theologians of the *nouvelle*

Not surprisingly, the theologians of the *nouvelle théologie* were quite critical of neo-scholastic theology and of the Church of that era. For example, in the immediate aftermath of World War II, Yves Congar sensed a welcome change in the air, one that could reverse the growing loss of Catholic faith in France and elsewhere. He reports that the laity, in 1946, "complained about the preaching they heard, the liturgies they attended, the place given to the proletariat (their place) in the church, and the outdated, inept, ineffective, and purely 'bourgeois' style of so many of the forms in which parish ministry was being exercised."[5]

Going further in his 1950 book *True and False Reform in the Church*, Congar deems that Catholicism today "is overloaded with all kinds of contributions from the history it has passed through and affected by all kinds of human circumstances.... Human and historical forms, developed throughout history, are linked to Christianity without pertaining to its essential reality."[6] The solution, he says, is *ressourcement*. He sees the possibility for a theologically rich "spiritual opening to the modern world" that "would avoid becoming a superficial amalgam of diverse elements and instead become a true development of Christianity."[7] Congar's basic concern is that the neo-scholastics are locked into post-Tridentine perspectives and discussions that are no longer fruitful. He remarks that "the church (even though it is changeless with respect to what it receives from on high) has to follow

théologie (or *Ressourcement*), focusing on Erich Przywara's complex relationship to the *nouvelle théologie*, see Aaron Pidel, SJ, *Church of the Ever Greater God: The Ecclesiology of Erich Przywara* (Notre Dame, Indiana: University of Notre Dame Press, 2020).

5. Yves Congar, OP, *True and False Reform in the Church*, translated by Paul Philibert, OP (Collegeville, Minnesota: Liturgical Press, 2011), 24.

6. Ibid., 47.

7. Ibid., 301. In additions to his text added (by Congar) in 1967, Congar argues: "It's not about dogma. At least, church dogma was not called into question by the reform spirit before Vatican II. If dogma is in question today in some writing or another (or if people think that it is), that is because things have changed. However, this book was written between 1946 and 1950 in a situation in which dogmatic issues were not being called into question any more than in any other of the great moments of the church. The real objective, rather, has been to grasp church dogmas according to the deepest meaning of the tradition. What really mattered was how to do catechesis, how to preach. The question was whether in some areas there is not some way (some obligation) to go beyond the way we habitually presented Catholicism, but that did not do justice to the fullness of its doctrinal traditions. For instance, in the light of a renewed understanding of the divine 'economy' and of eschatology, can't we say more concerning the 'last things' than what we find in most familiar treatments? If so, then naturally some improvements appear desirable in clergy education and in seminary book lists. We can find no example of an ecclesial reform that was serious that did not require a new perspective, a renewed impulse, and a return to the deepest wells of tradition—as well as a revision of clergy education." Ibid., 159.

humanity in expanding and evolving and thus experience a parallel development within itself."[8]

Writing in 1963 in the midst of Vatican II, Joseph Ratzinger puts matters in more pointed terms (as Congar sometimes also does in his Council diaries). Ratzinger criticizes the Catholic modernists Albert Loisy and George Tyrrell as "men who thought they could not save the faith without throwing away the inner core along with the expendable shell," and he recognizes that "[s]uch figures and their tragic schizophrenia show forth the mortal danger that threatened Catholicism at the first outbreak of the modern mind."[9] But he contends that the increasingly harsh ecclesiastical crackdown, joined to a neo-scholastic theology that was seemingly opposed to anything outside itself, became oppressive and counter-productive. In the original conciliar Schema on the doctrine of revelation, he finds a "spirit of condemnation and negation" and "a frigid and even offensive tone."[10] He bemoans its "cramped thinking" and its "theology of negations and prohibitions."[11] Among the areas in which he specifically criticizes deficiencies in neo-scholastic theology of revelation are the following: "the relationship of scripture to tradition and the way in which faith is related to history"; the "understanding of inspiration and of the historicity of events narrated in scripture"; and whether the Church could "turn over a new leaf and move on into a new and positive encounter with its own origins, with its brothers and with the world of today."[12]

For his part, in *Catholicism*—translated into English from its 1947 edition—Henri de Lubac raises sharply barbed concerns about "the combined influence of Aristotelian logic and Roman law on the formulation of theology during the Middle Ages."[13] Implicitly but clearly, neo-scholastic theology is his foil. He warns that the influence of Roman law produces "the danger of a legal outlook in expounding the mysteries—an outlook entirely foreign

8. Ibid., 130. For helpful background for ascertaining Congar's meaning here, see Andrew Meszaros, *The Prophetic Church: History and Doctrinal Development in John Henry Newman and Yves Congar* (Oxford: Oxford University Press, 2016); as well as Meszaros, "John Henry Newman and the Thomistic Tradition: Convergences in Contribution to Development Theory," *Nova et Vetera* 19, no. 2 (2021): 423–68.

9. Joseph Ratzinger, *Theological Highlights of Vatican II* (Mahwah, New Jersey: Paulist Press, 2009), 41.

10. Ibid., 40.

11. Ibid., 42.

12. Ibid., 43–44.

13. Henri de Lubac, SJ, *Catholicism: Christ and the Common Destiny of Man*, translated by Lancelot C. Sheppard and Elizabeth Englund, OCD (San Francisco: Ignatius Press, 1988), 307.

to their nature."[14] Likewise, Aristotelian logic cannot handle the "organic, unitary ideas which had formerly, in some respects, found an ally in the Platonic mentality," and neither can Aristotelianism handle the "spiritual continuity" of human action in time.[15] De Lubac praises the Middle Ages by comparison with the "later and by no means inevitable abuses"; and he adds regarding such abuses—implicitly with neo-scholastic theology in view—that "it is not always when it [theology] thinks itself particularly well-shielded that it offers the most effectual resistance" to negative modern trends.[16] I note that Ratzinger considered *Catholicism*, which he first read in 1949, to be "an essential milestone on my theological journey" and a demonstration, above all, of "how much more relevant theology is the more it returns to its center and draws from its deepest resources."[17]

Thus, the *nouvelle théologie* considered that neo-scholastic theology had replaced the richness of earlier theology with an intellectually narrow, indefensibly unhistorical (especially vis-à-vis Scripture), positivistic, ecclesiastically punitive, overly Aristotelian, ecumenically antagonistic theology. While the neo-scholastics charged the *nouvelle théologie* with modernism with respect to the truth of Scripture, the permanence of dogma, the authority of the Magisterium, and the gratuity of grace, the *nouvelle théologie* charged neo-scholastic theology with developing a reactive mirror image of the modernist errors—namely, by being all too modern (in the sense of too juridical, authoritarian, and dryly abstract) in the formulation of anti-modernism. According to the neo-scholastics, the leading representatives of the *nouvelle théologie* were hollowing out the truth of the Catholic faith. According to the *nouvelle théologie*, the neo-scholastics had so defensively shackled the Catholic faith that people were unnecessarily abandoning the faith, now ridiculed as a monarchist and medieval relic.

Thus far I have sketched the clash, surely a stark enough alternative. But in this essay, I argue that neo-scholastic theology and the *nouvelle théologie* can and should be united in theological work today. Those who have read the classic works of liberal Protestant theology will be cognizant of the characteristic elements that one finds in liberal theology: the reduction of faith to ethics, the rejection of the possibility of enduring biblical and

14. Ibid.

15. Ibid., 307–308.

16. Ibid., 308–309.

17. Joseph Ratzinger, "Foreword" (to the 1988 English edition), in de Lubac, *Catholicism*, 11–12, at 11.

dogmatic truth, the view that dogma is about the human community and is only "true" when it produces authentic human community, the denial of a stable human nature, a highly apophatic view of religious knowledge, the view that religions are human inventions inspired by figures who modeled liberative action and exalted consciousness, and so on. When one reads the writings of such varied figures as Congar, Ratzinger, and de Lubac, as well as Louis Bouyer, Jean Daniélou, and Hans Urs von Balthasar, one does not find these characteristic marks of liberal Protestantism or the Catholic variants thereof. These authors were not liberal theologians in the classic sense; they were not modernists.

If so, then the neo-scholastic theology and the *nouvelle théologie* (or Ressourcement) can be joined together in their best insights. I call this union "Ressourcement Thomism." As an example of how this can be done, I will focus upon two sources: Réginald Garrigou-Lagrange's constructive commentary on *Summa Theologiae* III, q. 1, a. 3; and Joseph Ratzinger's *Jesus of Nazareth*, volume 1, chapter 8. I argue that both of them defend, in very different but complementary ways, the integral link between the Incarnation and the Cross.[18] Garrigou-Lagrange employs a scientific-theological mode (in the technical neo-scholastic sense of the term) and Ratzinger in a biblical-theological mode. My proposal is that the two approaches have much to teach about the same dogmatic reality, namely, the intimate union of the Incarnation and the Cross.

By contrast, this intimate union goes by the wayside in classically liberal Catholic theology. For example, Balthasar aptly criticizes Karl Rahner, whose post-conciliar understanding of Catholic dogma exemplifies classical liberalism, for viewing (along Teilhardian lines) "the Incarnation of God as a world goal, even without the fall, certainly not the Incarnation as a function of salvation."[19] Liberal Protestantism and Catholic modern-

18. Although my topic (as will be clear especially in the survey of Garrigou-Lagrange's reflections) bears directly upon the controversy between Thomists and Scotists about whether the divine Son would have become incarnate even if Adam and Eve had not fallen, I am not attempting here to resolve that controversy— my exposition of Garrigou-Lagrange's perspective has a different goal, as I have indicated. For an explanation of the medieval roots of the controversy, see Justus H. Hunter, *If Adam Had Not Sinned: The Reason for the Incarnation from Anselm to Scotus* (Washington, D.C.: The Catholic University of America Press, 2020).

19. Hans Urs von Balthasar, *The Moment of Christian Witness*, translated by Richard Beckley (San Francisco: Ignatius Press, 1994), 107. Balthasar adds sadly, "This was not always Rahner's emphasis. Once he was a great exponent of the *Ecclesia ex latere Christi* and thus of devotion to the Sacred Heart." Ibid., 109.

ism advocate a Christ without the Cross, a cosmic Christ emerging from world processes who is the endpoint, rather than the cause, of salvation. Neo-scholastic theology and the *nouvelle théologie* can and should join together to oppose this reductive view of Christ.

In sum, although they devoted much time to fighting each other, their common opponent was what John Henry Newman called liberalism in religion. If they had realized more clearly that they had a shared opponent, theological liberalism might not have enjoyed such a heyday in the Church of the Seventies. In our time, exponents of the two theological modes should make peace with each other and should focus on developing a shared critique of the increasingly powerful liberationist or contextualist Catholic theology that takes its norms and goals primarily from the world rather than from divine revelation.[20]

II. Incarnation and Cross: Toward a Ressourcement Thomism

1. Réginald Garrigou-Lagrange, OP's "Christ the Savior". One of the things that stands out about Garrigou-Lagrange's neo-scholastic commentary on the question of the motive of the incarnation (*Summa Theologiae* III, q. 1, a. 3) is its spiritual richness. For example, he states, "Thus it is that the Son of God through His incarnation certainly stoops down to us with sublime mercy, so that the saints are moved to tears at the thought of it."[21] The incarnate Son's stooping down has the purpose not of reducing his glorious Godhead, but rather to show us what it means to be human. He comes to "[restore] the original subordination, by making us again subordinate to Himself and God the Father."[22]

Christ does this by his Cross and Resurrection, through which he takes away our misery, namely, our injustice and our slavery to sin and death. According to Garrigou-Lagrange, the Incarnation therefore has an intrinsic link to God's mercy toward us. Why, Garrigou-Lagrange asks, did God not

20. For work in support of rapprochement—recognizing the division between neo-scholastic and *nouvelle théologie* modes, but pointing out that the greater and more urgent division today is between these two modes and liberationist theology—see Tracey Rowland, *Catholic Theology* (London: Bloomsbury, 2017).

21. Réginald Garrigou-Lagrange, OP, *Christ the Savior: A Commentary on the Third Part of St. Thomas' Theological Summa*, translated by Bede Rose, OSB (n.p.: Ex Fontibus, 2015), 95.

22. Ibid.

take on angelic nature? The answer, which he draws from the *prima pars*, is that we humans were needier than were the blessed angels. Just as the sick servant receives the choicest wine from his or her loving master, so humans in our deep misery are given the greatest gift by God.

Does this mean that our neediness is the cause of God's action, so that God is subordinated to us causally rather than the other way around? Garrigou-Lagrange, indebted to Cajetan, explains that God's action is always causally ordered to God. The ultimate end or final cause of God's works vis-à-vis creatures is the glorification of God. Garrigou-Lagrange insists that when we say that the motive of the Incarnation is to remedy the fall, we do not causally subordinate God to us.

Yet, if we refuse to speculate about a hypothetical Incarnation that is *not* aimed at the remedy of human sin, must we also thereby refuse to speculate about why God permitted Adam and Eve's sin? Garrigou-Lagrange notes that Thomists such as Cajetan, John of St. Thomas, and Charles Billuart refuse to speculate about these topics, other than by granting that in the divine decrees, God's decision to become incarnate follows logically after God's permission of Adam and Eve's sin. But other Thomists, such as the Salmanticenses, argue that God always had the Incarnation in view, and that God permitted the evil of Adam and Eve's sin, precisely so that he could bring about the greater good of a redemptive Incarnation.

Inclining toward the latter position, Garrigou-Lagrange takes as "certain and *de fide*" the claim that God never permits an evil except with a greater good in view.[23] Otherwise, God's permission of evil would be wicked, whereas in fact God is infinite goodness. Does this mean, then, that we should say that God, having determined to become incarnate, allowed Adam and Eve to sin so that God could become incarnate? In Garrigou-Lagrange's view, this claim would not be in accord with the truth that God does not need evil in order to accomplish good. Thus Garrigou-Lagrange emphasizes, "It cannot indeed be said a priori that God permitted original sin because of some greater good."[24] We can move backward in our speculation, preserving the priority (as final cause) of God's good decree; but we cannot speculate from the opposite starting point by beginning with God's good decree in a manner that brackets original sin.

Is it possible, in Garrigou-Lagrange's view, to conceive hypothetically of

23. Ibid., 97.
24. Ibid.

an Incarnation that would *not* have taken place because of human sin? Certainly the answer must be yes. Citing Aquinas, Garrigou-Lagrange notes that God, in the simplicity of his divine knowledge, knows from eternity every possible scenario in which he could have become incarnate. Inevitably, one of these scenarios would have been in a pre-fall world. We should therefore affirm that "God, previous to any decree, saw by His knowledge of simple intelligence all possible worlds with all their contents, just as the architect has in mind various possible houses and all their component parts."[25] In his goodness, and "by a single decree," God chose to create and providentially order the world that we know, in which he permitted the Fall and in which he became incarnate as Redeemer.[26] In this regard, Garrigou-Lagrange takes the opportunity to point out that not only is Christ "the first of the predestined" (cf. Ephesians 1) as the incarnate Savior,[27] but also all things that bear upon salvation are included in this predestining decree. He explains, "In fact, it is evident that various events of the natural order, such as the death of a good person from some disease, which at first sight seem to depend solely on natural causes and the general provisions of Providence, are to be attributed to the supernatural operation of predestination."[28]

In his reflection on Aquinas's article about whether God would have become incarnate if man had not sinned, Garrigou-Lagrange begins by describing the debate as it stood in Aquinas's day. According to Alexander of Hales and Albert the Great, we can reason from the fact of the Incarnation to the supposition that God would also have become incarnate even if humanity had not fallen. But according to Bonaventure and Aquinas, it is more probable that God would not have become incarnate under such circumstances. Garrigou-Lagrange draws this position of Aquinas not from the *Summa Theologiae* (where Aquinas's view is less definitive) but from the *Commentary on the Sentences*, buttressed by the *Commentary on 1 Timothy*.

Having set the scene, Garrigou-Lagrange carefully goes through the objections and *respondeo* provided by Aquinas in ST III, q. 1, a. 3. He interprets Aquinas's *respondeo* as a theological proof whose arguments can be set forth in the form of a syllogism. The major premise is that "[w]hat depends solely on the will of God, and beyond all to which the creature is entitled, can be

25. Ibid.
26. Ibid.
27. Ibid., 96.
28. Ibid., 98–99.

made known to us only inasmuch as it is contained in Sacred Scripture."[29] The minor premise is that Scripture invariably teaches that God became incarnate in order to redeem us from sin. Garrigou-Lagrange thinks that the major premise is evident once one understands the terms, and the minor premise can be proven from Scripture. To do the latter, he cites Luke 5:31, Luke 19:10, 1 Timothy 1:15, Galatians 4:4, John 1:29, John 3:16, Romans 3:22, 1 John 1:7, 1 John 2:12, 1 John 3:5, 1 John 4:10, Isaiah 61:1, Daniel 9:24, and Zechariah 3:9. The conclusion of the syllogism is that it is more fitting, or more probable, to hold that "the sin of the first man is the reason of the Incarnation."[30]

Yet, Garrigou-Lagrange points out that this conclusion, strong though it is, does not rise to the level of "a theological conclusion."[31] He means that Aquinas purposefully stays in the realm of fittingness, rather than attempting a demonstrative theological proof. Given the consistency of Scripture's testimony, it is a strong conclusion, but because it is not "absolutely certain" it is not a scientific theological certainty. Nonetheless, its probability is further strengthened by Tradition. Here Garrigou-Lagrange points to the statement of the Nicene Creed: "for us men and for our salvation he came down from heaven." He also notes that both the Council of Sens and Pope Innocent I formally condemned the following statement of Abelard's: "Christ did not assume our human nature in order to deliver us from the devil's yoke."[32] He finds clear statements in the Church Fathers that Christ became incarnate because we sinned: among the Fathers he cites, the clearest are Irenaeus and Cyril of Alexandria, but Athanasius, Gregory of Nazianzus, John Chrysostom, and Augustine are quite clear as well. He also makes reference to the *Glossa Ordinaria*.

Given the above foundations, Garrigou-Lagrange briefly sketches the debate between Scotists and Thomists. According to Scotists, the above biblical and patristic texts show only that had humans not fallen, Christ would not have become incarnate *as Redeemer*. Scotists make much of Colossians 1:15–17. In addition to responding to the Scotist interpretation of this biblical passage, Thomists mount a logical argument that begins with the following claim: "Since God's efficacious decrees are not modified by

29. Ibid., 78.
30. Ibid., 79.
31. Ibid.
32. Ibid., 80.

Him, but from eternity include also all the circumstances of the thing to be produced, the present efficacious decree of the Incarnation from eternity includes the passibility of the flesh."[33] If this is so, then the Incarnation's rationale must be to redeem us from sin, because the passibility of the flesh (as Scotists agree) is the result of the fall. In other words, God's decree regarding the Incarnation includes within it the fallen (passible) condition of humanity. There is no "Incarnation," in God's decree, without this relation to human fallenness. At most, therefore, "the decree of the Incarnation considered in itself and not in passible flesh is a conditional and inefficacious decree," which has no reference to actually existing things.[34]

In Garrigou-Lagrange's view, this logical argument foils the Scotist position. The Scotist response, however, is that even if "the reparation of sin was an indispensable condition for the coming of Christ," still it is the case that an indispensable condition is not a motive.[35] Therefore we cannot know whether the motive for the Incarnation was solely to redeem sinners. If we cannot know this, then it is possible or even probable that God had other motives that would have ensured that God would have become incarnate even if humans had not sinned. In response, Garrigou-Lagrange again underscores that Scripture presents only the one motive for the Incarnation (other than the all-encompassing motive of the manifestation of God's glory), namely, the motive of redemption from sin.

Garrigou-Lagrange attends here to the nature of an efficacious divine decree. For Scotists, God makes an efficacious decree that he will become incarnate, and this efficacious decree is *distinct from* the motive, which depends upon the circumstances that humans find themselves in. An example of such a decree is: "I decree efficaciously that someone must be paid a debt of one hundred dollars, not considering whether this debt is to be paid in gold or silver."[36] On this view, God efficaciously decrees to become incarnate, and this efficacious decree can include diverse motives; thus his efficacious decree means that he would have become incarnate no matter what motives happened to be in play. Garrigou-Lagrange rejects this position, on the grounds that God's efficacious decrees are not vague in the way ours are. He reiterates, too, that God efficaciously decreed to become

33. Ibid., 82.
34. Ibid., 83.
35. Ibid.
36. Ibid., 84.

incarnate in passible flesh, which means that the Incarnation is connected intrinsically to our sinful condition—i.e. our loss of original justice—and to God's will to redeem us. Garrigou-Lagrange also notes that Francisco Suárez holds that God had two motives for the Incarnation: the redemption of the human race, and the sheer excellence of the incarnate Son. In reply, Garrigou-Lagrange observes that the latter motive is never identified in Scripture and therefore we have no basis for positing it.

Garrigou-Lagrange next carefully reviews Aquinas's responses to the objections included in q. 1, a. 3. He pays particular attention to Aquinas's replies to the third and fourth objections. The third objection is that both before and after sin, human nature is capable of the grace of hypostatic union; and God surely would not withhold a good from human nature that is possible for humans to attain, especially if God granted it to humans *after* sin. Garrigou-Lagrange explains that God is not obligated to complete every "obediential power"; God may do so, but this is sheer grace.[37] Still, why should it be right that humans, precisely by sinning, gained a greater dignity (the hypostatic union) than God already willed to give humans even had they not sinned? For Aquinas, citing Romans 5:20 and the Paschal candle blessing "O felix culpa," the answer is that it is perfectly fitting that God do what he pleases in this regard. Not only can God bestow grace abundantly whenever he wills, but also it is fitting that God allowed original sin with the purpose of drawing a greater good out of it.

The fourth objection comes from Romans 1:4 and has to do with the predestination of Christ. God foreknows human sin in predestining Christ. As Garrigou-Lagrange recognizes, this is where Scotists object most strenuously. Surely, Scotus suggests, in the order of intention God first wills (or predestines) Christ, and *only then* other things in relation to Christ. It follows that in this order, "God wills divine natural sonship to Christ before having foreseen Adam's demerit."[38] Garrigou-Lagrange thinks that Cajetan offers an adequate answer to this objection. Cajetan urges that we must distinguish between the "material cause" and the "final cause." The material cause here is fallen human nature that needs perfecting; the final cause is the incarnate Son. This material cause is what God, in predestining Christ, foreknows. It is not that the material cause enjoys the status of a final cause, however; rather, it is simply that the final cause is what it is *in light of* the

37. Ibid., 86.
38. Ibid., 88.

material cause. As Garrigou-Lagrange puts it, "Christ's predestination is dependent on the foreseeing of Adam's sin, not indeed that it is dependent on this latter as being the final cause, but as being the material cause that is to be perfected."[39] In a similar way, when God predestines Peter to salvation ("final cause"), God does so in light of the "material cause" that is Peter's coming into being as an embryo.

Of course, God *could* predestine the Incarnation without reference to human sin, but the revealed evidence indicates the contrary. Garrigou-Lagrange, indebted to Cajetan, notes that we cannot trust our reasoning about what seems best to us in matters that pertain to the mystery of God's will for salvation. For example, although it would seem best to us for God to show his goodness by saving all rational creatures, revelation indicates that God wills to save some but not all. Thus we cannot say what God *must* will, without scriptural evidence that tells us what God *does* will. It is only from revelation that we will be able to determine God's motive, and we cannot abstract from this revealed motive to determine what God would do if this motive were not in play.

Garrigou-Lagrange concludes his discussion of this article by taking a wider lens and asking why Scotus takes a position that seemingly gives God less liberty, while Aquinas a position that gives God more liberty. After all, Scotus is a voluntarist, continually emphasizing divine freedom. Why then would Scotus seek to pin God down to becoming incarnate whether or not humans sinned?

Garrigou-Lagrange responds to this seeming quandary by arguing that Scotus misunderstands the relationship of nature and grace. Scotus holds that "there is in our nature an innate appetite and not merely one that is elicited for the beatific vision."[40] Indeed, Scotus thinks that, if God willed, he could make beatific vision "natural" for humans. This, however, is to conflate what pertains to created powers and what can only be achieved by God's own power. Creatures, of their own powers, can do lots of things; but creaturely power simply does not suffice, as such, to share in the very life of God by knowing God as God knows himself. But it is within God's power to raise the creature to such unfathomably glorious knowledge. This is what the order of grace makes possible, by contrast to the order of nature. In the order of nature, humans are capable of being elevated to beatific vision,

39. Ibid.
40. Ibid., 99.

but for this actually to take place is entirely up to God's free determination. Rather unfairly, Garrigou-Lagrange accuses Scotus of a rationalistic viewpoint in this regard: Scotus "speaks finally, almost like the absolute intellectualists of the Leibnitz type, who think that the Incarnation is morally necessary for the world to be the best of all possible worlds."[41]

How is it, though, that God in his goodness would create humans without giving the perfect gift of hypostatic union, for which humans are capable and which is the most perfect expression of the divine love? Garrigou-Lagrange is aware that it may sound as if for Aquinas, the Incarnation is a nice thing but not the heart of God's plan, insofar as God might well have created humans without becoming incarnate (whether or not we fell). In response, Garrigou-Lagrange points out that, in fact, "in Thomism the Incarnation is seen to be the supreme fact of the entire universe."[42] Nevertheless, it remains the case that the Incarnation is entirely free, entirely contingent. John 3:16 announces glorious news, sheer mercy and love beyond anything required for God to do. As Garrigou-Lagrange replies that, "in the supernatural order, inasmuch as this order is gratuitous, divine liberty reigns supreme and its predilection is most free, the motive of which can be known only by revelation."[43]

At the end of his discussion, Garrigou-Lagrange circles back to the spiritual implications. He contends that it is imperative that the Incarnation not be separated from the redemption. If it were separated, then Christ could be seen as an exalted figure, a glorious man and great teacher, who also happened to overcome sin. Indeed, his conquest of sin could become so secondary as to be essentially forgotten—as happens in liberal or modernist theology. The center of Jesus' life, of all that he is and does, is his status as Savior. This explains why the Cross has such a central place in all the gospels and in the entire New Testament. The incarnate Son comes to conquer sin; he comes to enter into the fullest solidarity with sinners and to overcome sin from within. Spiritually, too, we become like the incarnate Son when we carry our cross (Lk 9:23). Our cross and our suffering are not secondary aspects of our discipleship to the exalted Christ. We are conformed not simply to the Incarnate Lord, but to Christ *crucified*, and this matters greatly.

In making this spiritual and dogmatic point, Garrigou-Lagrange cites

41. Ibid., 100.
42. Ibid.
43. Ibid.

John 12:24, Luke 24:26, and Romans 8:17, which emphasize that the center of Christ's identity is found in his suffering and the center of our Christian identity is found in our suffering in and with Christ. This contrasts with the view, expressed most recently by the Catholic spiritual writer Richard Rohr, that "Christianity's unique trump card is always and forever incarnation."[44] It is better to say that Christianity's uniqueness rests upon God crucified—thus joining together the Incarnation and the Cross.

2. *Joseph Ratzinger's* Jesus of Nazareth. I will focus on chapter 8 of the first volume of *Jesus of Nazareth*. In this chapter, titled "The Principal Images of John's Gospel," Ratzinger engages with historical-critical biblical scholarship, Jewish Second Temple literature (specifically Philo), and the Church Fathers. Ratzinger's approach is typical of the *nouvelle théologie* in that rather than beginning with the dogmatic tradition and refinements and debates within that tradition, he begins with Scripture as read by scholars who have expertise in the scriptural texts and their ancient near-Eastern contexts. Although Ratzinger brings to the scriptural texts his Nicene faith in Jesus as the incarnate Son, Ratzinger allows his dogmatic portrait of Jesus to emerge in full as he queries and explores Scripture in conjunction with historical-critical exegetes and the Church Fathers. This is a different method from the neo-scholastic task of beginning with dogmatic starting points and entering directly into the medieval and post-Tridentine dogmatic debates about such things as the nature of predestination, the relationship of nature and grace, and the divine decrees in light of divine simplicity.

Already from the Synoptics, treated in earlier chapters of his book,

44. Richard Rohr, OFM, *The Universal Christ: How a Forgotten Reality Can Change Everything We See, Hope for, and Believe* (New York: Convergent, 2019), 114. See also Ilia Delio, OSF, *Christ in Evolution* (Maryknoll, New York: Orbis, 2008), 127, drawing upon Raimon Pannikar, Pierre Teilhard de Chardin, SJ, and Karl Rahner, SJ: "Jesus is the symbol of what human beings really are and what is intended for all creation. As symbol, he provides the assurance that the infinite hopes and strivings of our human nature can be realized: God and the world can be one in unity.... When we say that Jesus is the symbol of God we are saying that God's self-utterance, his *ex*-istence is realized in the humanity of Jesus. Since the incarnation fulfills the potential of every human person, the incarnation symbolizes the union of God and humanity/creation for every person, whether or not they explicitly know Christ. To say that Christ is the symbol of God is to say that Christ is the Word of God expressed or projected outward in space, time, and history. This expression/projection of the symbol of the Word discloses and manifests what is present. The symbol makes real and reveals that which is otherwise hidden or concealed, that is, the centrality of divine life The symbol of Christ functions as the meaning of God for us and discloses to us the true meaning of our lives in God. Christ is symbol of the trinitarian mystery of God by which God is able to communicate God's life completely to another and to be united with the other as beloved in a perichoresis of love. The symbol of Christ as symbol of God helps us to understand Jesus Christ as the one in whom all humanity finds its permanent openness to God."

Ratzinger has gained the core insight that "the mystery of Jesus' oneness with the Father is ever present and determines everything, even though it remains hidden beneath his humanity."[45] Already, then, the basic elements of the dogmatic teaching of Nicaea and Chalcedon are at work. But in John, says Ratzinger, "Jesus' divinity appears unveiled."[46] Whereas earlier dogmatic theologians could take this for granted and move on to points of controversy or philosophical refinement, Ratzinger has to deal with the fact that, with respect to the Gospel of John, "modern critical scholarship" has denied "the historicity of the text" and has deemed it not to be "a reliable source for knowledge of the historical Jesus."[47]

Ratzinger has foremost in mind Rudolf Bultmann's influential commentary on the Gospel of John. Bultmann proposed that the Gospel of John reflects Gnostic Christian sources. On this view, the Gospel that grounded the dogmatic proclamation of the Church from Nicaea onward is actually rooted in a heretical form of Christianity: it was the Gnostic Christians who developed the notion of an incarnate Redeemer, and their worldview fueled the sharp dualism that one finds in the Gospel of John.

Catholic dogmatic Christology here encounters a challenge. Just as earlier dogmaticians turned to philosophy for clarifying errors (since bad philosophy often caused the errors), so Ratzinger must turn to biblical scholarship for his theological task. Ratzinger notes that Martin Hengel, in books published in the 1970s and 1980s, showed that no Gnostic redeemer text pre-dates the Gospel of John. Hengel and others also made clear that the author of the Gospel of John knew very well the Palestine of Jesus' day and drew heavily upon late Second Temple Jewish motifs. Therefore the Gospel is far from being "Gnostic" in its sources. Hengel offers his own reconstruction of the Gospel's origins, locating it in the circles of the Jerusalem priestly elite. Ratzinger accepts Hengel's view as plausible, in light of John 18:16 as well as the highly distinctive language of the Gospel of John.

Ratzinger points out that the Gospel itself attests to its veracity, claiming that its testimony comes from an eyewitness (Jn 19:35; cf. Jn 21:24). This eyewitness, the Gospel makes clear, is the "beloved disciple" who appears repeatedly in the narrative. In John 13:25, we find the beloved disciple leaning on Jesus' breast in a deliberate echo of John 1:18, "No one has ever

45. Joseph Ratzinger/ Pope Benedict XVI, *From Baptism in the Jordan to the Transfiguration*, vol. 1 of *Jesus of Nazareth*, translated by Adrian J. Walker (New York: Doubleday, 2007), 218.

46. Ibid., 219.

47. Ibid.

seen God; the only-begotten Son, who is in the bosom of the Father, he has made him known." The evangelist's claim is that the most important source for the Gospel of John "gained his intimate knowledge from his inward repose in Jesus' heart."[48]

Is this claim credible? According to the biblical scholar Ulrich Wilckens, the "beloved disciple" is not intended to be a historical figure. Ratzinger finds this idea to be mistaken, on the grounds that a witness is either a historical figure or else not a real witness at all. Ratzinger therefore presses further, exploring whether it is possible to identify the evangelist (and/or the beloved disciple) as Jesus' disciple John, the son of Zebedee—as Irenaeus and the Church's Tradition hold. Ratzinger notes that the identification of the evangelist with John of Zebedee has been defended from a historical-critical perspective by Henri Cazelles. Cazelles argues that the evangelist was a member of the priestly elite; but John of Zebedee was a fisherman from Galilee. Could a Galilean fisherman be a Temple priest? The answer is yes, because priests only served in the Temple twice per year, and they lived elsewhere during the year and often earned their living in other ways. Zebedee was wealthy enough to employ several helpers in his fishing crew. Cazelles speculates that Zebedee owned property both in Galilee and in Jerusalem; and indeed perhaps the Last Supper was held in property owned by Zebedee in the Essene part of Jerusalem. John of Zebedee would therefore have been the host of the occasion and entitled to sit at the right hand of the guest of honor, Jesus.

Continuing his review of the scholarship, Ratzinger notes that Papias, in the second century, mentions receiving the faith from the "Presbyter John" (or the Elder John) who is not the disciple John of Zebedee. Indebted to the biblical scholar Peter Stuhlmacher, Ratzinger puts the two together: the Elder John, on this view, "regarded himself as the trustee of the tradition he had received from the son of Zebedee."[49]

48. Ibid., 223.

49. Ibid., 226. For a different but basically complementary approach, arguing that the author of the Gospel of John was the Elder John who was an eyewitness (rather than tracing the Gospel back to John the son of Zebedee), see Richard Bauckham, *Jesus and the Eyewitnesses: The Gospels as Eyewitness Testimony*, 2nd ed. (Grand Rapids, Michigan: Eerdmans, 2017); Bauckham, *The Testimony of the Beloved Disciple: Narrative, History, and Theology in the Gospel of John* (Grand Rapids, Michigan: Baker Academic, 2007), chaps 2 and 3. Like Hengel and others, including Raymond E. Brown in his *The Community of the Beloved Disciple* (London: G. Chapman, 1979), 31–34, Bauckham considers that "the Gospel's portrayal of the beloved disciple makes most sense if he was not one of the Twelve, not one of the itinerant disciples who traveled around with Jesus" but

For Ratzinger, the point here is that this historical-critical research hardly rules out conceiving of the Gospel of John, with its emphasis on Jesus' divine Sonship, as rooted in eyewitness testimony. Yet, he notes that biblical scholars often still doubt whether the Gospel of John is "historical" in any commonly accepted sense of that term. Instead, the Fourth Gospel is often considered to be a poetic or theological meditation. Even Martin Hengel adopts this position; and Ingo Broer likewise insists that the Gospel of John, while intending to bear literary witness to Jesus, is not "historical."[50] Ratzinger challenges the notion of "historical" that underlies such perspectives. Certainly the Gospel of John is not modern-day historical work, governed by the effort to present the facts literally as they occurred. But if in fundamental ways the Gospel of John altered and violated what actually happened, then it could not be credible as a witness to historical events. The Holy Spirit cannot bear true witness to the truth through the evangelist John, if the evangelist has departed decisively from the historical events.

Here Ratzinger addresses the issue of historical remembering. Certainly, the evangelist expresses the intention to bear witness to what actually hap-

---

rather—as Bauckham argues distinctively—someone who was "a disciple resident in Jerusalem, who hosted Jesus and his disciples for the Last Supper and took the mother of Jesus into his Jerusalem home." *The Testimony of the Beloved Disciple*, 15.

50. For a critique of this widespread view, see a number of the chapters of Bauckham's *The Testimony of the Beloved Disciple*, including (among others) chapter 4: "Historiographical Characteristics of the Gospel of John" and chapter 8: "The Bethany Family in John 11–12: History or Fiction?" For the position that the Gospel of John was not composed by a single author (and indeed that chapter 11 came mainly from a later editor), see John Ashton, *Understanding the Fourth Gospel*, 2nd ed. (Oxford: Oxford University Press, 2007). For Ashton, by explicit contrast to Bauckham and others (including Hengel, Craig Keener, and Richard Burridge), the Gospel of John's genre is not that of Greco-Roman biography. In Ashton's view, the "two major sections of the Gospel, first the acrimonious controversies between Jesus and 'the Jews' in chapters 5–10, and secondly the farewell discourse and prayer in chapters 14–17" do not pertain to Jesus' life, but rather "display the concerns of a much later period" and show the Gospel to have been written "for readers whose circumstances were radically different from those of the few followers Jesus had gathered in his own lifetime." Ibid., 27. For other perspectives, see Tom Thatcher, *Why John Wrote a Gospel: Jesus—Memory—History* (Louisville, Kentucky: Westminster/John Knox, 2006); Harold W. Attridge, "Genre Bending in the Fourth Gospel," in Harold W. Attridge, *Essays on John and Hebrews* (Grand Rapids, Michigan: Baker Academic, 2012), 61–78. Thatcher emphasizes that John's "community viewed the memory of Jesus as a work of the Holy Spirit," and so John sought to place limits (governed by his own Spirit-guided "remembering") on who can truly "claim to be a remembrancer, able to recall Jesus and guided by the Paraclete in her interpretations of that memory.... The Gospel of John was born out of a desire to portray Jesus as a figure from the past and to keep him locked in that past, to draw a bold line between Christian experience and the events of 'the beginning,' to suppress the living memory of Jesus and replace that memory with a fixed image of a person who lived and died decades earlier." *Why John Wrote a Gospel*, 146, 165.

pened. But remembering involves more than—though not less than—facts. Indeed, Christian remembering is always something done "in and with the community of disciples, in and with the Church."[51] Remembering Jesus is not merely an individual task, as though Jesus had not established a community grounded precisely in remembering Jesus. When the evangelist remembers Jesus, then, he also has in view the broader remembering that understands and interprets Jesus within the memory of the community, that is, the memory of Israel and its Scriptures. Jesus' words and deeds take on their full depth when one knows and remembers Israel's Scriptures, since they point toward him and he fulfills them. Furthermore, all that Jesus says and does is re-thought after the Resurrection, when the full meaning of his words and deeds (and of the Scriptures of Israel) becomes more apparent. At the time of the events, Jesus' disciples may not have understood, but in hindsight, after the Resurrection, they remembered the events in a manner that exposed the events' interior depths and rootedness in Israel's Scriptures. In other words, the memory of the events of Jesus' early life is shaped by later events (especially Jesus' Resurrection) and also by the Scriptures that God has prepared over the centuries to help interpret Jesus. Such remembering is not only individual, because the individual shares in the "we" of the community of the Lord and does so by the indwelling Holy Spirit.[52]

It is apparent that Ratzinger is here moving toward a rich dogmatic understanding of scriptural and ecclesial remembering. It does not depart from real historical facts, but neither is it simply reportage. It has a depth and density that penetrates to the interior of outward realities. Here Ratzinger draws upon two crucial biblical passages about remembering, one from the Gospel of John, and the other from Luke. In the Gospel of John, Jesus states, "When the Spirit of truth comes, he will guide you into all the truth; for he will not speak on his own authority, but whatever he hears he will speak, and he will declare to you the things that are to come" (Jn 16:13). The truth will both be a historical truth, and a truth that, in its divine depth, has an eschatological fulness. In the Gospel of Luke, the Virgin Mary exemplifies this kind of remembering (and thereby stands as an icon or embodiment of the Church): "Mary kept all these things, pondering them in her heart"

51. Ratzinger/Benedict, *Jesus of Nazareth*, 1:231.

52. For the view that the remembering falsified Jesus profoundly—by contrast to the viewpoints offered by Bauckham, Samuel Byrskog, James D. G. Dunn, Robert McIver, and others—see Bart D. Ehrman, *How Jesus Became God: The Exaltation of a Jewish Preacher from Galilee* (New York: HarperCollins, 2014).

(Lk 2:19; cf. 2:51). The implication is that while others see only the external events, Mary begins to perceive the interior divine depth and power of Jesus and of his words and deeds.

Ratzinger next adds sacramental theology to the mix. John's Gospel receives its narrative structure from the liturgical feasts of Israel. These liturgical feasts, he argues, set the stage for Jesus to unveil the Eucharist (John 6) and baptism (John 7). Jesus' prayer at the Last Supper (his Farewell Discourse), too, draws upon the Jewish feast of Passover to interpret Jesus' Cross as the sacrifice of the true Passover lamb, redeeming the whole human race by the saving power of his blood. The connection of the feasts to the historical events surrounding Jesus is not an imposition upon these events, Ratzinger insists. Rather, the Jewish feasts each have a threefold aspect: a link with creation and ancient nature religion; a historical dimension as a feast of remembrance; and a hope on the part of the Jewish people "for the coming saving deed that is still awaited."[53] In this way, Jewish remembering and the evangelist's remembering come together in the saving work of the divine Messiah.

The remainder of chapter 8 explores what Ratzinger calls the "principal Johannine images": water, vine and wine, bread, and shepherd. After a brief review of water in the ancient near East and the Old Testament, where it is connected both with life and with the danger of chaos and destruction, he focuses upon the Gospel of John, beginning with Jesus' conversation with Nicodemus about being born again of water and the Spirit (Jn 3:5). He insists that baptism requires appreciating the centrality of Christ's Cross: we are not simply baptized into the incarnate One, but into the Savior. He also cites 1 John 5:6–8 to confirm that in addition to water and the blood of Christ, the Holy Spirit must also be present. He notes that according to the biblical scholar Rudolf Schnackenburg, the emphasis on the Spirit here (in 1 John) is related to the Spirit-guided Church of John 15:26 and 16:13.[54]

In Ratzinger's presentation of Jesus' words at the Feast of Tabernacles, it is not primarily to biblical scholars but to the Church Fathers that he appeals. He remarks that according to Origen, Jerome, and Augustine, when Jesus quotes Isaiah in John 7:38, Jesus means to say that living water (the Holy Spirit) will indwell the body of the believer and serve as a life-giving

53. Ratzinger/Benedict, *Jesus of Nazareth*, 1:238.

54. See Schnackenburg's multi-volume commentary, published in English as *The Gospel according to St John*, translated by K. Smyth (New York: Crossroad, 1968–82).

power leading to eternal life. By contrast, according to Justin, Irenaeus, Cyprian, Ephrem and others, Jesus is referring to his own body from which will come forth the life-giving Holy Spirit. Ratzinger observes that most modern interpreters follow the first interpretation on linguistic grounds, but, along with Schnackenburg, he deems the second interpretation to be more adequate in content. This is because, for the Gospel of John (cf. Jn 2:21), Jesus is the new Temple promised in Ezekiel 47:1 and in Zechariah 13:1 and 14:8. The connection between baptism, the Holy Spirit, and the Cross is suggested also by John 19:34, when the spear pierces Jesus' side and blood and water flow out—expressing the new creation through baptism and the Eucharist in the eschatological Temple, the body of Christ.[55]

Turning to the image of vine and wine in the Gospel of John, Ratzinger focuses upon the wedding feast at Cana, where Jesus reveals himself to be the bridegroom inaugurating the eschatological marriage of God and his people. Jesus connects his actions at Cana with his coming "hour" (Jn 2:4), namely, his Cross. Ratzinger remarks, "When at this juncture Jesus speaks to Mary of his hour, he is connecting the present moment with the mystery of the Cross interpreted as his glorification."[56] The inauguration of the marriage of God and humanity takes place in one sense at the Incarnation, but in a fundamental way at the Cross.[57] Ratzinger also links Jesus' "hour" and the eschatological marriage with the Eucharist, which is a sharing in the Cross and a celebration of "the marriage feast with us here and now."[58]

Ratzinger discusses the image of the vine (and vineyard), with particular attention to John 15. He argues that Jesus becomes the vine (Israel) through the Incarnation, and Jesus is a vine that bears fruit through pruning. As is his wont, Ratzinger connects this also to the Eucharist. Jesus' spilling of his

55. For further discussion, see Paul M. Hoskins, *Jesus as the Fulfillment of the Temple in the Gospel of John* (Eugene, Oregon: Wipf and Stock, 2007).

56. Ratzinger/Benedict, *Jesus of Nazareth*, 1:251.

57. See ibid., 252. See also Jens Schröter, *From Jesus to the New Testament: Early Christian Theology and the Origin of the New Testament Canon*, translated by Wayne Coppins (Waco, Texas: Baylor University Press, 2013), 65–66: "arrest, mocking, and crucifixion only appear to be an abasement of Jesus, whereas 'in truth' they are part of his exaltation and his divine origin. According to John, God does not act in such a way that he reverses the standards of wisdom and foolishness through the resurrection of the Crucified One. Rather, behind the events around Jesus there is a meaning that does not lie on the surface, which is only disclosed to the one who has learned to see Jesus as the revealer of God. Within the New Testament the Gospel of John can therefore be seen as the most considered attempt to think together the divinity of Jesus with his true incarnation."

58. Ratzinger/Benedict, *Jesus of Nazareth*, 1:252.

blood in love is the fruit or "wine" that comes forth from the Cross, inaugurating the marriage of God and his people; and we share in this through the Eucharist.

In treating the image of "bread," Ratzinger observes that the bread of life, for Proverbs 9:5, is the wisdom of the Torah.[59] But although Moses gave the Torah, he did not see God directly; rather he only saw God's back (Exod 33). Thus the true bread of life is Christ, who enables us to see God directly, because he is the divine Word incarnate. But the Incarnation by itself does not suffice, important though it is. Ratzinger explains that "a further step is still needed beyond even the Incarnation of the Word. Jesus names this step in the concluding words of his discourse: His flesh is life 'for' the world (Jn 6:51). Beyond the act of the Incarnation, this points to its intrinsic goal and ultimate realization: Jesus' act of giving himself up to death and the mystery of the Cross."[60] Here, Ratzinger reaches the conclusion pressed home by Garrigou-Lagrange. Describing the transition from the bread of life discourse to Jesus' words about eating his flesh and drinking his blood, Ratzinger notes that the point is not simply the Eucharist but also participation in Christ's Cross. He affirms, "the theology of the Incarnation and the theology of the Cross come together; the two cannot be separated."[61] Some scholars try to separate the two by arguing that John focuses on the Incarnation while the Synoptics and Paul focus on the Cross, but, as Ratzinger shows, this is a false opposition.

The final image that Ratzinger treats from the Gospel of John is that of shepherd. Applied to Jesus, the image signals his kingship: a point that is strengthened by the fact that, in the prophets and Psalms, God appears as Israel's royal Shepherd. On the journey to the Mount of Olives after the Last Supper, according to Matthew 26:31, Jesus tells his disciples that the prophecy of Zechariah about the slain shepherd is about to be fulfilled. In the Gospel of John, it becomes clear that the slain Shepherd and the slain Passover Lamb are one and the same. The incarnate God, the royal Shepherd of Israel, is the one who goes to the Cross. In dying on the Cross, he is also the one who gives life: "I [Jesus] came that they may have life, and have it abundantly. I am the good shepherd. The good shepherd lays down his life

59. Ratzinger is indebted to C. K. Barrett, *The Gospel according to John: An Introduction with Commentary and Notes on the Greek Text*, 2nd ed. (London: SPCK, 1978).

60. Ratzinger/Benedict, *Jesus of Nazareth*, 1:268–69.

61. Ibid., 269.

for the sheep" (Jn 10:10–11). The union of Incarnation and Cross involves bringing people into eternal life as adopted sons and daughters in the Son.

Drawing upon the insights of C. K. Barrett, Ratzinger notes that for Philo, "God, the true Shepherd of his people, had appointed his 'firstborn Son,' the Logos, to the office of Shepherd."[62] Philo here combines personified wisdom (Proverbs and the Wisdom of Solomon) with the prophets' depiction of God as Israel's Shepherd. God gives Israel true wisdom, and this wisdom, present in the wise among the people, leads the people. John's Gospel offers a more radical take on these themes. As the Logos incarnate, Jesus is truly God, and he leads the people to share in his own life by his self-sacrificial love. The link between divine Incarnation and the Cross is revealed to be not simply the divine wisdom, but, even more, divine self-giving love. Thus, as Ratzinger says, John goes beyond Philo not least insofar as "[t]he Cross is at the center of the shepherd discourse."[63]

Ratzinger makes a further important point. The Shepherd knows his sheep, but humans are not God's possessions. God does not order them around like puppets or servants. God relates to them as rational creatures, which means that God does not know them in order to use them. As their Shepherd, God knows them as creatures whom he loves and wishes to serve; God wills good to his flock. The knowledge involved here is not a mastery but a wondrous *communion*. In a nutshell, truth and love are intimately bound. Ratzinger concludes, "Just as Logos and Incarnation, Logos and Passion belong together, so too knowing and self-giving are ultimately one."[64]

He brings his chapter to an end by quoting Clement of Alexandria on the gift of following, and being led by, the Shepherd who is the crucified incarnate Lord. In light of Clement's words, Ratzinger urges us to ponder the unity of the Incarnation and Cross of the Shepherd who comes to carry home his wayward people: "In his Incarnation and Cross he brings home the stray sheep, humanity; he brings me home, too. The incarnate Logos is the true 'sheep-bearer'—the Shepherd who follows after us through the thorns and deserts of our life. Carried on his shoulders, we come home. He gave his life for us. He himself is life."[65]

62. Ibid., 279.
63. Ibid., 280.
64. Ibid., 282.
65. Ibid., 286.

III. Conclusion

My purpose has been to show that neo-scholastic theology and the *nouvelle théologie*—or Thomism and Ressourcement—are complementary theological modes that, at their best, can be joined together in expositing and defending the truth of dogma. Let me return here, however, to voices that insist upon the opposite.

The Methodist theologian D. Stephen Long contrasts "manualist Thomism" negatively with the "more biblical, patristic, and Catholic theology" that he thinks the *nouvelle théologie* (aided by Karl Barth) retrieved.[66] Long warns against those Catholic scholars who favor "a stricter observance of Aristotelian Thomism, now often called 'Thomist Ressourcement.'"[67] He bemoans the influence of Thomas Joseph White, O.P., who, says Long, "calls for theologians to retrieve much of what twentieth century Catholic theology left behind: Reginald Garrigou-Lagrange's neoscholastic theology, which was the kind of theology responsible for the modernist oath."[68] In a nutshell, Long deems the work of scholars whom he terms "Ressourcement Thomists"[69]—including White, Reinhard Hütter, and Steven A. Long—to be unfortunate, since their understanding of the *analogia entis* will encourage the full-scale retrieval of Garrigou-Lagrange and manualist Thomism.

D. Stephen Long of course is not alone. His book is about von Balthasar, and Michele Schumacher well summarizes von Balthasar's perspective when she writes: "It is precisely this Marian attitude [of receptive contemplation] that Balthasar found lacking in neo-scholastic theology, which … he perceived as failing to engage not only the experience of the contemporary world, but also and especially the lived encounter with the Word of God: an encounter requiring a true surrender of the self to the one (God) who is ever the first to surrender, or give, Himself."[70] For those who know von Balthasar's theology, know that for him there could hardly be a more damning assessment: he is suggesting that the neo-scholastics missed

66. D. Stephen Long, *Saving Karl Barth: Hans Urs von Balthasar's Preoccupation* (Minneapolis, Minnesota: Fortress, 2014), 154.

67. Ibid., 90.

68. Ibid., 91.

69. Ibid., 167. All the "Ressourcement Thomists" that he mentions are longtime friends and collaborators of mine.

70. Michele M. Schumacher, *A Trinitarian Anthropology: Adrienne von Speyr and Hans Urs von Balthasar in Dialogue with Thomas Aquinas* (Washington, D.C.: The Catholic University of America Press, 2014), 77. Michele Schumacher is a valued friend and collaborator of mine.

the very core of the faith, namely, receptive and contemplative surrender to the self-surrendering Trinity. Schumacher goes on to warn against a present-day "return to the neo-scholasticism of Balthasar's day," suggesting that neo-scholasticism "was perhaps motivated more by intellectual curiosity than by a reverent love of God and the obedience that it entails."[71]

Schumacher and White are my friends, as are the other living scholars named above. It will already be clear that my view is that these schools of thought are not incompatible. Garrigou-Lagrange and Ratzinger, proceeding in entirely different ways, both offer valuable theological arguments regarding the relationship of the Incarnation and the Cross.

Ratzinger's primary concern is dogmatic, but he addresses his topic by means of historical discussion—in this case, of the Gospel of John. In response to the challenges posed by historical-critical scholarship to the foundations of Catholic dogmatic faith, he returns to Scripture in critical dialogue with German-speaking biblical scholars, with whose work he is well familiar. In the chapter from *Jesus of Nazareth* that I examined, his purpose is to show the unity of Incarnation and Cross, and to set forth the ramifications of this unity. He advances a rich and fruitful *nouvelle-théologie* dogmatic project along biblical and patristic lines that reflect what one often finds in books by other representatives of the *nouvelle théologie*.

Garrigou-Lagrange's concern is primarily the refinement and clarification of dogma through instruments that require philosophical precision. He respects his Scotist opponents, even while he differs strongly from them. He draws upon Cajetan while also being critical of Cajetan, holding that later Thomists (such as the Salmanticenses, whose perspective here has been shaped not only by Aquinas but also by Scotus) were more insightful in certain respects.[72] He faces difficult mysteries such as the divine permission of evil, the biblical testimony to God's predestining will, divine simplicity and divine (non-discursive) knowledge, and so on. All of these mysteries have biblical and patristic grounding. Garrigou-Lagrange does not offer responses to these mysteries that can rightly be termed "rationalistic." Yet his method of seeking to understand arguments by identifying their syllogistic structure, his view of theology as a science capable often of demonstrative truth, his understanding of divine action vis-à-vis creatures in light of the four causes, and other Aristotelian patterns in his thought, can provoke frustration for non-Thomists.

71. Ibid., 381–82.

72. See Dylan Schrader, *A Thomistic Christocentrism: Recovering the Carmelites of Salamanca on the Logic of the Incarnation* (Washington, DC: The Catholic University of America Press, 2021).

One may disagree with particular points made by Garrigou-Lagrange or Aquinas; and many neo-scholastics (and Scotists) did firmly disagree. Neo-scholastic theology was never monolithic. Today, some theologians, of a more metaphysical or philosophical bent, will draw great riches out of reading the neo-scholastics but will tire quickly in the dense historical thickets of modern biblical scholarship. Other theologians will find the neo-scholastics off-putting but will delight in the historically nuanced and creedally delimited engagements with biblical scholarship that one finds in the *nouvelle théologie*. Not all Catholic theologians need to follow the same path. There are diverse ways to contribute to *sacra doctrina* of the kind that Aquinas modelled.

During the first modernist crisis in the early 1900s, great predecessors of the *nouvelle théologie*, including the Dominican biblical scholar Marie-Joseph Lagrange and the Jesuit theologian Léonce de Grandmaison, wrote stellar critiques of theological liberalism.[73] Many neo-scholastic thinkers did the same. Balthasar offers a trenchant critique of theological liberalism: "For modernism, dogmas are but crystallised forms of the existential faith-relationship to God, forms of vital religious intuitions and needs, valid as long as they foster the existential reality, but harmful once the life has gone out of them and they have stiffened into dead formulae."[74] Balthasar, de Lubac, and Ratzinger each attacked the liberal Catholicism ("liberal" in the classical theological sense of Schleiermacher, Albrecht Ritschl, and Ernst Troeltsch) that they saw emerging in Karl Rahner and Edward Schillebeeckx.

Today, we can benefit from both neo-scholastic theology and the *nouvelle théologie*. We can do so while still disagreeing with particular positions taken by representatives of one or the other approach. It is not a matter of "all or nothing." Fruitfully, we can combine elements from the two approaches in contemplating and defending faith in Jesus Christ. As I see it, this is the constructive project of Ressourcement Thomism, which can embrace within its bounds not only those who combine the two approaches, but also those who solely develop "Ressourcement" lines of inquiry or solely develop "Thomist" lines of inquiry.

73. See *Defending the Faith: An Anti-Modernist Anthology*, ed. William H. Marshner (Washington, D.C.: The Catholic University of America Press, 2017).

74. Hans Urs von Balthasar, *Seeing the Form*, vol. 1 of *The Glory of the Lord*, translated by Erasmo Leiva-Merikakis, edited by Joseph Fessio, SJ and John Riches (San Francisco: Ignatius Press, 1982), 177.

V

AS IF GOD POURED THEE

Is There a "True" Thomism?

DENIS A. SCRANDIS

Is Maritain's Metaphysics Authentically Thomistic?

I. Introduction

SOME CRITICS HAVE ALLEGED THAT Jacques Maritain was not a Thomist or was at best a flawed one. Others have even called him a rationalist. They have pointed to his use of suspect commentators or to his recourse to intuition as evidence of a compromised commitment. Yet, little or no credible analysis supports these claims and the question thus remains: Is Maritain's thought Thomistic? One wonders what measure could confirm or deny its authenticity? Well, here is a proposal. Since metaphysics is acknowledged to be at the center of Aristotelian-Thomistic philosophy, if the central principles of Aquinas's metaphysics are found to be also those of Maritain's metaphysics,[1] then Maritain's metaphysics will be found to be authentically Thomistic. Our standard is St. Thomas Aquinas's doctrine of distinctions as it appears in his commentary[2] on the *De Trinitate* of Boethius.

1. Maritain developed his metaphysics during the 1930s and 1940s. It appears principally in the three works cited here. Jacques Maritain, *Distinguish to Unite, or the Degrees of Knowledge*, 4th edition, translated by Gerald B. Phelan (South Bend, Indiana: University of Notre Dame Press, 1995); Jacques Maritain, *A Preface to Metaphysics, Seven Lectures on Being* (New York: Mentor Omega, 1962); Jacques Maritain, *Existence and the Existent*, translated by Lewis Galantière and Gerald B. Phelan (Garden City, New York: Image Books, 1947).

2. St. Thomas Aquinas, *The Division and Methods of the Sciences, Questions V and VI of his Commentary on De Trinitate of Boethius*, 4th revised edition, translated with Introduction and Notes by Armand Mauer (Toronto: Pontifical Institute of Medieval Studies, 1986).

II. Maritain, Before Thomas Aquinas

To understand the mature Jacques Maritain, it helps to know where he came from because his philosophical origins and culture presented challenges to be overcome. Jacques Maritain studied modern philosophy (not the thought of St. Thomas Aquinas) in the course of his formal education.[3] In fact, his preparation in Thomism only began years after graduation. He was in a sense self-taught although his circle of friends came to include some of the leading Thomists of the day. Maritain (the son of a prominent, secularized French Protestant family) and Raïssa Oumansoff (the daughter of an immigrant Russian Orthodox Jewish family) met as fellow students at the Sorbonne in 1901 beginning a collaboration that would run for almost 60 years.[4] The relativism of the scientists and the skepticism of the philosophers disillusioned them. However, the lectures of Henri Bergson in 1903 raised in them the possibility of attaining truth. Married in 1904, they came to embrace the spirit of the Gospels in the home of Leon Bloy and were baptized into the Roman Catholic faith in 1905 with Bloy as their godfather. At this point, Jacques and Raïssa had a religious way of life (unlike most elite moderns) but were intellectuals lacking a complementary philosophy.

1. Maritain's Interest in, and Disillusionment with, Bergsonism. Writing in the preface to the second edition of *Bergsonian Philosophy and Thomism*[5] in 1930, Jacques Maritain recalled a point at which he had turned from championing Bergsonism to rejecting it. It was in 1908, Maritain tells us, that he was troubled by the irreconcilability of Bergson's critique of knowledge with the formulas of revealed Christian faith.

Maritain faulted Bergsonism for "accepting the premises" of modern epistemology, such as Descartes' notion of an idea as a "mental picture interposed between the real and the mind" and Kant's notion of "the concept as an empty form."[6] He wrote: "As far as I was concerned it was upon the indestructible verity of the objects of faith that philosophical reflection rested in its effort to restore the natural ordination of the intellect to being and

3. Maritain passed the *agrégation* in philosophy in 1905, which entitled him to teach modern philosophy in a state high school. However, he eschewed such employment.

4. For an introduction, chronology, and early bibliography, see Donald and Idella Gallagher, *The Achievement of Jacques and Raïssa Maritain, A Bibliography 1906–1961* (Garden City, New York: Doubleday, 1962).

5. Jacques Maritain, *Bergsonian Philosophy and Thomism,* translated by Mabelle L. Andison and J. Gordon Andison (New York: Philosophical Library, 1955).

6. Ibid., 23.

to recognize the ontological genuineness of the work of reason."[7] Maritain required a philosophy that treated the creedal articles of faith and their certainty respectfully, that replaced rationalism's reflection on innate ideas with the intellect's natural ordination to being, and that articulated and defended the metaphysical truths that reason could discover. Certain criteria of Maritain's program (i.e., the defense of faith and reason) were starting to appear.

Did Maritain arrive at this juncture on his own or with the aid of St. Thomas Aquinas? Maritain recalled: "Nor was I at that moment familiar with the works of St. Thomas.... In thus completely accepting, without quibble or reserve, the authentic reality value of our instruments of cognition [i.e., the reality value of our senses, imagination, and intellect,] I was already a Thomist without being aware of it. When a few months later I came upon the *Summa theologica* its luminous flood was to find no opposing obstacles in me."[8]

2. *Bergsonian Intuition of Duration*. Bergsonian metaphysics begins with a psychological foundation, i.e., it begins with one's perception of oneself enduring through time. Maritain wrote: "This reality which the philosopher, by an exceptional tension of his will and his consciousness, succeeds in knowing on the fringes of the unconscious, with a knowledge impossible to fix indeed, a fading knowledge, Bergson calls *duration* or concrete time. I perceive myself enduring, I am, I am duration, that is the beginning of philosophy."[9] Duration or time constitutes the very stuff of our self and is the substance of all things. "Time, the flow of becoming, is reality itself."[10]

Intuition is the operation by which we grasp ourselves in becoming and through which we transport ourselves within the essence of things and assimilate to their most intimate reality, i.e., this intuition attains the "absolute."[11]

Bergson positioned his notion of intuition in opposition to reason: the domain of science, skepticism, and modern philosophy. Bergsonian intuition on the other hand is an experiential knowledge of singulars, viz., a form of sympathy with the presumptive real.[12]

3. *Maritain's Intuition vs. Bergsonian Intuition*. Bergsonian intuition and Maritainian intuition both involve perception of an object. Bergson per-

7. Ibid., 17.
8. Ibid.
9. Ibid., 67.
10. Ibid., 67–68.
11. Ibid., 68.
12. See ibid., 147–48.

ceives a subjective object, while Maritain perceives an objective object. Bergson's intuition involves consciousness turning back on itself and seeing its duration, while Maritain's intuition employs the intellect's illuminative power to render intelligible the architecture of real being.

Bergson's criticisms stretched Maritain beyond the restrictions of orthodox rationalism, scientism, and skepticism. Maritain may have received Bergson's doctrines as a mixture of insight and mischaracterization. In response, Maritain developed a foundational philosophy capable of serving faith and reason.

III. Aquinas and Maritain on the Division of Speculative Science

For St. Thomas, a speculative science is not just a body of true statements, definitions, principles, and so forth. It is also a comprehending intellectual grasp of the world that employs one of a range of conceptualizing habits of thought, each of which responds to the typical intelligibility unique to a science, and that facilitates the conception of ideas or objects of that science. These scientific objects may be employed as the subjects and predicates of scientific truths. Each scientific-type of intelligibility is uniquely defined, exists potentially in sensible beings, and thus provides knowledge of the world.

In *The Division and Methods of the Sciences*, Thomas explained why some thoughts or "intellectual objects" are properly objects of a speculative science while others are not. Ideas of sense and imagination are changeable since they can be or not be either in a certain respect (as when they change size or color) or absolutely (as when they cease to exist). They are changeable and thus uncertain because they contain a principle of change or potency called individual sensible matter. Ideas are rendered necessary when they are intellectually abstracted or released from individual sensible matter and thus from change and uncertainty. The objects of speculative science are divided into three kinds, and speculative science is accordingly and appropriately divided into three parts or domains, one for each kind of speculative object: natural science, mathematics, and divine science or metaphysics.[13]

Maritain shared with Aquinas the fundamental divisions of philosophical sciences into speculative and practical as well as the division of specu-

13. See Aquinas, *The Division and Methods of the Sciences*, q. 5, a. 1.

lative science into physics, mathematics, and metaphysics. Recognizing the vast development of natural science since the thirteenth century, Maritain added the spectrum of the modern physical sciences.[14]

1. *Aquinas and Maritain on the Objects of Natural Science.* For Thomas, the objects of natural science "are ... objects of speculation that ... depend on matter both for their being and for their being understood as do those things whose definition contains sensible matter and which, as a consequence, cannot be understood without sensible matter."[15] Natural science, on the one hand, is concerned with changeable, singular natural beings, such as cats and dogs but, on the other hand, scientifically studies them as necessary, universal natures, *felis domesticus* and *canis familiaris*, respectively. Now, individual or determined matter is the principle of materiality that makes a nature be an individual, changeable nature while common indeterminate matter is the principle of materiality that is in the definition of a universal, necessary nature, i.e., of a scientific object. For example, the nature *man* understood (a necessary object of natural science) is the nature considered with indeterminate matter, which matter is represented by the expression "flesh and bones," while the nature *man* in Socrates is defined with determinate matter or with "this flesh and these bones."[16]

Aquinas and Maritain both define objects of natural science as objects that exist in things with individual matter and that are conceived in thought with common matter.[17]

2. *Aquinas and Maritain on the Objects of Mathematics.* For Thomas, the objects of mathematics "are some things that, although dependent upon matter for their being in things, do not depend upon it for their being understood, because sensible matter is not included in their definitions."[18] Mathematical forms exist in sensible material things. For example, a snub nose is a short turned-up nose. The conspicuous mathematical feature here, i.e., "an abrupt upward turn," exists in matter since it exists in a nose. However, when understood, this mathematical object is defined without sensible matter and is the mathematical object "curved," which is conceived without reference to a material subject, namely without reference to a nose or an archer's bow.

14. See Maritain, *The Degrees of Knowledge*, 34–37.

15. Aquinas, *The Division and Methods of the Sciences*, q. 5, a. 1.

16. Aquinas, *The Division and Methods of the Sciences*, q. 5, a. 1; q. 5, a. 2.

17. See Maritain, *The Degrees of Knowledge*, 37–38.

18. Aquinas, *The Division and Methods of the Sciences*, q. 5, a. 1; q. 5, a. 3.

Thomas wisely informs us that Aristotle's doctrine of the categories sheds light on how mathematical objects are both material when they exist in material things and immaterial after they have been abstracted from material being.[19] Recall that accidents befall substance in a definite order: qualities (that is, the sensible qualities of sensible matter) depend upon quantity (the color red belongs to, or depends on, the apple's surface), while quantitative characteristics depend upon substance (the shape belongs to the apple), which is also called "intelligible matter." An accidental form contains in its definition its sustaining reality, which is (ultimately) its underlying substance. A quantitative form, when understood, contains in its definition its sustaining reality, i.e., contains intelligible matter, and is thus immaterial. Aquinas and Maritain agree that mathematical objects do not include sensible matter in their definitions.[20]

3. *Aquinas and Maritain on the Objects of Metaphysics.* Thomas[21] identifies two divine sciences or theologies that deal with beings that are immaterial and unchanging or, as he expresses it, that exist separately from matter and motion. One science is scripture-based and studies divine things as its subject matter, while the other is philosophical and studies divine things, not as its subject but, as principles of its subject. These divine objects[22] are separate from matter and motion in two distinct ways. Firstly, God and the angels are by nature or definition without matter and motion. Secondly, substance, act, potency, and the like are separate from matter and motion since their definitions do not depend on matter although they are sometimes found in matter and motion.

In *The Degrees of Knowledge,* Maritain agrees with Aquinas that metaphysical objects "not only can be conceived without matter, but can exist without it, whether they never exist in matter, as is the case of God and pure

19. See Aquinas, *The Division and Methods of the Sciences,* q. 5, a. 3.

20. See Maritain, *The Degrees of Knowledge,* 38.

21. See Aquinas, *The Division and Methods of the Sciences,* q. 5, a. 1; q. 5, a. 4.

22. Thomas's discussion of metaphysics brings together discussions of "first philosophy," "divine science," "theology," and "metaphysics." The fact that the objects of these investigations share a common intelligibility and the fact that Thomas uses the names somewhat interchangeably is consistent with taking them together in a single metaphysical science. First philosophy gives first principles (such as the principle of identity) to other, less general sciences. The metaphysical part of divine science studies immaterial objects (substance, essence, act, etc.) since they are parts of the metaphysics subject-genus. Another part of philosophical divine science proves the existence of God and the angels as causes and principles of being (i.e., as causes of the subject-genus) even though they are not parts of the subject-genus. Aquinas, *The Division and Methods of the Sciences,* q. 5. a. 1; q. 5, a. 4.

spirits, or whether they exist in material as well as immaterial things, for example, substance, quality, act and potency, goodness, beauty, etc."[23]

4. *Aquinas's Three-fold Theory of Abstraction*. Thomas's theory of abstraction includes abstractive and judgmental intellectual operations.[24] The abstraction of a whole[25] or universal nature (*abstractio totius*) serves physics, in particular, and all speculative sciences, in general. The abstraction of a quantitative form (*abstractio formae*) serves mathematics. And judgments of composition and division, especially judgments of separation (*separatio*), serve divine science and metaphysics.

Thomas shows how the intellect apprehends metaphysical objects. The intellect joins and divides objects while forming affirmative and negative statements, respectively. The intellectual operation bears upon the subject thing's act of being or *esse* (that results from the union of principles in a composite substance). An affirmative judgment can truthfully join what is joined in reality because the affirmation would truthfully signify a union in reality. And a negative judgment can truthfully separate what is separate in reality because the denial would truthfully signify a separation in reality. The negation "substantial being does not have to have quantitative properties" separates substance from quantity since substance does not depend on quantity (quantity rather depends on substance). Consequently, this negation considers substance without regard to quantitative properties and sensible matter, and substance stripped of quantity and matter is an object of metaphysics. John F. Wippel thinks that this judgmental grasp of substance is the starting point of Thomas's metaphysics. He wrote that the negative judgment's separation of substance from quantity "enables one to grasp [being] universally and *as* being," and that in this way "one discovers the subject of metaphysics."[26] Yet, substance is a part of being as being and is

23. See Maritain, *The Degrees of Knowledge*, 39.

24. See Aquinas, *The Division and Methods of the Sciences*, q. 5, a. 3.

25. The abstraction of a whole grasps a complete nature or whole in its essential character (say, taking man as a rational animal consisting of a rational soul and the body composed of the four elements in a proper mixture) in independence of all parts that do not belong to the species because they are accidental parts (say, leaving aside the individual's hand or foot). This abstraction is also described as the abstraction of a "whole from a part" because the abstracted object is a "whole nature" and the source-individual is understood in scholastic parlance to be a "part of the species." Aquinas, *The Division and Methods of the Sciences*, q. 5, a. 3.

26. John F. Wippel, "Aquinas on *separatio* and Our Discovery of Being as Being," in *The Discovery of Being and Thomas Aquinas, Philosophical and Theological Perspectives*, edited by Christopher M. Cullen, SJ, and Franklin T. Harkins (Washington, D.C.: The Catholic University of American Press, 2019), 32.

not the entirety of being as being, which includes act and potency, quality, *ens,* and *esse* as well as substance. Grasping substance is not grasping being as being.

5. *Maritain's Three Degrees of Abstraction.* Maritain's theory of the "three degrees of abstraction" as stated in *The Degrees of Knowledge*[27] differs from Aquinas's theory. Maritain's theory has two key factors. It is founded on the Aristotelian-Thomistic theories of categories and objects, which defined speculative objects ultimately in terms of the ontological architecture of the source realities. However, Maritain imported a problematic theory of abstraction that portrays the intellectual operations that abstract the objects from phantasms as variations (measured in degrees) of a common form of abstraction.[28] (Recall that Thomas's theory involves different kinds—not degrees—of abstraction and judgment, which also is abstractive.)

How does Maritain's theory characterize scientific objects? The first degree of abstraction considers "bodies in their mobile sensible reality" and populates a domain of objects called *physica* (literally, physical things). The second degree considers "quantity as such" or the domain *mathematica.* The third degree of abstraction considers objects "purified of all matter," which is *metaphysica* or being as being. And Maritain attributed the intelligibility of specific objects "in the final analysis" to "the mode of defining,"[29] which suggests that different scientific intelligibilities rest for Maritain upon different object-definitions.

How does Maritain's theory characterize scientific abstractions? Maritain cited Thomistic commentators and their theory of abstraction. "We should note here with Cajetan and John of St. Thomas that these three degrees of abstraction refer to the abstraction called *abstractio formalis.*"[30] There is one kind of abstraction and it has three levels of intensity. Moreover, "The speculative sciences differ from one another according to the degrees of this *abstractio formalis.*"[31] Each speculative science (or intelligibility) is distinguished by the level or degree of the common abstractive operation, which attributes scientific intelligibilities to psychological operations. The problem is perhaps more serious than that of a simple departure from the teachings of the founder of a school or tradition. While Thomas had taught that objects

27. See Maritain, *The Degrees of Knowledge,* 37–50.
28. See ibid., 39–40.
29. Ibid., 38.
30. Ibid., 39.
31. Ibid., 40.

provide content (a realist position), Cajetan may have taught that psychological operations determine content (a subjectivist position).

Gerald McCool, SJ, (who favors subjectivist neo-Thomists and is not sympathetic to Maritain's realism) criticized Maritain's reliance on Cajetan's degrees of abstraction without praising Maritain's faithfulness to the Aristotelian-Thomistic doctrines of categories and objects:

> Cajetan's three degrees of abstraction provide the epistemological justification for Maritain's three ascending levels of speculative science. Unfortunately for Maritain, later historical research has established beyond doubt that Cajetan's account of the three degrees of abstraction does not correspond to St. Thomas's own teaching. A new edition of St. Thomas' *In Librum Boethii de Trinitate, Questiones quinta et sixta,* published in 1948, led to a major revision of the accepted understanding of St. Thomas' theory of abstraction.[32]

McCool is correct that later research showed Cajetan's departure from Aquinas, which Maritain denied in *Existence and the Existent.*[33] However, Fr. McCool does not acknowledge that the distinction of the speculative sciences for Maritain involved "in the final analysis ... the mode of defining" not just their modes of acquisition.

IV. Maritain's Foundation of Metaphysics: The Intuition of Being

How does Maritain's metaphysician acquire being as being? We have seen that abstraction and judgment can attain metaphysical objects (such as substance, act, potency, etc.), yet, neither abstraction nor judgment attains the distinctive object of the metaphysician, namely, the object known variously as *ens in quantum ens* (being inasmuch as being) or *ens qua ens* (being as being). This object, unlike the essence *cat* or *dog,* has a content that is not limited to a single nature or singular analogate and is thus neither univocal nor equivocal but includes what Maritain describes as an infinity of analogates.[34] Being as being includes perhaps all created beings, all causes, all first principles, and all transcendentals.

32. Gerald A. McCool, SJ, *From Unity to Pluralism, The Internal Evolution of Thomism* (New York: Fordham University Press, 1992), 155–56.

33. Maritain, *Existence and the Existent,* chapter 1, "Being," especially n. 14, which runs from pp. 37–40.

34. See ibid., 29.

According to Maritain, the metaphysician's distinctive cognitive operation is the intellectual intuition of being:

> [There is a] higher intuition [in which] the intellect disengages being from knowledge of the sensible in which it is immersed, in order to make it the object or rather the subject of metaphysics; when, in a word, it conceptualizes the metaphysical intuition of being (seen now in the light of all the values proper to it, in its typical and primordial intelligible density), what the intellect releases into that same light is, here again, first and foremost, the act of existing.[35]

The object of metaphysics described in this quotation is the act of existing seen "in the typical and primordial intelligible density," that is, the act of existing seen as existing or able to exist without matter and seen "in the light of all the values proper to it," that is, seen in regard to the transcendentals (*bonum*, *res*, etc.) and first principles of being (*essentia*, *esse*, as well as the principles of identity, sufficient reason, and finality). When the metaphysician judges with regard, say, to his dog that "being is not necessarily material," his or her consciousness contains not only dog-being (*ens*), dog-essence (*essentia*) and dog-existence (*esse*) but also being as being, the principle of identity, etc. The foundation of metaphysics seems to be an immaterial and analogous object that is seen and conceived by the operation of an intellectual virtue in an act of judgment upon the act of existing of any, if not every, sensible being.

Another issue for Maritain was to account for the possibility and formation of concepts of being and existence. Being and existence are neither natures nor accidents and are not abstracted from sensible images in the ways in which physical and mathematical objects are abstracted. Now, simple apprehension conceives concepts, while judgment "lives" or "performs" acts of sensible existence. Simple apprehension does not abstract existence from a sensible species by illuminating a sensible species, but the intellect nevertheless forms valid concepts of being and existence. How does the intellect form a valid concept of existence?

> In judgmentally affirming the act of existence (say in affirming "the canary exists"), the intellect takes hold from the sensible species, not of an idea of existence but, of the very act of existing in order to perform or live that act of existing itself, which—as was observed before—is a super-intelligible object. It is at this point, that is, while the intellect judgmentally operates on its super-intelligible object, that the intellect

35. Ibid., 35.

in-act is itself intelligible in-act. Coincident with the intelligibility of the immaterial intellect, the intellect's operation and its operation's object (that contains existence) are also intelligible and thus available for apprehension and conceptualization. Simple apprehension can form at this moment and in this way a concept of existence and a concept of being.[36]

The being and existence of realities, as Thomas taught, are defined immaterially and understood immaterially whether they exist in immaterial subjects or material subjects. Because being and existence are immaterial by definition (or by "nature"), Maritain would not teach that being and existence can be abstracted from phantasms in the manner of concepts defined with sensible matter like those of physics. The concepts of being and existence, including those derived from material images and beings, are immaterial objects.

V. Wippel's Alternative: The Discovery of Being

John F. Wippel has commented on the relation of Maritain's theory of abstraction to the text of Aquinas studied here. In "Maritain and Aquinas on Our Discovery of Being," he considers Maritain's *Existence and the Existent* specifically in its treatment of *The Division and Methods of the Sciences*, q. 5, a. 3. He expresses some praise for Maritain's reading of Thomas but emphatically rejects any suggestion that the Cajetan-John of St. Thomas-Maritain theory of abstraction exists in Thomas and that Maritain's intuition of being is Thomistic. Wippel also proposes his own theory of the "discovery of being," i.e., the discovery of being as being or the subject of metaphysics, which rests upon novel notions of metaphysical separation and objects.

Thomas's *The Division and Methods of the Sciences* came to Maritain's attention only after the manuscript of *Existence and the Existent* had been sent to the printer, and Maritain's published reflections were thus limited to a few footnotes. Maritain commented on Thomas's presentation of the apprehension of being as being in a negative judgment: "This doctrine shows indeed that what properly pertains to the metaphysical concept of being is that it results from an abstraction (or a separation from matter) which takes

36. Denis A. Scrandis, "The Existential Metaphysics of Maritain's *Existence and the Existent*," in *In Search of Harmony, Metaphysics, and Politics*, edited by James G. Hanink (Washington, D.C.: The American Maritain Association, distributed by The Catholic University of America Press, 2019), 95.

place [in the second operation of the intellect]."[37] Wippel approves of Maritain's recognition of Thomas's specific use of separation to account for the apprehension of the subject of metaphysics[38] but disapproves of using both "separation" and "abstraction" to characterize this operation, which ironically is something that Maritain and Aquinas both do.[39]

1. *The Discovery of Being as Being: Ens.* Wippel's discovery doctrine[40] proposes a two-tiered notion of immateriality. On the one hand, there are "positively immaterial" objects that are never present in matter (i.e., God and the angels) and, on the other hand, there are "negatively or neutrally immaterial" objects that may or may not be present in matter although they need not be in matter at all, such as being, substance, quality, act, and so forth.[41] This conception of being present difficulties.

Firstly, the classification involved here seems to place God and his immateriality into both categories, i.e., as being both positively and negatively immaterial. Secondly, discovery-theory seems to involve metaphysical objects that, since they derive from material being, either cannot fully escape taint from their prior involvement with matter and become completely matter-free, or are not free of limitation to the material source being (i.e., perhaps this theory's notion of being is not analogous) and cannot thus be properly applied to God, man, and the sensible beings from which they came.

If discovery's metaphysical objects were defined without matter of any sort, they could not be segregated into "positive" and "negative" subsets. The notions of *ens* and *esse* are derived from sensible, material *ens*, are not derivable from non-sensible spiritual beings, but are nevertheless applicable analogously to God, the angels, and material being.

2. *The Discovery of Being as Being: Separatio.* The discovery-theory also proposes a corresponding form of separation, which it calls negation, to operate on its notion of *ens*. Discovery employs an intellectual operation that disassembles a being by undoing the creative operation that created

37. Maritain, *Existence and the Existent*, 37–40, n. 14, pp. 37–40.

38. See Wippel, "Maritain and Aquinas on Our Discovery of Being," 432n49.

39. See Maritain, *Existence and the Existent*, 39n14 for Aquinas's use of "*abstrahere* with reference to the separation that takes place in judgment." See Wippel, "Maritain and Aquinas on Our Discovery of Being," 432–34 regarding the usage of *abstractio* and *separatio* and Maritain's compliance.

40. Wippel, "Maritain and Aquinas on Our Discovery of Being," 433.

41. See ibid., 432–33.

the being, and which intellectual operation coincidentally precipitates the discovery of *ens qua ens,* subject of metaphysics. Restated, an intellectual negation (or *separatio*) negates an entitative negation (that restricts *esse* to an *ens*) and discovers *ens qua ens.* Wippel writes:

> It is this negative or neutral characteristic of being [characteristic of limited *esse*] that is recognized and expressed by the negative judgment (*separatio*). Through this judgment one recognizes that that by reason of which something enjoys being [i.e., by reason of *esse*] need not be restricted to that by which it enjoys any particular or restricted kind of being, such as material being or quantified being or living being or dead being [i.e., that *esse* need not be restricted to any sort of *ens*]. And thus, by negating any such limitation or restriction of being, by negating any such negation, one may say, one discovers the notion of being as being, the subject matter of metaphysics.[42]

Wippel is correct that separation separates *esse* from limitation by and to an essence. Yet, this negation, a form of separation, has too many functions and meanings: it makes an *ens,* un-makes an *ens,* and discovers *ens qua ens.* Is this not equivocation? Self-contradiction?

VI. Thomistic Realism

In a brief response to a question about scientific objects and singular natures, Thomas expressed in outline the realism inherent in his philosophy:

> Science treats of something in two ways: in one way, primarily and principally; and in this sense science is concerned with universal natures, which are its very foundation. In another way it treats of something secondarily, as by a sort of reflection; and in this sense it is concerned with the things whose natures they are, inasmuch as, using the lower powers, it relates those natures to the particular things possessing them. For a knower uses a universal nature both as a thing known and as a means of knowing.[43]

The universal nature serves both as the subject matter to be investigated and also as a means by which intellectual reflection traces the object to its source. In this reflection, the intellect confirms the object's origin in real being.

Maritain articulated his doctrine of critical realism in *The Degrees of Knowledge.*[44] He said that critical realism is a necessary task of metaphysical

42. Ibid., 433–34.

43. Aquinas, *The Division and Methods of the Sciences,* q. 5, a. 2; q. 5, a. 2, ad 4.

44. See Maritain, *The Degrees of Knowledge,* 75–107.

wisdom and essentially Thomistic. Maritain's critical realism refutes rationalism while confirming truth in science, philosophy, and theology. Four aspects of critical realism are: 1. The common starting point to philosophy and critique, 2. Knowledge is a metaphysical order and a form of existence, 3. The thing-object distinction, and 4. The concept and formal sign.

1. *Critical Realism: The Common Starting Point of Philosophy and Critique.* Maritain's analysis of knowledge recognizes two "movements" of knowledge, each of which is characterized by a distinctive form of knowledge. The first movement is by nature and function capable of being the starting point of philosophy. The second performs critique. In the mind's first movement, we have direct knowledge of something (principally of sensible being and the principle of identity), and, in the mind's second movement, we have reflexive knowledge of the preceding direct cognition. Maritain believed that if this act of reflection upon an act of knowing is utilized as the basic locus for the critique of knowledge, then realism is confirmed and this critique will not be contaminated by idealism.[45]

2. *Critical Realism: Knowledge Is a Metaphysical Order and a Form of Existence.*

Knowledge constitutes a metaphysical order and is not just a psychological operation:

> Knowing is an active, immanent super existence whereby a subject not only exists within an existence limited to what that subject is as a thing enclosed within one genus-as a subject existing for itself-but with an unlimited existence in which by its own activity it is and becomes itself other things.[46]

Analysis yields facts that describe a relation and union that extends beyond the knower's cognitive faculties to a thing in the extramental world and that gives determination to the knower's intra-subjective becoming an extramental thing as the other.

3. *Critical Realism: The Thing-Object Distinction.* How is one to understand the fact that to know is to become and be the other as other and that there is a kind of union between the known and the knower? This relationship and union allow Maritain to take the known nature or essence and to distinguish the thing as thing (i.e., the thing existing or able to exist for itself) from the thing as object (the thing as understood or present to the in-

45. See ibid., 79–86.
46. Ibid., 120.

tellect). The thing as object is neither an accident of the soul nor a terminus for direct knowledge. The thing as object is a means by which the thing as thing is known. The thing as thing and the thing as object are one and the same thing. The thing-object relation allows us to "confirm" that the terminus of direct knowledge is the extramental thing and that our direct knowledge is thus of things in the world.[47]

4. *Critical Realism: The Concept and Formal Sign.* Maritain's metaphysical description of knowledge employs the notions of sign and concept in order to explain the metaphysical realism of knowledge. Does the concept root direct knowledge in the things of the world? A sign in general is something that facilitates discovery of something else not otherwise evident. Maritain distinguishes two kinds of sign. Smelling smoke prompts a search. In the expression, "where there's smoke, there's fire," smoke is a sign (technically an instrumental sign) for fire since smoke, being first known, leads to its source, fire. In contrast to the instrumental sign, the concept or mental word functions as a means whereby something other than itself is known. It is called a formal sign. It is a means to knowing a fire directly before it is itself a terminus of knowing the fire-object in reflection.[48]

Secondly Maritain distinguishes two features of the concept. As an accident or modification of the soul, the concept has an entitative function. The word concept is used to name this entity because it conveys the notions of fertilization and development typical of embryonic conception. The possible intellect, when "fertilized" by an impressed species, receives ontological determinations originating in sensible reality and performs an operation that brings into being the concept. This concept, which is an accident, contains the object, which is not an accident. The object has an intentional function. The object serves as a formal sign of a thing through which an object in the thing is grasped by the mind.[49] We know things directly and our ideas of things subsequently. Maritain's analysis of the concept roots direct knowledge in things and not in our ideas.

47. See ibid., 96–107.
48. See ibid., 135.
49. See ibid., 127–36.

VI. Summary of the Evidence

Bergson's criticisms stretched Maritain beyond the limits of the modern orthodoxies. Bergson's intuition did not satisfy Maritain but it fostered an introspective search of consciousness and its contents wherein being as being reigns. Maritain established a purpose for his personal philosophy, i.e., that it foster the advance of faith and reason, and not long after began to read Aquinas.

Aquinas and Maritain taught: (1) that the objects of each science are drawn from the world, are ontologically defined, and provide knowledge of the world; (2) that the objects of physics depend on matter both in their physical being and in their cognitive being; and (3) that the objects of mathematics, although dependent on matter for their being in things, are not dependent on matter in thought since their definitions in thought involve no sensible matter.

In regard to metaphysics, Aquinas and Maritain identify two divine sciences or theologies that study beings existing separately from matter and motion. Scripture-based theology studies divine things as its subject matter, while philosophical divine science studies divine things, not as its subject but as the principles and causes of its subject. God and the angels exist by nature or definition without matter and motion. Substance, potency, act, and the like exist separately from matter and motion since their definitions do not depend on matter, although they are sometimes found in matter and motion.

In the course of explaining how scientific objects are acquired, Aquinas identified specific scientific forms of abstraction and judgment. Maritain ambivalently accepted Aquinas's theory albeit in combination with Cajetan's three degrees of a single form of abstraction. Maritain acknowledged a difference in terminology but not in doctrine between Aquinas and Cajetan. This study finds a difference both in regard to vocabulary and doctrine. Maritain and Aquinas agree regarding objects and definitions but disagree regarding abstractive operations.

Although numerous metaphysical objects were identified and accounted for by Aquinas, no operation had been found to acquire being as being. Yet, this object was part of Maritain's intellectual life, and the doctrine of the intuition of being was its explanation. Maritain described the object and operation of intuiting being in a realist and Thomistic way, i.e., in terms of sensible being (its structure), sense, and intellect.

The alternative account of the discovery of the subject of metaphysics and its critique of Maritain offered an opportunity to re-examine Maritain's doctrine and to let it prove itself.

In our reading, Aquinas and Maritain both present philosophical realisms. Aquinas describes a specific reflection upon a cognitive act that confirms the object's origin in sensible being. Maritain's critical realism describes this reflection more rigorously in terms of the thing-object relation, the concept, and the formal sign.

VII. Conclusion

Maritain's initiation into Thomism was a liberating and empowering experience. He was by then well versed in the failed projects and systems of modern philosophy, and the Aristotelean-Thomistic methodologies may have appeared to him as a toolbox set open before him with which to undertake his vocation.

This analysis recognized that Thomistic metaphysics is uniquely characterized by a doctrine of intelligible objects and corresponding cognitive operations. This evaluation finds that Aquinas and Maritain defined the same scientific objects and distinguished the same speculative sciences. However, Maritain's position on abstractive operations is ambivalent. Nevertheless, because, "in the final analysis," he attributed the intelligibility of objects to "the mode of defining (which is Thomas's position)," Maritain's position is more consistent with that of Thomas than with Cajetan.

Maritain's introduction of the intuition of being is seen as an advancement beyond the state of development left by Aquinas rather than as a departure from, or the repudiation of, Aquinas. The philosophically minded should bear in mind that subjectivism is the bane of our age and that the restoration of objectivity to human knowledge, which involves the intuition of being, is a major goal for Maritain.

Two points stand out in regard to critical realism. Firstly, Thomas described a reflection on an act of knowing a sensible being that confirms realism. Secondly, although Maritain's position was expressly in response to a serious issue of his day, he recognized critique (a metaphysical exercise) as an essential and necessary part of metaphysics.

With this evidence, this analysis concludes that Maritain's metaphysics, including his innovations (despite some discrepancies), is authentically Thomistic.

ANNE FRANCES AI LE, OP

A Thomist is a Thomist–A Must? A Must!

A Quest for "Mere Thomism"

I. Introduction

THERE ARE SEVERAL PROMINENT versions of Thomism, for example, Laval Thomism, Existential Thomism, Transcendental Thomism, Analytical Thomism. More often than not, the various interpretations of Aquinas's are in some meaningful sense, opposed to one another.[1] More positively stated, Thomism can be described as a fellowship of diverse views inspired and united by the thought of the *Doctor Communis,* and however diverse the views, they are generally accepted under the same flagship of "Thomism." Admittedly, some views are looked upon with more suspicion than others. Given such contentious interactions among them, one wonders, then, the degree of genuine commonality among Thomists, meriting the putative designation of "Thomism" for their views. Is the commonality more than simply inspiration by the Angel of the Schools, commendable though it may be, or simply invoking his name or authority in support of the various views? Does any substantial common ground exist, underlying these various views? Whose right is it to brand their position as "Thomistic" or by which authority are these views to be scrutinized?

To answer these questions, one could attempt to uncover a common, core Thomistic account, a "mere Thomism," as it were, among the variety of Thomisms. This would involve the daunting task of evaluating prominent

1. Helen James John makes a similar observation, specifically regarding metaphysics in the foreword to her work, *The Thomist Spectrum* (New York: Fordham University Press, 1966), x.

Thomisms.[2] Such evaluation, if failing to yield the desired result of uncovering genuine unity, would at least, I think, establish some grounds for reconciliation among them rather than stripping any view of the label outright. Towards that end, I will focus on the acknowledgement of a Thomistic pluralism and the manner in which Thomists should proceed from such a recognition. In short, I will formulate a standard for the label "Thomist" rather than for a unified "Thomism." To this end, I will consider the "unity" that is alleged by some to exist among Thomists despite divisiveness; then I will consider what it takes to be a genuine Thomist in the contemporary intellectually pluralistic terrain.

II. Unity within Thomism?

An introduction to the concept of a "school" or "tradition" is necessary and beneficial for purposes of clarity in discussing Thomism as a school of thought. The online *Cambridge Dictionary* defines a "school of thought" as "a set of ideas or opinions that a group of people share about a matter."[3] While I don't dispute the definition, I wish to place the emphasis on the group of individuals sharing a set of ideas or opinions on a particular matter. We can draw a link between the notion of a school of thought and a "tradition" that underscores the individuals behind the set of shared ideas and opinions. It should also be noted that within any school or tradition, a range of positions can be assumed, given the shared set of ideas and opinions on particular matters.[4] Within any school or tradition, a range of positions can be assumed, given the shared set of ideas and opinions on particular matters. Even regarding the shared set itself of ideas and opinions, degrees of acceptance and understanding may also occur as attested to in lived experience regarding any particular matter. In this way, there can be disagreement within the bounds of membership.

2. For this purpose, I had on hand as guide, Edward Feser's "The Thomistic Tradition," a recent, brief survey with an extensive bibliography. See http://edwardfeser.blogspot.com/2009/10/thomistic-tradition-part-i.html, http://edwardfeser.blogspot.com/2009/10/thomistic-tradition-part-ii.html.

3. https://dictionary.cambridge.org/us/dictionary/english/school-of-thought.

4. Even the "Wikipedia" definition of a "school of thought" mirrors these concerns. See: https://en.wikipedia.org/wiki/School_of_thought: "A school of thought, or intellectual tradition, is the perspective of a group of people who share common characteristics of opinion or outlook of a philosophy, discipline, belief, social movement, economics, cultural movement, or art movement."

Any consideration of the possibility of unity among Thomists requires a preface, honestly admitting and appraising the effects of the often divisive and dismissive attitudes among Thomists, who can often be contentious with one another. An illustration may not be needed but it may serve as a sober reminder for some measure of self-evaluation. In his introduction to a past Maritain volume, *The Future of Thomism*, Deal Hudson spoke of Thomists being "preoccupied with the failings of other Thomists"; the distinction between "genuine scholarly engagement" and "curt dismissal"; of "internecine quarrels" among Thomists.[5] Hudson, moreover, cited Maritain's writing about his disappointment in Thomists who

> use the formulas they have been taught in order to save themselves from regarding the thought of others, and to criticize it all the more peremptorily because they expect it to display only error. The universe of intelligible objects, to which first and foremost we owe our loyalty, is not that universe of verbal conclusions which serve all too often as material blinders which keep a man from gazing into the eyes of other men.[6]

In other words, the task and focus of Thomists, as of all philosophers, is to gaze upon "the universe of intelligible objects" rather than to look for and at one another's failed attempts or different outlooks. Gerald McCool similarly expressed the antagonism apparent among Thomists, saying, "too much time may have been spent deciding which philosophers could be called authentic Thomists. Too much time may have been spent as well debating" this or that.[7] Norris Clarke likewise remarked, "[G]ranted the new pluralistic setting,... Thomists must learn the skills, not just of polemics, as of old—which they have always been good at—but rather of peaceful, even creative co-existence."[8] Ralph McInerny, too, indirectly expressed similar sentiments about Thomists, saying, "The day of testing the adequacy of the Thomism of others, their Thomisticity, as it were, is behind us."[9] The apparent pattern of divisive argument is often displayed among Thomists

5. Deal Hudson, "The Future of Thomism: An Introduction," *The Future of Thomism*, (South Bend, Indiana: University of Notre Dame Press 1992),19–20.

6. Ibid. 20.

7. Gerald McCool, "Is Thomas's Way of Philosophizing Still Viable Today?" in Deal Hudson, *The Future of Thomism*, 64.

8. W. Norris Clark, "Thomism and Contemporary Philosophical Pluralism," in Deal Hudson, *The Future of Thomism*, 97.

9. Ralph M. McInerny, *Thomism in an Age of Renewal* (South Bend, Indiana: University of Notre Dame Press, 1968), 193.

in public lectures, yet despite acknowledging the prevalence of internecine quarrels, some Thomists still speak of a "discernible unity" in the fold.

III. Romanus Cessario's Vision of Thomistic Unity

In the opening words of his brief work on Thomism published in 2003, Romanus Cessario provides a definition of "Thomism," but also notes its fluidity from the outset. He writes:

> In the broadest sense of the term, "Thomism" refers to a body of tenets in both philosophy and theology that derive from and are held to represent faithfully the doctrine of the thirteenth century Italian priest Thomas Aquinas (1224/5–1274). But Thomism stands for more than an accumulation of teachings: it also embodies a conception of philosophical and theological enquiry that owes its genius to the insight and resourcefulness of the first Thomist.[10]

He continues later in the work to speak of the use of the term, "Although the epithet 'Thomist' has been used since the fourteenth century to identify those who subscribe to the principles of Thomism, scholars still debate the best way to identify the movement."[11] Cessario does due diligence in tracing various clarifications of the term by other Thomists and acknowledges in the end "a substantial unity exists that informs the Thomist school."[12] He is not ignorant of what he terms "moments of discontinuity in Thomism" arising from *inter-scholas* debates between Thomists and non-Thomists as well as from *intra-scholam* exchanges between Thomists themselves.[13] As a result, he acknowledges, "it is difficult to reach unanimous agreement as to what criteria should be used to identify a particular theologian or philosopher as one who stands within the Thomist circle."[14] He is confident that these moments of discontinuity do not outweigh the aforesaid substantial unity, though "this judgment may be made without necessarily endorsing the project of narrowly identifying true Thomists."[15]

10. Romanus Cessario, *A Short History of Thomism* (Washington, D.C.: The Catholic University of America Press, 2003), 1.

11. Ibid., 11.

12. Ibid., 15.

13. Here, the notion of a school or an intellectual tradition is distinctly manifest as "us" apart from "them." Those sharing a set of ideas or opinions about a matter, thus belonging to a particular intellectual tradition, distinguish themselves from those sharing a different set of ideas or opinions about the same matter.

14. Cessario, *A Short History of Thomism*, 15.

15. Ibid.

What does this substantial unity entail or consist in? Here, it is beneficial to introduce Weisheipl's distinction between "wide" Thomism and "eclectic" Thomism. One would think that "wide" and "eclectic" would bear similar connotations and would refer to the same or similar views of Thomism, but Cessario observes,

> Weisheipl distinguishes between a "wide" Thomism, which includes anyone who claims to follow the spirit and basic insights of St. Thomas and manifests an evident dependence on his texts, from what he calls "eclectic" Thomism ... [, both of which, though distinct from each other, are nevertheless more] easily [and clearly] distinguished from other intellectual traditions and movements such as medieval Augustinianism, Scotism, Protestantism, nominalism, idealism, and materialism.[16]

From such descriptions, the two views do not appear to be particularly diverse. Cessario further notes Weisheipl's understanding of the distinctiveness of "eclectic" Thomism as including "any author who gives the principles and conclusions of Thomas Aquinas a privileged place in the development of his own proper theological or philosophical reflections."[17] But in their effort to confront modernity through Thomistic principles and conclusions, as Cessario observes, "a number of authors who still held Thomas Aquinas as an authority began to work within a larger framework of thought than what up to that point had been considered Thomistic, even if one takes the term in the wide sense."[18] Thus the distinction between "wide" and "eclectic" Thomisms turns on the latter's explicit use and acceptance of or simply engagement with other traditions. Cessario's comments harbors a penchant for Thomistic purism that is suspicious of any collaboration of Thomism with non-Thomistic ideas, which he views as relativizing "the principles and conclusions that constitute the Thomism of Thomas Aquinas."[19] He identifies such adulteration, with systems such as Suarezianism, Molinism, casuistry, and even Salesian spirituality.[20]

Weisheipl's distinction between "wide" and "eclectic" Thomisms helps to focus Cessario's understanding of what he claims as the substantial unity informing Thomistic school According to Cessario:

16. Ibid., 16.

17. Ibid. Cessario also notes the difficulty of identifying instances of eclecticism, "especially since these forms mainly took shape in the modern period, that is, at a time when philosophy began to develop outside of direct ecclesiastical supervision."

18. Ibid., 17.

19. Ibid., 17–18.

20. By Salesian spirituality, Cessario is referring to the influential teaching of St. Francis de Sales (1567–1622) on the Christian spiritual life.

> Those who practice Thomism in the *strict* sense of the term observe a *pristine adherence* to the central principles of the philosophy and theology that Thomas Aquinas pioneered in the thirteenth century. This means that they *eschew large-scale importations* from other conceptual systems, while at the same time they aim in their own works to imitate Aquinas's appreciation for the rationality of the tradition.[21]

Clearly, this understanding of Thomism excludes any kind of "eclectic" Thomism. To cement his position, Cessario states:

> Since certain contemporary thinkers wonder whether it still is possible to identify a body of truths as Thomist, it is useful to identify what it is that recognized scholars generally hold concerning the major principles adopted and the conclusions elaborated by Thomas Aquinas in his writings.[22]

Cessario thus examines the opinions of "recognized scholars," opinions ranging from the liberal criteria of Leonard Kennedy[23] to those which can serve as "partial criteria" for Thomism from which he can begin his study of the history of Thomism more exactly: "[F]or the first centuries of Thomism, several key questions in philosophy can serve as bellwethers in order to identify those Thomists who adhered strictly to Aquinas's own principles."[24] Such key questions include those posed in natural philosophy, anthropology, moral philosophy, and metaphysical realism.[25] More specifically, Cessario maintains that the Thomist, then, is "preeminently a metaphysical realist insofar as the doctrine of St. Thomas hinges on that which is most formal in being and is its *sine qua non*: the *actus essendi*."[26] Thomism in this regard further entails "defending the reality of creation, the distinction between essence and existence in creatures, with God alone as pure act."[27] Moreover,

21. Ibid., 19; italics added. Interestingly, though he is seemingly promoting "wide" Thomism, Cessario's choice of words, as indicated by my italics, appears to create a further distinction, namely, a kind of "strict" Thomism.

22. Ibid.

23. Ibid., 20. Cessario notes further that "Leonard A. Kennedy, it is true, acknowledges that there are no universally agreed on criteria for answering the question: Who is a Thomist? Instead, he adopts what are described as fairly liberal criteria, such as an indication in the title of a work that the author aims to follow the mind of Aquinas ("*ad mentem Divi Thomae*"), or that an author produced a book of a certain kind,... or a statement of alleged Thomism by either the author himself or one of his historians." See Leonard Kennedy, *A Catalogue of Thomists, 1270–1900* (Houston: Center for Thomistic Studies, 1987).

24. Cessario, *A Short History of Thomism*, 21.

25. See ibid., 21–24.

26. Ibid., 23.

27. Ibid. 23. Cf. Helen James John, *The Thomist Spectrum* (New York: Fordham University Press, 1966), 17: "For any Thomist, metaphysics is of course the central discipline of philosophy, the source of the principles and insight which unfold into applications in all the other areas."

with a concern for theological endeavors of certain Thomists and acknowledging the engagement of Thomists in "widely diverse areas of the intellectual life," Cessario concludes that "what united all these followers of Thomas Aquinas, and continues to unite those who seriously study his works, is the conviction that the teaching of Thomas Aquinas provides a sure guide to the truth of the Christian faith."[28]

It seems, then, we have attained an understanding of a "substantial unity" among Thomists and Thomisms. Cessario's careful study and conclusion seems also to be supported by others as well. Deal Hudson concurs:

> There remains to be a large patch of common ground shared by what Henri de Lubac calls "The Big Family of Thomists." Their resemblances are so obvious, one must ask what discourages their cooperation on issues like the human person, the rational soul, its unity with the body, the importance of sense experience, the primacy of *esse*, the virtues and character, justice and the social order, and the interdependence of philosophy and theology?[29]

III. Thomistic Unity according to Ralph McInerny

Writing about four decades earlier and a few years after the closing of Vatican II while a spirit of renewal was in the air, McInerny examines the status of Thomism which to many at the time was thought (or hoped to be) in its last gasp. He similarly takes up the question of whether a "substantial" or "substantive" Thomism can be found among the various Thomisms and concludes in the negative.

Like Cessario (and all self-professed Thomists, in fact), McInerny accepts unity in the sense of some kind of loyalty to St. Thomas' teaching, although he puts the emphasis on adhering to Aquinas' "almost unique" method of philosophizing, namely, in discovering and accepting truth wherever it can be found.[30] He rejects the notion of a substantive Thomism

28. Ibid., 35.

29. Ibid., 20.

30. McInerny, *Thomism in an Age of Renewal*, 190. McInerny goes on to describe St. Thomas' unique approach to truth in this way: "One reads him [Aquinas] with the growing awareness that he was in principle interested in anything available to him, from whatever source it came; moreover, the sympathy with which he reads authors whose fundamental tenets are opposed to his own, he insists on finding wherever he reads, is something almost unique in the history of philosophy. Try if you will to imagine an Aquinas alive today who would not be well versed in Wittgenstein, Ryle, Wisdom, Russell, Whitehead, Heidegger, Jaspers, Sartre, and so forth. That is almost as impossible as imagining Aquinas a Thomist in the sense that designation has sometimes had."

that could be found on a list of some kind, as he fears it would bring about a sterility that spells almost certain death for Thomism itself.[31] Though fearing the inevitable fate of such expressions of Thomism, McInerny acknowledges the possibility of such a list, stating:

> There is little point in listing a series of key positions of Aquinas that would make up a substantive Thomism, though such a list could be made. Included in that list would be such items as his establishment of the spirituality of the human soul and of its immortality, together with such allied positions as the difference between intellection and sensation and the manner in which intellection is dependent upon sensation. All of this would lead to a statement of the essential realism of Aquinas.[32]

So it seems that despite his professed antipathy for any expression of Thomism as consisting of a list, McInerny expressly succeeds in conveying Thomism as an "essential realism." Nevertheless, McInerny has no intention of promoting such a view. After noting that the term "realism" itself has become so ambiguous that such a term for authentic Thomism would likely be differently construed, he focuses on the content of such a list: "Such a list as is envisaged would have to include Aquinas' proofs of the existence of God, his teaching on the basic principles of morality and the nature of the moral decision.... What I am saying is that any list that could be drawn up would have to be accompanied by a rather thorough commentary if its meaning were to be clear."[33]

So, for McInerny, the need for an extensive commentary on the contents of such a list would argue against actually creating such a list. He adds, moreover, that "[e]ven if such difficulties could be overcome, I doubt that very widespread agreement could be reached as to what would constitute

31. The rise of lists, famously the 24 Thomistic theses, resulted from a renewed interest in the writings of St. Thomas with the recommendation of Pope Leo XIII in the late-nineteenth century. McInerny viewed the use of lists in primarily an unfavorable light, describing them as setting up a standard against which to judge the authenticity of adherents and those studying St. Thomas' writings. Key positions of St. Thomas contained on a list would be easily accessible, containing quasi-requirements to adjudicate views of his would-be intellectual followers. In other words, the use of a list serves as a quick and easy checklist from which to determine whether one has met the requirements on the list to distinguish "them" from "us." Cessario, however, notes the initial aim of the list was "more toward promoting sound pedagogy than toward creating a narrow ideology" and later for "acknowledging Thomism as possessing a recognizable structure," agreed upon by then prominent European thinkers. (Cessario, *A Short History of Thomism*, 24 and 26, respectively.) That Cessario mentions "a narrow ideology" hints at the list devolving into something unintended, as McInerny feared.

32. McInerny, *Thomism in an Age of Renewal*,192.

33. Ibid., 193.

a list of the essential teachings of Aquinas."[34] Yet McInerny insists that the lack of agreement on the essential teachings of St. Thomas "does not really bother" him and in alluding to the renowned but, according to him, needless Twenty-Four Theses of Thomism, he maintains that "[t]he day of such lists is, I should hope, behind us. The day of testing the adequacy of the Thomism of others, their Thomisticity, as it were, behind us. To engage in that sort of thing is to be drawn away from the philosophical task, to lose the spirit of philosophizing, to want to identify the 'true believers' in an area where belief is not the point."[35] Clearly McInerny rejects the notion of a substantive Thomism that can be summarized as points on a list, which could then be understood as what unites alleged Thomisms, if they are really worth their salt. Having considered various key features of "the essentials" of Thomism, he directly affirms his having "certain ideas as to what a minimal and substantive Thomism would amount to."[36] Curiously, however, he insists on being "unwilling to lay it out lest it be construed as some kind of standard for others."[37]Yet he has in fact laid out certain ideas about a substantive Thomism, which would nicely correspond to what Cessario had termed a substantial unity among Thomists! It is my contention that though seemingly opposite in their presentations, both Cessario and McInerny are of the same mind, though with different emphases and purposes.[38]

Cessario and McInerny are simply concerned with what is done with such unity or list of essentials. Neither understands it as a strict measuring rod, the canon, if you will, against which to evaluate different kinds of Thomisms, though admittedly, Cessario's position is more ambiguous. Recall earlier, in speaking of the substantial unity between Thomisms as outweighing the moments of discontinuity in Thomism, that Cessario immediately qualifies his statement by stating that "this judgment may be

34. Ibid.

35. Ibid.

36. Ibid., 194.

37. Ibid.

38. The similarity should not be surprising since McInerny, after all, wrote the foreword to Cessario's work. One way of addressing their oneness of mind, despite their differences, is through the concept of analogy, a comparison of at least two unlike objects. An analogy exists precisely between two things that are apparently different, or better, the two are similar precisely because of, or in their, very differences. Explaining McInerny's and Cessario's views of Thomism (or Thomisms, in general) as analogical can be problematic, as the explanation would require identifying the analogate or primary instance in which the others participate. Identifying the analogate, however, is precisely the task at hand regarding Thomism.

made without necessarily endorsing the project of narrowly identifying true Thomists." In other words, Cessario does not regard the substantial unity he ascertained as the standard for orthodox or authentic Thomism. Moreover, his agreement with and use of Weisheipl's distinction between "wide" and "eclectic" Thomism highlights the tenuousness of the substantial unity he asserts. McCool made a similar distinction to speak of a "discernible unity" precisely within his acknowledgement of Thomistic pluralism:

> Philosophical pluralism within Thomism is a fact. Yet, despite that fact, a clearly discernible unity marks all its leading philosophers and theologians as followers of the Angelic Doctor. All are in the tradition of St. Thomas. Despite their misunderstandings of St. Thomas and the disagreements caused by their effort to adapt St. Thomas' thought to problems which he had never tried to resolve, the Thomists of the Second and Third Scholasticism, without exception, claimed St. Thomas as their master.[39]

In other words, McCool's "discernible unity" consists in nothing more than certain philosophers and theologians claiming St. Thomas as their master, separating them from other schools. Clear evidence of this tenuous unity is further seen in McCool's ensuing comments, redolent of Cessario's explanation earlier. McCool writes:

> For their philosophy of knowledge, man, and being, the systems of these Thomists could clearly be distinguished from the rival philosophies of Augustinians, Scotists, Ockhamites, Cartesians, Empiricists, Kantians, Husserlian phenomenologists, and Whiteheadian process metaphysics. They were closer to their master than to anybody else. A discernible unity in their philosophy of knowledge, man, and being linked them both to St. Thomas and to one another.[40]

Here, McCool spells out precisely the nature of this discernible unity of Thomists as simply that they were closer to their master than to anybody else. It is this affinity that linked Thomists of various persuasions to St. Thomas and to one another.

McInerny clearly rejects the possibility of a substantive Thomism that would unite all Thomists, though he did entertain the criteria needed for any such view of Thomism. First, taking what he interprets as the Church's injunction commending St. Thomas as a guide for Catholic philosophers, he insists, "When a Catholic philosopher reads Aquinas seriously and sympathetically, the only controlling criteria are those of reason, taking into ac-

39. McCool, "Is Thomas's Way of Philosophizing Still Viable Today?" 58.
40. Ibid., 58–59.

count particular criticisms of Aquinas."[41] The basis for this is the nature of the act of philosophizing itself: "What we have to keep absolutely clear is that there is no such thing as official orthodoxy so far as substantive philosophical arguments and positions go, unless of course a philosophical position is in open and flagrant opposition to revealed truth."[42] One's adoption of Thomism, in other words, cannot be simply because Aquinas has said so but that it resonates with and best manifests the act of philosophizing. McInerny's view finds ample support in St. Thomas' own method of approaching various views on diverse issues, through which he best exemplified the medieval adage: "Seldom affirm, never deny, always distinguish." Truth, the object of the act of philosophizing, can and should be sought out no matter its sources.

At this stage, we can ask what we have achieved in considering the relative unity among Thomists and Thomisms. Have we only managed to undo what was laboriously achieved by considering Cessario's understanding of a substantial unity within the Thomistic School? On the contrary, we have determined the tenuous character of such a unity and have seen it includes much latitude for diverse interpretations and views. So where do we go from here? It is now opportune to speak of the practical implications and responses to a Thomistic pluralism.

IV. Practical Responses to Thomistic Pluralism vs "True" Thomism

In speaking of the greater importance of philosophizing over philosophy as a tradition or any established system, McInerny distinguishes between personal and institutional responses to the study of Thomism. From a personal perspective, McInerny maintains that everyone can profit from a study of St. Thomas' teaching, allowing that some will agree more and others less with Aquinas. "Far better really," he insists, "to hold a few philosophical positions, which happen also to have been held by Aquinas, than to adhere to a whole host of unexamined philosophical tenets which one cannot adequately communicate or defend."[43] To do so would be contrary to the nature of philosophy itself. Concerning Catholic philosophers, in particular,

41. McInerny, *Thomism in an Age of Renewal*, 196.
42. Ibid., 195–96.
43. Ibid., 197.

who are consistently exhorted by Church authorities to look to St. Thomas as a guide, McInerny understands this exhortation to entail not a necessary obligation but an "antecedent deference to [Aquinas] of a special kind." This antecedent deference, however, "is not a prediction that there will be consequent deference, based on philosophical assimilation, or, if there is, that this will be homogeneous and on all points the same.... There is only one way to be a Thomist [for non-Catholics and Catholics] and that is by being a philosopher and there is but one set of demands that must be met by the philosopher."[44]

When St. Thomas is approached is this way, it can only bring about a Thomistic pluralism:

> It should be safe to predict that what we will move toward is not Thomism but Thomisms, any number of ways of truly and philosophically profiting from the study of Aquinas. This plurality of Thomisms will not simply be a function of diversity of talents; it will also be the result of the unavoidable division of philosophical labor.[45]

Thus, McInerny does not regard Thomistic pluralism in a negative light but views it as a necessary division of philosophical labor. He acknowledges that the common thread among Thomists is something flexible that allows them to adopt the spirit of St. Thomas, "which entails that they are in principle open and interested and sympathetic to whatever has been written on their principal interest."[46] McInerny recognizes that as Thomists engage with other adherents of other views and from different vantage points, their positions will be altered to the degree that they are able to "free themselves from the fact that Aquinas said it" and not to regard the "*opera omnia* of Aquinas as a repository of truth and nothing but the truth" to be defended at all costs.[47] The task of the philosopher who has benefited from this reading and study of Aquinas is "not to show that he can learn nothing from anyone else."[48] For McInerny, when Thomists are successful in taking on the spirit of St. Thomas rather than in committing to heart the letter of St. Thomas, they will have succeeded in manifesting "a family resemblance to one another" rather than in attaining "the cooky-cutter [sic] identity that

44. Ibid.

45. Ibid., 198; cf. John, *The Thomist Spectrum,* 49 about the transformation that Thomism will undergo.

46. McInerny, *Thomism in an Age of Renewal,* 199.

47. Ibid., 191, 199.

48. Ibid,. 199.

seems to have been the expectation of some past devotees of Aquinas."[49] In other words, they do not have to conform to a set of predetermined characteristics or to any particular list of teachings to be considered Thomists. By their open manner of philosophizing, they are in fact following in the footsteps of the master and can be called Thomists.

As an aside, Maritain's remarks on identifying himself simply as a Thomist are pertinent here, I think. He once affirmed, "I am not a neo-Thomist. All in all, I would rather be a paleo-Thomist than a neo-Thomist. I am, or at least I hope I am, a Thomist."[50] In *The Peasant of Garonne*, Maritain spoke of Thomistic philosophy in a similar vein:

> Given a chance to reveal its own nature, Thomistic philosophy exhibits the gait and demeanor characteristic of all philosophy; a demeanor and gait fully at liberty to confront the real. The philosopher swears fidelity to no person, nor any school—not even, if he is a Thomist, to the letter of St. Thomas and every article of his teaching.[51]

The goal, then, on the individual level in one's study of St. Thomas is to take after the spirit rather than the letter of St. Thomas in trying to grasp reality. Maritain's remarks on Christian philosophy, *mutatis mutandi*, also bear out McInerny's practical response on the individual level, specifically, Maritain's distinction between "nature and state," classically known as the distinction between the order of specification and the order of exercise.[52] Regarding Christian philosophy, Maritain explains that "nature" refers to what philosophy is in itself while "state" refers to the "concrete conditions of its existence and exercise" "in real fact, historically, in the human subject."[53] Applying this distinction to the topic at hand, the "nature" of Thomism, then, rather than being identified as a list of key positions or theses, can be said to be the spirit of St. Thomas to discover truth from all sources available to him. The "state" of Thomism would then correspond to the concrete conditions in which a philosopher or theologian exercises or imitates the spirit of

49. Ibid.

50. Edward Synan, "Jacques Maritain: A Believing Philosopher," in *The Future of Thomism*, 44; see also Helen John, writing in the 1960s, describing Maritain: "his creativity lies in his untiring application of principles already established to new areas of thought, thus offering the timeless truths of the 'Common Doctor' to the changing needs and interests of our century." *The Thomist Spectrum*, 16.

51. Vincent Colapietro, "History, Tradition, and Truth," in *The Future of Thomism*, 127, citing Maritain's *The Peasant of Garonne*, 161.

52. See Jacques Maritain, *An Essay on Christian Philosophy*, translated by Edward Flannery, §4. https://maritain.nd.edu/jmc/etext/aeocp04.htm.

53. Ibid.

St. Thomas, given the particular challenges or matters pertaining to a specific era as well as the various sources at one's disposal, including those not typically accepted as Thomistic or sympathetic to Thomism. Maritain's "nature"/"state" distinction makes room for the adoption of "non-traditional" sources into the Thomism while remaining authentically Thomistic.

This individual response, then, should, according to Maritain, influence the institutional-level response: "What we must seek is not the safe and closed and sterile, but the open and intellectually lively."[54] Achieving an open and intellectually lively philosophy department does not amount to having a cross-section of professors from prominent philosophical traditions, as something of a "philosophical zoo," McInerny humorously contends. For McInerny, the philosophy department of Catholic colleges "need not contain one analyst, one existentialist, one phenomenologist, one idealist, and so forth. But it should contain some men whose principal interest is analysis, others whose principal interest is phenomenology, and so forth."[55] McInerny regards the Thomism he envisioned as "the best hope of getting beyond the level of factions and schools and systems of philosophy" since it is "not one school among others."[56] Instead, McInerny envisaged Thomism as "the attempt to move out from a proved base in many directions, to assimilate, to grow, to renew itself as well as to correct misadventures, to be always open at the operative end of thinking."[57] In other words, Thomism is a method of philosophizing, as McInerny also adds, specifically regarding its substantive content: "Thomism, while principled and systematic, is simply not a system. It has substantive content, but that very content makes it more visible as a method of synthesis."[58] These remarks are reminiscent of Maritain's understanding of Thomism as "an assimilative philosophy," open to accepting truth from whatever source it came.[59] He is not alone in his envisioning of Thomism as a method of synthesis.

Norris Clarke, moreover, had occasion to speak of the assimilative nature of Thomism in its engagement with other, later views, specifically phenomenology. The starting point of phenomenology is with some empirically observed aspect of reality, setting aside questions about its underlying

54. McInerny, *Thomism in an Age of Renewal*, 202.

55. Ibid., 204.

56. Ibid.

57. Ibid.

58. Ibid., 204–205.

59. Maritain, *St. Thomas Aquinas* (New York: Meridian Books, 1958).

causes. Because of this omission or lacuna in phenomenology regarding the causal explanation of its object, it could benefit from the contribution of Thomism:

> It seems clear to me that one of the most significant contributions Thomism can make in the contemporary pluralist scene is the restoration of the validity of explanation by efficient causality, in particular when the cause required must by its nature transcend the horizon of our ordinary experience.[60]

Such positive interaction is always commendable in the development of Thomism. Negative interactions can also indirectly contribute to a development of Thomism and sharpen the Thomist's skill in acquiring truth in imitation of Aquinas.[61]

V. Conclusion

It is undeniable that McInerny's view would allow anyone engaging in philosophical endeavors to be called a Thomist, which would render the term too broad to be meaningful and would defeat the purpose of seeking real unity among Thomists. McInerny's proposal, however, would be fitting for a proper philosophical disposition or approach toward intellectual engagement in general. He is wary of a tradition that can be limited and limiting, especially if one does not have a good grasp of that tradition or what constitutes it. Cessario's vision of and recommendation for some established, common ground is better suited to elaborate the unity required by the Thomistic tradition. Cessario calls for a recognition of the certain key features or themes that constitute the Thomistic tradition, recognizably distinct from other traditions and yet united within itself.

Yet, the issue remains unsettled and an agreeable conclusion would be

60. Clarke, "Thomism and Contemporary Philosophical Pluralism," 103.

61. For example, Cessario admits, "the development of eclectic varieties of Thomism have pressed Thomists to articulate more clearly the non-gainsayable principles of their school, so as to keep Thomism from becoming too much of an expandable term"; *A Short History of Thomism*, 96. Helen John makes a similar observation regarding the development of the primacy of act-of-being in particular through engagement with twentieth-century Suarezian Pedro Descoqs, SJ, noted for his "critical and scholarly work of first importance for the Suarezian branch of neo-scholasticism; even more important is his indirect services to what he grimly referred to as 'the so-called Thomist school.' A voracious reader and relentless polemicist, he served the Thomists well in the role of a Devil's Advocate, constantly attacking what they regarded as well-established traditional positions, and so challenging his colleagues to a continual effort for greater historical and doctrinal precision in their interpretations of the Angelic Doctor"; *The Thomist Spectrum*, 72.

that no clear or really substantial unity can be found among Thomists, even though they take interest in and engage in similar topics. Despite his effort in identifying certain recognizable traits among Thomists, Cessario was led to concede that "Thomists are scholars of all sorts who have inserted themselves into a living tradition of historical, philosophical, and theological reflection that finds its origin and sustaining force in the work of a most eminent Christian figure who lived during the High Middle Ages."[62] In other words, the unity, even if and when acknowledged, is rather tenuous. Stated more positively, the unity within Thomistic thought is quite flexible and thus not only allows for but must accommodate diverse views. In so doing, one is not betraying the teaching of Thomism, but in fact is imitating the example of Thomas in his approach to understanding reality through philosophical and theological reflections. In short, one becomes a true, authentic Thomist rather than simply latching on to a tradition, even if it is the revered and coveted Thomistic tradition.

62. Cessario, *A Short History of Thomism*, 96.

MICHAEL DURHAM TORRE

Modest Reflections on Being a Thomist Today

I. Introduction: *Aeterni Patris* (1879) to Vatican II (1962)

I WANT TO INSIST ON THE WORD "modest" in the title of this essay. These reflections are indeed just that. They mean to answer, in very broad terms, how a Catholic today ought to think about the authority of Thomas in relation to theology and to philosophy, i.e., about how best today to appropriate and defend Thomas's thought.

Although the question is posed today, in 2020, it can only be understood by examining its "remote background": from *Aeterni Patris* (1879) to the Second Vatican Council (1962). I will then examine the question against its "proximate background" of Vatican II to the present.

For a little more than 75 years following Pope Leo XIII's encyclical, both Catholic theology and philosophy, as argued by Catholics, were largely and formally *ad mentem Thomam*. In philosophy, no doubt the "high-water mark" of this movement was the "24 Theses," approved by Pope Pius X in 1914. During the period prior to it, many manuals and textbooks were published, for a variety of audiences, including undergraduates at Catholic colleges and universities. The University of San Francisco, where I have taught for many years, was a typical example in having all its students take an ordered series of courses, one each semester, from logic through cosmology, rational psychology, ethics and politics, to metaphysics and natural theology. In effect, all of its students minored in Thomistic philosophy. The intent was forthrightly apologetic, namely, to prepare students better to respond to challenges to a theistic view of the world in a culture and society largely shaped by non-Catholic intellectual forces. In theology and seminary training, Thomas' *Summa Theologiae* likewise reigned supreme, offering an ordered and clear summation and rational account of the mysteries of the faith. In short, Catholic theology was scholastic, and Thomas was the principal scholastic doctor to be consulted and followed.

One should note, however, that even in this period there were Catholic thinkers recognized as "orthodox" who were not proponents of such a Thomism. Gabriel Marcel (1889–1973) in France is a case in point: a person coming out of the modern idealist tradition whose mature positions were more "empirically-minded," existential, and phenomenological. The German philosopher Dietrich von Hildebrand (1889–1977) can easily be cited as another instance. His thought was likewise strongly influenced by phenomenology and he was not a "scholastic Thomist." This did not prevent Pius XII from calling him "the twentieth-century Doctor of the Church". Many other important thinkers could be cited as well, as but just one instance, Maurice Blondel (1861–1949).

Nor was Thomism itself by any means monochromatic. Some Thomists, such as Garrigou-Lagrange (1877–1964), more-or-less wanted to continue the commentary tradition and simply follow in the footsteps of Billuart (1685–1757). Others could be far more critical of that commentary tradition, in the name of a greater fidelity to Thomas himself: Étienne Gilson (1884–1978) of course here comes to mind. Our own Jacques (1882–1973) certainly seconded the importance of *esse* in Thomas (with Gilson), while being more sympathetic to the main-line tradition of the Dominican commentators, such as Cajetan and John of St. Thomas. His great student and colleague Yves R. Simon (1905–1961) was of like mind. Others, such as Cornelio Fabro (1911–1995), emphasized the Neo-Platonic element in Thomas's thought. A Pole such as Joséf Maria Bochenski (1902–1995) emphasized its logical structure, and others, such as Mieczysław Albert Maria Krąpiec (1921–2008), emphasized the compatibility of Thomistic metaphysics with a realist phenomenology. Nor, in deference to the present Pope, should we overlook the remarkable work of the Argentinian Monsignor Octavio Derisi (1907–2002), founder of the journal *Sapientia*, who seems very much to be in the line and spirit of Maritain. The list could go on and on. Josef Pieper (1904–1997), for example, surely deserves to be on any list of important Thomists, as do Americans, such as Mortimer J. Adler (1902–2001) and

Ralph McInerny (1929–2010) or Norris Clarke (1915–2008) and Monsignor John F. Wippel (1933–2023)! There are in fact far too many fine Thomists and Thomistic works of note possibly to be named here.

Most such philosophers might broadly be said to agree that Thomas was a realist, and in the tradition of an Aristotelian Neo-Platonism, a tradition all of them in diverse ways defended. (Very few of them, for example, would likely quarrel with the 24 Theses, even though a few might demur on occasion and many might in relation to the usefulness or present relevance of such a list.) Many, perhaps our own Jacques at their head, would also have agreed that Thomism was by rights "assimilative" and thus should dialogue with contemporary culture and philosophy and take what was good and right in it within its own deeper philosophical perspective. Even aside from the more radical thinking of Transcendental Thomists (whether a Joseph Marechal, [1878–1944], Bernard Lonergan [1904–1984], or Karl Rahner [1904–1984] … and these varied quite a bit!), the first half of the twentieth century produced a rich variety of Thomist philosophers. Yet, even with the last three named again a bit to one side, there was still a great deal of unity within their diversity.

The period also produced an extraordinary number of important Catholic theologians, whose thought clearly influenced the documents of Vatican II. I will cite but six of the greatest: Henri de Lucac (1896–1991), Bernard Lonergan (1904–1984), Karl Rahner (1904–1984), Yves Congar (1904–1995), Hans Urs von Balthasar (1905–1988), and Louis Bouyer (1913–2004). Towards the end of their lives, de Lubac, Congar, and von Balthasar were all named cardinals. The "Thomistic revival" gave rise to an extraordinary flourishing of Catholic theology. Yet it is notable that, of the above six named, none could be described as a "scholastic Thomist." (For great theologians of their caliber who fit that description, some might cite Francisco Marín-Sola [1873–1932] or Santiago Ramirez [1891–1967]. Others might cite Garrigou-Lagrange [1877–1964].)

In truth, the explosion of Thomistic studies—and for its amplitude one need merely look at the bibliographies of Mandonnet, Bourke, and Miethe or the yearly reviews of the *Bulletin Thomiste* or the *Rassegna di Litteratura Tomistica*—had made it impossible for any one person to attempt a review of the entire *Summa* in the style of the past commentators. The bilingual *summas* produced by Dominicans themselves evidenced this: they were a *collective* work, calling upon the specialties of many Thomists (even if fairly "like-minded"). All one need do is consult the bibliographies attached to their work (as just one example, those of Francisco Muñiz in his work for the Spanish *Summa*) to realize that it would be a hopeless task for any one person to control the important published articles on all key questions and debated issues of the *Summa*. (Indeed, it would be hard enough just to control the material pertinent to Muñiz's own work on it.)[1] To see the daunting task facing a contemporary Thomist, one can simply consult the web article of Thomas O'Meara.[2]

To take a case in point, no doubt many an earlier Thomist, when coming to deal with the most important issue of analogical discourse, would more or less rely on Cajetan's commentary on *De Ente et Essentia*. No one could possibly do that today. Instead, he would need to *begin* by controlling the work on this subject of a Ralph McInerny, Santiago Ramirez, Battista Mondin, and Bernard Montagnes. And all of that work would not only put before him a number of arguments, but also a scouring of all the texts of Thomas himself on the subject, in a way that by rights should make a scholar far more conversant with Thomas's doctrine than anything he could find in Cajetan, however important a commentator he might be. Or, to take a disputed question in Thomism, it will no longer be enough to present Capreolus's and Cajetan's view of the supposit and support one or the other of them, Instead, just controlling the magisterial articles of Francisco Muñiz on this idea,[3] or the many other fine studies that have been made of Thomas's doctrine, would be necessary for anyone who wished to consider himself "au courant" with the best scholarship on the subject.

Not the *failure* of Thomism but its very *success* created new conditions for its study. The wealth of historical research on Thomas himself by rights makes it possible for good scholars today to have a better and deeper feel for Thomas than anyone before this Renaissance began.

My point here is not that the revival of Thomism gave rise to a pluralism that undercut the ability to present his philosophy; for, as earlier stated, most of the Thomists referenced, who took differing positions, were still

1. In addition to his over 350 pages of notes introducing and sometimes extensively commenting on the questions of *De Deo Uno*, his bibliography dealing with *just these 26 questions* runs to 8 pages: see *Suma Teologica de Santo Tomas d'Aquíno, Tomo I* (Madrid: Biblioteca de Autores Cristianos, 1947).

2. See https://opcentral.org/resources/2012/09/03/thomistic-bibliography-thomas-omeara.

3. See Francisco Muñiz, "El constitutivo formal de la persona creada en la tradición Tomista," *Ciencia Tomista* 68 (1945): 5–89 and 70 (1946): 201–293.

basically "friendly" to each another, and their emphases are largely compatible. No, it is the sheer richness of what was achieved that "problematizes" Thomism today. There is first the need to control his texts, which the wealth of scholarship makes a considerable task. Then there is the need to understand the various differing approaches to Thomas and to find one's own way amongst them: another task now made far more demanding. And, beyond both of these lies the task that Thomas himself gave us in his own work: of responding to the currents of contemporary philosophy to incorporate whatever is useful and true in them and to give adequate responses to what is not. It requires much time and dedication to be a creative Thomist today. Norris Clarke somewhere says that it takes ten years to begin to feel "comfortable" with one's understanding of Thomism. That is surely just to begin to do so. Arguably, it truly takes longer.

The great Spanish Dominican Francisco Marín-Sola points the way towards what one can reasonably hope to do at the level of creative scholarship: one must concentrate one's efforts on just a few controverted issues. Thus, he largely expended his considerable intellectual acumen and energy on but two problems: how the evolution of doctrine was rightly to be conceived,[4] and how our first causality in moral evil was to be reconciled with God's simplicity and sovereign will.[5] He intended in both simply to be stating or revealing Thomas's own doctrine and positions. By confining himself to these areas, he was able entirely to master his chosen *problematiks*, ones that included the entire commentary tradition, current scholarship, and the texts of Thomas himself. To achieve something lasting in Thomism today, one's scholarship perforce must be specialized.

4. See his *La evolucíon homogénea del dogma católico* (Madrid: Ciencia Tomista, 1923); the expanded second edition, *L'Evolution Homogène du Dogme Catholique,* 2 vols. (Fribourg: University of Fribourg, 1924); the Spanish version of this latter, *L'evolucíon homogénea del dogma católico* (Valencia: Biblioteca de autores cristianos, 1952); and its translation into English by Antonio T. Piñon: *The Homogeneous Development of Catholic Dogma* (Manila: University of Santo Tomas, 1988).

5. See "El sistema tomista sobra la moción divina," *Ciencia Tomista* 17 (July–August, 1925): 5–54, 11; "Respuesta a algunas objeciones acerca del sistema tomista sobre la moción divina," *Ciencia Tomista* 18 (January–February, 1926): 5–74; and "Nuevas observaciones acerca del sistema tomista sobre la moción divina," *Ciencia Tomista* 18 (May–June, 1926): 321–97. I have translated these articles into English: see *Do Not Resist the Spirit's Call: Francisco Marín-Sola, O.P.'s Teaching on Sufficient Grace* (Washington, D.C.: The Catholic University of America Press, 2013). Marín-Sola also wrote a three-volume work on this matter (still in manuscript) entitled *Concordia tomista entra la moción divina y la libertad creada,* the second volume of which is a sentence-by-sentence reply to the final criticism levelled at his work by Reginald Garrigou-Lagrange (in a pamphlet entitled "Principi Thomismi Cum Novissimo Congruismo Comparata: Thomismi Renovatio an Eversio?" [Rome: Angelicum, 1926]).

This again is not to say that one can no longer continue to range across the *Summa* and the entirety of Thomistic philosophy in one's teaching of undergraduates (as he himself did for seminarians). Nor is it to suggest that a series of courses with this range cannot still be taught, provided that there is the institutional will to hire a faculty to teach such courses. Yet the Thomism taught will surely be more "historically-minded" and less in need of defending a set of "theses" (which is hardly appropriate at the level of undergraduate studies, in any case). And surely it will be less inclined to a "scholastic" or "manual" style, from whose "baroque mindset" so many Catholics not very sympathetic to the Thomistic Renaissance finally fled. As our Jacques has insisted, Thomism needed to be understood and presented as a philosophy ever-new and ever-young, assimilating to itself whatever in the contemporary world of thought and culture was vital and deserved attention.

If contemporary versions of Thomistic philosophy might possibly be able to continue in importance for Catholic education, the situation was less clear when it came to theology. The reason again derived from the explosion of the sources authoritative to its undertaking. Sacred theology is rooted in Sacred Scripture and the patrimony of the Fathers of the Church. Our knowledge of both today goes far beyond that available to Thomas. (We might recall that the richness of the patristic patrimony now available to us gave rise to the call of the "Nouvelle Théologie" in the post-World War II years that scholastic theology seek to enrich itself through this patrimony.) It is perhaps enough to recall that Thomas was first an exegete (his scriptural commentaries) and an historian of patristics (the *Catena Aurea*)—thereby controlling the fundamental authorities for sacred theology—and both expert in the dialectical work-up of theological problems (the *Sentences*) and in apologetics (the *Summa Contra Gentiles*), before he attempted his systematic summary of theology (the *Summa Theologiae*), which covered dogmatic, moral, and sacramental theology. No one today could possibly be an expert in exegesis, patristics, apologetics, and the history of recent theology, as well as being expert in dogmatic, moral, and sacramental theology! And, given the need today to think both ecumenically and in an inter-religious context, a systematic theologian will also need to know the work of other Christian theologians, and the phenomenology or anthropology of religion, not to mention comparative religion. As with philosophy, so even more in systematic theology, one must depend on the expertise of others and be part of a collective enterprise. The sheer wealth of knowledge—and we again here see the influence of historical research on the discipline—must provoked the question: how can one attempt to do theology *ad mentem Thomam*?

II. From Vatican II (1965) to the Present (2020)

As I have said, my work here is modest, so I am going to turn now to what I will call "our" time, that of the last 55 years, since the end of the Second Vatican Council, seeking some answers.

One of the consequences of the turmoil and uncertainty provoked by the Council and its aftermath is that it saw a relative dearth of great Catholic theologians. Indeed, I dare say that future historians will hold that it really produced only one truly seminal figure. I refer of course to the work of John Paul II, rightly now being called "The Great." That he happened to be pope gave his work singular importance. I want to use two of the works of his pontificate to guide my reflections on how we should think of the authority of Thomas, and of appropriating his thought, in our day.

The first document is the single most important document for Catholic theology—indeed, it should by rights now be a *source* for it—that our time has produced. I refer of course to the *Catechism of the Catholic Church*,[6] a work of Her entire episcopate and drawing on Her whole tradition, yet published and approved under John Paul II's authority, in 1997. Just as the Roman catechism published after Trent became so essential for post-Tridentine Catholic thought, so this catechism should likewise be essential for that of post-Vatican II. Its seminal importance may not endure for four centuries, as the previous one did, but it remains of vital importance for us today.

As everyone who has read it knows, the *Catechism* is profoundly scriptural and steeped in the Fathers, who are referenced throughout. The index of citations to Scripture runs to over 30 pages, to the Fathers to over 10 pages. It is also clearly the work of the Second Vatican Council: it takes five

6. See *Catechism of the Catholic Church*, 2nd edition (Vatican City: Libreria Editrice Vaticana, 1997), English translation published by the United States Catholic Conference. Originally presented in 1992, the 1997 edition of the catechism is the official one, and incorporates several significant additions; for example, it incorporates (in no. 2267) what John Paul II had taught in the meantime regarding the death penalty (in *Evangelium vitae*, 1995). For the catechism's references (to Scripture, Fathers, and Thomas), see its pp. 689–772.

pages to cite all its references, whereas only two are necessary for *all* the previous councils. (Similarly, two pages are devoted to citations of *all* popes prior to Pius XII, two to those from Pius XII through Paul VI, and two to John Paul II himself.) This is a catechism for our time. What can we gather from it about the continued importance of Thomas for theology?

In the first place, it is notable that Thomas is cited by the *Catechism* over 60 times. By comparison, Bonaventure is cited twice, Anselm once, and Albert the Great and Duns Scotus not even once. Comparing Thomas to the Fathers, we find that only one—Augustine—is cited more frequently. (It is notable that it also pays a good deal of attention to the Greek Fathers. Collectively, the citations to Irenaeus, Athanasius, Gregory Nyssa and Nazianzen, John Chrysostom and Damascene roughly equal those to Augustine.) In the florilegium of "Ecclesiastical Writers" the *Catechism* cites, unsurprisingly Augustine and Aquinas stand as the most preeminent figures.

Yet Thomas's discourse is scholastic, not patristic. When it comes to the scholastic doctors who sought to understand the collective mind of the Fathers, the catechism turns almost exclusively to Thomas as a guide. His authority is, as it were, now set within a wider context, as a guide into the whole tradition. Perhaps we might make this comparison: just as some used to hold that, "*Roma locuta; causa finita est*", so they held that what Thomas said in relation to theological doctrine was the end of the matter; but now we should say that Thomas's views are not the *end* of the matter, but its *beginning* (and the same might be said of many a Roman statement). We cannot do without Thomas. He is a guide into the tradition. What he says (as what Rome says) is crucial and needs to be attended to; but his thought is a guide into a greater and richer tradition.

There is another way that Thomas's mind is at work in the *Catechism* and that is in the *order* of its presentation. As Thomas tells us, it belongs to a wise man to put truth in order, and Thomas's own wisdom is very much at work in the order of doctrine given by the *Catechism*. This is particularly notable in the way it organizes the moral life (Part Three). It takes up in turn our beatitude, our free acts, their morality and that of the passions, the virtues, sin, law, and grace. This is the order of the Prima Secundae, into which it makes only two insertions of more modern provenance: on the importance of conscience, and on social justice.

After learning what we can from contemporary exegesis of Scripture, confronting the search for the "historical Jesus," pericopes and texts in their

Sitz im Leben, and being attentive to the types of biblical texts and the need for a just hermeneutic; after understanding the rich idea of Tradition and being immersed in the riches of the patristic mind and the history of the early Councils, there is still the need to place in *order* the truths of faith and Catholic doctrine. And, for this task, Thomas remains our indispensable guide. The moral part of the *Catechism* invites us to see more broadly that the way Thomas orders the questions of the *Summa Theologiae* should remain perspicuous for us: his ample, fair, and formally-sober mind ordering our "theological matter." We may go "beyond" Thomas, but we should try to stand on his shoulders.

If this is the case, then neither can we do without his philosophy, for it is at work in ordering his theological wisdom. (We need only recall that his ways to demonstrate the existence of God make use of the distinctions between potency and act and essence and existence, a philosophical account of motion, and the principles of non-contradiction and causality.) To see how we should best understand and appropriate the philosophy of Thomas today, we need to turn to a work that John Paul II authored in the year following his confirmation of the *Catechism*, one that obviously was intended to do for our time what *Aeterni Patris* had done for its: I refer of course to his profound and beautiful encyclical *Fides et Ratio*.[7]

From its very first pages, we are placed in the new conditions of our time, confronting the world-wide pluralism of religious traditions. And, from the very beginning, the encyclical distinguishes a "legitimate plurality" from an "undifferentiated pluralism" (no. 4) that would simply be an illegitimate relativism. Thus, when it turns first to the broad "wisdom traditions" found in so many different cultures, it notes the *common* human questions embedded in them all: "Who am I? Where have I come from and where am I going? Why is there evil? What is there after this life?" (no. 1).[8] The questions are rooted in our common humanity and our desire to know the most fundamental truths bearing on our existence. Furthermore, it discerns a "core of philosophical insight" within this common natural effort: "the principles of non-contradiction, causality, and finality, as well as the concept of the human person as a free and intelligent subject, with the

7. See Pope John Paul II, *Fides et Ratio* (1998). The reference to it will hereafter be put in the text. (The number given refers to its paragraph.)

8. It returns to speak of these same basic questions in no. 26 (See also the discussion given in its footnote 28.)

capacity to know God, truth, and goodness" (no. 4). It thus speaks of our spiritual heritage possessing an "implicit philosophy" that can serve as a legitimate "reference point" (no.4) for differing philosophies. And it pointedly notes that "every truth—if it really is truth—presents itself as universal, even if is not the whole truth. If something is true, then it must be true for all peoples and at all times" (no. 27).

In its overview of the Church's relationship to ancient philosophy, it begins by noting the "dialectic" that marks its approach, one present from St. Paul on: on the one hand, being wary of a false pretense to some absolute and esoteric knowledge and critical—as St. Augustine later will be—of its failure to find or to embrace the right Way back to God; on the other hand, from Justin, Clement, and Origen on, willing to embrace what was right and good in Platonism and Neo-Platonism, that it might serve as a "hedge" or "protective wall" for the "vineyard" of the gospel (no. 38).[9] And, as this basic "Christian dialectic" continues to develop into the more rational analyses of the scholastic era initiated by Anselm, "at the summit of its searching, [philosophic] reason [ever] acknowledges that it cannot do without what faith presents" (no. 42).

In its history, the encyclical signals the "quite special place" (no. 43) that belongs to the thought of Aquinas: not only for his readiness to widen the reach of philosophical inquiry in his openness to dialogue with Jewish and Muslim philosophy, but also for the fearlessness of his approach to truth wherever it might be found, certain in his conviction that grace builds on nature and brings it to its perfection, just as the wisdom of faith does so for the achievements of rational wisdom (no. 43).[10] Thus, the Church has ever proposed (and now again proposes) St. Thomas as "the master of thought and the model of the right way to do theology" (no. 43). The encyclical also notes what, in the light of the past history it has traced, can only be regarded as an aberration, namely the increasing separation of reason from faith in modern philosophy and the consequent hostility of reason to faith, in contemporary scientism, agnosticism, atheistic humanism, skepticism, positivism, and nihilism. In the face of such trends, it will remind us of Leo XIII's "insistence on the incomparable value of the philosophy of St. Thomas" (no. 57), one that could stand as a corrective to the false roads down which many followers of contemporary philosophy wander.

9. Quoting from Clement's *Stromata*.
10. Cf. no. 44.

Nevertheless, it is worth noting here that, despite its critical review of modern philosophy, the encyclical is not entirely negative towards it. Just as it manifests a respect for non-Christian wisdom traditions, so it acknowledges that, in the currents of modern philosophy often inimical to the Church's historic tradition and mind regarding the accomplishments of human reason, there are nonetheless "precious and seminal insights." It thus lists its "penetrating analyses of perception and experience, of the imaginary and the unconscious, of personhood and intersubjectivity, of freedom and values, of time and history" (no. 48). Later, the encyclical will again laud the way moderns have enriched philosophical wisdom in the fields of "logic, the philosophy of language, epistemology, the philosophy of nature, anthropology, the more penetrating analyses of the affective dimensions of knowledge and the existential approach to the analysis of freedom" (no. 91). Neither is a short list. Together, they indicate that there is real work to be done to mine modern analyses so that their truth can be integrated into a deeper philosophical vision, one that is not inimical to Christian faith.

The encyclical reiterates the Church's tradition that She "does not canonize any one particular philosophy in preference to others" (no. 49). Still, in charting its way between the Scylla of fideism or a contemporary "biblicism," on the one hand, and the Charybdis of modernism or a contemporary uncritical adoption of Marxism, on the other, it is hard for it not to see "the incomparable value of the philosophy of Saint Thomas" (no. 49)[11] as charting the best way between such extremes. In the many philosophical truths it goes on to emphasize, any Thomist would be nodding his or her head in vigorous agreement. Nevertheless, and here again, the encyclical acknowledges the work of other Catholic philosophers: "some devised syntheses so remarkable that they stood comparison with the great systems of idealism. Others established the epistemological foundations for a new consideration of faith in the light of a renewed understanding of moral consciousness; others produced a philosophy which, starting with an analysis of immanence, opened the way to the transcendent; and there were finally those who sought to combine the demands of faith with the perspective of the phenomenological method" (no. 59). We would like to know of whom he is thinking here. He will later mention Rosmini and Newman with approval and possibly they fit the first two descriptions, just as possibly Max

11. Cf. nos. 52, 54, 55, and 57.

Scheler or Maurice Blondel fit the third. In any case, John Paul II does not cite just Thomists when praising contemporary Catholic philosophers.

When he does single out Thomists, most here are no doubt glad to see our Jacques cited, along with his colleague Gilson, and Edith Stein. It is again notable that directly following them, he cites Eastern Christians: Pavel Florensky, Petr Chaadaev, and Vladimir Lossky. We would be right, I believe, to recognize that John Paul II wants us here to remember his previous encyclical *Ut Unum Sint,* its claim that the Church breathes from its "two lungs," East and West, and its insistence on the need to search for an ever-greater unity between Catholics and other Christians, especially the Orthodox. Although its emphasis upon themes such as (1) the knowability of God (no. 67), (2) the objectivity of moral principles (no. 68) and our ability to grasp reality objectively (no. 82), and (3) the need to emphasize the sapiential dimension of philosophy (no. 81) and its "genuinely metaphysical range" (no. 83) cannot but be music to the ears of Thomists, we should bear in mind that these themes also fit the views and spirit of many an Orthodox philosopher, and even are welcomed by thinkers in the Indian and Chinese traditions of philosophy (which the encyclical again does not fail to mention [no. 72]).

III. Conclusion

The philosophical vision of the encyclical is far too rich to detail fully here. It has not been my intention, however, to go into all of its riches as the "way forward" for philosophy (although I think it does provide much wisdom and guidance). Rather, I have discussed it chiefly in order to help address my initial questions about the authority of Thomas in our day and how best we can appropriate his thought, using this encyclical simply as a "signpost." What conclusions might we draw from my brief survey of the *Catechism* and *Fides et Ratio*?

In the first place, then, I think an honest appraisal of these two documents cannot fail to see two clear truths. In the first place, the authority and the thought of Thomas continue to remain crucial for Catholics attentive to the voice of the *magisterium,* both for those who wish to pursue philosophy and for those who wish to pursue theology. The historic commitment to Thomas is in no way whatsoever being denied or diluted; rather, he continues to be recommended as master and model in these fields. Second, both fields are too rich to be reduced to simply reiterating what

Thomas held. He is an essential guide, but a guide into something greater.

I will leave theology here to one side, save to reiterate that Thomas should remain our principal guide to ordering the mysteries of Catholic faith and to beginning to think from its tradition. However diverse present explorations of Catholic theology may be, there is no better place from which to undertake them than to understand the substance of Thomas's own doctrine. That said, my remaining reflections here are directed to the undertakings of philosophy.

There, *Fides et Ratio* points us to many realms and many truths where work needs to be done to retrieve all that is right and good in contemporary modes of thought. The need to dialogue especially with Eastern Christians and their philosophical traditions is too clear to be missed. The need to widen that reach, not only to the Jewish and Muslim traditions, as Thomas himself had already done, but to Indian and Chinese traditions and the wisdom traditions found in places such as Africa and the New World (today, one thinks of the Amazon) is again too clear to be missed. Nor do we need to get lost in adjudicating niceties between differing Thomisms (although that certainly remains a commendable task). At least from the perspective of *Fides et Ratio,* not only do we not need to choose between a Maritain, Gilson, or Stein, but the latter could be taken to stand for the general effort to appropriate phenomenological analyses for a Thomistic metaphysics (as of course John Paul II had earlier tried to do). It seems that "whose Thomism?" requires "too fine" a distinction at the level of *praxis*. There are many "cousinly" versions within Thomism, and they all broadly share a common viewpoint and are part of the "same family." We do not need to decide between them when it comes to pursuing the fundamental philosophical project. They are far more united than divided.[12] In fact, it is evident that good work also is done and should be paid attention to by thinkers not in the strictly Thomistic tradition: ones who share the many commitments urged by the encyclical, but according to the light of their own wisdom.[13]

12. I think this is certainly true for those Thomists not of a "transcendental" stripe. Yet, even these are clearly within the same "broad Thomistic camp," the way a Bellarmine might have been regarded by a baroque Dominican or a Billot by an early twentieth century one. The first book of Marechal's *Le point du départ de la métaphysique* offers a brilliant analysis of what "went wrong" at the start of modern philosophy. Lonergan's early work on mind and freedom is clearly "Thomistic" in the usual sense, and much of value can be mined from his seminal *Insight*. Even while disputing the "transcendental move" they make (in differing ways), these men seem close to the "cousinly" agreement of other Thomists (Lonergan especially, it seems to me).

13. In the ancient world, an Aristotelian would have felt "at home" with Platonists who had

But, since I count myself a Thomist and am here writing primarily for "Maritainians," let me offer a few of my own personal reflections on John Paul II's stated difference between an "undifferentiated pluralism" and a "legitimate plurality", when it comes to Thomism itself. To put the question directly: What is the "unnegotiable core" that we need to defend in philosophy? To begin broadly, we must be committed to an Aristotelian Neo-Platonism. In truth, this is *the* tradition of philosophy within the Catholic tradition: from the Alexandrians through Damascene and the entire ancient and medieval periods and continued in the modern by Thomists. Later, "decadent" scholasticism should warn us off of an undue "sophistication," beginning with Scotus, and Ockham's Nominalist *via moderna* is the way *not* to be taken, leading to errors of modern philosophy and the separation of philosophy from theology. Again to keep it simple, we need to be able to defend the vision of Boethius's *Consolation of Philosophy*: the existence of God, and union with God as our perfection and happiness; our immortal mind and its destiny; our freedom to choose and to be the authors of our own "immoral miscalculation"; a philosophy of hope and prayer; and, above all, a philosophy recognizing we must follow a credible revealed truth accepted on faith if our natural desire is to be fulfilled. Yet there are things to learn from Ockham: the need to "keep it simple" (to which Thomas's "trajectory" from the *Sentences*, through the *Summa*, to the *Compendium* also points); its attention to Scripture alerting us to our need ever to stay connected to our philosophical sources; and its "empirical-mindedness" reminding us of the great unfinished business of incorporating modern and contemporary science within an adequate philosophy of nature and of making use of the empirical social sciences in a fuller practical philosophy. Not forgetting Thomas's dialectical method, as essential to his entire undertaking, by rights should keep his philosophy open to engagement with the other great traditions and truths that John Paul II references. As with Thomas in the *Catechism*, so with the "24 Theses": these are the beginning of, or part of, a wider and increasingly deeper philosophical conversation. Finally, the historical-mindedness from which we now have such a better

---

not taken a skeptical turn, just as the Neo-Platonists felt "at ease" with much of Aristotle, and both would have recognized (as Cicero did) their similarity to much of Stoic practical philosophy. In the medieval world, Thomas himself obviously was willing to learn from, and be in dialogue (and often in important agreement) with, not only a Bonaventure, but also an Avicenna, Averroes, or Maimonides (not to mention the fact that all the Semitic traditions sought to appropriate and be in positive relation to a pagan philosophical wisdom!).

sense of Thomas himself should remind us that Thomism today must be a collaborative effort. Its joyously difficult project remains viable. When it has "faltered," the fault did not lie with its intrinsic worth, but with the dearth of minds ready to rise to its great calling.

What, then, ought a philosophy department to look like on the campus of a Catholic university, were the vision of *Fides et Ratio* to be embraced? It seems to me that the right model is to think analogically. Thomism should be its "focal center." Departments should be forthright in defending the need to have Thomism remain central to their undertakings, thereby supporting the historic tradition of philosophy proper to a Catholic institution. Yet it also should not seek to have only Thomists in the department. On the contrary, it should look for other philosophers who share many of the underlying commitments to be found in Thomism, as well as being interested in representatives of the great non-Western traditions. And it can seek any philosopher whose work is true and compelling, even when not in accord with some Thomistic views. It has nothing to fear from such thought, provided that its commitment to Thomas's own thought remains central.

Could such a vision be acted upon generally? Is there some chance of succeeding in sustaining such a vision? Clearly not in some philosophy departments, ones that have abandoned anything resembling an interest in Thomas. Yet it seems this could exist or even thrive in some departments. And it seems to me, then, that this is what many of us should be seeking to create. It will be an uphill battle often or usually. Yet Thomas's philosophy clearly deserves to be accorded the respect and authority that the Church—now, as in the century before it—has urged for it. We should be about trying to make that vision a reality. Nothing ventured, nothing gained!

About the Authors

JAMES D. CAPEHART is originally from Dallas, Texas. He received his B.A. in theology from the University of Dallas in 1995, Ph.B. (B.A. equivalent) in philosophy from Regina Apostolorum Pontifical University in 2002, M.A. in philosophy from Holy Apostles College in 2009, and Ph.D. in philosophy from the Center for Thomistic Studies at the University of St. Thomas (Houston) in 2018. He has been teaching at the Middle, High, or College levels since September 2004, and currently serves on the faculty at Sacred Heart Apostolic School, Rolling Prairie, Indiana, and as an Adjunct Assistant Professor of Philosophy at Aquinas College of Grand Rapids, Michigan. His areas of expertise and interest are Thomistic philosophy, the thought of Étienne Gilson, and the general Catholic philosophical tradition.

JOHN J. CONLEY, SJ holds the Henry J. Knott Chair of Philosophy and Theology at Loyola University Maryland in Baltimore. A specialist in modern French philosophy, he has published *The Suspicion of Virtue: Women Philosophers in Neoclassical France* (Cornell University Press, 2002), *Jacqueline Pascal: A Rule for Children* (University of Chicago Press, 2003), *Adoration and Annihilation: The Convent Philosophy of Port-Royal* (University of Notre Dame Press, 2009), and *The Other Pascals: The Philosophy of Jacqueline Pascal, Gilberte Pascal Perier, and Marguerite Perier* (University of Notre Dame Press, 2019.)

TRAVIS DUMSDAY is Associate Professor of Philosophy at Concordia University of Edmonton. He works in analytic philosophy of science, bioethics, and Eastern Orthodox theology. His latest book is *The Marian Apparitions at Zeitoun: An Evidential Inquiry* (St Vladimir's Seminary Press, 2024).

FRANCIS FEINGOLD is Associate Professor of Philosophy at Kenrick-Glennon Seminary in St. Louis, Missouri. He holds a B.A. from Christendom College and a Ph.D. in philosophy from The Catholic University of America. His research interests center on Aquinas's metaphysics (especially God's relation to the world, angelic knowledge and time, and the nature of action) and ethics (chiefly the common good, friendship-love, and natural law); they also include medieval philosophy more generally, as well as figures such as Pascal and Dietrich von Hildebrand.

JAMES G. HANINK is a Los Angeles-based independent scholar. He received his Ph.D. in philosophy from Michigan State University. His research interests include metaphysics and social philosophy. He is editor of *Aquinas and Maritain on Evil: Mystery and Metaphysics* (American Maritain Association, 2013) and *In Search of Harmony: Metaphysics and Politics* (American Maritain Association, 2019). He is also a co-editor of *For Freedom, Set Free: Structure and Telos* (American Maritain Association, 2024). He served as the President of the American Maritain Association from 2016–22.

SISTER ANNE FRANCES AI LE, OP is a Dominican Sister of Mary Immaculate Province in Houston, Texas. Sr. Anne Frances holds a doctorate in Thomistic philosophy from the University of St. Thomas in Houston and a master's in theological studies from the Notre Dame Graduate School of Theology at Christendom College. Currently, Sr. Anne Frances is the Diaconate Assistant Director of Intellectual Formation for the Diocese of Fort Worth, Texas, where she teaches philosophy and theology courses in addition to carrying out administrative duties regarding the intellectual dimension of formation.

MATTHEW LEVERING holds the James N. Jr. and Mary D. Perry Chair of Theology at Mundelein Seminary. He is the author of more than thirty books and the co-editor of more than twenty. His books include numerous contributions to contemporary Thomism, most recently *Aquinas's Eschatological Ethics and the Virtue of Temperance* (University of Notre Dame, 2019), *Paul in the Summa Theologiae* (CUAP, 2014), *Reading Job with St. Thomas Aquinas* (CUAP, 2020), and *The Oxford Handbook of the Reception of Aquinas* (2021). He serves as co-editor of two quarterly journals, *Nova et Vetera* and *International Journal of Systematic Theology*. In 2021–2022, he was the president of the Academy of Catholic Theology.

CHRISTOPHER STEPHEN LUTZ is Professor of Philosophy at Saint Meinrad Seminary and School of Theology in Saint Meinrad, Indiana. After spending his college years with the Baltimore Province Redemptorists, he did his graduate work at The Catholic University of America. His publications include two books, *Tradition in the Ethics of Alasdair MacIntyre* (Lexington Books, 2004; paperback edition 2009) and *Reading Alasdair MacIntyre's "After Virtue"* (Continuum, 2012). He edited the *American Catholic Philosophical Quarterly* special MacIntyre issue (vol. 88, no. 4, fall 2014), and wrote for the "MacIntyre at ninety" special issue of *Acta Philosophica* (vol. 28, no 2, 2019). His research interests include Thomistic Aristotelianism and the history of moral philosophy. Dr. Lutz is a founding member of the International Society for MacIntyrean Enquiry, a multidisciplinary community dedicated to the theoretical and practical pursuit of the human good.

MATTHEW MINERD is a Ruthenian Catholic, husband, father, and translator. He serves as a professor of philosophy and moral theology at Ss. Cyril and Methodius Byzantine Catholic Seminary in Pittsburgh, Pennsylvania.

MARK MOES completed an M.A. in philosophical theology at the Aquinas Institute of Theology and a doctorate in philosophy at the University of Notre Dame. He just retired from the position of Professor of Philosophy at Grand Valley State University in Michigan, specializing in Ancient Philosophy. He is author of *Plato's Dialogue Form and the Care of the Soul* and articles on ancient philosophy and philosophy of medicine. He is currently doing research on two connected projects: (1) a book on Plato's *Republic*, and (2) a book on the whole corpus of the published writings of Alasdair MacIntyre.

CHRISTOPHER L. RAGUSA, Jr, Ph.D. is an Assistant Professor of Theology at Franciscan Missionaries of Our Lady University and a consultant for the United States Conference of Catholic Bishops. His interests are in natural law and virtue ethics and his recent dissertation was entitled "'Partakers of the Divine Nature' (2 Peter 1:4): The Role of Participation in St. Thomas Aquinas's Moral Theology" at The Catholic University of America. Christopher and his wife live in Baton Rouge, Louisiana.

HANNAH WOLDUM RAGUSA currently lives with her husband in Baton Rouge, Louisiana, where she teaches philosophy at Franciscan Missionaries of Our Lady University. Her interests are primarily in metaphysics and aesthetics, and her recent dissertation was entitled, "The Metaphysics of Image in the Thought of Thomas Aquinas" at The Catholic University of America.

ALICE M. RAMOS is recently named Professor Emerita of Philosophy at St. John's University in New York where since 1987 she taught metaphysics, medieval philosophy, early modern philosophy, and concentrated in aesthetics and ethics. She is currently Adjunct Professor at St. Joseph's Seminary in New York, teaching Natural Theology and Theological Aesthetics. She has a Ph.D. in Philosophy from the University of Navarra in Pamplona, Spain, where she worked primarily in St. Thomas Aquinas, and also holds a prior Ph.D. in French Literature from New York University. Among her publications are *Dynamic Transcendentals: Truth, Goodness, and Beauty from a Thomistic Perspective* (The Catholic University of America Press, 2012) and *Beauty and the Good: Recovering the Classical Tradition from Plato to Duns Scotus* (edited volume, The Catholic University of America Press, 2020). She is a past president of the American Maritain Association (2002–2004).

THOMAS ROURKE won the American Political Science Association's Aaron Wildavsky Award for the best dissertation written nationally on a topic of Religion and Politics in 1994. He taught at Florida International University in Miami before moving to WestPenn-Clarion. His research examines the intersection between political philosophy and theology; much of this has been in the context of Latin America. He has published five books and numerous articles. His last book was *The Roots of Pope Francis's Social and Political Thought* (Rowman and Littlefield, 2017). More recently, his work has focused on the Italian political philosopher, Augusto Del Noce.

DENIS SCRANDIS began his love of Maritain and the Aristotelian-Thomistic philosophy more than half a century ago when he found his vocation reading Maritain's *Preface to Metaphysics*. Although his undergraduate school (CCNY) could not nurture his development, subjection to Enlightenment thinking convinced him of its sterility before he came to understand its historic role undermining Western civilization. He remains convinced that Maritain is a beacon illuminating the path to truth and fullness of being in thought and in life.

MARCO STANGO is an Associate Professor of Philosophy at St. Bernard's School of Theology and Ministry, New York. He is interested in the Catholic philosophical tradition and all topics lying at the intersection of metaphysics, philosophical anthropology, and philosophy of history.

MICHAEL TORRE received his Ph.D. in 1983 and joined the Universtity of San Francisco Philosophy Department in 1989. He is now its senior member. He has served as the Chair of the Department and as the Coordinator of its Ethics sections. He has been a past Vice-President of the Institut Internationale Jacques Maritain and is currently serving on its Scientific Committee. He was the second General Editor of the American Maritain Association's series of publications from 2009–2013 and its President from 2012–2016, and he has regularly contributed articles to its Book Series for the past 40 years. His research interests have focused on the "interface" between reason and faith, nature and grace, and philosophy and theology, and with their common issues, such as the existence and nature of God, the relationship between providence and free will or providence and evil. He has published on various aspects on the thought of Thomas Aquinas and especially on the problem of God's permission of sin. As his presidency of the AMA indicates, he also has written widely on contemporary Thomists, particularly on Jacques Maritain and Yves R. Simon, and given courses on contemporary Thomists. He is the author of *Do Not Resist the Spirit's Call: Francisco Marín-Sola on Sufficient Grace* (The Catholic University of America Press, 2013), *What Is: Introductory Reflections on Thomistic Metaphysics* (Scepter, 2019), and *An Yves R. Simon Reader* (University of Notre Dame Press, 2021). His latest book, a selection of essays—*God is Love: Thomas Aquinas on the Being and Action of the Holy Spirit*—is due to be published by The Catholic University of America Press sometime in 2025.

KELSEY TUNING is a Master of Arts graduate from Franciscan University of Steubenville with special interest in the interdisciplinary (philosophy and psychology) study of virtue ethics.

Index

PUBLICATIONS OF THE AMERICAN MARITAIN ASSOCIATION

GENERAL EDITORS

Anthony O. Simon (1990–2004): vols. 3–14
Michael D. Torre (2009–2013): vols. 15–22
Giuseppe Butera (2013–2023): vols. 23–32

1. *Jacques Maritain: The Man and His Metaphysics*
Edited by John F. X. Knasas, 1988
ISBN 978-0-268-01205-2, (out of print)
Distributed by the University of Notre Dame Press

2. *Freedom in the Modern World: Jacques Maritain, Yves R. Simon, Mortimer J. Adler*
Edited by Michael D. Torre, 1989, Second Printing, 1990
ISBN 978-0-268-00978-6
Distributed by the University of Notre Dame Press

3. *From Twilight to Dawn: The Cultural Vision of Jacques Maritain*
Edited by Peter A. Redpath, 1990
ISBN 978-0-268-00979-3
Distributed by the University of Notre Dame Press

4. *The Future of Thomism*
Edited by Deal W. Hudson and Dennis Wm. Moran, 1992
ISBN 978-0-268-00986-1
Distributed by the University of Notre Dame Press

5. *Jacques Maritain and the Jews*
Edited by Robert Royal, 1994
ISBN 978-0-268-01193-2
Distributed by the University of Notre Dame Press

6. *Freedom, Virtue, and the Common Good*
Edited by Curtis L. Hancock and Anthony O. Simon, 1995
ISBN 978-0-268-00991-0
Distributed by the University of Notre Dame Press

7. *Postmodernism and Christian Philosophy*
Edited by Roman T. Ciapolo, 1997
ISBN 978-0-8132-0881-7
Distributed by The Catholic University of America Press

8. *The Common Things: Essays on Thomism and Education*
Edited by Daniel McInerny, 1999
ISBN 978-0-9669226-0-8
Distributed by The Catholic University of America Press

9. *The Failure of Modernism: The Cartesian Legacy and Contemporary Pluralism*
Edited by Brendan Sweetman, 1999
ISBN 978-0-9669226-1-5
Distributed by The Catholic University of America Press

10. *Beauty, Art, and the Polis*
Edited by Alice Ramos, 2000
ISBN 978-0-9669226-2-2
Distributed by The Catholic University of America Press

11. *Reassessing the Liberal State: Reading Maritain's Man and the State*
Edited by Timothy Fuller and John P. Hittinger, 2001
ISBN 978-0-9669226-3-9
Distributed by The Catholic University of America Press

12. *Faith, Scholarship, and Culture in the 21st Century*
Edited by Alice Ramos and Marie I. George, 2002
ISBN 978-0-9669226-5-3
Distributed by The Catholic University of America Press

13. *Jacques Maritain and the Many Ways of Knowing*
Edited by Douglas A. Ollivant, 2002
ISBN 978-0-9669226-4-6
Distributed by The Catholic University of America Press

30. *Facts are Stubborn Things: Thomistic Perspectives in the Philosophies of Nature and Science*

Edited by Matthew K. Minerd, 2021.

ISBN 9780997220520
Distributed by The Catholic University of America Press

31. *Restoring Ancient Beauty: The Revival of Thomistic Theology*

Edited by James F. Keating

ISBN 978-0-9972205-3-7
Distributed by The Catholic University of America Press

32. *Thomism and Tradition: From Rivulets to the Fountain's Source*

Edited by Heather M. Erb

ISBN 978-0-9972205-6-8
Distributed by The Catholic University of America Press

Thomism and Tradition: From Rivulets to the Fountain's Source
was designed in Arno and composed by Kachergis Book Design of Pittsboro,
North Carolina. It was printed on 55-pound Tradebook Natural and
bound by Sheridan Books of Chelsea, Michigan.